Serbia Between East and West

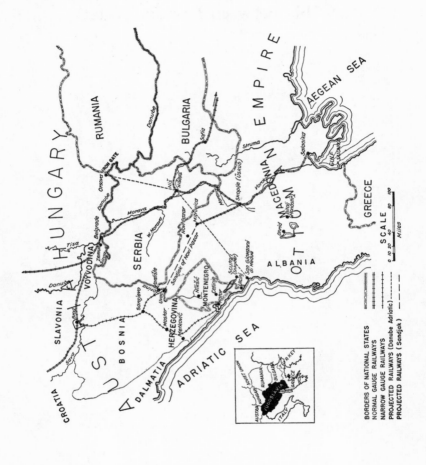

BORDERS OF NATIONAL STATES
NORMAL GAUGE RAILWAYS
NARROW GAUGE RAILWAYS
PROJECTED RAILWAYS (Danube Adriatic)
PROJECTED RAILWAYS (Sandjak)

HUNGARY

RUMANIA

BULGARIA

OTTOMAN EMPIRE

MACEDONIA

AEGEAN SEA

GREECE

ALBANIA

MONTENEGRO

SERBIA

VOIVODINA

SLAVONIA

CROATIA

AUSTRIA

BOSNIA

HERZEGOVINA

DALMATIA

ADRIATIC SEA

Sandjak of Novi Pazar

Danube

Tisa

Sava

Morava

W. Morava

Vardar

Struma

Sofia

Solonika

GULF OF SALONIKA

SCALE
0 10 20   40   60   80   100
Miles

Serbia Between East and West

The Events of 1903-1908

WAYNE S. VUCINICH

AMS PRESS
NEW YORK

STANFORD UNIVERSITY PUBLICATIONS
UNIVERSITY SERIES

HISTORY, ECONOMICS, AND POLITICAL SCIENCE
VOLUME IX

Reprinted with the permission of Stanford University Press
From the edition of 1954, Stanford
First AMS EDITION published 1968
Manufactured in the United States of America

Library of Congress Catalogue Card Number: 68-54304

AMS PRESS, INC.
New York, N.Y. 10003

Preface

The territories inhabited by the southern Slavs were for many centuries an arena of conflict between numerous political and cultural forces. The dominant conflict involved a struggle between the West and the East, a conflict which left a lasting imprint on Yugoslav society. The modern Serbian state from its very inception at the beginning of the nineteenth century was caught in the vise of the competing Austro-Hungarian and Russian imperialisms. No matter how much Serbia might have endeavored to build her state and shape her national destiny independently of foreign political interference, the somber reality compelled her to rely for diplomatic and military backing on Austria-Hungary or Russia. From 1878 to the end of the century Serbia for all intents and purposes existed as a political and economic enclave of the former power; by 1900 Russia had succeeded in undermining the exclusive position of Austria-Hungary in Beograd. From that time on, and especially after 1903, Serbia, beginning with a palace revolution and a dynastic change, undertook to free herself of foreign tutelage with the assistance of Russian diplomacy and Russian arms.

This study is an effort to interpret the dominant trends in the growth of twentieth-century Serbia by focusing the attention on the country's relations with foreign powers, particularly with Austria-Hungary, Russia, and the Balkan states. As such, it required a scrutiny of the complications which followed the murder of King Alexander Obrenović and Queen Draga: the question of eliminating the regicides from influential government positions on the demand of European powers, especially England, and the question of foreign recognition of the new king and the political order established by means of a palace revolution. Special attention has also been paid to Serbia's policy regarding the insoluble Macedonian Question, the relations with Bulgaria and Montenegro, and the effort to effect Balkan co-operation through a system of political and economic alliances. But, most important of all the contemporary problems was that of Austro-Serbian relations.

From 1903 until the outbreak of World War I Serbia and Austria-Hungary consistently ranged themselves on opposite sides in each of a series of Balkan crises. The determined efforts by Austria-Hungary to reassert its dominant position in Beograd evoked an equally determined attitude by Serbia to remain independent. The conflict between the two powers was especially manifest in the monarchy's policy buttressing the Albanians against the Serbs, in nurturing anti-Serbian sentiments in Bulgaria, in encouraging a rift between the dynasties of Montenegro and Serbia, in proposing to build the Sandjak railway that would permanently separate Serbia from Montenegro, and in employing a policy of oppression with regard to the South Slavs in Austria-Hungary. In the economic field the Austro-Serbian conflict developed into a tariff war, sometimes called the "Pig War," which lasted from 1905 until 1911, during which Serbia sought to free herself from economic dependence on Austro-Hungarian markets, industries, and banking institutions. Moreover, to assure herself of economic independence, Serbia proposed the building of the Danube-Adriatic railway that would have given her an Adriatic outlet and a trade route not crossing the territory of Austria-Hungary.

The conflict between Austria-Hungary and Serbia was sharpened by Austro-Hungarian annexation of Bosna-Hercegovina, that power's anti-Serbian policy during the Balkan Wars, 1912–13, and the Serbian national-ist activities inside Austria-Hungary. By 1914 the stage was set for World War I. But the treatment of these topics does not fall within the scope of this study.

Serbian and Yugoslav history since 1903 has been neglected by native historians, probably for two reasons: In the first place, the period is ex-tremely controversial and much material was withheld because of dynastic interests and the fact that many of the leading personalities were still living. In the second place, much of the archival material was lost during two world wars. The contemporary Communist writers have conspicuously ignored the period of our concern.

The author is deeply indebted to several Yugoslav historians and writers for a considerable reliance on their works. The monumental six-volume work by Slobodan Jovanović and the four-volume work by Živan Živanović, covering the period of kings Milan and Alexander Obrenović, have not yet been equaled for any subsequent period of Serbian history. These two multi-volume works and that by the noted littérateur, Dragiša Vasić (*Devesto treća*), were indispensable for the understanding of the immediate period preceding the fateful years of 1903, and they supplied the basic factual material in the first three chapters of the book.

In 1936 the distinguished Serbian historian, Vladimir Ćorović, who per-ished in the first days of World War II in Yugoslavia, published the only extensive study of Serbian relations with Austria-Hungary in the twentieth century (*Odnosi izmedju Srbije i Austro-Ugarske u XX veku*). Unfor-tunately, however, this work was confiscated by the censor. The reason for this official action has never been satisfactorily explained. Appearing at a time when the government coveted German friendship, it was probably con-fiscated because of the anti-German tenor of the work, or, as some allege, on the request of the German government.

All efforts by this author to obtain a copy of Ćorović's work were fruitless until a typewritten translation of a large portion of Ćorović's work was dis-covered in July 1951 in the files of the Hoover Institute and Library on War, Revolution, and Peace at Stanford. The translation, rendered by Stojan Gavrilović, a former Yugoslav diplomat now in the United States, is on the whole very good. The author used this translation and is indebted to Ćorović and Gavrilović for the privilege.

At long last, on the approval of the president of the Historical Institute in the Yugoslav Academy of Sciences, a copy of Ćorović from the Institute's library—now a rare item—was lent to the author in late 1952 for a period of three months. Ćorović's work, covering the period from 1890 to 1914,

did not change our knowledge of Serbian foreign policy. Its principal value
lies in the extensive use of archival materials of the Serbian foreign ministry,
a privilege given Ćorović to the exclusion of other historians, including the
author. It is unfortunate that Ćorović's study, monumental in its scope and
replete with significant data, has two serious shortcomings : it is unsystematic
and suffers from a pronounced nationalist bias.   This does not, however,
detract from the author's indebtedness to Ćorović for the numerous excerpts
from official documents and materials which would otherwise be unavailable.

Rather than transliterate Serbian names, the author used the Croatian
letters, and, with the exception of a few terms commonly known in the West,
he used the native geographical nomenclature. The transliteration of Russian and Bulgarian titles follows the Library of Congress style.

The author wishes to convey his deep appreciation for the assistance
given him by the staffs of many libraries. He is especially indebted to the
staffs of the *Slovanská knihovna* (Prague), Beograd City and University
libraries, and Hoover Library (Stanford). He is grateful to his teacher,
Professor Robert J. Kerner, Jane K. Sather Professor of History and Di-
rector of the Institute of Slavic Studies at the University of California, for
patient guidance and valuable suggestions, to Professor Ralph Lutz of Stanford University, for generous counsel, to Mrs. Mary Electa Brown for
stylistic suggestions, and to his wife Sara for unfailing help and encourage-
ment.

W. S. V.

STANFORD, CALIFORNIA
May, 1953

Abbreviations

A.P.S.	*Die Auswärtige Politik Serbiens, 1903–1914,* by Milosch Boghitschevitsch.
B.D.	*British Documents on the Origins of the War, 1898–1914,* edited by G. P. Gooch and Harold Temperley.
Borba	*Borba za narodno ujedinjenje,* by Jovan M. Jovanović.
D.A.	*Diplomatischen Aktenstücke über die Handelsvertragverhandlungen mit Serbien, 1905–1906.*
D.D.F.	*Documents diplomatiques français (1871–1914).*
D.P.	*Diplomatske prepiske o trgovačkom ugovoru s Austro-Ugarskom od marta 16-og do juna 24-og, 1906.*
G.B.C.R.	Great Britain, *Diplomatic and Consular Reports.*
G.N.Č.	*Godišnjica Nikole Čupića.* Izdaje njegova zadužbina.
Godišnjak	*Statistički godišnjak Kraljevine Srbije.*
G.P.	*Die Grosse Politik der Europäischen Kabinette, 1871–1914,* by Johannes Lepsius, *et al.*
H.A.Ö.R.	*Stenographische Protokolle über die Sitzungen des Hauses der Abgeordneten des österreichischen Reichsrates.*
K.R.	*Kraljevske Reči, Zbirka govora Kralja Petra I,* by Milan L. Zečević.
N.F.P.	*Neue Freie Presse,* Wien, 1903.
N.S.	*Stenografske beleške o sednicama Narodne Skupštine.*
Odnosi	*Odnosi izmedju Srbije i Austro-Ugarske u XX veku,* by Vladimir Ćorović.
Ö.-U.A.	*Österreich-Ungarns Aussenpolitik von der Bosnischen Krise 1908 bis zum Kriegsausbruch 1914.*
Ö.-U.K.	*Berichte der k. u. k. Österr.-Ung. Konsularämter.*
Parl. Deb.	*The Parliamentary Debates.*
US.D.	*Papers Relating to the Foreign Relations of the United States.*
S.K.G.	*Srpski književni glasnik.*
Vl. Al. Ob.	*Vlada Aleksandra Obrenovića,* by Slobodan Jovanović.
Vl. Mil. Ob.	*Vlada Milana Obrenovića,* by Slobodan Jovanović.
Z.T.U.	*Zbirka trgovinskih ugovora.*

Contents

PART ONE

The Turn of the Century

THE FOUNDATIONS OF THE MODERN SERBIAN STATE were laid during the first and second Serbian revolutions (1804, 1815), as a result of which Serbia gained a partial autonomy within the Ottoman political framework. The Treaty of Adrianople (1829), dictated by Russia to the Ottoman sultan, and the sultanic *hatti sherif* of 1830 based thereon, assured Serbia of an autonomous existence. This status of Serbia was guaranteed by the Great Powers collectively through the medium of the Paris Peace Treaty (1856). In 1867 the Serbs compelled the Turks to evacuate the Beograd garrison, their last military stronghold. The Serbo-Turkish War (1876–77) and the Treaty of Berlin, which for the time being at least settled the Balkan question, brought Serbia full political independence and additional territory. In 1882 Serbia was elevated from a princedom to a kingdom.

The internal development of Serbia during the nineteenth century was characterized by the country's progressive emancipation from Turkey and the substitution of Western for Ottoman political and socio-economic institutions. By the end of the century Serbia had become a parliamentary monarchy. She had developed a stable peasant society, a working administrative apparatus, and a political party system. Hospitals and schools were built and a number of thriving cultural centers grew up. Serbia had produced a small but vigorous intelligentsia and a fine group of literati and scholars. The basis was laid for a native industry, and a small proletarian class appeared.

Serbia's external relations throughout the nineteenth century were influenced by the struggle between Austria and Russia for control of Serbia. The two countries alternated in dominating the Serbian government. Both forced the Serbian government into political concessions and subservience. The feuding families of Karadjordje Petrović and Miloš Obrenović, the leaders of the two revolutions, had likewise alternated in ruling Serbia. It is not true, as is sometimes alleged, that the Karadjordjević family was always pro-Russian and the Obrenović family pro-Austrian. Indeed Alexander Karadjordjević (1842–53) leaned on Austria, while Mihailo Obrenović (1839–42, 1860–68) leaned on Russia. Prince, and later King, Milan (1868–89) was a firm Russophile before 1878, and thereafter, bitterly disappointed in Russian "Pan-Slavism" and the Treaty of San Stefano (March 1878), he embarked on an equally firm Austrophile policy.

1. THE UNCERTAIN FUTURE

Serbia entered the twentieth century in a state of political and financial instability. King Alexander I (Obrenović), who ascended the throne when his father Milan abdicated in 1889, had not married, and the end of the ruling house was in sight. One of the primary concerns of the feuding royal parents,

Milan and Natalija, was the marriage of their only son. The queen mother hoped that Alexander might take a Russian or Montenegrin princess for a wife and steer his country into Slavonic waters. The father favored marriage to a German princess, hoping thereby to cement friendly relations with the Triple Alliance.[1]

The marriage of King Alexander was often a subject of discussion in high official circles. That was one of the reasons Alexander visited Athens in 1896 and Cetinje in 1897. Responsible Russians were consulted with regard to a suitable Russian princess. Prince Lobanov-Rostovski, the Russian foreign minister, explained that the Russians had no available princess and suggested that Alexander find a wife among the German princely families of Protestant religion. The Serbian minister in Berlin, Milan Bogićević, cousin of King Alexander, tried in vain to promote a marriage between Alexander and a German princess. On one occasion, in 1898, Alexander had requested his cousin to make inquiries about "a certain princess." In the early autumn of 1899 the government itself took up the marriage question. On New Year's Day, 1900, in the presence of his father and other high dignitaries, the king* promised that he would marry, choosing a wife from a European princely family before the year expired.[2] He had apparently also misled his father into believing that he might marry a German princess.

When in March 1900 Čedomilj Mijatović, Serbian minister in London, stopped off in Vienna on his way to Constantinople, Count Goluchowski asked him to tell Milan and Alexander that it was vitally important for Alexander not to delay his marriage. He added that Austria-Hungary wished "to see the political consolidation of Serbia, which cannot be realized while the Royal dynasty has only one representative."[3] Goluchowski explained that when he had last spoken with Alexander the latter was aware of the importance of his marriage and had expressed the hope that Emperor Francis Joseph might help him find "a suitable princess." Unfortunately, he said, Alexander stipulated too many conditions. He expected the princess to be young, beautiful, and lovely, so as to win his love; further, she ought to be politically well connected, and at least have family relations with one of the first-class courts of Europe; further, she ought to be a highly cultured and gifted woman; and, at last but not least, very wealthy.

Goluchowski asked Mijatović[4] to tell King Alexander that both the Austrian and German emperors would join in the effort to find him "a suitable princess," but that a princess who possessed all his requirements "could do better than marry King Alexander of Serbia and spend her life in Belgrade." Goluchowski said that the two emperors had found a princess who possessed some of Alexander's stipulations and that she was "one of the most charming and most cultured Princesses in Europe."[5] The princess he had in mind was apparently Alexandra von Schaumburg-Lippe. Alexandra belonged to

---

* As in the Byzantine Empire, there were in Serbia at this time two kings. The formal king was Alexander, to whom his father Milan ostensibly bowed and to whom he swore allegiance. In reality, Alexander's father also ruled. He imposed his will and political ideas on his son by virtue of the superiority of his authority. (V. Čubrilović and V. Ćorović, *Srbija od 1858 do 1903*, p. 191.)

a minor princely family and could bring little in the way of dowry. Yet the interest shown in this marriage by the two emperors indicated that compensations in lieu of dowry might be anticipated. The German emperor was interested in the marriage because he had family ties with the princess and because he hoped to bring Serbia firmly into the orbit of the Triple Alliance. Count von Bülow, the German Imperial chancellor, suggested to the Serbian minister that the time had come for the king of Serbia to marry, "as the royal dynasty consisted of him and his father only."[6]

On his arrival in Beograd, Mijatović delivered Goluchowski's message to Milan, Alexander, and the prime minister. The three were much pleased. Alexander admitted that in the photograph Princess Alexandra looked beautiful. However, Alexander wished to see the princess in person before he agreed to marry her. Milan and Alexander requested Count Goluchowski, Austro-Hungarian foreign minister, to mediate between the Serbian court and the Schaumburg-Lippe house. Once again Alexander promised that he would marry before the year's end and he told Mijatović that he meant to keep his word.[7]

In June 1900 Alexander gave his father written authorization to make arrangements preliminary to the engagement. Milan accomplished his task devotedly and only one step remained in the negotiation—the meeting between the two young people, which was to take place at Karlsbad in August 1900. The father anxiously awaited the outcome. The marriage of his son to a German princess would relieve him of uncertainty regarding the future. It would cement Serbia's friendly relations with the Triple Alliance and assure Milan's continued control of political affairs in Serbia.[8] Yet outside immediate court circles few knew of the contemplated royal marriage.

Before he could meet the princess in person, Alexander explained that some delay was necessary. His father Milan wished to go to Karlsbad for the cure. Prime Minister Djordjević was likewise tired and planned to go to Franzensbad and then to the Serbian pavilion at the Paris Exposition. Alexander advised that all three "of us" ought not to be absent from Serbia at the same time, and he proposed that "papa" and Djordjević go first "to make their respective cures." He would, he said, depart for Vienna after Djordjević returned and go thence with his father to Paris and Germany "to see my Princess, and, if God so wills, give her the ring ; and certainly by the end of the year, if not sooner, you will see me a married man."[9] Alexander told Djordjević that Milan would leave Beograd on June 7 for Karlsbad and that he planned to meet with Emperor Francis Joseph to discuss the marriage question.[10] Since he, Alexander, wished to visit Karlsbad before his birthday, August 2, he urged Djordjević to make his contemplated trip as soon as possible. Djordjević agreed to leave Beograd on June 8. Mijatović, confidant of King Milan, saw here a deliberate plan of Alexander, Draga, and Pavel Borisovich Mansurov, Russian chargé d'affaires, "to have a clear field."[11]

No one could have guessed that in 1897 Alexander had already found in Draga Mašin his true love and future queen. Draga was one of the several daughters of Panta Lunjevica, who had been at one time mayor of Šabac.

She was a pretty youngster, and while still a school girl she had married Svetozar Mašin, son of a Czech who became a naturalized Serbian citizen. Svetozar was an engineer employed by the Ministry of Finance. After less than a year of married life, Svetozar died. Although there were rumors that Draga had poisoned him, Mijatović assures us that he died of delirium tremens, for he was "a hard drinker." Draga's pension as the widow of a government worker was rather meager. She had many admirers and was exposed to "temptations." Queen Natalija, who was noted for her charitable work, took an interest in her upon learning that Draga was a descendant of a close friend of Prince Miloš Obrenović. The queen mother paid "teachers of foreign languages" to instruct Draga, who eventually began to read German and French books. Natalija was seemingly proud "to introduce such a pretty, witty, and apparently cultured young Serbian lady to the families of the foreign diplomatists."[12] Draga soon came into contact with the highest social circles. Gossip about her began to circulate, and some alleged she was "the mistress of King Milan." Actually, from the very beginning of Draga's appearance in the court, Milan had had "an aversion to her," probably because he could not bear the favorites of his wife."[13]

When Natalija settled in France in 1890, she built a villa ("Sashino") at Biarritz and made Draga Mašin her *dame d'honneur*.* In this position Draga learned much from the high French, Spanish, and Russian nobility and from the "distinguished English and American families" who visited Natalija.[14] King Alexander fell in love with Draga while visiting his mother at Biarritz in 1897. He related to Mijatović and Vukašin Petrović, the acting prime minister in 1900, many details of his love affair, and assured them that Draga was virtuous. He was sure she was honest and honorable. He first made her acquaintance in 1894, and her modesty and wisdom impressed him. He took every opportunity to approach her, but she protested energetically. He once forced his way into her bedroom, only to be evicted by her. All the time she lived at Biarritz she did not allow him to come near her.[15]

The return of Queen Natalija to Beograd in 1895 must have been connected with Alexander's desire to have Draga near him. But his mother's interference with his life and government affairs and her determination to marry him to a Russian or a Montenegrin princess irritated Alexander, and he grew cold toward the queen. In July 1897 Natalija once again left Beograd; in the autumn of the same year Draga returned to Beograd[16] to assume her role as the king's mistress. She did so with the full knowledge of the prime

---

* After many quarrels King Milan and Queen Natalija were finally divorced on October 12, 1888. In 1889, in return for two million dinars which he received from the Russians, Milan renounced all dynastic rights and privileges as well as Serbian citizenship, and retired in Paris under the name Count of Takovo. Upon his departure from Serbia, the queen mother returned to Beograd. She was expelled from Serbia on May 7, 1891, and Milan returned on April 1, 1893, regaining the rights he had earlier renounced. In 1895 the queen mother returned to Beograd, and King Milan once again left Serbia. In 1897 relations between the queen mother and her son deteriorated, and King Milan replaced Natalija in Beograd. After Alexander's marriage the queen mother never returned to Serbia even for a visit. She gave her properties to Beograd University, became converted to Catholicism, and entered a monastery in Paris.

minister. Mijatović says that Djordjević "in discussion with the prefect of the Belgrade police" justified "this one and only mistress." He also writes that Archbishop Inokentije knew the whole situation and yet did nothing against such immorality. Moreover, adds Mijatović, "all the officers, all the citizens, knew about it; all the diplomatists, and even the most distinguished among them went to the weekly receptions of Madame Draga, and invited her to their dinners and entertainments."[17]

Alexander later said it was when Draga came to Beograd and he saw that without her he "could not live" that she gave herself to him. Alexander claimed that he was passionately in love with Draga and that life had no meaning without her. He told how he gave her money and how he had to persuade her to become his queen.[18]

In Beograd Draga was provided with a pretty little house, "sumptuously furnished," near the Old Palace. What a shock it must have been to father Milan, who had always found his son "a brilliant garçon" but in the company of women "absolutely gauche."[19] Milan hated the woman but abstained from interfering in the love affair of "his king and master"—as he affectionately called his son.

Correspondence between Alexander and Draga Mašin was replete with romance, sugary words, and naïveté.[20] Some of the letters throw light on the tactics Draga employed to force Alexander to marry her. On no less than three occasions she pretended pregnancy, and the last such pretense she utilized to press the king into a quick marriage decision.[21] Alexander had determined upon marriage; but he considered it necessary, before venturing upon that step, to free himself from his father's control and to establish friendly relations with Russia. Official Russia's single stipulation for granting this friendship was the expulsion of Milan from Serbia. Perhaps, the king thought, his decision to marry Draga rather than a German princess might be well received by the Russians and might serve as a starting point for negotiations.[22]

2. DID THE RUSSIANS PLOT ALEXANDER'S MARRIAGE?

During the preceding years Russia had appeared much interested in the affairs of Serbia. King Alexander told Mijatović in 1897 that Nikola Pašić, when he was minister to Russia, had entered "into negotiations with Russia to replace [him] by a Russian grand duke." He also related how Simić and Vujić took him to Cetinje, ostensibly to return the visit Prince Nikola had paid him a year before but actually to prevail upon him to marry the prince's daughter Ksenija. Time and time again, he said, the Russophile Radicals tried to devise schemes contrary to his personal and dynastic interests. King Milan told Mijatović that he had unmistakable proof of Pašić's negotiations with the Russians. It was for this reason that he decided to return to Serbia in 1897:

The Russian intrigue to get Serbia into her power is so persistent, great, and dangerous, that I consider it my duty to return to Belgrade, to be at the post of danger, and to help this poor and friendless young man to preserve his throne.[23]

After his return to Serbia Milan took up residence in the royal palace and became commander in chief of the Serbian army.[24]

Russia meanwhile suspected that Milan had returned to Serbia with Austrian connivance. It seems that on one occasion the Russian foreign minister remonstrated "in a friendly spirit with Count Goluchowsky, and wanted the Austro-Hungarian Government to use its reputed influence with King Milan to leave Serbia," since otherwise his presence in Serbia would signify Austrian preponderance in that country and would be contrary to the agreement wich the two powers had signed in 1897.[25] Mijatović concluded that Russia, having failed to obtain Austrian co-operation "for the amicable removal of Milan from Serbia," had embarked on a vicious propaganda campaign to discredit Milan everywhere. He adds,

In Serbia the "Asiatic Department," to which the Russian management of Milan and his country belonged, did not need special agents. The Radicals of Serbia, always intensely Russophil, many of them personally devoted to the Pretender, most of them opposed to Milan for his "Austrophilism," were only too eager to serve Russia. . . . the agitation, started and organised by the Russians, [was] carried on in Serbia by the partisans of Peter Karageorgevich and by the *bona fide* Russophil Radicals . . .[26]

The Imperial Foreign Ministry inspired press criticism of Milan, attributing to him a variety of crimes and evil intentions. Within Serbia Russian Minister Zhadovsky supported the Radical party's firm opposition to ex-King Milan. But despite attacks against him at home and abroad, Milan clung steadfastly to his new role. The press campaign having failed to destroy Milan, the Russians, according to Mijatović, decided to have him murdered. Mijatović quotes a letter Zhadovsky allegedly wrote in 1898, which asserted that "to save Serbia and to safeguard our own (Russian) interests, it is absolutely necessary to cut through this coil (personified King Milan) as soon as possible."[27] On July 9, 1899, an attempt was made on King Milan's life, but he and his aide escaped with only minor injuries.* Mijatović attributes this plot to the Russians but there is no conclusive evidence to substantiate that allegation.[28] Mijatović also believes that in order to liquidate Milan, the Russians decided to use Draga Mašin as "a wedge between the son and father, to separate them forever . . ."[29] King Alexander was deeply in love with his ambitious mistress, who was hated by King Milan. By the promotion of Alexander's marriage to Draga, the son and father would assuredly come into conflict.

Draga had come to the attention of the alert Russians during the winter of 1897 at Merano (Tyrol), where she was vacationing with King Alexander. Here they were visited by the Russian minister to Bavaria, Alexander P. Izvolsky, who came from Munich to spend a few days with them. It appears to Mijatović, who lacks concrete evidence, that Draga at that time "placed herself unreservedly" in the service of the Russian cause.[30] Professor

---

* The responsibility for the attempted assassination has never been fully traced. The would-be assassin was an unemployed worker from Bosna. The man who hired him was a Serbian official, probably a sympathizer with the Karadjordjević dynasty. This man, however, committed suicide in prison before he could be interrogated. King Milan blamed the Radical party, and since it was a "Russian agency," he also implicated the Russians. The would-be assassin was hanged, and several Radical leaders jailed.

Slobodan Jovanović says the same thing but dates Izvolsky's visit much later. He says that in 1899 the Russian military attaché, Baron Taube, and later one Pavel Borisovich Mansurov, had been in touch with Draga and through her had exerted influence on Alexander.[31] Subsequently, Mansurov was one of the first persons the king told of his engagement to Draga.

As the king's mistress, Draga Mašin joined the circle of the diplomatic corps in Beograd; she attended the parties of this socially favored group, and some diplomats—among them those of Russia—were present at her own weekly receptions. What particularly struck the eye were the cordial relations between Draga and the Russian military attaché, Baron Taube, and his wife. Mr. Nekliûdov, secretary of the Russian Legation and chargé d'af-aires, was also a frequent visitor at Draga's, and often met Alexander there. These weekly gatherings were known to both Prime Minister Djordjević and ex-King Milan.[32]

The eminent Radical party leader, Pera Todorović, recalls how a "distinguished" Russian diplomat, Mr. Z. I., told him that King Milan wished to arrange a marriage for Alexander which would draw Serbia "into German waters." He stated that this could be prevented by finding the right woman, and hinted that such a woman had already been discovered.[33] Curiously enough, on the very day of this conversation there was a court announcement to the effect that "the Court lady of Queen Nathalie, Mme. Draga Mashin, had been at her own request relieved of her duties on account of her bad health." Queen Natalija had apparently discovered the love affair between Draga and Alexander and decided to dismiss her court lady.[34]

Pera Todorović also tells how a mysterious Russian appeared in Beograd in March 1900, a man named Stakevich-Matushkin whom he had first met at Paris some twenty years earlier. This individual warned Todorović that within six months Serbia would find itself in turmoil, that King Alexander would marry a commoner, and that Serbian independence would virtually disappear. All this, the Russian was quoted as saying, would be done "by perfidious Russian policy, using as a tool a common woman, and . . . a Serbian woman!"[35]

3. THE ENGAGEMENT CAUSES A GOVERNMENT CRISIS

The king had confided his engagement to a handful of officers and government officials. Marshal of the Court Ljubomir Lešjanin, Secretary Vojislav Veljković, and Minister of Interior Djordje Genčić had all disapproved of the marriage. Other officials and generals had likewise discouraged it. But the attitude of the court dignitaries and cabinet ministers did not influence Alexander's decision. He consulted Mansurov, who told him that if he wanted official Russian approval he must improve his relations with the Radical party, which was friendly to Russia. Alexander was ready for any concession, especially if the tsar would accept an invitation to serve as his best man. On July 7 he broke the news of his intended marriage to his father, who was then at Karlsbad. The government found itself in a dilemma. The minister of interior urged Milan to return to Serbia "secretly," but the former king refused to go without an invitation from his son. To return "secretly"

would be, he said, "incompatible with my duty."[36] Prime Minister Djordjević and King Milan tried to communicate in code but were unable to decipher
each other's messages because Alexander purportedly had deliberately given
them the wrong code books![37] On July 8 the cabinet held a special meeting
to discuss the king's marriage. Acting Prime Minister Petrović and Minister
of Interior Genčić told the remaining members of the cabinet what Alexander
had confided to them. It was decided that the entire cabinet should resign
in protest.[38] Prime Minister Djordjević, then in Western Europe, was informed of the cabinet's action and promply tendered his own resignation.[39]
In response to various pleas that he change his mind, Alexander merely let
it be known that his decision was final and irrevocable.[40]

The king meanwhile went about his business. He ordered the rings,
engaged the priest, and invited the cabinet to a luncheon on July 8. The
ministers appeared at the court with their letter of resignation, which they
had signed that very morning.[41] Genčić and Borivoje Nešić were absent; they
had been sent to make one last effort to dissuade Draga from the marriage,
and, if she hesitated, to drive her out of Serbia.[42] Draga deceived Genčić by
agreeing to leave the country. She asked for a few hours to pack and agreed
to hide herself at a friend's house while the maid was packing. As though
suspecting Genčić and Nešić, the king ordered one of his aides to search for
them and to bring them to the luncheon. Suddenly the two absent ministers
appeared, and the apprehensive king slipped a note to Genčić, asking him in
French "*Vous avez été chez elle?*"[43] The air was tense. The host argued
with his guests. The king reprimanded Genčić for going to Draga's, and
Atanacković for saying that she was sterile. He then proceeded to address
the ministers in the following words:

> GENTLEMEN: I have the right as a man to be happy. That lady is the only con-
> dition for my happiness and I wish to take her unto myself. No one can deter me
> from that course. Neither in youth nor in adolescence did I have anyone who loved
> me. This woman understands me completely, and I wish to share both good and
> evil with her. I want to give her a ring. Of you I have the right to demand that
> you perform your duties. That right has been given me by the Constitution.

The king then reminded Genčić and General Atanacković of their official
duties, and pushed the proclamation of marriage into the hands of Petrović and dared him not to publish it.[44] The proclamation was written by
Vojislav Veljković, the king's secretary, on persuasion by the king after the
secretary had already resigned.[45] Acting Prime Minister Petrović suggested
that Alexander postpone his marriage for a year, but the king declared that
he would rather sacrifice the crown than Draga.[46] He complained to Petrović
that he had had no youth like others and had always been surrounded by
the quarreling of his parents.* On another occasion he told the chairman

---

* In 1905 King Alexander's personal physician, Mihailo Veličković, wrote an article
entitled "How They Reared Him" (*Pravda,* November 30, 1905), in which he argues
that Alexander was a victim of poor upbringing. In this connection the author relates
some episodes from Alexander's private life, such as his chase after irresponsible women
in Beograd and Vienna.

and the deputy chairman of the Skupština and a group of leading deputies, whom he had invited to the court to tell of his projected marriage, that he had no interest in ruling but that he was obliged to do so because it was a duty, that no princess from the big powers would marry him, and that he did not care to marry anyone from smaller courts. Consequently, he said, he decided to marry a Serbian woman, especially since everyone insisted that he must marry.[47]

The king refused to accept the cabinet's resignation, tore the letter of resignation to shreds, and once more ordered the deputy prime minister to send the proclamation of his intended marriage to the State Printing Office. Scores of court officials and servants gazed in astonishment at the conflict between the king and his ministers. The luncheon meeting broke up, and before the guests had departed, Alexander rushed out at 2:20 P.M., July 8, 1900, to meet Draga.[48]

When Alexander appeared at Draga's, her brother confided to him the whereabouts of his sister. Alexander found Draga and placed "a beautiful diamond ring" on her finger and thus became "formally engaged to her." Draga's title now became *svetla verenica*. A double guard was posted in front of her house.[49]

To prevent the marriage of the king, the acting prime minister even considered arresting the king in the palace or carrying him "forcibly out of the country!" This idea was abandoned, however, when the minister of war, General Atanacković, rejected the plan on the ground that it would demoralize the army. The cabinet remained in almost continuous session. Everything seemed unsettled at the moment, and friends of the dynasty anxiously awaited the return of King Milan, who was expected to force Alexander "either to give up Draga or the throne!"[50] Despite his opposition to the marriage, the acting prime minister on the king's orders sent the proclamation of the engagement to the State Printing Office. The king finally accepted the newly drafted resignation of the cabinet on July 8, and on the same day entrusted the formation of a new one to eighty-year-old Nikola Hristić.[51] On July 10 Mansurov conferred with the leaders of the Radical party and found them willing to approve the marriage if Alexander restored the constitutional regime, amnestied the imprisoned Radicals, and expelled King Milan from Serbia.[52]

The Metropolitan, head of the Serbian Orthodox Church, was persuaded to oppose the marriage. He apparently did try to persuade the king to give up his marriage, but soon perceived that his efforts were in vain and for that reason accepted the inevitable. Indeed, when the king ordered him either to recognize the marriage or to abdicate, the Metropolitan took the former choice.[53]

King Milan in sign of protest resigned his position as commandant of the army. At the same time the foreign press published the tsar's congratulations to Alexander. But Milan's letter to his son read:

MY DEAR SON,—With the best will to oblige you, I cannot give my consent to the impossible marriage for which you have decided. You ought to know that, by doing what you intend, you are pushing Serbia into an abyss. Our dynasty has sustained many a blow, and has continued to live. But this blow would be so terrible that the dynasty could never recover from it. You have still time to think it over. If your decision should really be, as you say, inflexible, then, nothing remains for me but to pray to God for our fatherland. I shall be the first to cheer the Government which shall drive you from the country, after such a folly on your part.—Your father,

MILAN[54]

Milan's resignation pleased Alexander, who had feared that his father might use the army to prevent the marriage. With a strong government leader such as Hristić, a man notorious for his police regimes in the past, and with the army deprived of the leadership of Milan, King Alexander felt much relieved.[55] Yet after some thirty-six hours of bickering with individual politicians, who resorted to dilatory tactics, the king and Hristić were unable to form a cabinet.[56] Hristić ultimately reconsidered the situation, probably under pressure from his friend Milan, and declined the royal mandate to form a government. Without a government that would assume responsibility for his marriage, King Alexander could do little.

The official gazette had meanwhile published the announcement of the proposed royal marriage—only fifteen hours after the engagement—which at once evoked widespread popular indignation.[57] There were errors of fact and exaggerations in the announcement. It stated that Draga was born in 1866, when in fact she was born in 1864. There were those who remembered that Draga's father had died in an insane asylum, and that her mother was a dipsomaniac. Draga herself was said to have had a shady past. Even the king had first frequented her house as one of the "friends." It was observed that Draga had no children by her first husband and that most probably she might not be able to bear them. The royal announcement, on the other hand, contained statements intended to raise Draga's social status. Her grandfather, Nikola Lunjevica, was referred to as the right hand of Prince Miloš Obrenović and as an active participant in the Second Serbian Revolution. He was titled *vojvoda*, which he was not. Draga was referred to by her maiden name, Lunjevica, and not by her widowed name, Mašin.[58] All this was calculated to make the public forget that the king was planning to marry the widow of an inconspicuous engineer.

4. THE "WEDDING CABINET" AND POPULAR INDIGNATION

The popular resistance to his marriage had obviously worried Alexander, and at times he acted as if dazed. Yet he was determined to go through with it. He won Metropolitan Inokentije[59] to his cause, and on July 11 entrusted Aleksa Jovanović, president of the Court of Appeals, with the formation of a cabinet. Jovanović found a group of men willing to enter his "wedding cabinet" and approve the royal marriage.[60] The cabinet was constituted of civil servants and military personnel amenable to the king's wishes, and by its very composition it lacked popular support. The opponents of the marriage continued to dissuade the king from the fatal step.[61]

The officers' corps especially resented the marriage. Not a single general was willing to accept the post of war minister in the cabinet. The king insisted that the military must take orders from him, but the generals argued that their obedience was restricted to military matters. There were stormy scenes between the king and his generals.[62] The king was in continuous battle with his first adjutant, Leonid Solarović. The marriage was discussed in all Beograd army commands. A few officers, although not approving the marriage, urged noninterference in the personal affairs of the king. On July 12 the king invited the officers of the Beograd garrison to the court so that he might personally sound them out on their attitude to his marriage. The war minister, however, declared it improper for the king to discuss his marriage with the officers. When, therefore, the officers arrived, the king merely read them the officer's oath and reminded them that the marriage was his personal affair. A few of the officers shouted approval, and what might have been the officers' protest turned out to be a faint confirmation of the royal decision.[63]

Those officers who felt strongly about the royal marriage awaited the return of King Milan, who, they hoped, might prevent the marriage, with the army's backing. Alexander lived in deep fear that his father might return at any moment. In a letter sent through the Austrian Legation on July 13, one of the generals requested Milan's immediate return to Serbia. But Milan did not venture to come back. He consulted with the Austrian Foreign Office about his son's marriage, and was received cordially, but the Austrians refused to become involved in the marriage affair, ostensibly on the ground that Russia might accuse them of violating the Agreement of 1897. Milan had lost his old fighting spirit; he no longer had the will for action.[64] Had he returned to Beograd he might have succeeded in preventing the marriage.

Even the Beograd women had their say. At no time in the recent history of Serbia had they concerned themselves so much with political affairs. They simply could not bear to see Draga become queen. Gossip was incessant, and invitations were dispensed and withheld in accordance with faction. Next to the Beograd garrison, Beograd "society" provided the bitterest opposition to the marriage.[65]

5. THE TSAR IS THE BEST MAN

On July 14 the official press announced that the Russian chargé d'affaires, Pavel Mansurov, had "at the order of his Imperial Majesty, Tsar Nicholas II," congratulated King Alexander and Draga on their approaching wedding. Four days later it was announced that the Russian tsar had agreed to serve as the king's best man (*kum*) and had ordered Mansurov to represent him in that capacity.[66] By virtue of these developments the marriage affair acquired a different complexion, and the king's position was improved. The Russian attitude was used as proof that Draga was worthy of her fiancé. There could no longer be any doubt that Russia in the person of Tsar Nicholas II "approved of the marriage of King Alexander with Draga Mašin. More than that, the Tsar had accepted to be the principal co-operator and co-officiator at the church ceremony of the wedding."[67] In the eyes of the people this agreement signified a Serbian political reorientation toward Russia. The

Radicals and many others welcomed this apparent liberation from King Milan and the Austrian domination. Alexander meanwhile took the opportunity to explain in his various speeches how right he was and how treacherous and un-co-operative were Vladan Djordjević and his cabinet.[68] On July 17 several thousand persons came to Topčider Hill to hear the king and Mansurov speak on the Russo-Serbian fraternal relations. The wedding, which had been originally planned as a modest affair, took place on July 23 amidst considerable festivity.[69] The wedding services were held in the Saborna Church. The tsar, however, not only did not take part in the wedding ceremonies but did not even send a special emissary to represent him. It might well be that Mansurov had represented the tsar on his own responsibility, without, it would seem, detailed instructions. In reappraising the situation, some historians note that the tsar's congratulatory message contained more sympathetic expressions in the Serbian translation than it did in its original Russian. Mansurov apparently chose his words shrewdly and incorporated whole sentences of his own composition. The tsar and his Foreign Office were probably not accurately informed about Draga. According to Professor Jovanović, Mansurov had so few scruples that he unhesitatingly dragged into the marriage affair not only the Russian government but also the tsar himself. Although Russian "official diplomacy," "secret diplomacy," and "secret police" all agreed that Milan had to be destroyed and that this might be done by supporting Alexander's marriage to Draga, Jovanović feels that no honest diplomat would have involved his government and dynasty in the affair.[70]

After he had found a government combination amenable to his marriage, Alexander started to search for broader political support. He began to flirt with the Radical party, which at the time was very popular among the common people. He granted amnesty to the Radicals convicted for the attempted assassination of King Milan in 1899.[71] He endeavored to associate himself with "Radicalism" and "nationalism," the two principal ideological forces of the day. The recent developments, moreover, had effected a regrouping of political forces. The former government parties (Progressive and Andonović's Liberal) went into opposition, and the former opposition parties (Radical and Avakumović-Ribarac Liberal) were slated to assume governmental power.[72]

6. DRAGA'S REACTION TO GROWING OPPOSITION

After the marriage Alexander unfolded a drive against his enemies[73] and at the same time instigated a variety of popular manifestations with which he hoped to enhance the prestige of the queen. He endeavored to transform Draga into a state cult. Regiments, schools, and villages were named after her. Her brothers and sisters were continually at the court and took part in formal audiences and receptions. The queen's birthday, September 11, was designated a state holiday.[74]

Love had blinded Alexander, and the power-thirsty queen held sway over all his actions. She interfered with trivial matters as well as with high matters of state policy, and interceded on behalf of her friends. She saw to it that her enemies were penalized and her friends rewarded. Draga aspired to become a real "Serbian queen," like Queen Milica of old. She was, however, not made of the true royal stuff. She had had some education, and followed Parisian styles, but under her the court became more bourgeois than royal.[75]

The possibility of his father's return to Serbia haunted Alexander. Vienna, where Milan now lived in exile, was too near to Serbia to suit Alexander. Who knew whether Austria might at a moment propitious for herself make use of Milan in an effort to regain her control over Serbia? When on one occasion a report came that King Milan was planning a trip to Bucharest, Alexander was beside himself. The Serbian borders were heavily patrolled to prevent Milan from crossing. Orders were issued for his immediate arrest, if by chance he should enter the country.[76] Special agents kept close watch on Milan's movements. The chief of the Russian intelligence, Colonel Grabov, charged with espionage activity in the Balkans, instructed his agents at Beograd, Budapest, and Vienna to keep an eye on the king, and his agent in Vienna took a house directly across the street from Milan's establishment.[77] Finally, in order to discredit his father, Alexander instigated a series of derogatory articles about him, which appeared in the *Mali Žurnal*.[78]

Next on the king's list of enemies were the court dignitaries and the members of the Djordjević cabinet. Placards smearing the Djordjević cabinet appeared on the Beograd streets. Some members of the cabinet, including Vladan Djordjević and Djordje Genčić, found it necessary to leave the country. But the most extensive drive against Draga's enemies took place within the army. The officers were divided—some were "loyal" to Alexander, some were "friends" of King Milan. The drive was concentrated mostly on higher-ranking officers. Four generals were pensioned.[79] These purges undermined the military discipline and morale of the troops, and instead of strengthening his control over the armed forces, Alexander achieved the opposite result. None of the king's repressive measures succeeded in curbing the popular discontent. Repression merely pushed the opposition underground. Alexander began to receive anonymous threatening letters. Leaflets against him and his dynasty were distributed and posted about the city. Criticism of the king and queen continued in private homes and gatherings. The police kept close watch for any activity injurious to the prestige and honor of the royal family. Spies were everywhere. Some undesirable and untrustworthy persons were questioned and threatened by the police on direct orders from the king. Djordje Genčić, who fled from Serbia, and whom the king accused of misappropriation of state funds, responded with blistering letters to the king and statements published in the press in which he accused the king of instituting a regime modeled on the "Central Asiatic khanates."[80]

Queen Natalija, who felt even more deeply about her son's marriage than did her husband, criticized Draga openly and abusively. On one occasion she sent an open postcard to a friend in Serbia in which she referred to Draga in a most vulgar manner. Under the king's own order an announcement appeared in the official gazette to the effect that all future intrigues against the royal house would be treated as acts of treason. The postcard sent by the queen mother was cited as an example of treason.[81]

It occurred to the king that Draga's prestige at home might be enhanced if she were received in some prominent foreign court. The first to enter his mind was the Imperial Court of Russia, and he sent General Jovan Mišković to St. Petersburg as his special emissary to explore the chances for a reception. On August 12, 1900, the tsar received General Mišković quite warmly but gave no indication of a desire to receive the Serbian king and queen.[82] In October the king sent Nikola Pašić to Russia to raise the question of the reception anew. The king believed that Pašić, for whom he himself had no special love, might as a leader of the Radical party be more successful in arranging a reception than General Mišković had been. But the tsar was again noncommittal.

Having failed to obtain a reception in St. Petersburg, Alexander resorted to other ways of improving the queen's position. Besides the wedding-day amnesty granted to civil and military persons convicted in connection with the Ivanjdan plot, a number of literati and artists were decorated on the queen's birthday. Such efforts to popularize Draga brought some results. The court was flooded with gifts from all over the country. The City of Beograd presented the royal family with a yacht which cost about 120,000 dinars. Three newspapers came out in defense of the queen's cause.[83]

Yet the king was not content so long as the attitude of the army remained unfriendly. At the first officers' ball attended by the royal pair the atmosphere had been distinctly chilly. The king continued to receive anonymous letters. On one occasion in late 1900, posters appeared on buildings in Beograd denouncing the royal house and glorifying the Karadjordjević family, and police discovered that these posters had been printed by the Cartographic Institute of the War Ministry. The king began to feel insecure, and when he went walking during his stay at Niš, special detachments of police and gendarmes accompanied him, all stores were closed, and various other precautions were taken.[84]

7. INTERNAL DEVELOPMENTS

Alexander lacked his father's skill in the conduct of internal affairs. In his address to the Skupština, which assembled at Niš on December 29, 1900, the king said that the queen was expecting an heir, and went on to censure his father and the Djordjević cabinet. The Skupština was expected to approve the royal address. It asked to be spared from subscribing to the attack on Milan, but Alexander insisted, so the Skupština was forced to oblige.[85] It remained in session until January 29, 1901, during which time it approved several acts of legislation. After his return to Serbia in 1897, Milan had detached the army command from the War Ministry and taken over the supreme command of the active armed forces. Now that Milan was permanently away from Serbia, the army command and the general staff were restored to the War Ministry. A law was passed making it possible for the king to employ the armed forces for domestic and foreign needs. Other measures taken dealt with training and organization of troops, military law, and discipline.

It was urgent that the government obtain a favorable loan with which to meet current state obligations and procure heavy artillery and other military equipment. By January 1901 three small loans, about 2.6 million dinars each, were made with domestic firms. Jovanović's cabinet succeeded in merging certain of its old loans, converting part of them through issuance of new 4 percent notes and part through a new French loan. Now that Russo-Serbian relations were improved, and Mihailo Vujić, a prominent Radical, appointed minister at Paris, the Russians were ready to help Serbia get a French loan.[86] The loan was obtained on condition that a French government representative be included in the Monopoly Administration established in 1895 by the Karlsbad Agreement. According to this agreement all earlier 5 percent loans were merged into a master 4 percent loan and representatives of various banks placed in charge of the Independent Monopoly Administration because the revenue from monopolies served as security for the master loan. Such foreign supervision over state finances was obviously in violation of national sovereignty. Several foreign loans were concluded after 1895— two in 1898, one each in 1899 and 1900. The 1902 loan was a monopoly loan concluded with a number of banks in the nominal amount of 60 million dinars at 5 percent interest, with amortization over fifty years. The subscription— and the amount Serbia actually received— was 48 million dinars, or 80 percent of the nominal amount.[87]

Despite all efforts to restrain popular expression, the press became bolder than it had been for some time. Some papers criticized the king and queen, others attacked Milan and Austria. Banditry and political murders increased. Activity among political parties intensified. The Liberals pressed the king for political concessions. The Radicals practically lived in the Russian Legation and sought through Russian influence, which at the time was all-pervasive at the court, to control the government. The king himself had many conflicts with individual members of the cabinet. All these developments were indicative of a growing political crisis.

8. THE DEATH OF KING MILAN

Those who had seen Milan during his last days in his home at Johannes Gasse 16 described him as a crushed man. He began to see in his unfilial son Alexander the "intellectual mover" of the plot to assassinate him on Ivanjdan, and in Draga "an ordinary Russian agent."[88] Mijatović writes that on one occasion Milan told Dr. Djordjević that he had "reason to believe" that his son Alexander and his mistress Draga, "assisted by Russia," organized the attempt on his life in June 1899.[89] Professor Jovanović gives little credence to the "imaginings" of the embittered Djordjević.[90] Mijatović himself states that Milan, who was unusually suspicious of everything, "did not suspect his son or his mistress . . . at the time of the attempt or a year afterwards." It was only after later bitter experiences that his suspicions were aroused.[91]

In January 1901 Milan contracted influenza, and after a brief illness died on January 29, 1901, in Vienna in his forty-seventh year. Kosta Hristić, minister at Vienna, had informed Alexander of his father's serious condition. On January 27 Alexander had instructed Hristić to visit Milan, inquire about his health, and wish him a speedy recovery. Milan received Hristić and asked him to thank his son for the thoughtfulness which he apparently had not expected.[92]

Instead of visiting his dying father, Alexander sent an emissary, Lazar Petrović, his first adjutant. Alexander was severely criticized for his attitude, although it seems that sharper censure should have been directed toward the queen. Petrović spoke at length with Milan, who invited him for another day's talk. But suddenly Milan took a turn for the worse, and died at 4:20 P.M. on January 29. A number of political refugees (Aleksandar Konstantinović, Vladan Djordjević, Djordje Vajfert, Milan Bogićević) and the Hungarian Count Eugen Zichy, Milan's close friend, recorded their impressions of Milan on his deathbed; but these reports are not in accord. It is impossible to know what the feelings of the father or son were during the last days of Milan's life.[93] In Beograd the death was announced by the customary ringing of church bells. The Skupština adjourned. The king announced the death of his father in touching words, and with the queen returned from Niš to Beograd. The Skupština and the cabinet followed them. A funeral committee was appointed, and Milan's body was to be laid to rest next to Princes Miloš and Mihailo in the Saborna Church. A six-month memorial service was planned.[94]

While one set of funeral arrangements was going forward at Beograd, another was being made in Vienna by the Habsburg court. Petrović was instructed to request an audience with Francis Joseph and to ask him for permission to bury Milan in Serbia. The emperor explained that King Milan had asked him in case of his death not to permit the transfer of his body to Serbia, but instead to bury him in one of the Serbian monasteries in Srem. The burial plans were dropped in Beograd, and Alexander dispatched a personal representative to Vienna to attend the funeral.[95]

The body of Milan was embalmed and dressed in a general's uniform; the Star of Miloš the Great and an icon were placed on his chest and the rosary from his pilgrimage to Jerusalem in 1889 in his hands. The body was then taken to the Serbian church. The emperor requested Serbian Patriarch Georgije to officiate and selected the long-famous monastery, Krušedol, in Fruška Gora for Milan's resting place. The funeral services were held on the afternoon of February 2 in the presence of the emperor, all the archdukes, foreign representatives, cabinet ministers, and other dignitaries. An Imperial deputation, Patriarch Georgije, and representatives from Serbia accompanied the body in a special train to Karlovci, where it arrived on the morning of February 3. The next day, in the morning, the body was laid to rest near the remains of Princess Ljubica. Later in the same year Francis Joseph placed an inscription on the grave.[96]

In Serbia, where the peasants had no special love for Milan, there was no strong reaction to his death. On the other hand, Alexander was angry at Austria for not allowing Milan to be buried in Serbia. He was successful in retrieving a large quantity of Milan's papers, but by no means all. Draga appeared relieved, and hereafter she probably could breathe more easily. The "wedding cabinet" had completed its mission, and the king awaited a propitious moment to change the government and grant a new constitution.[97] On February 8 the cabinet was reconstructed by the inclusion of two Radicals —Mihailo Vujić as minister of interior and Milovan Milovanović as minister of economy. It now became this reshuffled cabinet's task to draw up a constitution.[98]

9. THE APRIL CONSTITUTION

After Milan's death the Radicals pressed for the return of a constitutional regime in which they might participate. The time favored the Radicals, and Alexander's concurrence was inevitable. He dismissed the Jovanović cabinet on March 1, 1901, and asked Radical Mihailo Vujić to form a new one. The new government, a coalition of Radicals and Progressives, promptly took up the constitutional question. On April 6 the king proclaimed the new constitution—the April Constitution.[99] This royal action was in itself a violation of the Constitution of 1869, which specified that only the Grand National Assembly could decide on changes affecting the Constitution. Nonetheless, it was important that the personal regime the king had established in 1894 had come to an end. At the king's suggestion, the Radicals and Progressives "fused" into a single political bloc, and published a common newspaper, *Dnevnik*.[100]

The Constitution of April 1901 was conservative, yet it guaranteed many of the usual civil liberties and provided for a bicameral legislature. The lower house and half of the Senate were elective, and the remaining half of the Senate was appointed by the king. The royal prerogatives and privileges in legislative matters, provided by the Constitution of 1869, were appreciably curtailed; they were now equally divided between the king and the Parliament.

What were the motives behind the king's apparent readiness to grant a constitution curtailing his power? He explained this shift in policy on the grounds of changed political conditions. His enemies had been liquidated, and the Radical party had altered its uncompromising attitude.[101] Živanović, however, believes that the real reason for granting the new constitution was the expected "blessed event." He finds the clue in Articles VI and XXI of the Constitution, which established the succession for female children of the king, and the queen's right to serve as regent for minor children.[102] The king had apparently feared that he might not have male offspring and wished to secure the succession of his dynasty whatever the sex of his children. There is, moreover, evidence that the Russian minister Charykov and the chargé d'affaires Mansurov had supported Alexander's action.[103]

The Progressives alone were satisfied with the new Constitution. The Liberals opposed it and under the leadership of Stojan Ribarac took a firm stand against the king. The Radicals were divided. The "old" Radicals favored the tactics of bargaining with the Crown, and saw in the April Constitution a good beginning. The "young" Radicals preferred war against the Crown rather than a policy of opportunism. They were firmly for the original 1881 program of the Radical party,* which called for a real constitutional monarchy, and became known as the Independent Radical party.[104] The split

---

* The Radical party's 1881 program stipulated internal improvements and betterment of the people's lot, a real constitutional government, and a limited monarchy. It called for liberation and unification of Serbian nationals.

in the ranks of the Radicals served the interest of the king, who was still maneuvering for some form of personal rule.

10. THE QUEEN FAKES PREGNANCY

The king chose to grant the Constitution on the eve of the expected birth of a royal child, but, as it turned out, this was to cause one of the most embarassing moments in Alexander's life. The story began when, following an order from the king, the government announced on August 25, 1900, that the queen was an expectant mother.[105] The king was gladdened by the news, which he believed might arouse popular sympathy for Draga and check the widespread rumors of her sterility. The announcement was certainly unprecedented, for it meant the king's public admission of intimate relations with the queen before their marriage.[106]

About the middle of April a French obstetrician (Dr. Caulet) and two Russian obstetricians (Dr. Vladimir Feodorovich Snegirev and Dr. Gubarov) arrived at Beograd. Dr. Caulet had been Draga's physician before and was the one who had diagnosed pregnancy in August of the preceding year. Snegirev had been invited by Minister Charykov on instructions from his government. It seems that the queen mother Natalija had warned the Imperial Court that Draga could not bear children and urged caution lest the Russian tsar serve as godfather to an adopted child. Natalija's suspicion was shared by Colonel Grabov of the Russian intelligence service. For these reasons, the Russian government decided that some Russian obstetrician should verify the queen's pregnancy. Dr. Snegirev and his assistant, Dr. Gubarov, were sent on this unprecedented mission. Dr. Caulet told Snegirev that his examination of Draga in August was definitely perfunctory and that under pressure from a Serbian colleague he had signed an affidavit that the queen showed symptoms of pregnancy. The three obstetricians for the first time in April 1901 gave the queen a complete examination. They discovered that she was not pregnant and signed a protocol to that effect. They diagnosed a tumorous condition and recommended a suitable cure.[107]

The court had made all arrangements for the birth of the royal child. Appropriate ceremonies had been planned. Gifts were beginning to shower the court. Draga was lying in bed as if suffering from pain. Then suddenly came the shattering news that the queen was not pregnant at all. The whole truth could not be given to the king at once; he was fed in doses. The news upset him terribly. He denounced the doctors, rejected their diagnosis, and suggested that someone beat Snegirev and expel him from the country. Other doctors were invited to examine the queen. One of them was from Vienna and the other from Budapest, and, like Caulet, a friend of the queen. They confirmed Snegirev's diagnosis, but Alexander still hoped that Draga might some day be a mother.[108] His disappointment did not cause him to turn against the queen, for he continued to love his Draga.

The *Srpske Novine*, which followed up all the developments concerning the forthcoming "blessed event," suddenly ceased reporting on the subject. On May 5 another newspaper published an official statement explaining that the earlier diagnosis of the French physician Caulet was mistaken and that the queen was not pregnant in truth. Unofficially the entire blame was put on Dr. Caulet for his mistaken diagnosis.[109] The news of the "false expectancy" caused widespread popular resentment of the queen's deceit, despite assurances by the official announcement that the queen had at one time shown definite symptoms of pregnancy. The rumors had it that Draga had planned to adopt the child of her sister, who was pregnant at the time. This scheme allegedly failed because sister Hristina had a miscarriage and Snegirev arrived before Draga could make new arrangements.[110]

Draga was apparently a master at "faking pregnancy." Once, according to reports, she had done so in an attempt to coerce a Frenchman working in Serbia into marrying her. During her premarital intimacies with King Alexander she had twice made trips outside Serbia ostensibly for reasons of abortion. Even after Snegirev's diagnosis, Draga twice in 1901 reported pregnancy. On these occasions, however, the king was wise enough not to advertise it! These latest court scandals had completely deprived the queen of any respect she might have enjoyed. As time passed it became increasingly apparent that she had willfully deceived Alexander. The domestic press was muzzled on the subject of the queen's trickery. But not so the foreign press, which sensationlized the affair.[111] The reports of at least one of the medical experts were published in full.[112]

Baffled and perplexed, Alexander became obsessed with the idea that if he and Draga should be received by the Russian Imperial Court, they might rehabilitate themselves in the eyes of the Serbian people. He once again requested such reception in St. Petersburg, and would even have been satisfied with a minor reception in Crimea during the summer vacation of the Imperial family. While not refusing the reception outright, the tsar did not commit himself to an exact date. Plagued by anxiety, Alexander wanted to visit St. Petersburg as soon as possible, but an official communication from Russia indicated that the reception would have to wait until autumn. Subsequently Alexander was told that the reception could not be arranged even in the autumn. Meanwhile, the royal pair made a tour of Serbia. "Spontaneous demonstrations" were arranged by the police along the itinerary. Everywhere the king was purposely placing Draga in the limelight. But personal appearance made no impression on the discontented masses. The king's drive against enemies of the Crown was therefore resumed.[113]

11. RADICALS WIN ELECTION

The Skupština elections of July 22, 1901, gave the "old" Radical party eighty-four of the one hundred thirty seats in the Skupština. The Progressives came out second best with only twenty-six seats. Of the eighteen elective senators, the Radical party won seventeen in the elections held on August 5. With the Radical senators appointed by the Crown, the Radical party thus acquired a plurality in the Senate. The legislature convened on October 1 and adjourned on May 11, 1902, and sat in special session from July 11 to 25. The Skupština passed several important laws affecting the press, public assembly and meetings, various administrative organs, communes, tobacco monopoly, secondary schools, criminal law, military organizations, and parliamentary procedure.[114]

During this period a renewed attempt was made to settle Serbian financial problems. The Karlsbad Agreement of 1895 made it possible to reduce the annual payments of the state debt and thereby provided one of the first prerequisites for a balanced budget. But the loan concluded in France in 1902 was not for various reasons consummated until later.

The 1901 Skupština, unlike other sessions which followed the king's coup d'état in 1894, enjoyed real parliamentary opposition, represented by able critics, mostly from the ranks of lawyers and professors, all men of peculiar oratorical power. The government parties—the "old" Radical and the Progressive—were also blessed with able speakers.* But most of their orators were in the Senate.[115]

The democratic forces, unleashed after seven years of personal rule by the king, were felt at once so strongly that the king himself was led to complain about growing attacks on the dynasty. The question of sovereignty was widely debated. The opposition press criticized the existing situation with vehemence. *Srpska zastava*, organ of the Liberals, *Dnevni list*, organ of the Independent Radicals, and the *Srpski književni glasnik*, which marshaled many intellectuals and literati under the able editorship of Bogdan Popović, were the most effective opposition publications. Among the contributors to the *Srpski književni glasnik* were such noted figures as Jaša Prodanović, Svetislav Simić, Ljubomir Stojanović, Vojislav Veljković, Milan Grol, Jovan Skerlić, and Stevan Luković.[116] Milan Grol vividly described the deplorable state of affairs in Serbia. An excellent story writer, Radoje Domanović, ridiculed and satirized the government with its bureaucracy, the widespread corruption, the leaders of the government parties, and also, indirectly, the king and queen. Domanović's story "Stradija," which appeared in the *Srpski književni glasnik* (1902), was widely read.

The king simply could not adjust himself to the Constitution and was continually stepping out of bounds. He continued to interfere in all government affairs, opposed legislation proposed by the Vujić government when he felt it smacked too much of democracy, and, failing to check such legislation in the Skupština, he intervened in the Senate to defeat it. The king insisted that the Skupština should reprimand those of its members who criticized him. When these measures failed, he resorted to personal attacks via the semiofficial *Dnevnik*. The police systematically hunted out and persecuted enemies of the king and queen. They interfered with the opposition papers, threatened editors, insisted on their replacement. Even in his official pronouncements Alexander found time to denounce the opposition.[117]

After the "false expectancy," the question of succession came up again. Since Draga had failed to produce an heir to the throne, one had to be

---

* Of the Liberals the prime movers were Avakumović, Stojan Ribarac, Vojislav Veljković; of the Independent Radicals, Ljubomir Živković, Svetislav Simić, Ljubomir Stojanović, Ljubomir Davidović, Ivan Pavićević. The most effective government spokesmen were Pavle Marinković, Stojan Protić, Milan Kostić, Mihailo Popović, Nastas Petrović, and Milovan Milovanović.

provided. The question was whom Alexander would designate as his successor. The Russians were first to call the king's attention to the question of succession. They allegedly told him that they would wait two and possibly three years for the birth of an heir, and, if one was not born, Russia would have to concern herself with the question of future rule in Serbia. It was widely believed in Serbia that the king was planning to designate the queen's younger brother, Nikodije Lunjevica, as his successor. Rumors to this effect were so widespread that Alexander found it necessary in a speech at Niš on September 23, 1901, to deny them publicly.[118] Meanwhile Draga's brothers enjoyed a privileged position in the court. On festal occasions they were in the immediate presence of the royal pair. The foreign diplomats, and particularly the Austrian minister, resented Draga's relatives and favorites.

The king continued to nurture the cult of his wife. A "queen's medal" was introduced for decorating women distinguished in service of "the king, royal house and state." The family of Lunjevica continued to be treated as if they were members of the royal family, and the king intervened on all sides in behalf of his wife's relatives. The April Constitution permitted the king to designate members of the royal family by statute. There was some fear that the king might exercise this special prerogative and confer royalty on the Lunjevica family.[119]

The funeral of the prominent Radical leader Kosta Taušanović, in early 1902, was turned into a political demonstration against the royal despotism. The passage by the Senate in March 1902 of a law restricting the right of meetings and associations was the occasion for a demonstration by students, many of whom were beaten by the police, who invaded their quarters. In a resolution addressed to the Skupština, the students complained of "brutal attack," and demanded satisfaction for the injury to "academic honor." They threatened not to attend lectures, and because of this the Academic Council dismissed nearly two hundred students from school for a half-year or a year. Twenty students had been jailed for a month. *Dnevni list* denounced the treatment of the students as "brutal, despotic, unprecedented."[120]

The army and the public servants suffered as a result of the depleted state of the treasury. Yet while the number of military recruits was being reduced for reasons of economy, the king was making new generals. The promotion of adjutant Lazar Petrović to the rank of general was much resented. The officers' salaries were in arrears for some months during 1902. The Austrian military attaché reported the Serbian army as poorly dressed and hungry; even the horses lacked fodder. The military machine built up by King Milan was obviously disintegrating.[121]

The king needed a strong government to protect him; he could not rely on the Radicals. The latter were turning against the enacted legislation, characterized as a Radical-Progressive mixture, and were groping for the restoration of the laws based on the Constitution of 1888. The king was beginning to blame the Radicals for everything that went wrong, and the Radicals, having won an electoral majority, wanted exclusive government control. The cabinet formed on October 4 by Pera Velimirović did not give them this control, and because it lacked the Radical majority it was forced to resign a month later. With Velimirović's fall the "fusion" of the Progressives and Radicals came to its final end. The last issue of their joint newspaper, *Dnevnik*, appeared on November 17.[122]

12. KARADJORDJEVIĆ PROPAGANDA AND THE ALAVANTIĆ AFFAIR

The growing dissatisfaction with Alexander gave occasion for a revival of activity by the followers of the Karadjordjević dynasty. Jakov Nenadović, maternal cousin of Peter Karadjordjević, sought to resuscitate Karadjordjević propaganda. On December 12, 1901, as "a political plenipotentiary" of Prince Peter Karadjordjević, Nenadović established contact with the chief of the information section of the Austrian Foreign Office. In his letter to Nenadović, Prince Peter expounded his political program, in which he expressed a desire for friendly relations between Serbia and Austria-Hungary, for reasons of economic necessity.[123] In Budapest a Serb-owned press printed postcards with Peter Karadjordjević's portrait on them, and published a Karadjordjević newspaper and a yearbook.[124]

On February 20, 1902, an inconspicuous supporter of the Karadjordjević cause by the name of Rade Alavantić secretly entered Serbia from Austria-Hungary. He appeared at the border in a general's uniform with an escort of three men. The customs officers respected his rank and took orders from him. He entered the *gendarmerie* quarters at Šabac and proceeded to take over. The commanding officer became suspicious. An altercation ensued, shots were exchanged, and Alavantić fell dead, shouting "Long live Karadjordjević!"[125]

Needless to say, Alavantić's plan to overthrow the dynasty was childish. Yet it seems that Nenadović and the agents of the Russian secret police knew of it. They did not expect the plan to succeed; they were primarily interested in the impression that it would create. It was hoped that the incident might arouse Alexander's suspicion of the Radicals and add to his worries. Once separated from the Radicals, Alexander would have no politcal group to rely on. Some believed that Austria-Hungary was implicated in the affair, and rumors persisted that Peter Karadjordjević was ready to move into Serbia with Austrian backing.[126]

King Alexander had evidently felt insecure even before the Alavantić affair. Toward the end of 1901 the police guard around the court had been increased and the Beograd army garrison was ordered under semipreparedness. To alleviate the king's fears, his first adjutant, General Petrović, slept at the court. At the beginning of 1902, the king was once again in fear of an attack, and appropriate military preparations were made.[127]

13. THE "NEUTRAL" CABINET OF CINCAR-MARKOVIĆ

On November 6, 1902, General Dimitrije Cincar-Marković formed a "neutral" cabinet, including four so-called "court Radicals" and three generals. The program of the new government, made public on November 21, called for a change of constitution, a necessary requisite, no doubt, if the king's personal rule was to be re-established.[128] The king urged the political parties to cease their mutual strife and lend their support to him. A press war ensued between the government and opposition newspapers. The police began interfering with the public meetings. On March 23, 1903, students demonstrated (the "March Demonstration") against the police regime and demanded a democratic constitution. Police, army, and gendarmes were used in dispersing the demonstrators, killing and wounding several. Over a hundred persons were imprisoned, most of whom were freed after brief detention. [129] During the demonstration voices were heard demanding a republican form of government. Some of the army officers appeared to have been implicated in the demonstration; two of them were arrested. The demonstration had in fact reached such proportions that the king and queen feared for their lives.

The opposition accused the police of having deliberately instigated the March disturbance in order to use the incident as a pretext for suspension of the Constitution. On the other hand, the king was convinced that the disturbance had been instigated by his political enemies. [130] The repercussions in the country were tremendous. Popular indignation increased when on March 24 the king suspended the Constitution of 1901, ostensibly on the grounds that the Skupština did not respect its own provisions and that the press abused the privilege it derived from the Constitution. The political parties, the king averred, exploited the Constitution to demand that which it did not provide. He also alluded to the serious foreign problems in the Balkans which required national discipline and unity. The Constitution of 1901 was suspended for only one hour, a length of time sufficient to enable the king to change several important laws—the electoral law and the laws dealing with the press, meetings, and associations. He then dismissed the Skupština, Senate, Privy Council, and judges of the courts. The royal proclamation restoring the Constitution contained also a list of new appointments. [131]

The Radicals in protest against the new electoral law refused to take part in the election held on May 19. Intimidation and police terror were so great that no party could freely participate in the elections. Those who were elected were mostly Liberals and "neutrals." The result was a complete government victory. Seventy-two parliamentary seats went to the right-wing Liberals, thirty-four to the right-wing Progressives, and twenty-four to the so-called "court" Radicals. Alexander was once again relinquishing his role as a constitutional monarch and establishing a personal regime which secured for him all governmental functions. [132]

PART TWO

Foreign Relations, 1901-3

AFTER HIS MARRIAGE ALEXANDER TURNED TO RUSSIA for aid and protection. The Russians helped him achieve his marriage and from time to time backed Serbia's interests in Macedonia and Old Serbia, but they were at no time ready to accord Alexander full and unequivocal support. Relations with Austria-Hungary correspondingly deteriorated, and they were characterized by a series of minor crises and mutual suspicion and distrust. Efforts were made to reach an agreement with Bulgaria over Macedonia, but without success. Nor was Alexander able to establish cordial and friendly relations with Montenegro. Of all the problems involving the country's foreign relations, the problem of Macedonia caused the most grief; it involved not only Serbian relations with the Balkan states but also relations with the Great Powers.

1. THE MACEDONIAN QUESTION AND RELATIONS WITH BULGARIA

Relations between Serbia and Bulgaria were dominated by the "insoluble" Macedonian Question. The continuing disintegration of the Ottoman Empire and the imminence of a complete Ottoman eclipse intensified the Macedonian problem, which became a corollary to the broader Near Eastern question. For the Balkan nations Macedonia was a source of continuous friction and conflict. Greeks, Serbs, and Bulgarians all considered "Macedonians" their unliberated nationals and Macedonia their ancient land. The absence among the Macedonians of national consciousness, as well as of religious and ethnic homogeneity, gave each one of the neighbors an opportunity to claim Macedonia as its own land. Lengthy studies and statistical compilations were prepared to prove that Macedonia historically and ethnically belonged to this or that Balkan nation. A great deal of polemical literature appeared on the subject in Balkan and in the major European languages. Just what constituted territorial Macedonia depended on the interests of the claimant power. However, until 1903 the Balkan states had for the most part resorted to peaceful means—the founding of schools and churches—in furthering their Macedonian aspirations.

Originally the Greeks had had for centuries a distinct advantage in Macedonia, thanks to the fact that the regional Orthodox Church had been subject to the Constantinopolitan patriarchate. In the course of the nineteenth century, rapidly growing Slavic nationalism led to a movement toward the establishment of an independent Slavonic Orthodox Church in order to check the "Hellenization" of the Slavs by the Greek clergy. The Bulgarians were the first to emerge as the defenders of Slavonic Orthodoxy, and their activity ultimately attained pronounced results. On February 28, 1870, on Russian recommendation, the sultan issued an edict permitting the creation of the

Bulgarian exarchate;[1] that is, an autocephalous Bulgarian Church with its seat at Constantinople.

The exarch was the head of the Bulgarian Church and partisan of the Slavic liturgy. He represented the Bulgarian people before the sultan and his ministers, protected their interests, and promoted the cause of Bulgarian nationalism. The jurisdiction of the exarchate covered at first only Bulgaria proper, but was gradually extended to embrace also Rumelia, Old Serbia, and Macedonia.[2]

After the Congress of Berlin (1878) Serbia showed an increasingly active interest in Macedonia. Article VII of the secret Austro-Serbian Convention (June 28, 1881) states:

If, as a result of a combination of circumstances whose development is not to be foreseen at present, Serbia were in a position to make territorial acquisitions in the direction of her southern frontiers (with the exception of the Sandjak of Novipazar), Austria-Hungary will not oppose herself thereto, and will use her influence with the other Powers for the purpose of winning them over to an attitude favorable to Serbia.[3]

This clause was made more precise in the Convention renewed in 1889: Article IV stated that the territorial extension forseen by Article VII in the 1881 Convention "may be carried in the direction of the valley of the Vardar as far as the circumstances will permit."[4] Two additional developments after 1878 served Serbian interests in Macedonia: the Russian fiasco in Bulgaria, 1878–85, and the Bulgarian unification with Rumelia in 1885 which alienated the Ottomans. After that year the Turks became more tolerant of Serbian activity in Macedonia. The Society of St. Sava was organized in 1886 at Beograd for the purpose of educating the "Serbs" in Turkey in the spirit of nationalism.[5] In 1887 Serbia was allowed to open consular offices at Skoplje and Salonika, and subsequently at Bitolj (1888) and Priština (1889). In 1901 permission was granted for a consular office at Prizren, but the unsettled conditions there prevented its establishment.[6]

In 1889 Nikola Pašić visited Sofia in hope of promoting an entente between his country and Bulgaria. Stefan Stambolov, then all-powerful prime minister of Bulgaria, suspected the Beograd government, which had given refuge to many of his political enemies, and Pašić's mission bore no fruit. The Serbs next turned to Greece for an agreement. In this way they also hoped to befriend the Greek Patriarch, who would give Serbia permission to establish churches in Macedonia and send clergy thither. The preliminary discussions with the Greek envoy were begun in 1890 in Beograd. Kharilaos Trikoupis, in the hope of bringing both Serbia and Bulgaria into a Balkan agreement, visited Beograd and Sofia. The agreement he envisaged included two basic points: defensive league against Turkey, and partition of Macedonia. The Bulgarian government rejected the proposal, while Serbia in 1892 submitted a draft for an agreement. The negotiations did not materialize, primarily because the Greeks feared the Serbo-Greek agreement would serve to cement Bulgaro-Turkish relations.[7]

In the period from 1889 to 1892 the Serbian government took the leadership in Macedonian work away from private groups. It now directly sought Russian backing of Serbia's Macedonian claims. Russia was urged to exercise pressure in Istanbul with the view of obtaining for Serbia religious and educational privileges in Macedonia. At a special conference in the latter part of 1891, the consular agents from Macedonia and other appropriate Serbian officials prepared a plan for action in Macedonia. They proposed to open girls' and boys' schools wherever possible and necessary, distribute free textbooks, give regular salaries to teachers, disseminate literature, and, finally, they proposed to create a Macedonian propaganda section within the Ministry of Foreign Affairs.[8] It was also planned to organize the émigrés from Old Serbia and Macedonia into brotherhoods (*bratstva*) under a central leadership, publish selected books in the Serbian literary language, establish a newspaper service, introduce literary Serbian into church services, and to found at the Monastery of Hilendar (Mt. Athos) a school of theology which would offer, in addition to regular theological subjects, courses in business, medicine, and certain other skills.[9] This program was adopted and by and large remained the basis of Serbian activities in Macedonia until the First Balkan War (1912). Within the next ten years the Serbs achieved marked success in Macedonia and Old Serbia. The number of their schools in these regions grew rapidly. In 1901 there were 226 primary schools, four gymnasia, one school of theology, and three high schools for girls. The total number of schools of all kinds soon reached three hundred.[10]

On the religious side the Serbs were less successful. It was not until 1896 that they were able through Russian pressure on the sultan and the Ecumenical Patriarch to receive the right to name their first bishop in Turkey—at Prizren. This was the first important victory on the religious front in Macedonia. However, in the struggle with the Greeks for an episcopal right at Skoplje,* the Serbs lost out.[11]

Unstable political conditions in Serbia from 1892 to 1898 caused the government to stress diplomatic means toward furtherance of its interests in Macedonia. The official policy during this period has sometimes been described as Turkophile, because the government believed that through a policy of friendship with Turkey that power would allow Serbia to build additional schools and churches in Turkey.[12] Furthermore, traditionally pro-Austrian, Novaković embarked temporarily on a pro-Russian and a "Slavophile" policy, expressed in his efforts to effect a *rapprochement* among the Balkan states. Under Russian auspices, in April 1896 Prince Ferdinand of Bulgaria visited King Alexander at Beograd. This was a "purely diplomatic visit," in contrast to the visit by Prince Nikola of Montenegro on St. Vitus' Day, 1896, which turned into a great manifestation of Serbian national solidarity. The Austrian press was very much alarmed, particularly over the patriotic sentiments uttered by the Montenegrin prince.

Despite this deterioration in relations, Alexander could not bring himself to break completely with Austria-Hungary, as is evident from his inopportune decoration of Benjamin von Kállay, minister for Bosna and Hercegovina.

* Skopje in Macedonian; Üsküb in Turkish.

Because he acted without consulting his government, Novaković resigned in December 1896.[13] The new cabinet, which was formed by Djordje Simić on December 17, 1896, consisted primarily of Radicals. Four months later, in April 1897, Turkey declared war on Greece. The war stirred up Muslim against Christian in the Ottoman Empire. The Muslim Albanians, recognizing the Serbian threat to their national cause, engaged in terroristic acts against their Serbian neighbors. The Serbian government feared that the war might open up the entire Near Eastern question. The Bulgarians proposed to negotiate with Serbia to provide for any eventualities. After lengthy discussions on the occasion of Alexander's visit to Sofia, on February 19, 1897, the two states signed the *Ugodba*, which affirmed that neither would undertake any political or military action that might affect the status quo in the Balkans without prior agreement. Until the two powers could establish their spheres of interest in the Ottoman Empire, they would allow each other complete freedom in the field of educational, religious, and national work there.[14] Montenegro was invited to join in the agreement.

Prince Nikola of Montenegro was not unwilling to enter into an agreement with Serbia and Bulgaria at that time. But during Alexander's visit to Cetinje in April 1897, the prince raised the question of delimitation of Serbian and Montenegrin spheres of interest in the Ottoman Empire, and specifically laid claim to Plevlje, Prizren, Djakovica, and Debar. Both Serbian states wanted Prizren, and for that reason they failed to reach an agreement.[15]

Simić's cabinet had won a few minor successes in Macedonia. The Porte removed the Greek bishop from Skoplje and allowed temporary appointment of a Serbian archimandrite as episcopal administrator. Simić's efforts to separate the Serbian Church from the Greek and to establish a Serbian patriarchate were without result.[16] Nor had the Turks yet shown willingness to recognize officially the existence of the Serbian as a separate nationality in their empire.[17] The minor educational and religious concessions that were made by the Turks were principally the result of Russian pressure on the Porte and the Turko-Greek war which forced the Turks to bribe the Serbs in order to keep them neutral.

The Serbo-Bulgarian understanding never became effective because the two parties failed to agree on the delimitation of spheres of influence in the adjacent, dominantly Slavic areas of the Ottoman Empire.[18] Simultaneously, the relations with Russia worsened as a result of King Milan's return to Beograd in October 1897. The Simić cabinet resigned, and when the new one was formed (October 11, 1897–July 8, 1901) by Vladan Djordjević, a personal friend of King Milan, the pro-Austrian foreign policy was revived.[19] Russia withdrew her support of Serbian claims in Macedonia and once again befriended Bulgaria. Because of trivial irritations, said to have been caused by the Serbian government, the Russian minister was recalled from Beograd, and the Russian chargé d'affaires, Pavel Mansurov, was left to maintain the delicate relations with the Serbian court and government. In December 1897 the tsar, showing his disgust with the Obrenović dynasty, gave Prince Karadjordjević, pretender to the Serbian throne, an official audience. The "diplomatic strike" by Russia lasted from October 1897 to

June 1898, when Zhadovsky was appointed minister to Beograd. Relations with Russia, however, remained strained.[20] From the end of 1897 to the beginning of 1899 a series of diplomatic conflicts between Serbia and Bulgaria followed in succession over Macedonia. In the beginning of 1899 a new government came to power in Sofia, less subject to Russian influence, and the Serbs took the opportunity once again to approach Bulgaria for her friendship. The situation in Macedonia had become critical, and responsible persons in Serbia felt that their country should not find itself on bad terms with both Turkey and Bulgaria. They also worried over the rumors of Bulgaro-Montenegrin understanding. But efforts to negotiate an agreement with Bulgaria failed.

Djordjević, who had received an offer from the Greek government for common action in Macedonia, attempted to reach a formal agreement with Greece. In 1899 the treaty negotiations with Greece collapsed as a result of Serbia's unwillingness to meet the Greek request that the Serbian government abolish the consular offices at Serez and Salonika before Greece recognized Firmilijan as Bishop of Skoplje and a Serbian metropolitan for the Veles-Debar region.[21] For a variety of reasons, therefore, Serbia had failed to reach agreement regarding Macedonia with either of the three Balkan states—Bulgaria, Montenegro, Greece—and had lost both the Austrian and the Russian backing for her national claims.

By the turn of the century Macedonia was in a state of veritable chaos, and was inundated with bands and revolutionary groups, the most active of whom were those organized and directed from Bulgaria. In 1893 there had come into existence the so-called Internal Macedonian Revolutionary Organization (IMRO), which represented a group of Macedonian refugees. The IMRO attracted supporters from all social strata under the leadership of two Macedonian nationalists, Damian Gruev (1871–1906) and Goce Delčev (1872–1903). The two leaders organized a revolutionary movement in Macedonia and gave it its "basic ideological direction." The original IMRO objectives were twofold: to obtain an autonomy for Macedonia in which all Macedonians regardless of their nationality would enjoy full equality; and to oppose partitioning of Macedonia. Likewise, in 1893 was organized the first Macedonian socialist group, headed by Vasil Glavinov, a cabinetmaker from Veles. Other important socialists included in this group were Nikola Karev, Vele Markov, and Nikola Rusenski. Both the IMRO and this small socialist group initiated a program of educational, political, and organizational work. The communist sources tell us that the IMRO at this time was "a progressive-populist" type of organization, led by prominent and distinguished revolutionaries—Gruev, Delčev, Djordje Petrov, Jane Sandanski, and others. Delčev was considered especially able and "an inflammatory tribune." He maintained a close contact with socialists, some of whom were also members of the IMRO. IMRO, in fact, became a broad popular front representing the "oppressed masses" of Macedonia.[22] It became a well-knit organization supposedly based on "democratic revolutionary principles." The main object was to prepare the masses for an armed struggle toward national liberation. Delčev was sure that outside aid would not serve the cause of the Macedonians, and he took a stand that national liberation must be the work of the Macedonians themselves.[23]

The IMRO developed from a local committee into a "national liberation movement." It took four years (until November 14, 1897) and an incident known as "Vinishkata afera" for the Turkish authorities to track down the conspiracy. Meanwhile, having lost control over the revolutionary activity in Macedonia, the Bulgarian government decided to establish a Macedonian political organization that could be controlled. Under the auspices of the Bulgarian Crown, the so-called Supreme Macedono-Adrianopolitan Committee (Supremists) was organized in Sofia in 1894. Its members were known as "Supremists" (Vrkhovists) or the "External Organization," and ostensibly represented the Macedonian immigrants in Bulgaria. The purpose of the Supremists, among other things, seems to have been to transform the IMRO into an instrument for furthering the cause of "Greater Bulgaria," and to strive toward annexation of Macedonia to Bulgaria. Supremists at once sent bands (*cheti*) into Macedonia and provoked armed conflict with the Turkish garrisons. The Turkish authorities carried out severe reprisals on the population and seriously damaged the IMRO organization, killing many of its leaders. A communist source tells us that the aim of the Supremists was to demoralize the Macedonian masses, to kill confidence in their own power for a liberation struggle.[24]

The actions of the Supreme Committee were at the very beginning controlled by Stefan Stambolov,[25] the noted Bulgarian prime minister. After his fall in 1894, the Stoilov government permitted the Supremists to terrorize Macedonia and to plan an uprising in 1895, which was unsuccessful. The Supremists became especially active when Tsonchev, ex-general of the Bulgarian army, assumed control over them.[26]

Mihailo Vujić's coalition cabinet (March 23, 1901–October 4, 1902), although divided on internal matters, was in full agreement on foreign policy. Both parties in the cabinet had pro-Russian leanings, and the Russians lost no opportunity in making their influence felt in Beograd. They apparently advised the establishment of close relations with Bulgaria and Montenegro, in an endeavor "to tie all their Balkan protégés into a single package."[27] The Radical party was particularly cordial to any such suggestion, since it had always favored Serbo-Bulgarian agreement as a step toward a broader Balkan alliance.

In 1901 discussions were started by Serbia and Bulgaria with a view toward achieving a general agreement which would have included the eventual partition of Macedonia between them. The Serbian policy was outlined in a Foreign Ministry circular (April 9, 1902) which recommended an understanding with Bulgaria because their mutual rivalry weakened the resistance of the people of Macedonia. The circular stressed the dire consequences to the Slavic cause that would arise if Austria-Hungary were to establish itself in Kosovo. The Serbs proposed that they and the Bulgarians abstain from disturbing peace in Macedonia. They also desired by diplomatic means to persuade Turkey to renounce the policy of favoring the Albanians and not to wait for foreign intervention before cleaning its own house. Both the Serbian and Montenegrin rulers favored a policy of status quo rather than an aggressive action with regard to Macedonia that might precipitate a Macedonian uprising.[28]

The Macedonian revolutionaries at the time had also embarked on a policy favoring Serbo-Bulgarian solidarity. Boris Sarafov (1872–1907), who had been elected president of the Supreme Committee in 1899, began to soft-pedal the idea of a "Greater Bulgaria," and emphasized the principle of Macedonian autonomy. This policy made it possible for the Supremists to enlist followers from all Macedonian nationalities. The Supremists even made their way to Serbia to solicit aid. Svetislav Simić, chief of the propaganda section in the Beograd Foreign Office, served as their principal contact with the Serbian government. Both government and king rejected any co-operation with the Supremists, whose true objective remained Bulgarian annexation of Macedonia.

The latest attempts to reach an agreement with Bulgaria were no more successful than earlier ones. The Bulgarians insisted on "autonomous" Macedonia, the Serbs on "partition" of Macedonia.[29] If an agreement could not be reached on partition of Macedonia between Bulgaria and Serbia, the Serb leaders preferred to maintain the status quo. In exchange for western Macedonia, Premier Vujić was prepared to relinquish the eastern part of the province to Bulgaria. The Bulgarians ostensibly refused to sign any agreements involving lands belonging to their suzerain, the Turkish sultan, but in fact opposed the partition of Macedonia, and continued to claim the whole province. An autonomous Macedonia would have favored Bulgaria by virtue of her religious control in the province and the power of the Bulgaria-orientated revolutionaries. It was also a more popular policy. Indeed, by rejecting the autonomy of Macedonia, the Serbs alienated many Macedonians who were anxious to win freedom from the Turks, and thereby pushed them into the Bulgarian fold.[30] The Austrian military attaché, Joseph Pomiankowski, reported on March 27, 1902, that Serbia, suspicious of Bulgaria's attitude regarding Macedonia, "sincerely desires the maintenance of the status quo." A month earlier Alexander himself assured the Austrian minister that he would not "even move a finger" with regard to Macedonia. In 1902–3 Bulgaria once again took the offensive in Macedonia, while Serbia, for the most part, remained on the defensive in fear of Austro-Hungarian action and because of domestic uncertainty.[31]

2. RELATIONS WITH MONTENEGRO

The Vujić government restored friendly relations with Montenegro, and in June 1901 sent a special representative to Cetinje. King Alexander, however, lacked confidence in the Montenegrin court. He envied Prince Nikola, who had been received by the Russian tsar at the time when Alexander had failed to obtain a reception.[32] He suspected that two daughters of the Montenegrin prince who were married to Russian grand dukes might have deliberately spoiled his chances of reception at the Russian court. Moreover, Alexander's lack of confidence in the Montenegrin court seemed confirmed when he learned from the Bulgarian prince that Nikola had suggested a Bulgaro-Montenegrin alliance. Such an alliance, Alexander believed, could be directed only against Serbia. Alexander would appoint only trusted confidants as ministers in Sofia (Pavle Marinković) and in Cetinje (Miloš Našić), although the Serbian government and Prince Nikola favored Jevrem Velimirović, brother of Pera Velimirović. Alexander disapproved of the friendship the Radical party nurtured for Montenegro and Bulgaria and found it expedient, therefore, to appoint personal friends as representatives to these countries.[33]

An incident in the spring of 1902 contributed toward the further deterioration of Montenegrin-Serbian relations. The second son of Prince Nikola had married the daughter of Colonel Alexander Konstantinović, a relative of King Alexander, and after his marriage Konstantinović had resigned from the Serbian army and left the country. Suspicious Alexander saw in the marriage an ulterior motive on the part of Prince Nikola, an effort to establish blood ties with the Obrenović house as he had done earlier with the Karadjordjević house. The marriage would strengthen the prince's claims to the Serbian throne. Nikola assured Alexander that no significance should be attached to the marriage, but nonetheless Alexander declined to participate in or be represented at the wedding.[34]

3. RELATIONS WITH AUSTRIA-HUNGARY

Serbian relations with Austria-Hungary left much to be desired. Throughout 1901–2 the Vienna press reported alarming rumors regarding a Serbo-Bulgarian alliance against Turkey, a Russo-Serbian military convention, and Serbo-Montenegrin preparation for invasion and occupation of Old Serbia. These rumors did much to strain the relations between Serbia and Turkey,[35] as was most probably intended by Austria-Hungary. Alexander's marriage and behavior at the time of his father's burial were much resented in Vienna. The Austrian press spared no words in criticizing Serbia and her dynasty, and reported and sensationalized the "false expectancy" in all its unpleasant detail. The tone was so provocative that the Russians expressed serious concern to the Austrian archduke, who was visiting St. Petersburg at the time.[36]

In 1901 there were widespread rumors that Austria was planning to annex the Sandjak of Novi Pazar. There were reports of expanded Austrian garrisons in the Sandjak. An official announcement of the Sarajevo-Sandjak railway project gave credence to these reports.

Alexander was convinced of the inimical attitude of his neighbor when in July 1901 Austria began applying repressive measures against Serbia's foreign trade. This was a traditional recourse whenever Austria wished to punish Serbia or exact a political concession from her. Austria-Hungary stopped the importation of horned cattle from the Beograd district altogether on the pretext that the animals were infected, and allowed imports from other districts only under special conditions. In December imports were stopped from two other districts. Normal relations in trade were not restored until June 1902. Serbia, whose trade was almost exclusively directed toward Austrian markets, suffered considerable economic loss.[37]

Alexander tried to improve his relations with Austria-Hungary; he assured Austria of his honest intentions and suggested a visit to his father's grave at Krušedol, a procedure which might end his quarrel with the emperor. Vienna, however, no longer trusted Alexander. His latest overtures were considered to be merely endeavors to intimidate Russia into giving him and Draga an Imperial reception. He was permitted to visit Krušedol, but the Austrian government refused to attach any political significance to the visit.[38] Vujić's government failed to improve relations with Austria-Hungary.

4. TURKEY AND ALBANIAN NATIONALISM

Nor were the relations with Turkey always harmonious. Abdul Hamid had congratulated Alexander and Draga on their marriage and sent Draga a decoration. For a brief period the Turkish minister was among the most favored friends of the court. Alexander had planned to pay his respects to the sultan after the projected Russian visit and take up the question of Serbia's interests in Old Serbia and Macedonia. The Russians, who had ignored Serbian interests in Turkey during the time of Djordjević's cabinet when King Milan's influence was paramount in Beograd, now made frequent interventions at Constantinople on behalf of Serbia. Russian support was decisive in connection with the appointment of Bishop Firmilijan. The Russian ambassador in March 1902 reminded the sultan that the Patriarch had chosen Firmilijan as Bishop of Skoplje in 1899, and that he had been waiting three years for the Porte's approval. In May 1902 the long awaited *berat* was issued by which Firmilijan was confirmed Bishop of Skoplje. The installation services were held in the monastery of Skalota near Enos.[39] This Serbian success backed by Russian diplomacy was not viewed favorably in Austria-Hungary; a responsible official reminded his friends that Serbia "still lies within the range of Austrian guns."[40]

Albanian nationalism and Serbo-Albanian conflict in Old Serbia for the first time assumed importance during the period of the Djordjević cabinet (1897–1900), causing frequent tension in Serbian relations with Turkey. A number of Albanians had volunteered in the Turkish army in the recent war against the Greeks. Upon demobilization they retained their arms, which they used to molest their Christian neighbors. In a note to the Porte, May 26, 1898, Serbia cited four hundred cases of crimes against Serbian elements committed by the Albanians during 1897. The Serbs demanded at various times a commission of inquiry, intervention by the Great Powers, and permission to make a military demonstration on the frontier. The Turks employed dilatory tactics, and Austria-Hungary, which could not allow Serbian success against the Albanians, rejected Serbian proposals outright. In June 1899 and in the course of 1900 the Albanians crossed into Serbia proper and carried on raids in the frontier villages.[41] In 1901 the situation became even worse. The Austro-Hungarians, having lost their favored place in Beograd, increased their support to the Albanians. The Serbs in turn began to smuggle arms to their hard-pressed kinsmen in Old Serbia, and the Turks countered by severe measures in searching for arms. Ćorović says that after 1878 Turkey's policy was to prepare Albania as a kind of military frontier against Serbia. The Albanians were, he said, favored in the court of Abdul Hamid.

As soon as the Porte started oppressing Serbian nationals, the Albanians joined in. In the summer of 1901 one Isa Boletin was particularly notorious in persecution of the Serbs, especially in and around Kolašin, where a "massacre of Serbs" took place. The Serbian government suspected that his activity was backed by the Porte as well as by Austria-Hungary. It believed the latter hoped to see the elimination of the Serbs in Old Serbia in order to create a compact Albanian region which would serve as a check against possible Serbian expansion. Because only the Orthodox Christians were attacked by the Albanians and not the Roman Catholic Albanians, many observers, among them Russian Ambassador Zinoviev in Constantinople and the sultan himself, alleged that the most recent Albanian attacks were inspired by Austria-Hungary.[42]

Russia sympathized with Serbia on the question of the Albanian terror. Her consul at Skoplje examined the areas of terror and confirmed the authenticity of the Kolašin massacre. The Russian ambassador demanded that the Porte cease searching the Serbs for arms, release those imprisoned, and replace Asaf-Pasha, the *mutesarif* of Priština, who was apparently implicated in the Kolašin massacre. The Russian demands were met, and persecution of the Serbs subsided. Unfortunately, about 1,500 refugees who had arrived in Serbia dared not return home, despite promises of protection by the Porte, and had to be maintained at Serbian expense. The Serbs were indignant, and Vujić was forced to declare in the Senate that if massacres did not cease the government would request the intervention of the signatories of the Treaty of Berlin.[43]

Suddenly a serious conflict occurred among the Albanian leaders, principally between Mola Zeka and Adem Zajim. The resultant anarchy in Old Serbia did not spare the Serbs ; strong men were virtual lords over individual districts. Isa Boletin established himself over the *nahis* of Mitrovica and Novi Pazar, and issued demands to the sultan. The Porte was unable to stop Albanian terrorism against the Serbs. In order to observe the situation more closely, the Russians on May 7, 1902, opened a consulate in Mitrovica ; their first consul, Grigorii S. Shcherbina, who had served in Scutari, was disliked by the Albanians and suspected by the Austrians. Indeed, the Turks cautioned him not to proceed to Mitrovica at once but to await the pacification of the district.[44]

On August 14, 1902, with Russian backing, the Serbian government sent to the Porte a note which demanded improvement of conditions in Old Serbia. It called for replacement and punishment of the incompetent officials, increased military protection for Serbs living in regions heavily populated by Albanians, and the disarming of the Albanians. If the Albanians could not be disarmed, the Serbian government requested permission for the Serbian population to bear arms in self-defense. The note further asked for the correct application of existing laws and general amelioration of the adverse conditions by means of a series of reforms. The suggested reforms specified the recognition of Serbian nationality, greater participation of Christians in the courts, administration, *gendarmerie*, and improvement of agrarian relations and the tax system. The note was followed by a large demonstration in Beograd protesting the terror in Old Serbia and Macedonia, and the Russians backed the Serbian note as "very reasonable and justifiable." The compliance with the note, it was believed, would not affect the status of Turkey; it merely meant the *status quo amélioré par les réformes*.[45] The Russians, however, were not yet ready to give Serbia unequivocal support, and so long as relations with Russia remained uncertain it seemed impossible for Serbia to pursue a successful policy in Old Serbia and Macedonia.

5. RELATIONS WITH RUSSIA

After his marriage Alexander geared his country's foreign orientation toward Russia but erred in depending too much on the good will of his "best man." The Russians made it known in no uncertain terms that so long as the Radical party was not in power they would not engage in serious political discussions with Alexander. They were, however, ready to assist Serbia in getting a loan in Paris, something they had previously steadfastly refused to do. On the other hand, they refused to sponsor at Alexander's suggestion a Serbo-Bulgarian agreement for division of Macedonia into spheres of influence. Such an agreement was, they felt, premature, since it might open the whole "Eastern question."[46] Alexander was denied an Imperial reception until he settled first the internal problems in his own country. But to compensate for their refusal to honor Alexander's request, the Russians, late in 1900, arranged a meeting at Niš between the Bulgarian Prince Ferdinand and Serbian royalty.[47]

Officially at least, the Russians minimized the importance of Alexander's reorientation. They told the Austrians that it meant nothing more than restoration of normal diplomatic relations. The Austrians in turn assured the Russians that they considered the situation in Beograd Alexander's personal affair although they were concerned over the political instability of Serbia, and declared that whatever happened in Beograd they would not allow the prince of Montenegro to succeed to the Serbian throne. This seemed to imply that they were willing to accept some other candidate, possibly even Peter Karadjordjević.[48] In 1901 and 1902 there were rumors that Austria-Hungary and Russia were conspiring to replace King Alexander by Prince Peter Karadjordjević. During his visit in Vienna in January 1902 Mijatović had the impression that the matter of replacing Alexander by Peter "was completely arranged" between the aforementioned powers. By the end of 1901, Austria and Russia, according to Mijatović, must have come to an understanding on "the possible, or even probable, change on the throne of Serbia."[49] But in May 1900 Count Goluchowski told Count von Bülow, the Secretary of State for Foreign Affairs of Germany, that "Austria-Hungary will never allow a union between Serbia and Montenegro."[50] Likewise Count Goluchowski told the German ambassador, Prince Eulenburg, on January 6, 1901, that "we shall simply strangle Serbia should anything serious happen in the Balkans and Serbia adopt a line of policy we did not like."[51] By breaking his promise to marry Princess Alexandra von Schaumburg-Lippe, King Alexander had angered Francis Joseph, and his estrangement from father Milan brought an end to the Austrophile foreign orientation of Serbia. Nor could Emperor Wilhelm forgive him. Alexander subsequently explained that his interest in Alexandra had been but "a simple courtesy to the Kaiser."[52]

Soon after Milan's death in the spring of 1901, the Russians sent N. V. T. Charykov, their new minister, to Beograd. The king suspended the official mourning for his father in order to give as fine a welcome as possible to Charykov, who found his post at Beograd as difficult as the one he had held in Bokhara.[53] After many years of Austrian predominance in Serbia, Charykov found much work to be done "to re-establish cordial relations." The Russian objectives were, he said, to improve relations between Serbia and Bulgaria, "to develop Russian navigation on the Danube in conjunction with that of Serbia, to prepare for the construction of the 'Adriatic Railway,' which should join the Danube to the Adriatic through Serbia and Montenegro, to study the possibility of growing cotton in south Serbia, and to help, as much as possible, Serbia's renaissance to an economic independence."[54] With these Russian interests in mind he describes in his memoirs how he made a trip down the Danube to Radujevac on the Serbo-Bulgarian frontier, and thence to Niš "along the probable course of the Adriatic Railway." He says that no Russian minister had ever been seen in those parts, and the inhabitants accorded him "a glorious welcome." The Imperial interests in Serbia were, it would seem, as far-reaching as those of the Soviet Union in Yugoslavia!

The Russians felt uncertain of Serbia's friendship so long as foreign affairs remained in the hands of the king. Paradoxically, absolutist and autocratic Russia supported a constitutional regime in Serbia. The Radical party, which was the strongest popular party and which stood for a constitutional regime, was traditionally Russophile; hence the Russians insisted that power be turned over to the Radicals.

Since Alexander's marriage the Russians had held a dominant position in Beograd, and Minister Charykov acted as principal councilor for the Crown and the government. He interfered in all matters of foreign and domestic policy. He kept in close association with the leaders of the Radical party and on occasion mediated between them and the court. In 1901, on the tsar's nameday, there was a big reception at the Russian Legation; hundreds of invitations were sent out, and Charykov received Serbian delegations from Old Serbia and Bosna. Colonel Grabov—in charge of Russian espionage—placed his agents in strategic posts, and only he and King Alexander knew of their activities. Together the Russian diplomats and the intelligence agents worked on the Serbo-Bulgarian *rapprochement*, and quite probably sponsored the aforementioned meeting between Svetislav Simić and the Macedonian Boris Sarafov.[55]

Alexander had surrendered to the Russians primarily for personal reasons. After the "false expectancy" of the queen he realized that he and she had lost what public esteem they might have enjoyed. The prestige of the royal family, he believed, might be restored if they were recognized by the Russian tsar. For that reason he still strove to arrange the reception at the Russian court. But the tsar, who had recently received princes of Bulgaria and Montenegro, kept postponing the reception of the Serbian royalty. Charykov repeatedly assured Alexander that his reception in St. Petersburg was certain and that upon his return from a leave, which he took toward the end of 1901, he would announce the exact day of the reception. Charykov's return was impatiently awaited. But when he did return, he brought no news concerning the reception, ostensibly because he had been unable to see the emperor. Nevertheless, Alexander and Draga continued to hope. Charykov led them to believe that the reception would surely come about in the autumn of 1902.[56] This was confirmed in June by Lamsdorff, the Russian foreign minister, who informed the Serbian government that the tsar would receive the royal pair at Livadia. The Russian and Serbian press featured the trip. Alexander was expecting the tsar's formal invitation in September or early October, but on September 4 a note from Lamsdorff informed him that owing to the illness of the tsarina the reception was again postponed.

The daughters of the Montenegrin prince, wives of Russian grand dukes, had apparently ruined whatever chance Alexander and Draga might have had of being received in St. Petersburg. They passed on to the tsarina all the scandals attached to Draga's past life.[57] Lamsdorff had hoped to prevail over the tsarina notwithstanding, and this hope accounts for Charykov's optimistic belief that the royal pair would be received sooner or later. Charykov found himself in an awkward position; he had personally assured Alexander that he would be received. He rushed to Niš to explain and apologize. The furious Alexander refused to listen to him, and returned to Beograd, to accuse Vujić's cabinet of failing to bring about the reception in Russia and of having been unduly influenced by Charykov; he asked for the resignation of the cabinet.[58]

Charykov tells us how the king pressed him to secure a definite date for the projected reception at the court of St. Petersburg, and how he [Charykov] transmitted the request to Lamsdorff, but received dilatory answers. The reason for this "could be traced to irresponsible feminine influences directed against Queen Draga." Charykov felt that the political importance of a refusal was so great that he wrote to Lamsdorff again and again, telling him that unless the royal pair were received "a breach would inevitably result between King Alexander and his people and endanger the peace of Serbia."[59]

6. THE MACEDONIAN TURMOIL AND LAMSDORFF'S VISIT

The feud in 1902 among the Macedonian revolutionary leaders temporarily precluded large-scale insurrection in Macedonia, although in the autumn of 1902 there were signs of possible trouble. Prince Ferdinand and the war minister, General Paprikov, seemed ready to avail the revolutionaries of Bulgaria's support. *Ergo* Alexander decided Serbia must be militarily prepared in case the trouble in Macedonia flared up. In 1902 he had ordered 25 million bullets and obtained from the Skupština a special military credit of 360,000 dinars to meet the costs of mobilization. The Cincar-Marković government ordered 45 million bullets, 50,000 trench coats, 40,000 pairs of shoes, and a battery of rapid-firing guns. Premier Cincar-Marković and War Minister Milovan Pavlović, aware of the country's unpreparedness, favored a policy of peace. King Alexander felt that war was unavoidable, and was determined to prepare for it. He believed that the year 1903 would bring partial liberation of the Serbs in Turkey and declared that no Balkan power would get Macedonian territory without Serbia obtaining her share.[60] Austria and Russia took a serious view of these latest Balkan developments, and exerted pressure on Serbia and Bulgaria to cease their warlike preparations.

In December 1902 the Russian foreign minister, Count Vladimir Nikolaevich Lamsdorff, paid Alexander a visit to discourage him from taking any rash action "after the king had made a bellicose speech to his officers at Niš." Lamsdorff apparently felt that written dispatches to Bulgaria and Serbia on the question of Macedonia were insufficient; a personal talk with the heads of the two Balkan nations was necessary.[61] He was also anxious to see Alexander and soothe the ill feeling caused by St. Petersburg's refusal to receive him and Draga. Lamsdorff arrived in Beograd from Vienna on December 23, and before he saw the king he heard a detailed report from Charykov on the situation in Serbia. Instead of rushing from Niš to Beograd to meet Lamsdorff, Alexander had him come to Niš. Lamsdorff pressed upon Alexander the necessity "to pursue a policy of peace." He frankly stated that Russia was preoccupied with Far Eastern matters and needed peace in the Near East. He let Alexander know that unless Serbia and Bulgaria maintained peace, Russia would not assist them in their educational and religious work in Macedonia, and that in accordance with the Russo-Austrian agreement of 1897, the status quo must be maintained in the Balkans. Lamsdorff apologized for the tsar's failure to receive Alexander and Draga but no longer showed any particular interest in the internal affairs of Serbia, and Alexander got no satisfactory answer to his query about what Russia would do if Austro-Russian diplomacy failed to preserve peace in the Balkans.[62]

The question of the succession was a vital concern to Alexander. Alexander feared that Lamsdorff might suggest for the successor Prince Mirko of Montenegro, who he believed was the Russian preference for the Serbian kingship. Lamsdorff however did not even broach the question of succession.[63] At a court dinner that followed the audience, the atmosphere was rather cool.

Lamsdorff's impression of Draga was not too favorable although he found her beautiful and intelligent. From Niš he continued to Sofia, and when he passed again through Beograd on the way to St. Petersburg he told Muraviev, secretary of the Russian Legation, to tell Charykov "not to meddle with the internal affairs of Serbia, but to take care that its foreign policy continued to be in complete harmony with that of Russia." Charykov concludes that neither Lamsdorff nor he knew that "this order was the death warrant" of

Alexander and Draga.[64] On his return to Russia, Lamsdorff told General Kuropatkin that it would be unwise to enter into a military convention with Serbia because it would probably be betrayed to Austria-Hungary. He added that if Alexander should be designated as commander of a Russian regiment, the gesture would be most pleasing to him.[65] Indeed, immediately upon Lamsdorff's departure Alexander had informed the Austrian minister, Count Heidler, of his entire conversation with Lamsdorff.[66]

In Beograd and Sofia Lamsdorff made it clear that "Russia would not allow herself to be drawn on any pretext into armed intervention in the Balkans, or again sacrifice Russian lives and treasure to further the aims of the agitators against Turkish rule."[67] In Vienna Lamsdorff elaborated with Goluchowski a program of Macedonian reforms, the so-called "Vienna scheme."[68] The principal points of the program specified reorganization of the *gendarmerie* and police, and improvement of the tax system.

On February 22, 1903, the Turkish Council of Ministers approved the Imperial irade accepting the reforms proposed by the government of Austria-Hungary and Russia.[69] When the reorganization of the *gendarmerie* under the European officers made no progress, the Austrian and Russian governments intervened anew with the Turkish government. They demanded action, and threatened otherwise "to withdraw the guaranty previously given for the conduct of the Balkan states."[70] The Porte was reluctant to accept any new infringements upon its national sovereignty, but under the combined pressure of Austria and Russia, and subsequently of others of the Great Powers, it accepted the reform project, initiating thereby an era of reforms which was to extend from 1903 to 1908.

Meanwhile Serbia's relations with Russia worsened. Alexander could not forgive the Russians for denying him an imperial reception. On the other hand, the Russians did not approve the latest political developments in Serbia, and, although Charykov was a representative of an autocratic ruler, he did not hesitate to censure the Serbian regime for violation of the Constitution.[71]

The Serbs, however, had promised Lamsdorff that they would not disturb the peace, and at the beginning of February the government of Cincar-Marković, in a note to the powers, stated its official Macedonian policy as that of peace and tranquillity, and of furtherance of the pacific reform of the administration in Macedonia.[72] But in the spring of 1903, when Turkey concentrated troops on the Serbian frontiers, Alexander said he would consider mobilization unless he received official assurance "from Russia and Austria-Hungary that Turkey would not invade Serbia."[73] Vienna and St. Petersburg warned him to abstain from any military action, and the Russians reminded him that complications might force a decision relative to future Obrenović rule. The threat touched on a sensitive issue, and Alexander, who had ample reasons to suspect the Russians, was profoundly shaken.[74]

7. BELATED OVERTURES TO AUSTRIA-HUNGARY

The accession of the cabinet of Cincar-Marković and the king's return to personal rule had been signs of a change in foreign policy. Indeed, overtures had at once been made to Austria for an improvement of relations which might be symbolized by the reception of the Serbian royal family at the Habsburg court. After Lamsdorff's visit to him, Alexander intensified his effort to befriend Austria. At the end of 1902 Alexander and Draga paid homage to Milan's grave at Krušedol, hoping that this gesture might induce Francis Joseph to forget Alexander's behavior on the occasion of his father's death. But Vienna was adamant on this issue, even though the usual courtesies were extended the Serbian royal family, the *ban* (governor) of Croatia, Count Charles Khuen-Héderváry, coming out to meet them on the emperor's instructions. These belated efforts were not taken very seriously in Austria, for Alexander's policy shift appeared to be merely a tactical move to induce Russia to take Serbia back into favor. The visit to Austria-Hungary was interpreted as a move on the part of Alexander to arrange a royal reception for Draga in Austria-Hungary and perhaps to engage in some nationalistic strutting before the Serbs in Hungary.[75] On February 11, 1903, the *Neue Freie Presse* warned that recent developments have proved "the line of policy which King Alexander has embarked upon to be a fatal mistake."

During the final months of his life Alexander repeated his overtures to Austria. He feared that the Russians were planning to replace his dynasty in Serbia with some other and that they favored Bulgaria over Serbia in their Balkan objectives. The increase of Bulgarian guerrilla activity in Macedonia in early 1903 made him doubly suspicious of both the Russians and Bulgarians. It would be dangerous to go against Austria-Hungary and so Alexander envisaged a plan "of action in the south with her aid." He sent former Minister Andra Djordjević on a secret mission to Vienna to express his readiness to restore the policy of his father and to offer a secret treaty. He was ready to surrender the railways, conclude a military convention and a customs union, and for all intents and purposes to reduce Serbia to a virtual dependency of Austria.[76] He asked in return Austria's support of Serbian claims in Old Serbia and north Macedonia—the regions of Prizren and Skoplje—to which Serbian bishops had been appointed. The king also broached the question of the succession. He had been thinking of adopting a male child from the female line of the Obrenović dynasty, a resident of Austria-Hungary and a citizen of that country, with the agreement of the Vienna government. It was in the interest of both Alexander and Austria to prevent the Montenegrin Prince Mirko, believed at that time to have been a Russian candidate, from ascending the Serbian throne. It is interesting to know that Charykov on one occasion found it necessary to assure his Austrian colleague that Russia had no candidate. At the same time he was prompted to ask why Austria should oppose the candidacy of the Montenegrin prince.[77] He received an ambiguous reply.

The despondent king got nowhere with Austria, which either ignored his proposals or gave him vague promises. Goluchowski ostensibly rejected Alexander's offer of a secret treaty because it involved annexation of Turkish territory and was thereby a violation of the Russo-Austrian agreement of 1897. It should be noted that Alexander's offer to Austria-Hungary was made in the strictest secrecy and nothing was known of it in Russia.[78]

In May 1903 Alexander inquired whether the Austrian emperor might invite him to witness the military maneuvers scheduled for autumn in the vicinity of Temišvar, southern Hungary.[79] He had hoped in this way to be received with Draga by the emperor at Vienna or Budapest. This was his final attempt, but Austria remained noncommittal. Historian Jovanović thinks that in the final months Alexander was sincerely seeking an understanding with Austria. He may have feared Macedonian upheaval; perhaps he was excessively worried over the future rule in Serbia. On the other hand, he may have merely wanted to win recognition for Draga through a reception at the court of Vienna.[80]

The Austrian policy, although ignoring Alexander in the spring of 1903, was one requiring control of Serbia. Lamsdorff was told, for example, that if Serbia interfered in Macedonian disturbances, the Austrians would simply take Serbia.[81] Yet, Constantin Dumba, the Austrian minister to Serbia, who arrived at Beograd in February 1903, says that his country's Balkan policy "failed for want of a definite aim." He writes that the Treaty of Berlin had given the impression that Austria wished to safeguard her plans of expansion in the Balkans, with a view to eventually reaching the Aegean Sea at Salonika. But in Central Europe, he adds, "the leading politicians were ultimately convinced that the Dual Monarchy, even if it had so desired, was not in a position to carry through such a policy purely on nationalistic grounds and owing to the opposition of the Magyars."[82]

According to Dumba, repeated assurances from various Austrian foreign ministers that they had no plans for expansion in the Balkans were meant seriously. Count Kálnoky and Count Goluchowski had adopted the policy of avoiding "any action that might lead to a forcible solution of the Eastern question and possibly to a general European war." As Dumba saw it, the Austrian policy was conservative. It consisted of "pursuing in the main commercial aims in the Balkan Peninsula—the protection and enlargement of a market for our exports." So far as the ministers sent to Beograd were concerned (Count Khevenhüller, Baron Schiessl, Baron Hengelmüller, and Dumba himself), they were never given instructions as to what really constituted the Imperial policy. On his petition for instructions on that score, the only reply Dumba claims he obtained was: "In no circumstances can we permit a union of the Kingdom of Serbia and the Principality of Montenegro; we shall prevent it even if it means going to war to do so," and he was informed that the Agreement of 1897 might serve as the guide for his conduct.[83]

The Austro-Hungarian policy in the Balkans, however, was a frequent topic of discussion in the official press and in the two parliaments. Some citizens described the monarchy's Balkan mission in glowing phrases, some found that the Balkan policy lacked sufficient aggressiveness, and still others found it ruinous and destructive. The typical attitude of the latter type of citizen was that of an eminent Austrian deputy of Czech nationality whose words take us to the Austrian Parliament:

Austria-Hungary had besides political also economic interests in the Balkans . . . she is seeking . . . to make the Balkan markets inaccessible to other European powers . . . For this resason primarily . . . she is trying to subjugate politically the Balkan peoples, after which complete economic subjugation would follow . . . The aim is to prevent the creation of a strong Slavic state in the Balkans, particularly . . . that of . . . Serbia, which would as a geographical barrier impede the German-Magyar policy and block their way to Salonika and the Aegean Sea. This clearly explains the present anti-Slavic Balkan policy.

What does one see in Bulgaria and Serbia after twenty-five years of Austro-Hungarian domination? Economic chaos unequaled in Europe.[84]

8. ALBANIAN UNREST GROWS

Meanwhile, despite the Porte's acceptance of the Russo-Austrian Reform Program, no apparent improvement was visible in Old Serbia and Macedonia. Repeated Albanian attacks on Serbian nationals in Turkey, motivated by a desire "to drive the Serbs out of those districts in which the population was mixed," caused considerable anxiety. Aside from Turkish indifference regarding the Albanian terror, the Serbs believed that the Albanians were encouraged and subsidized by Austria-Hungary. The Albanian and Austrian interests coincided; both strove to make the Sandjak "a great canal separating Serbia and Montenegro."[85] Dumba, however, implies that such incorrect allegation is grounded only on the fact that "the Emperor of Austria had from time immemorial held a protectorate over the Catholics in Albania," and that "Austria had supported Albanian culture by keeping up numerous churches and schools as well as by publishing school books in the Albanian language."[86]

In the memorandum of February 17, 1903, on the reforms in the Ottoman Empire, Austria-Hungary and Russia recognized that the Albanian atrocities were "among the chief causes" of unrest.[87] Yet the Austro-Hungarian policy regarding the reforms in Albanian districts was from the start "rather equivocal."[88] The Russian ambassador in Constantinople, Zinoviev, was heard saying that "for the Austrian ambassador [Baron Kalitsche] the Albanian atrocities do not exist, for they are not committed against the Catholics—who, like the Albanians, go about armed and enjoy all privileges—but against the Orthodox Serbs, who are treated like serfs that have no rights."[89] According to Ćorović, there is ample evidence showing that the Austro-Hungarian consuls worked openly against the reforms, encouraging Albanian resistance to them. The Austrian agents even went about persuading the local Serbs to oppose the reforms. They discouraged the Russians from establishing a consulate in Mitrovica, and resented the investigations by foreign consuls of activities in districts where Albanians lived.[90] Yet in public the Austrian government steadfastly avowed innocence. Austrians accused the Serbian consul general at Skoplje, Kurtović, who worked closely with his Russian colleague, of spreading rumors that Austrians inspired the Albanian atrocities. The Austrian minister was consequently instructed to request the Serbian government to recall Kurtović. Only after considerable pressure by Austria did the king recall Kurtović, a relative and protégé of the royal family.[91]

In March 1903 Albanian attacks on the Serbs reached their height.

Albanian bands disarmed the Christian *zaptiehs* in Vučitrn and then advanced on Mitrovica. The Turkish authorities here employed artillery to prevent the Albanians from entering the city. During these troubles the Russian consul, Shcherbina, was fatally wounded and died on April 10.[92] Two non-Muslim reforming judges were killed on April 18. The situation even evoked alarm in Berlin, and the kaiser advised the sultan to do everything possible "to become master of the situation," but the Austrians preferred a policy of status quo. Count Goluchowski told the Italian Count Nigra that "eine Albanische Frage für ihn nicht existiere."[93] The monarchy's press, and particularly the *Neue Freie Presse*, urged diplomacy rather than force in settling the Albanian question.[94]

The Serbs were very much disturbed by the Albanian terror, and protested that the Turkish authorities were not taking firm enough measures "for the protection of the Christian people."[95] The troop concentration by the Porte along the Serbian frontier at this time as a precaution against possible Serbian military action, and for reasons of establishing order in Old Serbia and Macedonia, caused uneasiness in Serbian official circles. Alexander worried lest the Turks launch an attack on Serbia, and only under pressure from Austria and Russia did he abstain from ordering a general mobilization which might have precipitated war with Turkey.[96]

9. ALEXANDER NEGOTIATES WITH BULGARIA AND TURKEY

There was still another question which concerned Alexander. Should there be an uprising in Macedonia, he believed that the Bulgarians might effect a rapid mobilization and seize a large portion of Macedonia before the Turkish armies arrived. This belief largely explains why he was so anxious to obtain foreign support for Serbia's claims in Turkey. Having failed to secure such support, Alexander was prompted to discuss with Bulgarian Premier Danev a joint Serbo-Bulgarian attack on Turkey. The Danev government accepted his proposal in principle, but because Alexander insisted first on division of Macedonia into Serbian and Bulgarian spheres, Danev prolonged the discussions and delayed any final action on the proposed agreement.[97]

The Danev government, which was "Russophile," and which under Russian pressure had disbanded the Macedonian committee, encountered internal difficulties.[98] War Minister General Paprikov disagreed with the new line of policy and no high ranking officer could be found willing to accept the vacated post. Prince Ferdinand was at the mercy of his officers' corps. During this political tension the Bulgarian-inspired bands secretly entered Salonika, and on April 28, 1903, detonated bombs in various parts of the city. There were many casualties, among them the German consul. The Ottoman bank was almost completely destroyed. The Turks denounced this action of the bands and initiated reprisals against the "Bulgarophile" elements. The persecutions which began at Salonika spread to other parts of Macedonia.[99]

However, the threat of war disappeared when in May 1903 Racho

Petrov's government replaced that of Danev. The new government, representing Austrophile and Stambolovist elements, favored agreement with the Porte. The aim was "to cultivate good relations with Turkey, while extracting concessions by working on her fears of foreign intervention."[100] The revolutionary work was stopped. D. Nachovich, a special Bulgarian diplomatic agent of pro-Turkish orientation, was sent to Constantinople to request the release of the imprisoned Bulgarian patriots and effect an agreement with the Porte.[101]

Like the Bulgarians, King Alexander also made overtures to the Turks. He sent Colonel Mihailo Rašić on a mission similar to that of Nachovich. Rašić was instructed to ask the Porte to recognize Serbian educational and ecclesiastical demands regarding Macedonia. Serbia wished to strengthen her cultural position among the Serbs living in Turkey. Alexander hoped for favors from the sultan because he, unlike the Bulgarians, had incited no uprising in Macedonia. The Serbian government vehemently reacted to reports that "bands were being formed in Serbia, and that a contraband trade in arms was being carried on." It pointed out that although some arms might have been taken across the frontier, there was "no organized system of smuggling."[102] But Rašić returned with empty hands. The Porte considered Serbia's changed attitude one of necessity and not of choice, and neither Austria nor Russia was at this time disposed to support Serbian demands for new religious and educational privileges in Macedonia.[103]

Alexander wished to make sure that in case of war his troops would occupy Skoplje before the Bulgarian troops could take over.[104] But if the Turko-Bulgarian operations were concentrated in the region of Adrianople, the Serbs might stay out of the war. In light of this probability he offered to the Turks an alliance which, he hoped, would be joined by Rumania. Working thus simultaneously on agreements with Bulgaria and with Turkey, Alexander's dealings obviously evinced opportunism. He reasoned, no doubt, that in case of a Turko-Bulgarian war, if the Bulgarians appeared stronger than the Turks, he would at a propitious moment invade Turkey and drive toward Skoplje. If, on the other hand, the Turks appeared stronger, he would attack Bulgaria and seize Vidin and Lom Palanka.[105]

In the spring of 1903, Macedonia being on the verge of revolution, the Powers agreed to a policy of status quo in the Balkans and the improvement of conditions in European Turkey. Russia made it plain in Beograd and Sofia that before she would favor Macedonian autonomy, conditions in that province would have to be improved.[106] Germany, friendly to the sultan, opposed the reforms.[107] Italy and Austria-Hungary vied jealously with each other, and the Albanian turmoil prompted the Italians to approach the Austrian government with regard to reforms.[108]

To check any possible future Austro-Hungarian expansion along the Adriatic the Italian government was endeavoring to make its influence in Albania as strong as possible. The Austro-Italian agreement of December 20, 1900,[109] like that between Russia and Austria-Hungary, had provided for maintenance of the status quo in the Balkans. The autonomy of Albania was agreed upon if the status quo could not be maintained; nevertheless, the

Italians intensified their propaganda in Albania. They printed pamphlets and books in which they stretched the Albanian frontiers to include not only the region of Skadar (Scutari) but also Ioannina and large parts of the vilayets of Kosovo and Bitolj. Victor Emmanuel himself had called attention to the fact that Bitolj was inhabited by "compact masses of Albanians."[110] From the Serbian national point of view, the Italian policy was as detrimental as was that of Austria. Yet for the moment the Serbs welcomed the former to neutralize the activities of the latter, and one notes after 1903 a steady growth of the Italian influence in Beograd.[111]

The most pressing question for the Serbian government in 1903 was how to counteract the Bulgarian and Austrian encroachments on Macedonia. This, it was believed, could be done only by a firm expansionist policy which would widen Serbian influence in Macedonia. The advisers of Alexander recommended an agreement with Rumania with regard to Macedonia in order to offset the Bulgarian predominence in that region. Preliminary discussions with Rumania actually took place, although the latter could hardly claim any part of Macedonia in the name of the mere handful of Kutsovlachs living there. Moreover, Macedonia was not territorially contiguous to Rumania. But since there were Kutsovlachs, racial kinsmen of the Rumanians, in Macedonia, Rumania might speak on their behalf and throw her support behind those who wished "to prevent the exaggerated Bulgarian claims."[112]

Because relations with Montenegro were strained, Serbia could expect no backing for her Macedonian policy from Cetinje. As a matter of fact, the Beograd government suspected that Italy would support the territorial aspirations of the prince of Montenegro at the expense of Serbia. Subsequent events* showed that the Italian king did not allow family ties with the Montenegrin court to influence his country's foreign policy.[113] The responsible factors in Rome believed that the major Balkan questions could not be solved without Serbia, and that through Serbia alone Italy might extend her influence in the Balkans.[114]

After Alexander's murder there was much speculation about the nature of his last plans. Some believed that he had actually planned to invade Macedonia and to take a firm stand in the name of Serbian nationalism against Austria-Hungary, so that he might satisfy the aspirations of the Serbian nationalists. Since Alexander had lost Russian and failed to regain Austrian support, and because close co-operation with Italy or France was not yet possible, there is indication that Alexander had hoped to find in England the backing he needed for his foreign policy.[115] On June 10, 1903, he submitted to the English government a memorandum in which he analyzed at some length the anti-Serbian character of the Austro-Hungarian activities in Macedonia.

Likewise, there are hints that just before his death Alexander had contemplated divorcing Draga to pacify his enemies.[116] She was first to be sent to Franzensbad for a rest, and, once outside Serbia, she was not to be allowed to return. There are signs of Alexander's changed feelings toward Draga.

* In 1896 Victor Emmanuel married Jelena, daughter of the Montenegrin prince.

For example, he made decisions on political matters and a number of appointments disagreeable to her. The king was said to have flirted with Draga's sisters, and to have quarreled with Draga over the question of succession. Draga wanted her brother Nikodije to succeed, whereas Alexander wanted a descendant of a female member of the house of Obrenović.[117] But there is no conclusive evidence to show that he contemplated a divorce. Notwithstanding all these rumors, even if Alexander had planned to adopt a more popular foreign policy and to divorce Draga, these plans had come too late. The movement against the Obrenović dynasty had gained such momentum by 1903 that nothing short of a miracle could have saved Alexander and Draga ; and that miracle did not occur.

The Conspiracy

BY MARRYING DRAGA, "UNEQUAL TO HIM AND OF ILL REPUTE," Alexander as the supreme commandant of the army had in the eyes of officers dishonored the entire officers' corps. One of the tragedies of Alexander's reign was his failure to appreciate the extent of the popular discontent; he was under the illusion that it was restricted to a small group of die-hard friends of his father Milan, who resented the latter's inglorious eclipse.[1]

The royal marriage, the sterility of the queen, and the rumors that one of the queen's brothers might inherit the Serbian throne, enraged many officers. Moreover, King Milan had paid special attention to the army; he had equipped and paid the officers with regularity. But under Alexander officers went for months without pay, undeserving officers were promoted, and the queen's brother, Nikodije Lunjevica, though lacking in rank, took precedence over the king's adjutants, and lived in luxury at the royal court.[2]

Under the protection of the Constitution of 1901, the opposition press with its tirades against existing affairs encouraged the military opposition to the king. The press pulled no punches, and, through implication, even the person of the king became subject to criticism. The opposition press was blessed with a powerful battery of caustic critics and some exceptionally good writers. These writers described the political situation with artistic effect and with persuasive eloquence. Writing in the popular tongue, they exaggerated the deplorable state of affairs in the form of satire, poetry, and fiction, leaving an impression that Alexander was a tyrant, responsible for Serbia's retarded civilization, and incapable of defending the nation and promoting the national cause. With such a pilot as Alexander* at the helm, it was widely believed that the country could not possibly anticipate a favorable settlement of the Balkan question.[3]

---

* Kaljević and many others say that Alexander was not as stupid as critics made him out to be (Vasić, p. 163). The following description of Alexander and Draga by the Austrian minister is probably accurate: "It is quite a mistake to suppose that the King [Alexander] was physically or mentally deficient or abnormal or that he submitted to the baneful influence of Queen Draga for pathological reasons. His appearance was certainly not prepossessing. Nevertheless King Alexander was not devoid of brains, was of quick perception, possessed a good memory, and displayed a lively interest in literature by devouring large quantities of books without at the same time always thoroughly digesting their contents." As for Draga, the same source has this to say: "Queen Draga . . . was, when I came to know her, a rather small, insignificant-looking woman of about forty, to whom no traces of beauty remained, with the sole exception of her large dark eyes. Instead, however, of making friends with people by being kindly and pleasant after her miraculous rise in the world, Draga revealed herself as ambitious, avaricious, greedy; and persecuted unmercifully any who did not at once hurry to Court to do her homage or who did not believe in her ability to bear children." Dumba, *Memoirs*, pp. 94–97.

1. PLANS AND PREPARATIONS

It was this situation which provided a background for the conspiratorial movement which began in the army and was later extended to civilians. In August 1901 a young army lieutenant, Antonije Antić, confided to friends a plan to murder the king. He complained that he could not undertake such a task alone, and expressed readiness to co-operate with any others who might want to support him. He also believed that action by a single person could not achieve the necessary results and that a broader revolutionary movement was required. Antić's friends, among them Dragutin Dimitrijević-Apis, unhesitatingly accepted the plan. The first meeting of the group of young conspirators took place in Antić's home. Seven officers were present, and they are considered the founders of the military conspiracy.* They agreed to murder the king and queen on September 11, the anniversary of the queen's birth, at an evening ball at the "Kolarac." This naïve plan to kill the royal pair was essentially the work of Dimitrijević, who was to obtain the poison. Two officers were to seize the electric power plant on the Danube and one of the officers the "Kolarac" power plant. At a designated time the lights would be shut off and the four officers attending the ball would ignite the curtains, sound a fire alarm, and in the midst of the ensuing chaos liquidate the royal pair. The poison was successfully tried out on a cat. When the time for action came, the officers who were assigned the seizure of the electric plant on the Danube failed in their mission because the plant was too well guarded. Furthermore, the king and queen failed to appear at the ball. The plan of the "big uniformed children" failed.[4]

The conspirators did not give up but made new plans to assassinate the king. A plan to kill him in the autumn of 1901 during the military maneuvers at Ub failed, but the conspirators did not lose heart. They were mostly junior army officers; an exception was Colonel of Engineers Damjan Popović, who became the leader of the military conspiracy. Since he was not widely known in the regular army, an effort was made to find a leader of wider reputation and higher rank. Such an officer could not be found among those on active duty; the conspirators satisfied their needs with a retired general, Jovan Atanacković, who had been persecuted for his opposition to the king's marriage, and he was won over to the conspiratorial cause by his godfather, Aleksa Novaković. Atanacković, whose name attracted many new officers, was associated mostly with the civilian component of the conspiracy. He was of the strong conviction that the military should not meddle in politics and that the civilian conspirators would remain passive until after the liquidation of the king, when they would offer their services to the conspirators from the military. Unlike Atanacković, Colonel Damjan Popović associated with the young officers and inspired them in their work. He was the spark plug in the whole conspiratorial work.[5]

On November 1, 1901, the military conspirators established their first contact with civilian leaders. It had been agreed that Lieutenant Antić should

---

* The seven officers were Milan Marinković, Nikodije Popović, Radomir Arandjelović, Milan Petrović, Dragutin Dimitrijević, Antonije Antić, Dragiša Dulić.

inform his cousin Djordje Genčić of the conspiracy.[6] Genčić, former minister in the Djordjević cabinet, who had been released from the Požarevac prison only a few weeks before, joined the conspiracy wholeheartedly. His sincerity, confidence, and political experience—qualities which the conspirators badly lacked—were positive and tangible contributions to the movement. The task entrusted to Genčić was to organize the conspiracy among the civilians, and the first recruit was his own father-in-law, Aleksa Novaković, a Beograd lawyer. The original plan called for the inclusion in the conspiracy of representatives from all the major political parties. The civilian component of the conspiracy as ultimately constituted included Djordje Genčić and Jovan Avakumović (Liberals), Aleska Novaković and Dragomir Rajović (Progressives), and Nikola Hadži Toma (a supporter of the Karadjordjević dynasty). Genčić, Avakumović, and Rajović were former cabinet ministers and had some reputation as politicians. Novaković and Hadži Toma, although active in the movement, were not experienced in politics. Because of their negligible role, Avakumović and Rajović were conspirators in name only. The three most active civilian conspirators were Genčić, Novaković, and Hadži Toma.[7]

The first meeting of the civilian conspirators was held on Topčider Hill in the home of Aleksa Novaković. Here the "patriotic readiness" of the officers was accepted, and at once discussions were initiated with regard to the composition of the "revolutionary" government and the succession to the Serbian throne.[8]

The military conspirators had no particular philosophy or political convictions. They were merely opposed to the king, some for personal and some for patriotic reasons. Under the influence of the opposition press they became inclined to favor the constitutional regime and a Russophile policy. Nor, for that matter, were the political convictions of the civilian conspirators crystal-clear. Indeed, they had previously been supporters of the king's personal regime. Genčić was minister of interior in the Djordjević cabinet. Rajović at that same time was vice-president of the Skupština. Atanacković was also a member of the Djordjević cabinet. Novaković and Hadži Toma, who were not politicians, leaned toward the personal regime, probably because they opposed the Radicals. Of the civilian conspirators, only Avakumović was consistently opposed to the personal rule of the king.[9]

Little difficulty was encountered in winning the Liberal and Progressive parties to the conspiratorial cause. The Radicals did not have a single person in the conspiracy. The unsuccessful Timok uprising (September 28, 1883) had apparently made the Radicals wary of revolts and conspiracies. They included, to be sure, a larger number of critics of the regime and followers of the Karadjordjević dynasty than did other parties, but the heads of the party pursued a cautious policy. Neither Nikola Pašić nor Stojan Protić nor Ljubomir Živković wished to be involved in the plot. Some of the Radical leaders approved the conspiracy but avoided taking an active part in it.[10]

By party affiliation Genčić and Avakumović were Liberals; Hadži Toma was not active politically, but through family connections favored the Liberals. Of the officers, Damjan Popović, Anta Antić, Dragutin Dimitrijević, and Milan Milovanović also leaned toward the Liberals. Two great Liberal families—Baba Dudići and Hadži Toma—were in the conspiracy: Baba Dudići through Jovan Avakumović, and Hadži Toma by way of Nikola Hadži Toma. "King Alexander began his rule with a coup d'état against the Liberal regency and the Liberal cabinet. The conspiracy which cost him his life was in a sense the Liberal revenge."[11]

While the military conspirators planned the liquidation of the Obrenović rule, the civilian conspirators concerned themselves with the selection of a successor to the vacated throne. A Russian or German or Austrian prince for Serbia was dismissed as inexpedient. The former would not be acceptable to the two German states, nor the latter two to Russia. The leaders concluded that Peter Karadjordjević as a representative of a native dynasty would be more readily accepted by both the Serbian people and the foreign powers, especially since he already enjoyed considerable popular backing. It was now necessary to consult with Peter and ascertain whether he would accept the Serbian throne. There is little information on the discussion between Peter and the conspirators. Of the conspirators only Hadži Toma and Vukašin Petrović, "a quasi-conspirator, abroad at the time," had dealings with Peter. All that is known about these meetings, according to Jovanović, comes from verbal reports made by Hadži Toma.[12]

Having agreed on Peter to succeed to the throne when it should be vacated, the conspirators dispatched Hadži Toma to establish liaison with Peter and consult with him. Toward the end of November 1901 Hadži Toma journeyed to the Swiss-Austrian border and there met with the future king. This was the only meeting with Peter. Hadži Toma's report was hailed as satisfactory, and both Hadži Toma and Petrović assured the conspirators that Peter would accept the crown if it should be proffered, although Peter was apparently noncommittal at first. Hadži Toma was later quoted as saying that Peter had been hesitant and expressed lack of confidence in the Serbian politicians. He showed interest only after he discovered that the young officers constituted the backbone of the conspiracy. Nonetheless, at the last visit with Hadži Toma, he stated that he preferred not to become involved. Hadži Toma kept from the conspirators this attitude of the future king.[13]

The conspirators maintained contact with Peter, who lived in Geneva, through his cousin Jakov Nenadović, prominent exponent of the cause of the Karadjordjević dynasty, who resided in Vienna. Despite Peter's vacillation, Nenadović backed the plot wholeheartedly, later admitting to Constantin Dumba that he had been "one of the most active among the conspirators." He regretted that there had been no resistance to the conspirators during the crucial days of May and June, because in that event "nobody would have called it murder, but only revolution!"[14]

Until December 23, 1901, Lieutenant Antić was the only officer in touch with the civilian conspirators. On the evening of that day, the conspirators met in Antić's home to examine various questions, including that of the future rule. To allay suspicion, the conspirators arrived at the meeting pretending to be drunk, and in the company of street musicians.[15]

During the meeting Genčić dwelt on the deplorable political situation in which Serbia found herself and on her future King Peter. On this occasion the officers, with great exuberance and confidence in the future, renounced their oaths to King Alexander and swore that they would hereafter take orders exclusively from Genčić. Only one of all the officers present refused to accept the plan to kill the king, although two officers eventually dropped out. This lone officer felt that it would be sufficient to expel Alexander from the country, and after having promised not to betray the conspiracy he withdrew from the meeting. The remaining thirteen conspirators now for the first time discussed in detail the actual assassination plans. It was agreed that the job of dispatching the royal pair would be that of the officer conspirators, and that the civilian conspirators would be responsible for organizing a coalition government representative of all major parties, and for preventing foreign complications. Convinced by Hadži Toma that Peter would accept the proffered crown, the conspirators next concerned themselves with the international complications that might develop from the royal murder.[16]

Genčić and the civilian group made a study of the possible political situation and of the international complications that might ensue as the result of a palace murder. In the course of 1902 Genčić made several trips to Vienna, hoping in vain to learn from the Russian ambassador something more concrete about the policy his country would adopt, should the Serbian dynasty come to an end. In early 1903 Genčić again approached Russia and Austria and inquired what their attitude would be in case the Serbian dynasty should suddenly expire. The discussions were conducted mostly through Constantin Dumba (February 1903–May 1905), Austrian minister at Beograd, and Count Kapnist, Russian ambassador at Vienna. Genčić spoke with both these men; he did not divulge the existence of the conspiracy but spoke in general terms about the future rule in Serbia. The two diplomats did not commit their respective governments to any definite policy. The Russian ambassador opined that if a Russian prince should become king of Serbia, Austria would probably object strongly. Similarly, the Austrian minister expressed the belief that a German prince ruling Serbia was out of the question, because of inescapable Russian opposition. From this, Genčić concluded that Peter Karadjordjević would be accepted more readily by Austria and Russia than a candidate put forward by either one of them.[17]

Two other men were also busy exploring the possible attitude of Austria and Russia when and if the Serbian dynasty came to an end. These were Vukašin Petrović and Jaša Nenadović, both exiles in Vienna. Petrović, who had special contacts with Baron Kállay, learned that the extinction of the Serbian dynasty would not cause major complications, that no trouble might be anticipated from Russia or Austria-Hungary, and that neither would oppose the election of Peter Karadjordjević as king of Serbia.[18]

Professor Jovanović argues that a plan to return the Karadjordjević dynasty to the Serbian throne did not originate in Karadjordjević circles. "Neither Peter nor a follower of his dynasty had initiated it." He adds that the conspirators decided to remove Alexander and Draga, not primarily in order to bring Peter to the throne but because they could no longer bear the Obrenović rule, and had selected the Karadjordjević dynasty because it would be accepted more readily than would a foreign prince, or the Montenegrin prince or one of his sons. The next step on the agenda of the civilian conspirators was the composition of the revolutionary cabinet, which would take over the government after the death of the king. Avakumović was offered the premiership and accepted.[19]

On October 19, 1902, the conspirators once again met in Antić's home. Twenty young officers were present, and the discussion centered on the question of the oath. Genčić had felt all along that he and the civilian conspirators depended too much on the mere word of the officer conspirators, who continued to organize but without any definite plans of action in the near future, and he insisted that the officers take some sort of written oath. The first conspiratorial oath stated that the undersigned planned to kill the king and bring to the throne Prince Peter Karadjordjević, provided that the political conspirators assured them that "their work would not precipitate danger from abroad which might be detrimental to the interests of the people." Only nine officers on this occasion signed the oath, which was at once delivered to Genčić. The paper was kept by Mrs. Novaković and was brought out of hiding whenever additional signatures were taken. When on one occasion the war minister hinted to General Atanacković that the king suspected him because of his associates, Genčić destroyed the oath in fear that the conspiracy might be exposed.[20]

Subsequently another oath was drafted; it was dictated by Dragutin Dimitrijević, who was at the time ill in bed, and it was kept by Dimitrijević himself. Like the first one, this oath was not signed by all the conspirators; some declined in fear that the document might come into the hands of the police. The text of the second oath is particularly significant for its content:

Anticipating certain collapse of the state if the existing situation continues even for the shortest time, and blaming for this primarily the king and his paramour Draga Mašin, we swear that we shall murder them and to that effect affix our signatures. In place of these dishonorable individuals, we shall bring to the Serbian throne Peter Karadjordjević, grandson of the Leader (*Vožd*) and the legitimate son of Prince Alexander Karadjordjević.[21]

During the disturbances of March 1903, when the officer conspirators were imprisoned and there was danger that the conspiracy might be disclosed, Dimitrijević, with the knowledge of only one officer, again destroyed the document. The other officers remained until the end under the conviction that they were bound by a signed oath which no longer existed.[22]

The number of civilian conspirators remained the same throughout, the two principal ones being Genčić, who maintained liaison with the officers, and Hadži Toma, who was in touch with Prince Peter. The number of military conspirators, however, increased, thanks to Dragutin Dimitrijević-Apis, who was especially fitted to attract new recruits. To avert a general revolution, the conspirators enlisted officers from Beograd as well as from the garrisons of the interior. The Niš garrison supplied a number of conspirators. The officers there had been bitter over the irregularity of salaries and the favoritism shown in the distribution of military posts. For the conspiracy, the year 1902 was one of preparation and of numerical and geographical expansion. Some leaders, however, discouraged a huge conspiratorial organization lest the movement become vulnerable to internal dissension.[23]

In early 1903 the severity of Cincar-Marković's government, the March Demonstration, the coup d'état of March 24, and other developments intensified the resentment against the king, and the number of conspirators correspondingly grew. Before, the conspirators had had to be recruited, but now they flocked to the movement voluntarily. No new follower was asked to sign the oath, because none existed. The unpopularity of Alexander had seemingly reached its zenith and the conspirators began to think that the moment for final action was at hand. The conspiracy was no longer a monopoly of a few young officers.[24] Money apparently played a negligible role in the conspiracy, a fact which makes Jovanović conclude that the principal conspiratorial group was constituted not of profiteers but of fanatics —"the people who might commit crime, but could not be bought."[25]

Perhaps the most enthusiastic officer conspirators were those of the Niš garrison. The continued delay annoyed them and they decided to act on their own. Such a task appeared easy to accomplish because the king and queen were visiting Niš. They tentatively selected February 22, 1903, the anniversary of the proclamation of the Serbian kingdom, as the day when the royal pair would be slain, while they were witnessing the play to be staged in the Hotel Evropa. In order to carry out this assignment, the conspirators were in need of revolvers and poison. Furthermore, their plan had to be approved by their comrades in Beograd, who would also have to procure the tools of death. With these purposes in mind one of them was sent to Beograd, but his mission was a failure. The Niš plan was not approved on the ground that it would not achieve the real objective. Earlier, a similar plan to dispatch the royal pair during their visit to Smederevo had been turned down. It was rightly reasoned that the attack on the king had to be made in Beograd, in order to permit prompt seizure of the government.[26]

Two months after the proposed Niš plot, the Beograd conspirators were ready for action. During the last phase of preparation they were anxious to receive into the movement some of the royal guards and additional political men. The enlistment of the guards was of course the hardest task yet. Vasić gives us a detailed description of the various efforts to infiltrate the royal guards, and of how second lieutenant of the cavalry Petar Živković, who had just been assigned to the guards, was won to the cause.[27]

By spring 1903, when the number of officer conspirators had reached one hundred twenty, a definite plan was made to kill the king in his Beograd palace. However, for a successful *putsch* it was held necessary to have collaborators within the very inner sanctum of the court.[28] The conspirators finally secured "the co-operation of Lieutenant Colonel Naumović, a high official in the war ministry and the king's aide-de-camp." According to Dumba, "only with his connivance was it possible to obtain leave during the

Whitsuntide holidays for those officers who came from the provinces and thus to collect them unostentatiously in Belgrade. Since Naumović slept in the palace, he also undertook to open a heavy oaken door from the inside at a given signal." Captain Kostić, commander of the king's bodyguard, was another valuable enlistment. It was he who let the conspirators into the courtyard of the palace and surrendered his unarmed guards to them.[29]

The liquidation of Alexander and Draga was to be followed by seizure of the government, and in order to accomplish that feat a revolution was required—a military revolution; yet the conspirators did not have control of the army. They were strong in the Beograd and Niš garrisons; they were sure of only a few followers and sympathizers in other garrisons. In Beograd, where the conspirators were strongest, only a single regimental commander was on their side. The troops everywhere were still, by and large, loyal to the king. An open call to uprising would not find sufficient response even in the Beograd garrison.[30]

Influenced by the reasoning just outlined, the conspirators decided that the revolution could be effected only if they should kill the king and queen, immediately seize the government, and proclaim the existence of a new regime. This was all to be the work of the conspiring officers. The troops employed would not know that they were being accomplices to a murder. After the murder and seizure of the government, the world would be informed of a *fait accompli*.[31]

The king was well guarded. The armed defenders of the palace included the following: General Lazar Petrović; the duty adjutant; the court guard, consisting of three officers and forty-five cavalrymen of the guard squadron; and a *gendarmerie* detachment of one officer and six men. To subdue all these officers and men, and kill the royal pair to boot, appeared a risky venture. It must be remembered that there was a smaller number of officer conspirators who could be used in the attack on the palace than there were armed defenders of the court. For this reason it was absolutely essential to find collaborators among officers in the palace.[32]

The conspirators successfully found supporters in the palace, and with their aid they planned to break into the palace and, in case the king summoned the Beograd garrison to his aid, put the troops into motion. They had their own men in all the regiments. The commandant of the Sixth Regiment, Lieutenant Colonel Petar Mišić, was their man, and through him they could remove part of the army from the barracks and station them before the palace until the murder. This army might be used to halt any troops that came to the defense of the king. Only after the murder would the troops be told of the royal tragedy. But then, as Jovanović says, no serious trouble could be anticipated because "a dead leader has no followers."[33]

The plan as outlined, however, required a superb supreme command. Colonel Damjan Popović was originally placed in charge of the revolt, but because of his recent transfer from Beograd, the command was entrusted to Colonel Alexander Mašin, brother of Draga's first husband. He hated his former sister-in-law; when she became queen he was pensioned.

The conspiracy became increasingly difficult to conceal. By spring 1903 it had more than a hundred members, including several women. The number of persons who were not in the conspiracy but knew of its existence grew daily; the king and his government learned about it. The neurotic king feared a violent death; he ordered military readiness, increased police protection of the palace, and from time to time he stayed at Niš to dodge any possible assassins. He received the first inkling of a conspiracy soon after its plans were laid, but curiously enough he did not then fear the military but the civilian elements, who, he believed, were trying to instigate a quarrel between him and the army. He had issued orders for investigation of the Karadjordjević followers, left-wing Liberals, Independent Radicals, and government officials. The king found no reason for suspecting the officers.[34]

Not until the March disturbances in 1903 did the king become distrustful of his officers. On that occasion two officers of the conspiratorial circle were imprisoned, but because their guilt could not be established they were freed. From then on, reports of the military conspiracy increased, and the police took these reports seriously. Premier General Cincar-Marković and the king's first adjutant, Petrović, persisted in believing that the police fear was unwarranted. These two officers saw in the conspiracy something morally impossible and were ready to defend the army's reputation against the "vicious" reports of the police.[35]

The king and queen meanwhile were much disturbed and emotionally upset. In an audience he had with the queen, Pera Todorović was criticized for his bad taste in publishing matters appearing in the *Male Novine*. In a serial, "A Prophecy," he presented "the prophecies of the clairvoyant peasant, Mata of Kremna," a highly suggestive story which much disturbed the king, especially when references were made to death and assassination. The queen thought it was especially offensive to publish the royal portraits just above the article reporting the assassination of the Italian King Humbert.[36] The king and queen seldom appeared in the streets. The queen did not leave the palace for about six weeks. The king did so but always in company of a large group of people. The palace guard was doubled, and gendarmes were stationed on all sides. What Alexander and Draga did not know, says Jovanović, was that the attack on their lives would take place in the palace itself.

On May 24–26 a huge celebration was sponsored by the "Beograd Singing Society." About two thousand persons came to Beograd—singers and delegates from the interior and abroad. In the midst of these festivities the king received an anonymous letter about the conspiracy and was told that an attempt on his life might be made on the occasion of the laying of the foundation to the Home of Art, or at the concert on May 26. He did not appear at the laying of the foundation but instead sent his court marshal. The king and queen were present at the concert but were surrounded by police.[37]

There is a report that during the evening of May 28 the king had quarreled with General Cincar-Marković. The king demanded that a fairly large number of officers suspected of conspiracy be imprisoned and tried, and that martial law be proclaimed in Beograd. Cincar-Marković defended the officers and threatened to resign. Meanwhile, the fear of conspiracy had so overtaken Alexander in the last days of May that Draga and he felt secure only in the palace. Naumović cautioned the conspirators that the king had received word of the conspiracy; that very evening the conspirators assembled in the mess hall of the Sixth Infantry Regiment, Colonel Mašin presiding, to decide on final action.[38]

It is interesting to note that the Russian intelligence service had been informed of the conspiracy. On May 25 one Alexander Vaïsman rushed from Sofia to Beograd to tell King Alexander about it. Alexander replied that he had already been informed of the conspiracy by Bulgarian Prince Ferdinand, and that he would take appropriate steps against it. This knowledge may have hastened Alexander's plans to send the queen away from Serbia and eventually to divorce her.[39]

After the March disturbances the conspirators were as nervous as the king. Two of them had been imprisoned and one of them transferred into the interior. The conspirators feared that they had been betrayed and that if their plans were to succeed they must strike before the king launched a drive against them. These developments hastened the final action by the conspirators. At a meeting held on May 26, at which Colonel Naumović was present, they decided to attack the palace on the night of May 28. That night was chosen because Colonel Naumović, the king's aide-de-camp, and other friends would then be on duty in the palace. At midnight, or at a propitious moment, Naumović was to dispatch a guard with an appropriate sign signaling the advance on the palace.[40]

The detailed plan of action called for a group of twenty-eight officers to attack the palace. The leaders had chosen for this purpose officers from the interior who commanded no troops and who were apparently candidates for the general staff or attached to the military academy. Three battalions of the Sixth Regiment, the entire Seventh Regiment, an artillery battery, and a squadron of cavalry were to be taken from the barracks and stationed around the palace. In this manner the palace would be separated from the rest of the city.[41]

2. THE FINAL HOURS

At their last meeting on May 26, the conspirators agreed to invade the palace at two in the morning. The evening before, they were to separate into groups of five and disperse to five different coffee shops until quarter of two in the morning, when they were to gather at the Officers' Home, and, when the battalion led by Lieutenant Colonel Petar Mišić (commandant of the Sixth Regiment) appeared, fall in at the head of the column and proceed to the main gate of the palace. A company of infantry guards, a battalion from the Seventh Regiment, and a battery of artillery were later to take up positions at various places around the palace court. Lieutenant Petar Živković agreed to open the gate for the attackers. Captain Panajotović, commandant of the guards and ordnance officer on duty, would meanwhile be drugged with opium, which had been procured with great difficulty. It was decided that the brothers of the queen must be killed and that a detachment of troops should guard the homes of the premier, General Cincar-Marković, Minister of War Milovan Pavlović, and Minister of Interior Velimir Todorović, in order to prevent their escape.[42] Arrangements were also made to surround the house of the senate chairman, Dimitrije Nikolić, and to take over post and telegraph offices and the municipal government. The first group of officers would penetrate the royal bedroom and dispatch the royal pair. The second group, under Dimitrijević, would demobilize the ordnance detachment on duty. The third group would seize Laza Petrović, the king's adjutant. The fourth would take care of the *gendarmerie,* and the fifth would keep watch on the palace windows to forestall possible escape. In case the conspirators fell short of their objective, they intended to retreat from Beograd to Topčider Hill and there unfurl the banner of revolution and call upon the people to rise in general revolt. The conspirators tried their arms and sharpened their sabers. Watches were adjusted against the clock in the railway station.[43]

Dragiša Vasić vividly and dramatically describes the evening of the fatal May 29 (O.S.). That night there was a formal dinner ⌐⁺ ⁺ʰᵉ court and a concert by the royal guards. At midnight the guests departeα ⌐ ¹⁻ᵃ royal pair retired. At one o'clock in the morning complete stillness prevailed.[44] Kaclerović writes that a letter from Major Milosav Živanović was delivered to the war minister, General Milovan Pavlović, during an evening party a few hours before the assassination, warning of the plans of the conspirators, but that the general stuck it in his pocket without reading it.[45]

In its initial stages, the conspiracy followed the plan substantially as outlined at the May 26 (O.S.) meeting. It was to be a revolt of the officers and not of the troops. Alexander Mašin donned his discarded uniform and took charge of the bloody operation. The battalion of the Sixth Regiment led by Mišić was late in arriving, and at first treachery was feared; but at two o'clock they finally arrived, and the conspirators advanced on the palace in double time, followed by a company of guards. Shortly thereafter, a battery of artillery and the battalion of the Seventh Regiment also appeared. The palace was isolated and besieged. According to the arrangement, communications were seized to prevent the news from reaching the interior and the troops, and guards were posted at the homes of the ministers.[46]

The conspirators reached the main gates of the palace. Lieutenant Živković struggled "several long seconds" before he managed to open them. Explosions began to shake the very foundation of the palace and fire broke out. The conspirators first attacked the guards, and pushed into the quarters of the duty officers, Colonel Mihailo Naumović (a conspirator) and Captain Jovan Miljković, who knew of the conspiracy but had refused to betray it. Both were killed, the former because the attackers did not know he was a conspirator, and the latter because he resisted.* It had been expected that

* According to Živanović (IV, 348–49), Miljković was asleep. He knew of the conspiracy but did not belong to it; he was on the conspirators' approved list, and they would have spared his life.

Colonel Naumović would surrender the palace keys, which were in his charge and which could not be located after his death.[47]

The heavy oak door leading to the main chamber was dynamited, and the twenty-eight conspirators rushed in; their position was precarious, for they had attacked the palace before all the troops they counted on had reached their designated positions. Hastily and without system, they rushed through the palace rooms in groups, searching for the king and queen. Dimitrijević fell upon the quarters of the interior guard; they opened fire, and he dropped, badly wounded. The battle with the guards in the subterranean hallways ended in victory for the conspirators. The search went on. Door after door was destroyed with dynamite. Finally the conspirators found their way into the royal chamber, only to find the king and queen gone, and no clue to their whereabouts. Fearing that someone might summon the army to the king's defense before they found him, they proposed destroying the palace with dynamite and artillery, to make the death of the royal pair certain, supposing they were still anywhere in the building. The guards and the gendarmes had been silenced, and all the army units that were expected had finally arrived and taken up their positions around the palace.[48]

Petar Panajotović, whom the conspirators had doped with opium the evening before, was awakened by the palace alarm and drowsily began to collect such guards as he could find, but the battalion of the Sixth Regiment plunged through the gates of the palace, shooting, and Captain Panajotović fell wounded. The battalion then took charge of the courtyard, and opened the *gendarmerie* gate to let in Captain Kostić with his company of guards. Additional troops began arriving at the palace under the command of other rebelling officers. The palace was by now completely in the hands of conspirators, who had not yet found their victims.[49]

Fear of treachery was constantly in the minds of the conspiring leaders. Their position was improved but was by no means safe! They could not trust the troops surrounding the palace, who did not know the purpose of their presence; only the commanding officers knew. Once the troops learned the truth, it was always possible that they might turn against the officers in charge of them. The destruction of the palace seemed to be the only possible alternative, but Colonel Mašin temporized, and suggested immediate seizure of the government and continuation of the search for the king. Djordje Genčić was instructed to occupy the Ministry of Interior and to proceed as if the king were already dead. Orders were issued to kill the prime minister and the minister of war. Although they were surrounded in their homes, there was constant fear that they might somehow establish contact with the army and the police. If that should happen, the whole state machine would be turned against the conspirators.[50]

The search for the royal pair still continued, but now it was more methodical. If anyone knew the king's hiding place, it would be his first adjutant, Lazar Petrović, whose quarters had been surrounded by conspirators as soon as they entered the palace yard and who had ordered the electricity turned off, forcing the conspirators to wander in confusion through the palace hallways. After shooting it out with the conspirators he had been forced to surrender and hand over his revolver, but he had kept another revolver hidden. Despite his repeated assurances that he did not know the whereabouts of the king and queen, the conspirators demanded that he locate the royal pair within ten minutes. He was conducted through the halls, calling at the door of each room for "Your Majesty?" There was no answer. Then the conspirators returned once again to the royal chamber. Suddenly one of the conspirators (Velimir Vemić) noticed that on the side of the chamber which faced the street there were no windows behind the draperies. Instead, there was a cleverly concealed door opening into an alcove. To divert the attention of the onlookers, General Petrović assured them there was nothing there.* When the conspirators called for an ax to break down the door, Petrović agreed to ask the king to step into the room.[51]

For almost two hours the king had been hearing explosions and shooting. He had concealed himself and the queen as well as he knew how. Now suddenly he heard the voice of his own adjutant asking him to step out. Petrović called the king twice. Certainly Alexander must have felt that the storm was over and that his army had saved him. The king inquired who was calling, and Petrović responded: "I am, your Laza, open the door to your officers!" The king asked, "Can I depend on the oath of my officers?" The conspirators replied that he could. The king opened the door, and before he knew what had happened, a volley of shots felled him; then Draga toppled forward over the king as if protecting him. Shocked and overwhelmed, Petrović pulled his concealed revolver to avenge the king, but it was too late. The conspirators shot first. Thirty bullets had riddled the body of the king and eighteen that of the queen. Then the two corpses were put to the saber.[52]

Alexander and Draga were dead at 3:50 A.M., two hours after the conspirators had broken into the palace. The troops outside the palace, still puzzled as to their mission and most of them under the impression that they were there to protect the king, suddenly heard the shout from the palace window: "The Tyrant is no more!" Petar Mišić, commandant of the Sixth Regiment, jubilantly stepped in front of his troops, and, waving revolvers in both hands, announced that the king and queen had been killed. Shooting into the air, he shouted: "Long live Peter Karadjordjević!" The soldiers followed suit. Bullets were raining everywhere and the officers had a difficult time stopping the demonstration. The troops were at last brought into the revolution. In the midst of the excitement that ensued, two young officers hurled the bodies of the king and queen out of the window into the garden below. "The two bloody and nude bodies" crumpled to the earth.[53]

Besides the king and queen, several other persons had been killed during this short-lived revolution. Among those killed were Prime Minister Cincar-Marković, Minister of War Milovan Pavlović, and both of the queen's brothers, Nikola and Nikodije Lunjevica. Minister of Interior Velimir Todorović was left for dead, but survived. Other cabinet ministers and the mayor of Beograd, Maršićanin, succeeded in escaping the conspirators. The

---

* A report by a Russian agent ("Majevci," p. 227) states that Petrović refused to co-operate with the conspirators and that they shot him before the royal couple were discovered. The same source states that Alexander and Draga were hidden in a closet.

commandant of the Danube Division, Dimitrije Nikolić, was also killed. Most of these murders had not originally been planned.*

The conspirators had successfully controlled communications. Indeed, military aid could not have come in time even if it had been summoned. There had been only one attempt at a possible counterrevolution, which was nipped in the bud. This was the work of the commandant of the Danube Division, Dimitrije Nikolić, who disappeared from his guarded home, reached Banjica, and there alerted the Eighth Regiment. The conspirators sent word informing Nikolić of the king's death, and appointed a new commandant to succeed him. Nikolić requested that one of his own officers authenticate the report. The officer (Lieutenant Colonel Ljubomir Milić), accompanied by two conspirators, arrived at Banjica to assure Nikolić of the king's murder. Shooting began. What precipitated it is not clear. It seems that the conspirators opened fire first. In the scuffle, Commandant Nikolić and both conspirators were killed. Lieutenant Colonel Milić then took over the command and explained to the army that the king had been assassinated and a new government established. This ended the only immediate threat of counterrevolution.[54]

After taking over the government, the conspirators did not at first release the authentic version of what had happened. At about 5:00 A.M. on Terazije Square, Ljuba Živković announced to the crowd that the king, wanting to rid himself of the queen, had been involved in a palace war, that the army had entered the palace, and the royal pair had been killed in the struggle. He repeated this version of Beograd developments in later statements—the murder a result of a family quarrel! During one of his speeches, shouts were heard: "Long live Serbia!" and "Long live the Republic!"[55]

The bodies of the king and queen were moved from the garden into a near-by room of the palace on the lower floor. An autopsy was performed and a protocol drawn up. The bodies were then placed in caskets and taken into an antechamber on the upper floor.[56]

* *Vl. Al. Ob.*, III, 370. The source states that Mašin had ordered the murder of the prime minister and the war minister; Vasić, p. 89, writes that only the queen's brothers were ordered killed; see also "Majevci," p. 227.

Establishment of the New Regime

1. THE REVOLUTIONARY GOVERNMENT

IMMEDIATELY AFTER THE DEMISE OF THE ROYAL FAMILY, the conspirators formed a "provisional" government to take charge of national affairs, maintain peace and order, and prevent any possible counterrevolution.[1] Its official name was "The Government of the Kingdom of Serbia," but the press alluded to it as the "Revolutionary Government."[2] This government included the conspirators and representatives of the three political parties. At the time of its organization none of the party leaders were in Beograd. Having been informed when the palace revolt would take place, Nikola Pašić* of the Radical party departed for Abazzia "on cure." Stojan Ribarac of the Populist party was staying at the time in his summer home in Požarevac. Jovan Žujović of the Independent Radicals had gone on a "scientific trip."[3] In the absence of the party leaders, the conspirators sought other prominent political figures, to inform them of the royal murder and, if need be, drag them to a meeting in the Ministry of Interior. Stojan Protić and Lj. Živković were upset by the unexpected visit of the officers, and received them reluctantly. Živković begged to be left out of the government, but at the point of a pistol changed his mind. At about 5:00 A.M. on May 29 (June 11, N.S.) the government, including the political representatives, was formed. Besides four conspirators, there were included six representatives of political parties.† Ljubomir Kaljević refused the premiership, which was then offered and accepted by Jovan Avakumović.

2. THE BURIAL OF ALEXANDER AND DRAGA

The first phase of the revolution was now complete. Constant vigil had to be maintained against a possible counterrevolution. At the same time there remained certain nasty jobs still to be done, such as the burial of Alexander

---

* According to Wegerer (*Weltkrieg*, I, 38) Pašić was in touch with the conspirators but remained behind the scenes. This cannot be substantiated.

† Živanović, IV, 355–56. The members of the government were: Jovan Dj. Avakumović, prime minister and minister without portfolio (a conspirator and a member of the Liberal party); Ljubomir Kaljević, minister of foreign affairs (an old Karadjordjević supporter with no party affiliation); Jovan Atanacković, minister of war (a conspirator); Dj. A. Genčić, minister of economics (a conspirator, Liberal party); Colonel Aleksa Mašin, minister of public works (a conspirator); Stojan Protić, minister of interior (Radical party); Lj. Živković, minister of justice (Independent Radical party); Lj. Stojanović, minister of education (Independent Radical party); V. S. Veljković, minister of finance (Liberal party). Vasić (p. 114) gives Kaljević as a member of the Progressive party. According to Živanović, the Progressive party was not included (p. 356 n. 1). Kaclerović (p. 75) writes that conservative men such as Avakumović, Genčić and Veljković, at one time servants of Alexander Obrenović, amply indicated that the government was not to be "revolutionary."

KING ALEXANDER

From Chedomille Mijatovich, A Royal Tragedy (*New York: Dodd, Mead & Co., 1907*)

QUEEN DRAGA IN 1901

From Chedomille Mijatovich, A Royal Tragedy (*New York: Dodd, Mead & Co., 1907*)

KING PETER I OF SERBIA

From Djurdje Jelenić, Nova Srbija i Jugoslavija *(Beograd, 1923)*

Nikola P. Pašić, Prime Minister

From Djurdje Jelenić, Nova Srbija i Jugoslavija (*Beograd, 1923*)

and Draga. The king and queen and the other victims had been placed in caskets early on the morning of June 12 in the presence of duly designated witnesses. The most expensive caskets available in Beograd were provided for the king and queen. Indeed, they were too large for the usual hearse so a special one had to be borrowed from the Fire Department. Then, Vasić says, "In the silent moonlit night the funeral procession started for the old cemetery along the deserted street bearing the king's name." The procession reached the Church of St. Mark at 1:15 in the morning. The church was surrounded by *gendarmerie*. Two conspirators were present as witnesses to the funeral service and burial, at which five clergymen officiated. The grave-diggers had not yet completed the excavation, and the final rites were delayed beyond expectation. When the senior clergyman uttered the final words of the ritual, no one stepped forward to kiss the deceased, as was customary. At 3:00 A.M. the caskets were at last lowered into the grave inside the small Chapel of St. Mark—the same grave in which rested the bones of the king's grandmother, Anka Obrenović, who had been murdered with Prince Mihailo in May 1868. Two cheap little crosses on the grave bore the names of Alexander and Draga. The protocol of the burial was prepared and at 3:30 in the morning delivered to Stojan Protić, minister of interior. In the same night other casualties were brought to St. Mark's Cemetery and buried there.[4]

A stone marking the graves was erected by the Austrian occupation authorities during 1915–18. It bore the names of Alexander and Draga, and recorded that they were victims of "criminal hands." It is a sad commentary on the last two Obrenović rulers, writes Živanović, that Austrians had to build monuments to them both.[5]

3. THE CONSTITUTION OF 1903

One of the first acts of the revolutionary government was the official announcement on June 11, informing the people of the royal death and appealing for order and co-operation in "this critical moment." At the same time the government ordered the restoration of the Constitution of 1901 and the convocation of the Skupština and the Senate at Beograd on June 13. The order expressly applied to the Skupština elected on July 20, 1901, by "constitutional means," and not to that elected on May 19, 1903, less than two weeks before the royal tragedy, which consisted principally of Liberals and Progressives. Likewise it applied to the Senate constituted in accordance with the Constitution of April 6, 1901, and not to that which came after Alexander suspended the Constitution on March 25, 1903, and which had not yet been completed.

The true situation was not immediately conveyed to the people. In its announcement on June 11, 1903, the government merely stated that the king and queen had been killed (*Noćas su poginuli kralj Aleksandar i kraljica Draga*), without reference to the conspiracy. Following the day of the murder, the press released bitter attacks against the king, who was vilified for his alleged inquisitorial methods and persecutions. The action of June 11 was glorified and at the same time the misdeeds of the dead king were greatly magnified.[6]

At the opening of the joint session of the Skupština and the Senate, Prime Minister Jovan Avakumović explained in the form of a declaration the existence of the "Government of the Kingdom of Serbia." He told how June 11 had found Serbia without a king, and how at dawn of that day a group of patriots had assembled for consultation to decide on a course to follow in the best interests of the state and the people. From these consultations there had emerged the existing government, which, due to popular backing and the support of the patriotic army, was able to maintain peace and order. "Convinced that it has fulfilled its duty toward the Fatherland at so critical a moment, the government leaves to the national representatives judgment of the act of June 11, and its subsequent work." Thus the government declaration mentioned "the act of June 11" but left it to the national representatives to pass judgment.

In response to the government's declaration, the Senate and the Skupština passed resolutions recognizing the new situation. The Senate, under the chairmanship of Pera Velimirović, passed a resolution hailing the "new order" with enthusiasm. It declared the existence of complete harmony between the people and the army, which was granted full recognition for its action in saving the nation from certain disaster.[7] The Senate identified the conspirators with the army and recognized the "event of June 11." The Skupština resolution was similar to that of the Senate; both were formal sanctions of the palace assassinations. The national representatives also approved all decisions and measures taken by the government and resolved that it should continue to conduct affairs of state until the election and arrival of the new king.[8]

On June 15 the Skupština raised the question of the Constitution. The Radical party, still the strongest political unit, had played an insignificant part in the overthrow of the dynasty, but now demanded a new constitution before the election of a king who would be expected to swear allegiance to it. Two of the most prominent Radicals, Paču and Geršić, suggested that the Constitution of 1901 serve as the basis for a new constitution. Liberals Stojan Ribarac and P. Maksimović, irreconcilable opponents of an upper house, demanded the restoration of the Constitution of 1888.[9] After a great deal of discussion, both houses voted to restore the Constitution of 1888 and all laws passed on the basis of it, with appropriate modifications and amendments to meet present needs. The new constitution became known as the "Constitution of 1903," but in reality it was nothing but a modified version of the Constitution of 1888, promulgated on the eve of King Milan's abdication and suspended on May 21, 1894, by King Alexander. Provision for the abolition of the Senate was the principal change in the new Constitution; it was argued that parliamentary affairs are more speedily and effectively dealt with in a unicameral legislature. The "Government of the Kingdom of Serbia" signed the Constitution on June 18.[10]

4. THE ELECTION OF PETER KARADJORDJEVIĆ

Having decided on the form of a new constitution, the Senate and the Skupština met jointly on June 15 in a spacious room of the new court, and after three-quarters of an hour elected Peter Karadjordjević* king of Serbia.[11] Before the election a group of political leaders (Jaša Prodanović†, Voja Veljković, and Jovan Skerlić) had hoped the conspirators might proclaim Serbia a republic; but at the formal meeting of the conspirators in the Officers' Home on the eve of Peter's election, the form the future government must take was so obvious that it was not even discussed. A contemporary—himself a conspirator—writes that the monarchical spirit in Europe was so strong at the time that, had Serbia proclaimed itself a republic, the European powers would most likely have intervened. For this reason, "as a historical necessity" the monarchy was the form of government accepted from the very beginning of the conspiratorial movement, although among the young conspirators there were those who favored a republican form of government.[12] However, a Russian intelligence agent, Vladimir Tržecjak, saw the situation in a somewhat different light. He noted in his report to St. Petersburg that after the palace murder there was widespread talk of a republic, and the Beograd school youth, in particular, had manifested republican tendencies. The Austrian agents, who had recently flooded Beograd, allegedly worked toward this same goal, on instructions from Vienna. Minister Charykov, whose duties had formally terminated with the death of King Alexander, found it necessary to maintain contact with the revolutionary government through a Russian agent called Vaïsman. Through this agent he advised the Serbian government to do everything possible in order to paralyze the republican agitation and to prevent further complications which might invite Austrian occupation. In response to Charykov, Colonel Mašin appeared at a gathering of students, who had assembled to discuss "the necessity and propitiousness" of a republic, and threatened to use the army against them unless they disbanded.[13]

Minister Charykov, also through Vaïsman, informed the Serbian government that, in order to avoid further difficulties and to assure the unanimous election of Peter by the Skupština, it was necessary to obtain the tsar's approval of Peter's election. The Russian agent, Tržecjak alleges that the formal election of Peter "killed the republican movement." It is interesting to note that Charykov introduced Tržecjak to Foreign Minister Kaljević as a representative of a "Russian foreign revolutionary agency," and that Kaljević reportedly promised to facilitate the work of this agency in Serbia. Charykov had also hoped to introduce Tržecjak to King Peter and to secure for him Peter's co-operation.[14]

The protocol announcing the election of Peter was read and, except for a single abstention, signed by all senators and deputies. The assembly then forwarded to Peter, who was at Geneva, heartfelt congratulations on his election. Peter replied, thanking the national representatives for the honor and promising "to be the real protector of national liberties and the most ardent defender of the National Assembly." Various patriotic institutions

* Of 158 deputies and senators, all but one voted for Peter: 119 representatives and 38 senators. One senator, Jovan Žujović, abstained from voting.

† Prodanović lived to see his dreams realized in the proclamation of the Federative Peoples Republic of Yugoslavia, on January 31, 1945. He died in July 1948.

and the government hastened to congratulate the newly elected king; in his acknowledgments Peter reiterated his promise. A deputation of twenty-four was sent to Geneva to deliver to Peter the credentials announcing his election. The deputation reached Geneva on June 20, 1903, and was received by Peter the following day at 10:30 in the morning. Four days later, accompanied by the deputation, Peter arrived in Beograd by special train.[15]

King Peter did not arrive as a stranger arbitrarily imposed on the Serbian people; his return culminated a long-standing dynastic feud between the Karadjordjević and Obrenović families. Peter had been selected to be the future king of Serbia long before Alexander was killed. If Serbia had to continue as a monarchy Peter was certainly the best selection that could have been made at the time, despite the fact that he was already on the elderly side, and had spent most of his life away from Serbia. Experience and education in Europe had given him, as one author put it, a perspective on the political problems of Serbia which in a sense counterbalanced the disadvantages of his lack of intimate knowledge of the country.[16]

As the third son of Prince Alexander Karadjordjević (1842–59), Peter received his elementary education at Beograd under the instruction of imported foreign teachers.[17] Later on he studied at Geneva and in French military schools. The French government awarded him the medal of the Legion of Honor for distinguished service during the Franco-Prussian War (1870–71). When the Balkan insurrections began in 1875, Peter saw action in Bosna under the name of Petar Mrkonjić. When, in 1883, the Austrian forces quelled the rebellious peasants of Boka Kotorska, Bosna, and Hercegovina, Peter moved to Montenegro. Here he found a warm welcome, was awarded the Order of Danilo of the first degree, made honorary senator, and on July 30, 1883, married Zorka, the eldest daughter of Prince Nikola. The marriage alarmed Prince Milan of Serbia, who was especially apprehensive because it took place at the time when he was having to deal with an uprising caused by the Russophile Radical party. He appears to have felt that Peter's marriage and the Radical party's action against him constituted an intentionally co-ordinated Russian plot, since Peter was favored by both the Russian and the Montenegrin courts and his political ideas were very much in harmony with Russian policy and pan-Slav activities. Milan's personal pride was injured when Peter received a medal identical with one he had been awarded by Prince Nikola, and he refused to credit the assurance of Nikola that he had given his daughter to Peter only after the latter had renounced his rights to the Serbian throne. In an informal sort of way Nikola even invited Milan to serve as Peter's best man, an overture which Milan declined, realizing full well that it was not an indication of genuine friendship.[18]

Princess Zorka died on March 4, 1890, after less than seven years of married life. Peter and his children—Jelena, Djordje, and Alexander—left Montenegro and settled in Geneva, where they remained until 1903. His earlier and later experiences in Western Europe left a deep imprint on his character and political thinking. He was by nature liberal and in Switzerland and France learned to appreciate the fruits of civil liberties and parliamentary democracy. He became an admirer of John Stuart Mill and translated into

Serbian his essay "On Liberty." Peter's liberalism and strict adherence to the principles of constitutionalism and parliamentarianism contributed toward a remarkable socioeconomic and political transformation of Serbia. His deep patriotism was a significant contribution to the strengthening of the national movement. "The national energy was unharnessed. Henceforth begins the real national—Serbian and Yugoslav—policy."[19] No longer was there a serious question which of the two Slavic states—Montenegro or Serbia— should be foremost in the struggle for national liberation and Yugoslav unification. There was a time before 1903 when Montenegro, though much smaller than Serbia, had enjoyed more prestige among the yet unliberated Slavs.[20] But after Peter's accession, Serbian primacy was indisputable.

Prior to 1903 the prestige of Montenegro had been strengthened by the unpopularity of the Obrenović dynasty. Although Prince Nikola, like Milan and Alexander, had had dealings with Austria-Hungary, he had never allowed himself to be drawn into the Austro-Hungarian orbit. He was loyal to Mother Russia, and on one occasion was recognized by Tsar Alexander III as Russia's "only true friend." The political relations of Montenegro with Russia had been cemented through marriage alliances; two of the daughters of Nikola married Russian grand dukes. Yet toward the end of the nineteenth century Serbia had definitely forged ahead of Montenegro as leader in the national struggle. Economically she was far ahead of the poverty-stricken Montenegro with its mountainous and nonproductive regions. The same was true in the field of culture and learning. Serbia had developed an intellectual class, a rapidly expanding university,* the Royal Serbian Academy of Arts and Sciences, and many other learned societies. Beograd was the natural rallying point for all Yugoslavs, since it represented both spiritual and physical strength.[21] And so when Peter arrived—a friend of Russia,† a son-in-law of the Montenegrin prince, and an anti-German by political conviction— Serbia clinched the leadership in the struggle for Yugoslav unification.

5. POLITICAL REORIENTATION

When Peter arrived in Beograd, he was formally welcomed at the station.[22] His first proclamation to the people came on June 25, the day he took the oath to uphold the Constitution. In the proclamation he stated that he wished "to be the real constitutional king of Serbia," that he would remain loyal to the "tradition of the Serbian people and of my ancestors," that he would conduct foreign relations in accordance with the traditional aspirations of the Serbian people, and that he would seek to maintain friendly relations with the neighboring states.[23] Five days later at a court banquet he added to his program a promise to concern himself with establishment of justice and freedom in the country, stabilization of finances, betterment of

---

* By the law, signed on February 27, 1905, the so-called Beograd "high school" was raised to the status of university with faculties of Theology, Philosophy, Medicine, Law, and Technical Sciences. *N.S.* (December 15, 1904), II, 999–1004, records most illuminating debates on the subject.

† Regarding Peter's poor financial situation and dependence on Russia, see Svetozar Pribićević, *Diktatura kralja Aleksandra* (Beograd, 1952), pp. 338–41.

the economic position of the people, and development and modernization of the army. In his first speech from the throne (September 24),[24] he expressed a wish for "traditional relations with powerful brotherly Russia," the best possible relations with the neighboring Dual Monarchy, and "sincere and cordial relations with the Balkan peoples." King Peter placed the Macedonian Question high on the agenda, and welcomed the program for Macedonian reforms and Austro-Russian co-operation with the Ottoman sultan therein. He expressed himself as particularly pleased by the official recognition the Ottoman Empire had accorded Serbian nationality in a special irade and by the inclusion of a Serbian representative on the reform commission. The government, at that time under General Grujić, had finally persuaded the Porte to issue an irade by which the existence of Serbian nationality in Macedonia was recognized. For six years the Serbs had sought such recognition in order to free their kinsmen from the "inquisitorial" activities of the Bulgarian exarchate.[25] Peter expressed great satisfaction with the way he was received everywhere by the people during his first tour of the country; he recognized the "patriotic" service of the revolutionary government in preventing turmoil during the absence of royal authority. Peter urged internal stability, financial and administrative, in order to improve the country's international position.

Peter's first address from the throne and his other declarations were received enthusiastically by the Skupština. In its acknowledgment of the royal address,[26] the Skupština emphasized the import of the news that Serbian nationality had been officially recognized in Turkey, because that recognition was said to have removed an obstacle which had long hindered cultural and socioeconomic improvements among Serbians then living in Turkey. The Skupština viewed with optimism the Macedonian reform projects, which it believed would secure peace and order in the provinces, toward which Serbia could not be indifferent. But the Skupština recommended that the country must be prepared to assume its responsibilities in case of "further developments in our neighborhood." Each statement of the king in his address from the throne was carefully weighed, and after a parliamentary debate both his internal and foreign policies were approved.

On October 6, 1903, Stojan Protić submitted to the Skupština the government's program, which touched on all phases of national life. The restoration of the freedoms provided by the Constitution of 1888 was not, it said, enough, and the government proposed a long list of reforms aimed to democratize the country by eradicating all vestiges of the former bureaucratic and police regime. They touched on the administration, judiciary, local government, personal and property security, military and press. The government planned improvement of economic conditions through financial stability and industrial development. It also sought to secure more advantageous commercial relations with foreign countries through new trade treaties based on the general customs tariff law to be shortly submitted to the Skupština. The government proposed development of transportation and communication networks, technical works, educational reform, and a new surtax (*prirez*) to meet the added costs. The latter would also provide partial funds for construction of new railways. A society would be organized for this purpose to attract foreign capital.[27]

These first statements by the king, the Skupština, and the government represented in a way an enunciation of the new Serbian foreign and domestic policy. It soon became obvious that in foreign policy the government aimed to maintain close relations with Russia and the Balkan states. From the very beginning, therefore, the new regime had indicated the political trend it would follow in its domestic and foreign relations; it gave the country a "national policy." A constitutional-parliamentary regime was installed. Civil and political freedom and local self-government were guaranteed.* For the first time in Serbia's history the Parliament adopted a constitution independently of the Crown and thereby "imposed" the popular will on the king.† Indeed, some observers considered the Constitution too liberal and too advanced for the Balkan peninsula![28] But in fact, although Peter himself respected the Constitution, the cabinets after 1905 usurped some parliamentary prerogatives; they appointed officials, controlled the budget and, to an extent, the army as well.[29] There were irregularities accompanying elections as well as political discrimination against and intimidation of the opposition by the government party.‡

6. DEVELOPMENT OF THE PARLIAMENTARY REGIME AND THE PARTY SYSTEM

The Constitution of 1903 gave Serbia a parliamentary regime of the English type. The Radical party continued to be the strongest political party and retained control of the government. The few cabinets formed by other parties were short-lived. Perhaps the most important single development was the fact that the leading political parties pursued the same basic foreign policy and that even internal policy varied, at least in practice, very little. There existed nevertheless an interparty rivalry, bitter indeed, but never intensive enough to weaken the national solidarity that came with the new regime. The king stood above party politics, and conducted the formation of the cabinet in accordance with parliamentary rules. Party life was free, and several new parties appeared after 1903, among them the Social Democratic party. The two wings of the Radical party, split in 1901 into "old" Radicals and "young" Independent Radicals, were the best-organized parties and had the largest popular support.[30]

* During the November 1, 1904–March 3, 1905, session, the Skupština passed laws for communal and district administration, the press, and many other laws.

† Kaclerović, p. 74. This socialist writer found that the Constitution actually strengthened the royal prerogatives, that it deprived several hundreds of thousands of persons of the right to vote, that it did not provide for proportional representation in the Skupština nor in lower councils, and that it did not assure genuine autonomy for local governments.

‡ The debates on the law for public security and the question of liberties during the Skupština session, November 1, 1904–March 3, 1905, throw much light on the actual political situation in the country. See, for example, N.S., II (December 20, 1904), 114 ff., and II (February 21, 1905), 1735 ff. The opposition *Srpska zastava* frequently reported violations of public security regulations. On one occasion (No. 58, December 14, 1904) it complained that the *gendarmerie* was used to silence political rivals.

The change in political orientation after 1903 induced the political parties to adapt themselves to the new conditions. The two Radical parties, Old and Independent, least discredited in the eyes of the masses, could so adapt themselves without any serious changes in their program. The new policies fell in with their party program: a parliamentary and constitutional rule, a national and Russophile foreign policy, civil liberties, a defense and promotion of the interests of the peasants, who comprised the majority of the population, full political and economic independence, and military preparedness.

That group of the Radicals which rejected the 1901 understanding ("fusion") with the Progressives had formed their own party, the Independent Radical party. Unlike other parties, the Independent Radicals refused even to recognize the Constitution of 1901. They remained loyal to the original 1881 program of the Radical party, in contrast to the "opportunism" of the Old Radicals. Their party leadership was younger and more spirited than that of the Old Radical party. The principal organ of the Independent Radicals was *Odjek* (Echo); the party's leader until May 11, 1905, was Ljuba Živković, and then until January 29, 1912, Ljuba Stojanović. The struggle between the two Radical parties centered on technicalities and personalities rather than on basic issues. In 1903 they settled their differences, but the coalition broke up again on October 12, 1904, with the demise of Grujić's cabinet. Henceforth the two factions of the Radical party continued to develop independently. From 1903 on, the struggle for political power was primarily between the two Radical parties, giving the country considerable stability and the character of a two-party system.[31]

Besides the two major parties there were a number of smaller ones. The Liberal party, founded in October 1904 under the leadership of Stojan Ribarac, resembled the two Radical parties in foreign policy. Nor did its domestic program basically differ from that of the two Radical parties. It was a strong advocate of a reorganized and modernized standing army, military preparedness, and universal military training. It emphasized the need for compulsory education, new educational institutions and centers of learning. Later the Liberal party and the Liberal Democratic party, headed by Dr. Vojislav Veljković, merged to form the so-called National party (*Narodna stranka*), led by Stojan Ribarac; in all essentials, the program resembled that of the Liberal party. The Populist was the third largest party, and, for tactical reasons, always supported the strongest opposition group in the Skupština.[32]

The old Progressive party was formally dissolved in 1897, but its leaders continued to attract followers. On January 30, 1906, the party was re-established with a new platform. It continued to support a bicameral legislature system, a conservative constitution, and political liberalism. Like most other parties, the Progressives laid stress on the need for economic and social improvement at home, and in foreign relations demanded the realization of Serbian national rights through peaceful and legal means and the elimination of foreign influence in Serbian affairs; they also declared themselves in support of the principle "The Balkans for the Balkan people." The titular head of the party was Stojan Novaković, the noted philologist and historian, but because of his advanced age the real leaders were the brothers Pavle and Vojislav Marinković.[33]

In October 1903 the Serbian People's Peasant Solidarity was founded as a new political party, which had little popular appeal and only once won a single parliamentary seat. Its platform, of course, emphasized the need for the betterment of the lot of the peasants. It demanded compulsory education, agrarian schools, lower taxes, and reduction of the army. In the field of foreign relations it demanded unity for all Serbs, friendship with Montenegro, and close relations with the other Balkan peoples.[34] All the political parties except the Populists demanded universal suffrage—at least on paper. The Social Democratic party was the only one which actively suggested universal suffrage, with a direct and secret ballot for all citizens twenty years of age, regardless of sex.[35]

The change in 1903 gave impetus to the growth of socialism and republicanism. The socialist movement had originated in Serbia and in the Yugoslav provinces under Austria-Hungary in the 'seventies. Its followers first gathered around socialist newspapers, later founded societies and clubs, and finally, after 1903, organized a political party. The origin and growth of socialism among the Yugoslavs followed the same characteristic development one finds in other countries, and it passed through the same crises caused by "revisionism, opportunism, reformism, and open betrayal and compromise."*

The Serbian socialist movement developed independently of similar movements in Slovenia, Croatia, and Bosna-Hercegovina. The first exponent of socialism in Serbia was Živojin Žujović (1840–70).[36] He was essentially a "Socialist utopian." His work did not produce permanent results because conditions in Serbia in his time were not suitable for socialistic activities. His successor—and the greatest socialist mind in Serbia during the latter nineteenth century—was Svetozar Marković,[37] who was educated under the influence of the Russian *narodniki*. He applied his socialist theories to founding co-operatives and organizing the workers. He founded the first workers' newspaper, *Radnik* (Worker), which appeared on July 1, 1871. Other papers and periodicals soon appeared—*Javnost* (The Public), *Rad* (Work), and *Oslobodjenje* (Liberation). The idea of Marković was that liberation of the Serbs should come through a general Balkan revolution, directed against all states which sought to prevent the Balkan union. The union should be built by the working class—a union of equal workers, communes, counties, and states. Marković is the precursor of the Serbian co-operative and syndicalist movements.

The Serbian socialist movement in the 'seventies and 'eighties was almost completely of the guild character and was of course not widespread. It represented a confused theoretical mixture of utopianism, anarchism, and distorted

* Josip Broz Tito, *Political Report of the Central Committee of the Communist Party of Yugoslavia*, pp. 4 ff. One of the principal tasks of postwar Yugoslav historians is the collection of materials and investigation of the history of Yugoslav socialism. Many invaluable fragmentary materials have already appeared. See Wayne S. Vucinich, "Postwar Yugoslav Historiography," *The Journal of Modern History*, XXIII, No. 1 (March 1951), 41–57.

Marxism. It was not until the 'nineties that so-called scientific Marxism took hold and found expression in the paper *Social Demokrat*, first published in 1895, and in the *Radničke novine* (The Workers' News), which appeared in 1897. The first May Day celebrations were held in 1896.[38]

The first congress of the Social Democrats was held on July 27, 1903, from which emerged the first Marxist party—the Social Democratic party. The leading organizers were Dimitrije Tucović (1881–1914) and Radovan Dragović (1878–1905).[39] The program adopted by the congress was similar to that of the Erfurt Congress. As the "most consistent" Marxist, Dimitrije Tucović led the struggle against those who advocated co-operation with the bourgeois elements (Skerlić, Lapčević, and others). The opponents of Tucović and his group founded their own newspaper, called *Svest* (Consciousness). The two wings of the socialist movement conducted a verbal and press war. After 1904 dissension in the ranks of the socialist movement continued. One group, led by Milorad Popović, stood for independent trade unionism, while another group, under Tucović, believed in the control of trade unionism by the Social Democratic party.

In the elections of 1903 the Social Democrats entered candidates in two districts and two cities, and elected one, Dr. Mihailo Ilić, to the Skupština.* Ilić was an energetic and vocal defender of socialism and the rights of workers, giving a great deal of trouble to the government with his numerous interpellations.[40] After 1903 a small proletarian class was gradually emerging, which clamored for recognition. Already in 1904 there were conflicts in the city of Kragujevac, the center of the war industry, between the workers and employers, workers and officers.[41] The socialist movement did not develop into a mass movement, but it did become an organized political force, with its own party machine, publications, and theoreticians. The age was still that of nationalism; only those parties which had strong nationalistic programs were able successfully to cater to the masses.

7. COUNTERCONSPIRACY

Captain Milan Novaković was the prime mover of the most important counterconspiracy. He was an intelligent young man who had graduated with an excellent record from Nikolaevska General Staff Academy at St. Petersburg and had been sent to Paris for further study in the field of military science. He was there when the assassination of King Alexander occurred, and on July 6, 1903, he returned to Beograd. The death of the king had apparently filled him with shame; upon his return to Serbia he was shocked to learn that the murder had been every bit as bloody as described by the foreign press. Furthermore, he sensed an open break in the army, which widened as the official announcements indicated "house cleaning."

---

* Mitrović, p. 100. In the 1905 elections the Social Democrats polled a mere 2,608 votes and won two seats, one in Beograd, one in Pirot. In the next year's elections they won 3,133 votes but only a single parliamentary seat (in Kragujevac). They retained this seat in the 1908 elections, when they polled 3,143 votes. In the last elections before World War I, the Social Democrats polled 4,250 urban and 24,787 rural votes.

The officer conspirators, via their committees and friends, were shifting commandants of divisions, brigades, and even smaller military units. Some officers were pensioned off. In the eyes of Novaković this was a dangerous situation, in which something like eighty conspirators were trying to control the entire Officers' Corps. He noted that new appointments to high military posts did not always correspond to qualifications and seniority.[42]

Immediately after the dynastic change the conspirators filled all the better military and government posts. Atanacković became war minister; Mašin, minister for public works; Genčić, minister of economy; all the adjutants were conspirators (Colonel Bogdan Damnjanović and Majors Gojko Djurić, Steva Milovanović, and Branko Jovanović); all ordnance officers were also conspirators, as was the chief of the postal military section in the War Ministry (Petar Mišić), and so on through a long list of responsible positions. These developments weighed heavily on Novaković's mind. In July and August he thrice noted in his diary that the officers who had been most responsible for the conspiracy and for current corruption and praetorianism in the army should, in the interests of peace, "the fatherland, the king, and the army," put off their uniforms. He had friends who shared his views wholeheartedly. They condemned the assassination on the basis that it was immoral. They had hoped the Skupština might be able to handle the situation, and felt it to be a mistake for the revolutionary government to continue in power after the king's election. But since the Skupština was showing itself unable "to save the fatherland and the king" from the conspirators, then someone else should—and this could be Novaković and his officer friends.[43]

On August 11, 1903, Novaković arrived at Niš to assume his duties with the Sixteenth Infantry Regiment. He brought with him a proclamation he had prepared, addressed to the Officers' Corps. The proclamation listed sixty-eight conspirators who, it was claimed, had dishonored the uniform and violated their sworn oaths when they killed the king and queen in a most inhuman manner. According to Novaković, the officer conspirators should have removed all signs that they were sworn officers; having failed to do so at that time, they should do so now. Such action, he asserted, was required in the interests of peace, and for the honor of the fatherland, king, army, and Officers' Corps. Instead, the manifesto continued, the officer conspirators acted in their personal interest and had interfered in the appointments of royal adjutants and ordnance officers, and in the appointment of the marshal of the court. When Colonel Lešjanin, military attaché in Constantinople, was appointed court marshal (court chamberlain), the conspirators had stormed the State Printing Office, where they "tore up the issue of the official gazette which announced the appointment, and demanded a second edition with the omission of the announcement, Lešjanin was obliged to return to Constantinople."

Novaković appealed therefore to his comrades to see to it that responsible authorities removed the officers in question from state service. He urged that they all unite, regardless of rank, behind the slogan "Remove uniforms, they or we!" (*Mundire dole, oni ili mi!*) The proclamation was printed and circulated for signature. On August 15 Novaković began enlisting collaborators.

There were rumors at the time that King Peter himself was trying to eliminate the conspiratorial atmosphere from the court.[44]

In August 1903 the king undertook his first official sojourn in the country. When he reached Niš, the largest prewar military garrison, the authorities discovered traces of a "counterconspiratorial" movement among the officers. At a ceremonious reception prepared in his honor in the Hotel Evropa, mutual apprehension was apparent among the officers. Most of the younger conspirators attended the reception with concealed revolvers. There was danger that evening of an armed attack on the royal family, and the conspirators came ready to defend "His Majesty." This was the first organized movement against the new regime, and was of course of Novaković's making. The aim of the Niš counterconspiracy was allegedly to eliminate conspirators from the army, and through peaceful and legal means to restrain the political influence of the conspirators. The counterconspirators steadfastly insisted that their movement was not directed against the new dynasty and the new order, but was intended merely to remove the officers who had violated their oath and soiled their uniform with blood. Yet some hold that the movement was directed against the king as well. One source, seeing broader ramifications in the movement, states that its failure was also due to the lack of an acceptable candidate for the throne. There was no native candidate except the illegitimate son of King Milan and Artemiza Hristić, and during the first years after the tragic palace murder a foreign ruler was unthinkable.[45]

As soon as the counterconspiracy was discovered, an emergency meeting was held at the Ministry of Interior in Beograd with several of the original conspirators present. The existence of the movement was confirmed by the Russian diplomatic agent Chakotin. Captain Dimitrijević was dispatched to Niš to investigate the situation, reaching there on August 21. He obtained a copy of Novaković's proclamation the day he got to Niš by bribing a noncommissioned officer. That very evening the commandant of the Morava Division, General Božidar Janković, ordered the imprisonment of twenty officers who had signed the proclamation.[46] The investigation of the counterconspiracy ended at the beginning of September. Twenty-seven officers were tried, all from the Niš garrison. Captain Novaković defended the accused very ably; he argued that the conspirators who had raised their hands against their commander in chief were traitors, because in so doing they had violated their given word and broken the faith vested in them. Their action, he said, violated the basic principles of military "honor" and abused the confidence of the troops. The murder of the ruler, he explained, was unnecessary and could not be justified. If the conspirators remained in the army, there was danger that the armed forces might disintegrate. Novaković noted that control of the government by conspirators could only bring a prolonged ostracism of Serbia by foreign powers.[47] He deprecated the selfish motives of the conspirators and their lust for personal power. At the time that the military deputation was selected to accompany the newly elected king to Serbia, the conspirators had imposed on the government a list of deputies of their own choosing, and later on, in the form of a reward, had accepted promotions to which they had no legal right from the not-too-well–informed king. A case in point was Damjan Popović, whom the king made a general and then was forced to demote when Stojan Ribarac pointed out the legal irregularity. Novaković pointed out that the conspirators not only controlled the court and the government but continued to meet secretly and to enforce their will on the executives, especially with regard to military appointments. There were instances of the destruction of printed orders for military appointments, in order to reserve the rank or post for a fellow conspirator. The Officers' Corps resented this nefarious influence "from below." Whatever Novaković's intentions may have been, one thing is to his credit: he brought the problem into the open, and in that way hastened the elimination of conspiratorial influence on national politics. His criticism of the activities of the conspirators was cogent, and he risked his career when he boldly decided to lead the hard fight against them. He argued, however, that the military code permitted his espousing a selection of a deputation to discuss the conspiratorial question with responsible authorities. His group, he said, did not advocate a revolt and insubordination, the two charges brought against them. He explained how strong the feeling against the conspirators was among the officers and how on July 27 he had prepared his proclamation to the "Serbian Officers' Corps."[48]

Novaković put up an able and effective defense, but nevertheless on September 16 the military court found him and his friends guilty and sentenced them to varying degrees of punishment. The ringleaders, Milan Novaković and Dobrivoje Lazarević, were given two years in prison. The grand military court confirmed the sentences on September 26, 1903.[49]

The conspirators, making use of the friendly press, undertook to refute every charge Novaković had made against them. They argued that their motives for killing Alexander arose from a sincere and honest desire for the betterment of their country. They admitted that they had made some mistakes, and regretted that there had been unwarranted promotions, such as occurred when the war minister, General Jovan Atanacković, transferred his son from the interior to Beograd. They admitted having interfered with certain military appointments, but offered what they thought to be convincing explanations in each case. They had opposed the appointment of Lešjanin as court marshal because he had served in the same capacity under Alexander. They had criticized the war minister for his abuses of ministerial prerogatives, probably principally for the reason that they wished to replace him with their friend, General Putnik.[50]

The counterconspiracy was probably larger in scope than appeared at first glance. The list seized from Captain Milan Novaković consisted of about twenty names, all rather inconspicuous individuals. It no doubt included the less prominent counterconspirators only, the late-comers, so to speak. Other garrisons must have had members in the organization, but for a variety of reasons the investigation was restricted to the Niš garrison, and therefore the real size of the counterconspiracy remained unknown.[51] Novaković boasted that in a very short time he could have enlisted two hundred fifty followers, had not the counterconspiracy been uncovered. But, as Vasić says, there is always a "Judas" in an organization of that type.

Some of the alleged counterconspirators had believed that the mere elimination of the conspirators from influential positions was not sufficient. Unless physically eliminated, they feared, the conspirators might resume their work from the outside. This group would have preferred something like an exemplary punishment of the assassins, as a warning to any future officer who might wish to raise his hand against his monarch.[52]

The Niš counterconspiracy ended without bloodshed because it was discovered at the outset. Its only lasting result was the division of the officers into two opposing camps. Between 1903 and 1912 there were to be other conspiracies afoot among officers and noncommissioned officers, but they were all minor ones of local import.[53]

PART FIVE

Foreign Recognition

1. EUROPEAN REACTION TO THE PALACE MURDER

THE NEWS OF THE ASSASSINATION IN BEOGRAD shocked the outside world. The whole affair was so sudden that the foreign powers were unprepared for any immediate action, and before they could communicate with each other, Beograd resumed its normal activity. The British ambassador in Vienna observed that the Serbian people had "not only forgotten, but apparently rejoiced in, the murderous extinction of the late royal family."[1] Europe was surprised by the calm acceptance of the royal murder by the Serbian people. The foreign diplomats at Beograd had been unaware of any conspiracy. They were not certain at first who the killers were and what their motives were. Some were inclined to think that the assassination had been engineered by the supporters of the Macedonian revolutionary movement. The British ambassador at Vienna, usually well informed on Balkan affairs, reported that "the terrible catastrophe was not only not foreseen by the Austro-Hungarian government but that, odd as it may seem, the contingency of King Alexander's possible death had not been provided for in the arrangement come to between Austria-Hungary and Russia in regard to the Balkans."[2] The American consul, probably the only impartial and neutral observer, reported the palace revolution in a series of brief telegraphic communications, and transmitted several statements from the Serbian revolutionary government to the Department of State. These were not addressed specifically to the American State Department but were copies of identical documents transmitted to other foreign governments. Within four days after the assassination a government was formed, the Skupština and Senate were assembled, and the new king was elected.[3] Constantin Dumba, Austro-Hungarian minister, notes that the people's matter-of-fact acceptance of the new order was surprising.

The capital had accepted the new order. No shooting was going on and there would be no more bloodshed. I might wander all over Belgrade without being molested. The officers had been so certain of their power that they had not held up the 5:30 A.M. train from Belgrade to Budapest and Vienna, and the local steamers were departing from Semlin [Zemun] every hour as usual.[4]

The Russian minister, Charykov, observed the attack on the palace from the window of his Legation across the street.[5] On the morning after the murder, Dumba found Charykov "terribly shaken." Charykov told how "a stray bullet fired from the garden of the palace had penetrated the window of the nursery and had passed close to the bed of his child." The incident had so shocked Charykov that, with his concurrence, Dumba reported the Beograd developments by telegraph to St. Petersburg, *in claris* from Zemun. Earlier in the day Dumba had visited the Serbian Foreign Office, where he received from Colonel Mašin detailed information regarding the composition of the revolutionary government and its avowed policy, and was requested to pass this same information on to the Russian Legation.[6]

From the memoirs of Dumba and Charykov and many official materials, one has the impression that the Austrian and Russian ministers were innocent bystanders and knew nothing about the conspiracy. But if the Russians did not know of the conspiracy, why did they organize a group of special agents to protect Alexander's life?[7] An English writer, Wickham Steed, an expert on Central European affairs, has another version. He writes that the plot may have been hatched, as has been alleged, under Russian auspices, but that its existence was certainly known to the Austro-Hungarian government as well. The latter was fully informed of the meetings held by the conspirators in Vienna's well-known Ringstrasse. Early in March 1903 Benjamin von Kállay, joint Austro-Hungarian finance minister, told Steed that "King Alexander was in a perilous position and might not have many weeks to live." When, immediately after the assassination, Steed reminded Kállay of his earlier remark, he replied, "Quite true; and that will prove to you that what I tell you about the East is apt to be well-founded. Alexander was doomed and the intrigues of Nicholas of Montenegro have been nipped in the bud."[8] Some interesting speculation transpired on both sides of the conversation. Kállay elaborated on his earlier statement by saying that the relations of Peter Karadjordjević with his father-in-law, Prince Nikola of Montenegro, were "so bad that he is not dangerous. Besides, the Karadjordjević dynasty had always had two elements in its policy—not to quarrel with Austria-Hungary and not to quarrel with Turkey." However, explained Kállay, Peter's accession might cause some trouble in the Balkans. He might be obliged

to make himself popular by engaging in some national enterprise, though, as he is no longer young, I do not anticipate trouble in that direction; it is Nicholas of Montenegro, who seeing the defeat of his schemes to put his second son, Mirko, on the Serbian throne, may try to push forward to Prizren through the Albanian Catholic country so as to work round towards Serbia from the South. It will be the business of Turkey to deal with him.[9]

On June 12 the official *Fremdenblatt* published a statement to the effect that the change of regime in Serbia was of comparative indifference to Austria-Hungary, which required only the maintenance of friendly relations. Goluchowski confirmed this statement in his conversation with the French ambassador. Some other newspapers, such as *Zeit*, launched a violent attack on the official *Fremdenblatt* for the attitude it took toward "the assassination of crowned heads," and forced it to abandon its moderate position. Nevertheless the impression persisted in Vienna that the Austro-Hungarian policymakers were by no means displeased with the dynastic change in Serbia. Steed further notes the fact that "when Peter passed through Vienna on his way from Geneva to assume the crown, the Austrian authorities refrained from interfering with the crowd of Serbo-Croatians that assembled to welcome him at the Western Railway Station, although, among other manifestations, cheers were given for 'Peter, King of Croatia!' "[10]

At Bucharest little sympathy was felt for Alexander Obrenović, although there was much speculation about the future Serbian government and its foreign orientation. As a sign of disapproval, however, King Carol resigned as honorary colonel of the regiment whose officers had participated in the conspiracy, and the Rumanian diplomatic agent in Beograd was recalled for a brief period.[11] Serbo-Rumanian relations deteriorated and became particularly strained in April 1904, when Serbian officials on the Danube failed to greet the Rumanian royal family, then sailing to the Black Sea.[12]

In Bulgaria General Petrov, the prime minister and foreign minister, gave it as his opinion that the Serbian affair was "a matter which did not concern the Bulgarian government at all." Only in case of civil war did the Bulgarians plan "to take steps to secure the tranquillity of the Bulgarian border." As far as Petrov was concerned it made little difference who the next Serbian king would be, although he suggested that Serbia elect "a sovereign from among the royal families of Europe."[13]

Monsieur Delcassé, the French foreign minister, expressed to the Serbian minister the profound condolences of his government.[14] In several countries —Russia, Spain, Rumania—court mourning was ordered. The British prime minister, Balfour, severely criticized the Serbian murders before the House of Commons. Lansdowne went so far as to seek means by which Serbia could be punished. Edward VII was particularly alarmed, and England sought to influence the Great Powers "to recall their ministers from Beograd in sign of protest for the act of May 29."[15] Italy for the moment refused to recognize the new government, but Admiral Morin in the Senate cautioned that despite "this terrible tragedy, the Government must remember that the events which took place at Belgrade . . . relate to internal affairs."[16]

The interests of Montenegro in the Serbian palace revolution were of course unique. Official circles in that country were fully aware of Queen Draga's unpopularity in Serbia and of the wide disapproval of the actions of King Alexander. The French minister to Montenegro had reported that some people thought King Alexander might remain on the throne by marrying Ksenija of Montenegro (fifth daughter of Prince Nikola) or by adopting as his successor Prince Mirko (the second son of the prince). Only a few hours before the assassination, the *Piccolo* of Trieste carried an article outlining the conditions under which Prince Mirko could be invited to accept the hereditary title of Prince of Serbia.[17]

2. AUSTRIA AND RUSSIA CO-OPERATE

Whatever the attitudes of the various foreign governments, the provisional Serbian government was sure that "on pursuing the course adopted it would assure the sympathies of all the European powers with the new state of affairs."[18] Internal strife, it was feared, might provide Austro-Hungary with a ready pretext for occupying Serbia, ostensibly to re-establish peace and order. Some Serbian historians claim that there were those in Austria-Hungary who urged prompt military intervention.[19] In his *Memoirs*,

Dumba says, as we noted earlier, that no such action was contemplated. He argues that "the dual monarchy, even if it had so desired, was not in a position to carry through any such ambitious expansionist policy purely on nationalistic grounds and owing to the opposition of the Magyars."[20] According to Dumba, the success of the assassins relieved him of "the necessity of communicating directly with the corps commanders in Agram [Zagreb] and Temesvar by telegram." Finally he concluded that

In any case, a request for military intervention would have been quite useless— apart from the fact that I was not entitled to ask for it. We had scarcely five hundred rifles in Semlin [Zemun]. On the other hand, Belgrade was garrisoned by five or six regiments, several thousand men strong.[21]

Dumba notes that only if Alexander and Draga had taken refuge with Charykov or himself would the question of requesting military assistance have become a reality.

On the morning following the assassination, Dumba requested from Colonel Mašin of the Serbian Foreign Office permission to communicate with Austrian consulates throughout Serbia regarding the popular reaction in the provinces. Mašin granted this permission on the grounds that it would be of interest to Serbia to keep the Austro-Hungarian government "promptly and accurately informed," and during the same afternoon Dumba was in contact with the consulates. The news from the provinces was so favorable to the new regime that Dumba on June 13 requested permission from his superiors "to negotiate with the new government . . . as a *de facto* government, without recognizing it *de jure*."[22]

When conditions appeared to have returned to normal, Austria-Hungary and Russia accepted the *fait accompli* and endeavored to make the best of the "bad" situation. The official spokesmen of Austria-Hungary and Russia assured the world on several occasions that the Serbian crisis would cause no complications between their countries. Goluchowski stated that Russia and Austria-Hungary were inclined to let the Serbs themselves choose their future king.[23] The Austrian prime minister confirmed this very policy in a statement before the Reichsrat.[24] Count Lamsdorff stated that "Russia had no intention of intervening in the internal affairs of Serbia and would no doubt recognize any legally constituted government if other powers did so."[25] For the time being, however, the Russians continued to ignore the provisional government, and the Serbian minister left St. Petersburg because the Russian authorities refused to acknowledge communications transmitted to him by the new Serbian foreign minister.[26] The British representative at St. Petersburg reported that Russia and Austria-Hungary were taking "a sober view of the situation" in Serbia, and that they would be prepared to recognize any legally constituted authority capable of maintaining order. The provisional government seemed to them "equal to the occasion."[27]

On June 12, 1903, Goluchowski communicated with Lamsdorff concerning the policy their representatives should follow at Beograd. Both emphasized the need for a speedy settlement of the internal political situation by ending the provisional government and recognizing Peter Karadjordjević as a "relatively lesser evil." They were acting on the assumption that the new king would be able to bring to justice the officers by whose hands the Obrenović dynasty had fallen. Dumba, however, was not ready for such hasty recognition.[28] Nevertheless, he was ordered to remain at Beograd and to accept the provisional government as the *de facto* authority for the transaction of any current business."[29]

Pursuant to their policy of maintaining the status quo in the Balkans, the governments of Russia and Austria-Hungary agreed to work together in all matters pertaining to Serbia; the major steps taken with respect to the Avakumović government were identical. Their representatives sent written notes in the third person, and avoided meeting with the Serbian cabinet ministers. "They jointly read their telegrams and jointly composed them."[30]

The Austro-Hungarian and Italian representatives at London, upon inquiry at the Foreign Office,[31] were told by Lansdowne that the British minister would temporarily return to his post at Beograd, in order to supply information and to watch over British interests, but he would not be "accredited to or have official relations with the new Government." He added that the British would "probably be in no hurry to accord official recognition to them."[32]

The British Foreign Office, however, ordered its representative to leave before the arrival of Peter, and sent Vice-Consul Wilfred Thesiger to take charge of the Legation. The revolutionary government was informed of these changes in an unofficial note transmitted by the British minister.[33]

The Italian government decided for the time being to employ its minister at Beograd only for the transaction of *les affaires courantes*, without accrediting him officially to the new government.[34] The Italian minister was instructed to conduct any necessary communications with the Serbian government by impersonal *notes verbales*, without suggesting recognition of the existing government.[35]

The instructions sent to the French minister at Beograd were practically the same as those sent to the British minister by his government.[36] The German government concluded that inasmuch as the Austrian and Russian governments were leaving their representatives at Beograd, the German minister would remain also; and the German emperor "decided not to declare any court mourning for the late King and Queen of Serbia."[37]

3. THE BRITISH TAKE A FIRM POSITION

The Serbian question was hotly debated in London, both in the Foreign Office and in the House of Commons. In response to a question from the floor regarding the Serbian affair, the undersecretary of state for foreign affairs, Lord Cranborne, explained that formal relations with Serbia were suspended. He continued by saying:

It has been usual to recognize the right of a Legation to retain the customary extra-territorial and diplomatic privileges in spite of a temporary suspension of the Minister's official functions. British consular officers in Serbia do not enjoy extra-territorial privileges, but in accordance with usage the only British consular officer in the country will continue to exercise the consular functions.

The functions of the Serbian minister "accredited to the Court of St. James in London . . . lapsed with the death of King Alexander, just as Sir George Bonham's lapsed at the same time."[38] A. J. Balfour defined British-Serbian relations thus: "They came *ipso facto* to an end with the death of the King of Serbia, because our representative in Serbia was accredited only to the King."[39] When he was asked if he could, before diplomatic relations with Serbia were renewed, convey to the Serbian government "an expression of the feeling of this country," the prime minister and first lord of the treasury pointed out that "it would evidently be impossible to make any remonstrance of representation to the Serbian Government until diplomatic relations are renewed." It was decided, he said, that "the people guilty of these murders should be punished."[40] Lord Newton severely criticized the revolutionary Serbian government in the Upper House and asked that the government express in "the most emphatic manner its abhorrence to this crime." He went on to say: "So far as Serbia itself is concerned, the feelings of nobody appear to have been outraged at all. On the contrary, the assassins are glorified as heroes, the national assembly has passed a vote of thanks to them, and their action has been effusively and solemnly blessed by the clergy."[41]

Lansdowne told the Russian ambassador at London that British public opinion had been so greatly aroused over the Beograd murder that it was impossible for the British "at present" to enter into official relations with the new Serbian government. He was pleased with the Russian expectation that the authors of the Beograd crime would be punished, but doubted that this could be effected, since some members of the government were directly involved in the murder. According to Lansdowne, the Russian ambassador (Count Benckendorff) apparently shared the British attitude and had remarked that the British "should certainly be in no hurry to accredit a representative to the Serbian Government."[42]

Thus, British-Serbian diplomatic relations remained suspended, though no court mourning was held in England. The British representatives abroad were instructed to inform the governments to which they were accredited of the British policy toward Serbia.[43] The Dutch minister was the only other minister permanently withdrawn from Beograd. None of the other powers was willing to take such firm action, and although the conditions in Serbia for months after Peter's arrival left much to be desired, the new regime was in to stay.

4. AUSTRIA AND RUSSIA RECOGNIZE PETER

Events at Beograd moved so fast toward the selection of Prince Peter Karadjordjević that Vienna and St. Petersburg considered it undesirable to take steps to imperil his immediate selection, especially since they had no objection to him.[44] Upon his acceptance of the Serbian throne, Peter advised the two emperors of his election by telegraph from Geneva, and requested their recognition and assistance. In the replies which arrived from Vienna and St. Petersburg "with startling rapidity," the two emperors acknowledged Peter's election to the Serbian crown by the legally constituted assembly, and recognized him as the sovereign of Serbia. In explaining the precipitate recognition of Peter, Count Lamsdorff said that "the risk of seeing a republic proclaimed could not be incurred."[45]

In replying to Peter, the Russian tsar addressed his telegram to the "King of Serbia," acknowledged the announcement of his having accepted the crown "from the legally constituted Representative Assembly," and recognized him as "the sovereign of Serbia." The tsar probably shared the views of his foreign minister that one of Peter's first acts must be "to mark his reprobation of the abominable and indefensible tragedy of the 11 [sic] of June, by bringing the regicides to condign punishment."[46]

Russia therefore condemned the Serbian atrocities, but decided not to make the punishment of the regicides a condition for continuing friendly relations with Serbia. Although the Russian government operated on the supposition that the punishment of the murderers was a question of internal Serbian concern, it asked for an impartial investigation and "the production of all documents discovered . . . bearing on the subject."[47]

The recognition of the new dynasty and the Russian activities in Beograd were on the whole well received by the St. Petersburg press. *Svet* and *Novoe Vremîa* particularly followed the Beograd events, but took their government's line in reminding the Skupština to punish, after thorough investigation, those found to be implicated in the murder of the king.[48]

The Austrian emperor's reply to Peter's message, carefully drawn up by Goluchowski, condemned the assassination and expressed the hope that Peter might lift Serbia "out of the state of profound depression into which it was lately fallen."[49] The official explanation of the Austro-Hungarian recognition of Peter was that the monarch's primary concern was the establishment of stable conditions in Serbia, and that the Karadjordjević regime seemed to offer the best prospect of attaining such conditions. He added that "a conditional recognition or the categorical command to punish those who were at present in power could only result in shaking Peter's thr one, kindling a civil war, and leading to international complications."[50] Public opinion and the press in Austria-Hungary meanwhile became less violent. There was now a growing sentiment that the Serbian tragedy was, in the final analysis, the concern of the Serbian people themselves.[51]

After learning that his son-in-law Peter had been recognized by the tsar, Prince Nikola of Montenegro gave his blessing to the new Serbian dynasty, and sent a telegram to Peter conveying his congratulations, thus completing the roll of those from whom the Karadjordjević regime had won recognition.[52]

5. CHARYKOV VERSUS DUMBA

Encouraged by his royal master's recognition of Peter, Russian Minister Charykov on June 17 hastened on his own initiative to recognize the revolutionary cabinet of Avakumović as the *de jure* government of Serbia.[53] This incident alarmed his colleague Dumba and the Austrian Foreign Office, on whose request Charykov was ultimately removed from Beograd.[54] Dumba tells in his *Memoirs* how he and Charykov were instructed to act in consultation with each other before taking any step, and to view the revolutionary government exclusively as a *de facto* government. The correspondence with the government was carried on in the third person by means of *notes verbales*. Dumba says that he "kept to the letter as well as to the spirit" of his instructions, and read his telegrams to Charykov. He was therefore astounded when Charykov told him that he had "acknowledged the revolutionary Government as the *de jure* Government of Serbia" on June 17. Dumba reminded Charykov of their instructions, but Charykov retorted that "the Tsar's telegram contained a recognition of the new regime; that he understood the East from A to Z; that he knew what he was doing; and that he could now exercise a decisive influence in the formation of the new Cabinet to be appointed by the King and would try to eliminate the compromised ministers." Dumba took this attitude of Charykov as a personal affront. He felt that Charykov had hoped, by "recognizing the revolutionary Government without—indeed against—the instructions of his superiors, to get the better of me and to give Russia the ascendancy in Serbia." Count Lamsdorff, says Dumba, was greatly disturbed and told Austria's Foreign Minister Aehrenthal confidentially that he had decided to recall Charykov "as soon as things had returned to normal in Belgrade."[55]

It was obvious from the very beginning that the new Serbian regime was pro-Russian. This trend was an expression of a general reaction against the unpopular Austrophile policy of the Obrenović house, which had dominated the Serbian political scene for twenty-five years. The Russians were not slow in exploiting the situation, although they could not make a sudden and unqualified acceptance of the new order, since that would have aroused widespread suspicion in the capitals of Europe. Certainly Charykov's actions were not without support in St. Petersburg, even though Count Lamsdorff personally might not have approved the method by which Charykov extended Russian recognition of the Serbian government.

6. PETER'S ARRIVAL AND AUSTRO-RUSSIAN RIVALRY

When the entry of Peter into Beograd was set for June 24, 1903, an official welcome at the railway station was decided upon, and the question arose as to the attitude the diplomatic corps should take on this occasion. The Russians were the only power which had recognized the revolutionary government as yet; the Austrian, Dumba, considered it a mistake "to leave the King, on his very first appearance in his capital, tête-à-tête with the Russian Minister who behaved as if he were the protector of Serbia."[56]

The "preponderant role" played by the Russian minister at Beograd worried Austria-Hungary, whose prevailing sentiment was that she could no longer "sufficiently count on the sincerity of Russian friendship." Moreover, Austria-Hungary could not have been expected to view with disinterest "the politics of her neighbor" Serbia. Goluchowski felt that after the emperor's "public manifestation of the indignation" caused by the Beograd murders, the Austro-Hungarian government could not enter into relations with the revolutionary government. Yet the Austrians realized that a "complete abstention would not have been politically wise." Therefore, Dumba was instructed to attend the welcoming of Peter in a private capacity and to allow himself to be presented to the king by Charykov. So, as Dumba says, "in view of the great interests which Austria-Hungary had in Serbia, moral considerations had to take a back seat."[57]

Consequently, Dumba arranged with Charykov that the latter and his staff, wearing uniform, "should await the King on the platform in company with the ministers and be presented to him," that Dumba and his staff "would wear morning dress and be presented to His Majesty in the royal waiting room by Charykov without coming into touch with the ministers in any way." The motive behind this arrangement, according to Dumba, was to demonstrate to the Serbian nation the co-operation between Austria-Hungary and Russia and to stress "the difference in [their] attitudes towards the revolutionary Government." The Serbian foreign minister apparently was satisfied with this arrangement.[58] The British chargé d'affaires reported the final arrangements in Beograd as follows:

The ministers of France, Turkey, America [sic] and Holland left Belgrade today and the representatives of Germany, Italy, Belgium, Greece, Roumania and Bulgaria, although remaining in Belgrade, will take no part in the celebrations of the next three days. The question as to what action was to be taken by the ministers of the various countries was only decided at the last moment. It was for some time uncertain whether M. Dumba, the Austrian Minister, would go to the station in uniform or not, but the hand of the Austrian Government was forced by the action taken by the Russian Minister, and, in order not to imperil their future influence in Serbia, Austria has practically been obliged to follow the lead of Russia in this question, with the sole stipulation that the presentation of the Austrian Minister to the King should not be made by the Foreign Minister or any other member of the provisional Government. The Russian Minister, who has already acknowledged the existing Government, will be presented by the Serbian Minister for Foreign Affairs and will then present his Austrian colleague.[59]

The reception plans were carried out as outlined. The Russian minister met the king at the station and was presented to him by the minister of foreign affairs. The Austrian minister remained in the waiting room. After a brief reply to the welcoming speech of the prime minister, the king climbed into his carriage and was escorted to his home by a group of military officers and members of the cabinet. The Russian minister in grand style followed the royal carriages to the palace. The Austrian minister came much later. A *Te Deum* service was celebrated at the cathedral. Along the road, the crowd remained indifferent; only the soldiers acclaimed the king.[60] The Austro-Russian entente was further "demonstrated at a gala performance at the opera and at the Court at which Charykov and [Dumba] alone appeared accompanied by the staffs of the Legation."[61]

The French minister at Beograd, M. Benoit, was instructed not to join the diplomatic corps which was to welcome Peter, and had made arrangements to leave Beograd on June 22 for Budapest, where he intended to remain until the end of the week. After learning that the German, Italian, and a majority of the other foreign representatives were instructed to meet the king at the railway station but to abstain from entering into official relations with the government,[62] the French Foreign Office reversed its position and hastened to instruct M. Benoit to do what most of his colleagues had decided to do. Should he be absent from Beograd, as was actually the case, M. Desportes was instructed to take his place.[63] The foreign diplomats had apparently refused the invitation to the feast. They were expected, however, "to hang out flags and to illuminate their official quarters."[64]

Immediately after Charykov had presented his credentials at a formal audience, he was ordered by his government to leave Beograd before the king's name-day, which was to be celebrated on July 12, and Muraviev was accredited as chargé d'affaires. "It was inadvisable for my government," Charykov wrote, "to be represented in the palace of the murderers of King Alexander and Draga." His leave was prolonged until April 1905, when he was appointed plenipotentiary at The Hague.[65]

On June 25, 1903, King Peter sent a letter to M. Loubet, president of the French Republic, explaining his election by the National Assembly and his accession to the throne, and thanking him for the "sympathy of France toward Serbia."[66] Since France had more to gain than to lose in recognizing the new Serbian regime, especially because Russia had already recognized it and possibly to keep Serbia from falling into the orbit of the Triple Alliance, France officially recognized the Serbian regime on July 1, 1903.[67]

7. GENERAL GRUJIĆ'S GOVERNMENT

After the enthronement of Peter, the revolutionary government of Jovan Dj. Avakumović considered its work accomplished and submitted its resignation to the king. Peter accepted the resignation *pro forma*, and with the approval of the Skupština entrusted the formation of a new cabinet again to Avakumović.[68] By this action of the king, the revolutionary government was thus "transformed into legal Government appointed by the King," and the Austrian minister at once recognized it as *de jure*.[69] On August 2, 1903, the Avakumović government was reshuffled because of a conflict over political favoritism and spoils. Two Independent Radicals (Ljubomir Stojanović and Ljubomir Živković), one Liberal (Dr. Vojislav Veljković), and the war minister and conspirator (General Jovan Atanacković) were ousted from the government. The first parliamentary elections since Peter ascended the throne were held on September 8, 1903. The pre-electoral campaign was fought principally between the Radicals and Independent Radicals. The former won seventy-three and the latter sixty-four seats in the Skupština. After final counting of the votes, the Radicals received an additional three seats.* As neither party had received a majority sufficient to form an exclusive party cabinet, the two parties agreed (September 16, 1903) on a coalition cabinet under General Sava Grujić (1840–1913) of the Radical party. The cabinet was formed on September 21, and consisted of four members

* Other parties received the following numbers of seats: Liberal 18, Progressive 1, and Social Democratic 1.

from each of the two parties and one neutral member.* Because of both foreign and domestic pressure, the conspirators were excluded from the cabinet.[70] This was the first regular government of the new regime.

A coalition between the two Radical groups was necessary at so critical a time. The united labors of the two strongest political parties seemed to be essential for the strengthening of the new regime. However, the agreement between the two Radical parties was not accepted by all their respective leaders, and it was therefore apparent from the beginning that the Grujić cabinet represented but a "temporary compromise."[71] The bickering continued inside both parties and between them. Some thirty-eight Independent Radical party deputies, who did not accept the agreement with the Radical party, in their party organ *Dnevni list* (Daily Sheet), continued to criticize Pašić and certain other Radicals.

The Grujić government had two important jobs: in the first place, it was necessary to improve the country's general economic position; in the second place, the government was faced with the task of re-establishing normal diplomatic relations with the foreign powers as soon as possible. So far as the economic program was concerned, it was in essence a national program which every subsequent government adopted. The establishment of an economic system based on national needs necessitated the concluding of new trade treaties to provide wider additional markets for Serbian exports, thereby facilitating an economic independence which had been impossible before 1903, when Austria-Hungary had controlled about four-fifths of Serbian trade.

The Austrian minister persuaded his foreign minister, M. Goluchowski, to agree with Lamsdorff on "a kind of diplomatic strike" against King Peter in order "to induce [him] to take the required measure" regarding elimination of the conspirators from influential positions, with appropriate punishment. Dumba asked for several weeks' leave "from January 1, in event of the non-removal of the officers in question before that date." France, Germany, and the smaller states followed this example. The English and Dutch ministers had been recalled after the murder. The secretaries and military attachés were to absent themselves from court functions or receptions. The reception arranged for January 1, 1904, was now canceled and instead a centenary celebration of the Karadjordjević dynasty was held at Topola.[72]

On January 12, 1904, the French, Belgian, and Rumanian ministers had left Beograd. The Turkish and Greek ministers were instructed to remain in Serbia. This step on the part of the foreign powers influenced internal affairs in Serbia to a considerable extent. The opposition press was "urging upon the Government the necessity of ceding to the opinion of Europe on the question of the officers," because spring would find Serbia isolated

* Prime Minister, and minister without portfolio, Sava Grujić (Radical), Foreign Minister Andra Nikolić (Radical), Finance Minister Milić Radovanović (Radical), Minister of Interior Stojan Protić (Radical), Minister of Education and Church Affairs Ljubomir Stojanović (Independent Radical), Minister of War Colonel Milan Andrejević, Minister of Justice Nikola Nikolić (Independent Radical), Minister of Public Works Vladimir Todorović (Independent Radical), and Minister of Economy Todor Petković (Independent Radical). *N.S.*, 1903–4, I, 6; Popović, *op. cit.*, p. 93.

at the moment when she would most need the good will of the powers. The British co-operated with other powers in order to leave the impression that they were "unanimous in requiring the dismissal of the conspirators from Court." The absence of the whole diplomatic corps from the court ball in the first week in February led to a cabinet crisis.[73]

Inability to obtain the necessary funds to meet various financial needs, together with leftover complications from the conspiracy and the "diplomatic strike" of foreign powers against the Serbian government, and, finally, continued party bickering forced the Grujić cabinet to resign on February 2, 1904. The king invited Stojan Protić (Radical) to form the new cabinet, but he declined the privilege. On February 8, at the king's request, Grujić once again formed a cabinet. It included a number of prominent persons who influenced the course of political development for many years. The Foreign Ministry went to Nikola Pašić (1845–1926, Radical),[74] who laid the basis of a foreign policy that remained unchanged until 1918. Finance was entrusted to Dr. Lazar Paču (1855–1915, Radical)[75] under whose wise administration the country averted bankruptcy, emerged into financial solvency, and despite many difficulties made steady financial and economic improvement. The Ministry of War went to General Radomir Putnik (1847–1917), an able strategist and military leader, who led Serbia's armies with great skill during the Balkan and World wars. By political conviction General Putnik belonged to the Independent Radicals, and when he was not on active duty he served as a member of the executive committee of that party. The Ministry of Education was given to Ljubomir Davidović (1863–1939, Radical),[76] who was responsible for some basic improvements in the elementary and secondary school systems.[77]

At the end of March by royal decree "all the compromised officers were removed from their positions at Court in so far as they still occupied them. The majority were promoted." The decree was to go into effect on April 1. Dumba returned to Beograd before the Orthodox Easter celebrations and had an audience with the king. Toward the end of April Russian Minister Gubastov presented his credentials in a ceremonial audience.[78]

The Grujić government, which contained no conspirators, did not affect Anglo-Serbian relations in the aggregate. In a subtle way, however, the Serbian Foreign Office endeavored to ascertain the British attitude. Hitherto all communications from the Serbian Foreign Office had been addressed to the British Legation unsigned; the Grujić government proceeded to address its communications, signed by the foreign minister, to the British agent, Mr. Thesiger, in person. The latter pointed out this discrepancy in protocol and called the attention of the Serbian Foreign Office to the fact that he had never been present "on any of the public occasions when the diplomatic body has been officially represented." He explained his position as that of second secretary of the Legation and *chargé des archives*, authorized only to carry on the current business of the Legation and communicate unofficially with the Serbian Foreign Office.[79] Realizing that England was not yet ready to renew diplomatic relations, Serbia decided not to treat Mr. Thesiger as a full-fledged diplomatic representative.

During the first year of King Peter's rule a number of patriotic organizations mushroomed in Serbia, and accelerated political and nationalist activity was noted among the Yugoslavs in Austria-Hungary, Montenegro, and Macedonia. The period of Grujić's cabinet witnessed many scenes of general Serbian and South Slav solidarity. In the course of the year 1904 several congresses and exhibits were held in Beograd: the Congress of the South Slav Youth, the first Yugoslav Art Exhibit, and the Medical Congress, in which doctors from all Yugoslav lands participated. On April 23 Bulgarian students visited their Serbian counterparts to manifest Serbo-Bulgarian youth solidarity. On June 29 Peter's birthday and his first anniversary as king were celebrated with great pomp and fanfare. This year also marked the centennial of the First Serbian Revolution (1804), which had been led by Peter's grandfather. Thus the year seemed a propitious one. At the Saborna Church in Beograd Peter became the first-crowned (*prvovenčani*) king of new Serbia.

8. THE CORONATION

Despite strong opposition from the cabinet and the press, the coronation of Peter took place on September 8, 1904. According to tradition, "former sovereigns had simply been annointed at the Abbey of Žiča." King Peter, if we are to trust Dumba, "insisted on a coronation ceremony," which for want of suitable accommodations at Žiča had to be held at Beograd. He is said to have hoped that a Russian grand duke and an Italian prince would be sent to Beograd for the occasion, but neither came. Of all the European royalty, only the Montenegrin Crown Prince Danilo and his "beautiful" Milica were present. Italy sent Marquis Guiccioli "as special Ambassador for the period of the coronation at which he acted as *doyen* of the diplomatic corps." Dumba observed that "the fact that Guiccioli was very desirous of acting as *doyen* . . . showed that Italy was not proposing to be as retiring as she had hitherto been in Belgrade."[80]

Dumba notes several other interesting details. "All the representatives of the smaller powers" requested their governments that they "be appointed special envoys for the coronation. Gubastov received a very flattering personal letter from the Tsar for presentation to King Peter," but "to the great annoyance of the Serbs he refused to change his status as Minister for the period of the coronation ceremonies." Since Dumba "was the permanent *doyen* of the diplomatic corps in Belgrade, the unpleasant task fell to [him] of settling the disputes among [his] somewhat small-minded colleagues on matters of precedence." He only succeeded in making "an urgent appeal to their *esprit de corps*," and warned that unless they co-operated "we should all permanently lose prestige in Serbia."[81]

So far as the coronation ceremony itself is concerned, few eyewitnesses described it in such detail as did the Austrian minister. He noted that the ritual was closely copied from that followed at the coronation of Rumania's King Carol.

The church ceremony lasted for two hours and, although there had been but one rehearsal, everything went off very well. King Peter displayed remarkable powers of endurance. The Crown weighed over nine pounds and gold-embroidered coronation robe about thirty-one pounds. He was obliged to take off the Crown from time to time during the service in the cathedral. Nevertheless he managed to walk on foot in his regalia from the cathedral to the palace—a distance of over half a mile. Owing to the numerous uniforms and the rich—perhaps a little too ornate—vestments of the priests, the cathedral presented a magnificent spectacle of colour. After days of grey or rainy skies, the sun burst through the clouds at the very moment when the King took his seat on the throne. Either by chance or design the rays fell obliquely through the window directly upon him and made him the resplendent centre of the ceremony. The most conspicuous member of the congregation was the beautiful Princess Milica in a marvelous white and gold robe which appeared to have been copied from a Byzantine model. The enormously tall Montenegrins, with their martial, clean-cut features and their picturesque native costumes, certainly made a splendid show. A remarkably large number of young officers wearing the new Karageorge Star, which showed that they were members of the conspiracy, were present in the cathedral.[82]

The coronation was followed by "a reception of the high ecclesiastical dignitaries" and then "a reception of the diplomatic corps." The king continued "to receive deputations for hours after the two receptions." Dumba describes how the foreign representatives were lined up in a long column, "according to seniority." Marquis Guiccioli, as *doyen*, made "a honeyed speech in Italianate French, whereupon those Ministers who had not been honoured with a special audience approached at a quick step, gently murmured their congratulations, and rapidly returned to their places. It was all rather like a figure in a quadrille with *pas seuls* performed by the gentlemen. I am afraid this exhibition did not increase the respect in which we were held by the Serbian public."[83] The American consul observed that

The Italian Minister congratulated His Majesty in the name of the sovereigns and chiefs of the states represented by it. The Italian, Austrian, French and German ministers had presented letters to the King prior to his coronation; the Russian, Rumanian, and Greek ministers presented similar letters at the reception that followed, and at the same time verbal congratulations were presented by the Turkish and Belgian ministers and myself.[84]

The next evening a dinner was given at the palace at which the Italian minister spoke again, after King Peter had drunk to the health of the represented sovereigns and chiefs of state.

The hereditary Prince and Princess of Montenegro and a special Bulgarian mission were present at the fetes, all other countries being represented by their regularly accredited Ministers. The fetes included a gala performance at the National Theater, a military review, a ball at court, races, and a sham battle. Belgrade was filled with visitors, foreign and native; the city was appropriately decorated and quite prettily illuminated on the evening of the coronation itself.[85]

According to Dumba the festivities "went off very well" although the people "took extraordinarily little part" in them. Only a few peasants from neighboring districts had come to witness the spectacle.

There was only a sparse row of spectators behind the double ranks of soldiers lining the streets and they simply watched the procession passively. There was no sign of enthusiasm and excitement. Even the press had made no attempt to arouse any special ardour; on the contrary, it accused the Court and the city fathers of extravagance and styled the coronation a superfluous luxury.

The ceremony of the annointment would, according to the press, have been sufficient. "This ceremony did eventually take place in October at the Abbey at Žiča and caused great difficulties in the matter of the accommodation of the royal suite, which as always was far too numerous. It was a purely national ceremony in which the diplomatic corps took no part."[86]

A few weeks after the coronation a group of forty French officers, classmates of King Peter at St. Cyr, came to visit him. "He had regularly attended the annual meeting of his classmates in Paris, excepting only the year 1903, while he was living in Geneva." He now received his friends "most magnificently and acted as their host for the several days." They took all their meals in the palace and were "charmed with the hospitality and cordial welcome accorded them." The conspirators "tried to make capital out of this visit and . . . invited the French officers . . . to a vast banquet at their Club." The invitation, however, was refused.[87]

"At a great reception at which the diplomatic corps was present, the King was positively beaming with pleasure." Dumba then adds, "this renewal of his old relations with his St. Cyr friends also strengthened his natural preference for French guns, rifles, etc.—a circumstance which very soon grew to be of real importance."[88]

In his speech from the throne, on the occasion of the convocation of the Skupština on November 1, 1904, King Peter reviewed foreign and domestic accomplishments in 1904 and recommended further action. He recalled that friendly states, "represented at my Court," had witnessed the coronation, and was especially pleased with Prince Nikola of Montenegro, his father-in-law, who sent his "loving son" and heir, Danilo, to witness the coronation. The king was likewise thankful to Prince Ferdinand of Bulgaria, who sent a special mission to the coronation ceremony. After the coronation Peter went to the second *lavra* of the "seven-door" monastery of Žiča, and there was annointed. Peter was happy to report that during the coronation and annointment ceremonies and his subsequent travels through Serbia he encountered everywhere popular enthusiasm and genuine loyalty.[89]

King Peter warned that the situation in Macedonia and Old Serbia, affecting Serbian "conationals," had not changed much in 1904. He still hoped, however, that the reform action begun in 1903 might bring relief and improvement to the two long-suffering regions. Serbia, the king said, was especially interested in improvement of the situation along her southern frontiers, because her territory was constantly being invaded by refugees and was exposed to endless Albanian attacks.[90]

In his address from the throne the king commented on the internal developments in the country in the first year of his rule. He listed several basic laws which were enacted in order to stabilize the country and give it international prestige. The state treasury in one year's time had met all its obligations. State revenues, despite failure in achieving expected results in the harvest, surpassed those of preceding years and the most optimistic forecasts. Money circulation was normal. All annuities for the year were met, as well as half of those for the next year. For this reason it was possible to drop the special 40 percent surtax (*prirez*) for the coming year. Improvements in the economy and defense were planned for the near future. New laws were passed giving popular representation to districts and regions. The government was planning to initiate new and better trade treaties.[91]

During the second Grujić cabinet a pro-Russian foreign policy became most apparent. On November 14, 1904, in answer to the king's speech from the throne the Skupština again confirmed the foreign policy outlined by the monarch, adding in its declaration that "the traditional sympathy for Russia, deeply rooted in the people, is certainly strengthened by the war which the great Empire carries on in the Far East. Slavic Serbia naturally considers every Russian success as a strengthening of the Slavic cause." The Skupština furthermore hailed with enthusiastic approval the news regarding more friendly relations between the Serbian and Montenegrin courts.[92]

In the face of the Austro-Hungarian menace, the governments of Serbia and Montenegro began, in September 1903, discussions tending toward an agreement that would provide for joint defensive action against any threat to the Serbian people.[93] The Skupština, likewise in response to the king's speech, welcomed the founding of close friendship between Serbia and Bulgaria by the exchange of visits between Peter and Ferdinand. Finally, the Skupština expressed ardent hopes that the reform program in Macedonia would produce satisfactory results. Relations with neighboring Austria-Hungary were, it declared, "cordial and correct."[94]

The royal address and the Skupština's reply evoked many stormy discussions in the Skupština. Stojan Ribarac and Vojislav Veljković, speaking for the opposition, did not agree with the government's policy regarding Macedonia, Bulgaria, guns, loans, and trade. They felt that it was ill-advised for Peter, "an independent ruler," to visit Prince Ferdinand, "a foreign vassal." The opposition likewise felt that the coronation "parading" was poor taste while "brotherly" Russia was suffering in the Far East. They complained because the government had not already initiated trade discussions with foreign powers. The opposition approved the modernization of the army by the purchase of new equipment, but preferred for the purpose a short-term rather than a long-term loan.[95]

There was much for Serbia to worry about in 1904. The question of disposal of the conspirators had not yet been settled. Conditions in Macedonia, despite the reform project, had become more and more chaotic. Relations with Austria-Hungary had deteriorated. "Mother" Russia was engaged in what was to become a disastrous war in the Far East. These foreign problems and internal parliamentary squabbles, coupled with the unceasing intracabinet friction between Independent Radicals and Radicals, forced Grujić's resignation on November 19, 1904. There was disunity within the Radical party itself, for one wing, displeased with Grujić, sought to replace him with a more powerful leader such as Pašić. The immediate pretext for the resignation, however, was the question of parliamentary immunity of the socialist deputy, Dr. Mihailo Ilić (from Kragujevac). The Old and Independent Radicals disagreed over the proposition to deprive Ilić of his parliamentary immunity to bring him to trial for the insulting manner in which he had denounced the army. The cabinet's resignation had been actually precipitated on October 31, 1904, by the decision of the deputies of the former Independent Radical party to separate themselves from the "united front" and form a parliamentary group of their own. Henceforth the two Radical parties developed independently and carried on a relentless struggle for political supremacy. By 1906 the tide definitely turned in favor of the Old Radicals, who continued to control the government until 1918, although there were coalition governments in times of crisis—the Annexation Crisis and World War I (November 22, 1914, to June 10, 1917).[96]

9. THE FIRST GOVERNMENT OF NIKOLA PAŠIĆ

After the resignation of the second Grujić cabinet some time elapsed until the new cabinet was formed. In the intervening period ways were sought to heal the schism between the two Radical groups. King Peter himself had hoped that the two parties might mend their differences, and when reconciliation failed he invited Nikola Pašić to form a new cabinet. On November 27, 1904, Pašić formed a homogeneous Radical cabinet, which gave him his first chance at government. The cabinet included the Radical party's entire heavy battery: "Paču, the mouth; Protić, the pen; Pašić, the brains."* With several friendly Independent Radicals in the Skupština, the Radicals acquired the necessary working majority.[97] This uneasy "honeymoon" between the Radical and Independent Radical parties ended in December when the latter's press started to attack Pašić. The Independent Radicals issued a declaration of final separation and reaffirmed their unequivocal stand on the original 1881 program of the Radical party. *Samouprava* (Self-Government), the organ of the Radical party, and *Odjek* (Echo), the organ of the Independent Radicals, opened a press war on each other. For a time the Independent Radicals abstained from acting as a parliamentary obstruction and allowed Pašić a free hand. However, the head of the Independent Radicals, Ljubomir Stojanović, made it plain that his party, although not represented in the cabinet, would support after close scrutiny all major financial and economic proposals of the government.

The international position of Serbia in early 1905 was even more critical than it had been in the preceding two years. Her "protector," Russia, had been defeated by the Japanese on February 26, 1905. There was fear of imminent Austrian invasion. The Macedonian turmoil continued and the uncertainty of the Bulgarian attitude gave Serbian leaders grave concern. Pašić was anxious to conclude a foreign loan which would enable Serbia to construct

---

* Among those entering the cabinet were Pera Velimirović (Public Works), Andra Nikolić (Education and Church Affairs), Mihailo P. Jovanović (Justice), and Svetolik Radovanović (Economy), and such stalwarts as Radomir Putnik (War), Lazar Paču (Finance), and Stojan Protić (Interior).

her badly needed railways and to modernize and equip her army. The loan, and the "gun question," as it came to be called, stirred up political dissension at home.[98] The opposition approved the loan in principle but criticized Pašić on the kind of loan it should be and on matters of procedure. Rumors about the loan, aimed toward undermining the government, emanated from hostile groups in Beograd. During December *Štampa* (Press) and *Dnevni list* (Daily Sheet) carried especially devastating articles against Pašić. The Radicals reasoned that this "irresponsible group" wished to destroy the parliamentary system established by the Constitution of 1903. What irritated Pašić most of all was that the leader of the campaign against him was Živojin Balugdžić, the king's secretary. Balugdžić, a man who spent many years abroad as foreign correspondent, was accused of having written articles in Vienna's *Neue Freie Presse* in which he criticized Pašić over the loan and gun questions. Balugdžić's censure of the government appeared in the domestic press as well. Among other things he accused the government of planning to buy guns without testing the six selected models. The *Neue Freie Presse*, inspired no doubt by Balugdžić, alleged that Pašić had bribed War Minister Putnik to withhold tests of the guns under consideration in order to place the contracts with a firm of his own choosing. On January 11, 1905, the government officially denied these charges. The official gazette on the following day announced that Pašić had brought to the attention of the king the activities of his secretary, and that the king regretted the circumstances and had again assured the government of his faith in the constitutional and parliamentary regime.[99]

But the gun question continued to cause political discussion. It seems that the king, in a slip of the tongue, had told a group of officers that the government planned to buy French guns. This statement was picked up by some newsmen and circulated. The opposition wished to know if the government had in fact tested the various gun models or if it wished to obtain the French guns from sheer favoritism. Stojan Ribarac reviewed in the Skupština the gun question. He pointed out that a special commission had been appointed nearly a year and half before to test and compare the six gun systems—two German, two French, one English, and one Austrian. He wished to know what the results were and if the commission had been dissolved. Pašić explained for the government that the gun tests had not been made, that no special commission had been appointed, that there always existed a permanent technical-military committee in charge of procurement of new equipment, and that this committee had been touring European capitals and visiting various gun factories.[100]

Reports of government crisis persisted, although the government enjoyed the confidence of the Skupština. There were still rumors of "irresponsible elements" trying to impose their will on the nation. The parliamentary system founded in 1903 was weathering its first major crisis.[101] Pašić logically assumed that because of Balugdžić's activity these recent attacks had royal backing, and decided to test the king's confidence in him by resigning on January 23, 1905. The king's reply was not only to request Pašić to withdraw his resignation but to promise him unwavering support and to assure him that the "constitutional and parliamentary regime" would not be infringed upon from any quarter.[102]

The friendly press attributed the fall of the government to Balugdžić and the "irresponsible elements." Public opinion clamored for a prompt but by all means parliamentary solution of the government crisis. The newspaper *Politika* was in the vanguard of the struggle for preservation of the parliamentary system. In an editorial on January 25 the editors described the situation, deprecated those who sought to abuse parliamentary rule, and urged the immediate formation of a new government by the political party which had the majority in the Skupština. Likewise the Independent Radicals, the largest opposition party, advised the king that they advocated the strictest adherence to parliamentary principle in resolving the current crisis.[103]

Pašić, after consulting with the individual parties and ascertaining that only a small group opposed majority rule, withdrew his resignation. In a declaration before the Skupština on January 28[104] the government explained that the press campaign had begun to cause confusion and to shake public faith in the constitutional and parliamentary regime; the government had therefore resigned in order to test its power and the effectiveness of the parliamentary system. The king's request that Pašić withdraw his resignation was interpreted as tangible evidence of the king's confidence in Pašić and respect for parliamentary procedure. Thus the parliamentary system was victorious—and this victory was final, for attempts to destroy it did not come again.

But Pašić's government was soon shaken by another question. This time the crisis was precipitated by a loan of 110 million francs contracted in Paris by Lazar Paču, minister of finance. When a special session of the Skupština convened on May 8, 1905, the Independent Radicals threatened to kill the loan by parliamentary obstruction, on the grounds that it was harmful to the country. In the Skupština, where the government had meanwhile lost some of its support, there appeared little chance of the loan agreement being ratified. The chairman of the Skupština, Aca Stanojević, representing the Radical party as majority leader, had just resigned, explicitly because the narrow margin of support he retained made it impossible for him to exercise his function with sufficient authority. Pašić now advised the king to dissolve the Skupština and order new elections; otherwise he would resign. The king rejected the proposal, and Pašić resigned for the second time.

10. STOJANOVIĆ'S GOVERNMENT

On May 16, 1905, Ljuba Stojanović organized the first Independent Radical government. The Skupština adjourned and new elections were scheduled by the government for June 10, despite Radical opposition. All the parties agreed that elections should be held. The big question after Pašić's government had resigned was who by law could schedule the elections.* The Radicals took the position that they as the majority party enjoyed that privi-

* *N.S.*, I (October 22, 1905), 277–78. Ljubomir Stojanović criticized Pašić on procedural matters on grounds that only the Crown had the right to dissolve the Skupština and schedule new elections. See also M. Popović, pp. 98–99.

lege. The Independent Radicals, on the other hand, took the stand that a minority party might also under certain conditions be authorized by the king to order elections.* They noted that Pašić proposed the elections after he resigned and this only after he realized that Ljuba Stojanović of the Independent Radicals was ready to accept the royal mandate for the formation of the new cabinet. The Radicals insisted that the minority Independent Radical party could not schedule elections. In the forefront of this attack on the Independent party was the Radical party's leading theoretician, Stojan Protić, who, writing in *Samouprava*, demonstrated the legality of his own party's stand. Questions regarding the right to schedule elections and the right of obstruction by the parliamentary opposition constituted from that time until 1908 a perennial controversy between the two parties. The question of the right to obstruct was very much debated when the Independent Radicals resorted to that tactic in 1907–8. The Radical party held that only a majority party could order elections and that a minority party should not exercise parliamentary obstruction, but instead should strive to become a majority party itself. The Independent Radicals, on the other hand, argued that the king was free to entrust the minority party with the right to schedule elections, and that obstruction offered the only medium by which a minority party could countervail the majority in a constitutional monarchy with a unicameral legislature.[105]

There were of course other less important points on which the two parties disagreed, but the above two were paramount. It is interesting to note that while they criticized the obstructionist tactics of the Independent Radicals, the Radicals at a later date used those tactics themselves. By the end of 1906 the Radicals' idea that on the question of scheduling elections the king was bound to the wishes of the government in power was definitely accepted. The problem of obstruction was eventually settled by foreign developments which required united political action at home, and from 1908 to 1917 Serbia was ruled by a series of coalition governments. Obstruction, however, came into vogue again during the World War when the political opposition in exile (on Corfu) employed it, after the demise of the coalition government in June 1917.[106]

During their electioneering the Independent Radicals were not backward in censuring the practices of their Radical rivals, disapproving especially of the loan the Radicals had contracted on terms felt to be injurious to national interests. The election returns gave the Independent Radicals eighty-one of a total of one hundred sixty parliamentary seats, only after a special commission had decided in their favor disputed votes in the Morava district. This one-seat majority appeared even smaller when viewed against the superior quality of deputies which the Radical party elected. The future of the Independent Radical cabinet became uncertain, and of necessity a cautious bipartisan-like policy was adopted.

* *N.S.* (May 16, 1905), p. 4; (July 25, 1905), p. 18; (August 1, 1905), p. 21; M. Popović, p. 99. Jaša Prodanović, an authority on constitutional procedures, shared this view, while Stojan Protić, the Radical stalwart, argued that Pašić proposed elections at the time he resigned.

The Stojanović government remained in power eleven months, during which time it suffered continuous parliamentary reverses. In particular, the cabinet bungled the loan and gun questions. They refused the loan of 110 million francs which the Radicals had arranged in France,* and then proceeded despite strong opposition to find a loan in which Austrian capital would have a share. Austro-Hungarian intransigence in commercial discussions and domestic opposition forced the government to abandon the loan it had negotiated with the Union Bank of Vienna.[107]

Another development which affected Serbian foreign relations took place in 1905. On March 30, 1905, Serbia and Bulgaria concluded secretly a Treaty of Friendship and a Treaty of Alliance. On the basis of the former, they signed a Customs Treaty at a later date. These arrangements will be discussed in some detail below, but here it is sufficient to point out that Austria-Hungary in no uncertain terms demanded suspension of the customs agreement, and this controversy with Austria-Hungary marked the prelude to the Austro-Serbian "Pig War" which began in 1906 and continued with brief intervals until 1911.

Whatever support Austria-Hungary might have given Serbia in the preceding months against English demands for elimination of the regicides from government was nullified by her insistence on controlling Serbian economic life. By the end of 1905 the conflict with Austria-Hungary had reached serious proportions. The government's unflinching stand against the neighboring monarchy enjoyed wide popular backing. There was hardly a political combination that would have accepted the Austro-Hungarian economic demands.

The press harped on the need for immediate restoration of diplomatic relations with England, especially after the disastrous Russian defeat in the Far East, which made Serbia feel more than ever isolated. National interest called for improvement of foreign relations regardless of sacrifices, all the more so after England had indicated a readiness to restore relations with Serbia.

Public opinion was strongly opposed to "secret influences" and "mysterious meetings." There was a strong feeling against the army's intervention in political affairs. In October 1905 the Populist party incorporated this popular sentiment into its platform. Its spokesman assured the government that the party favored a strong national army but that they wanted this army to be morally strong and imbued with comradely spirit and military discipline. They also asked for improved relations with foreign countries and restoration of normal diplomatic relations with England. The latter they considered especially urgent because the English had of late become more interested in "our brothers in Old Serbia and Macedonia," and because the powerful voice of Britain would be decisive in any solution of the Balkan questions.[108]

One of the Populist deputies in the Skupština (V. S. Veljković) called the attention of his fellow deputies on October 27 to the dissension in the army, and urged the Skupština to concern itself with the question of army

* Independent Radicals campaigned with the slogan, "Not a cent of loan!"

morale. He criticized the foreign minister for allowing the break in relations with England to continue and demanded to know why English demands were not accepted.[109]

In the midst of heated discussions over the status of the conspirators, *Štampa* reported a meeting of officer conspirators, in which they allegedly discussed plans for future action. The news got into the major European papers. On October 31, 1905, once again the Populist deputies, Stojan Ribarac and Vojislav Veljković, demanded an explanation from the foreign minister as to why the government had not renewed relations with Britain, and what if anything had been done in that direction. In addition, they asked what the foreign minister planned to do about the regicide question.[110]

Meanwhile one new power had begun to exercise influence in Serbia. Ever since the turn of the century Italy had shown a good deal of interest in the Balkans. The role of Italy in recognizing and befriending the new king has been noted earlier. Her policy regarding the Balkans was corollary to her Austrian policy, which called for a *rapprochement* between the Balkan peoples and resistance to any future Austro-Hungarian expansion in the Balkans. And this Italian policy coincided with the political tendency manifest in official circles in Sofia and Beograd at the time. Dumba writes that King Peter kept up "a frequent correspondence with the King of Italy" and adds that

A new factor had entered into Balkan politics—even though only in vague outline. Italy began to take interest in the western Balkans, even apart from Albania, and to raise her voice in discussions over the Macedonian Question. It was clear that the passive role forced upon Italy by the Mürzsteg Program and the Austro-Russian entente would not be accepted in Rome much longer.[111]

The first attempt to solve the question of the regicides and to renew diplomatic relations with England came in December 1903, with the Italian king, Victor Emmanuel, playing the role of intermediary. The Serbian minister in Rome meticulously posted the Italian king on Serbo-British relations. Aside from official Italian interest in Serbia and the desire to maintain the status quo in the Balkans, Victor Emmanuel's relationship to King Peter by way of marriage contributed to mutual friendship.* During his visit to Paris and London in 1903 the Italian king spoke favorably of Serbia and sought the restoration of British-Serbian diplomatic relations. In this connection Victor Emmanuel also urged the Serbian government to remove from influential positions those regicides who had played leading roles in the murder of King Alexander.[112] The efforts of the Italian king brought no results, and the problem of the regicides and of relations with the English was passed on from government to government. Pressure for settlement of the regicide question became especially strong in 1905 during the government of the Independent Radicals. Opposition in the Skupština, especially from the Populists and Progressives, demanded settlement of the persistent problem. The government of Ljuba Stojanović hesitated; Foreign Minister

* Both married daughters of Prince Nikola of Montenegro.

Jovan Žujović sought a way out in vain. He co-operated closely with the Italian government and all those who wanted to see the settlement of the controversy. The intransigence of King Edward VII and of certain elements in Serbia regarding the regicides was blamed for the unclosed breach between Serbia and England. Writing on one occasion from Karlsbad to his prime minister, Žujović stated : "If the British would formulate their demands, and if they are not exaggerated, and if we could . . . perhaps even issue an ultimatum to those who are so stubborn at home, something might be done."[113]

The 1905 government seemed ready and willing to make reasonable concessions, i.e., the removal of two or three regicides. Žujović received the English demands through his Italian colleague, Tittoni. The English government demanded the pensioning of Colonels Damjan Popović (commandant of the Danube Division), Alexander Mašin (chief of general staff), Leonid Solarević, Petar Mišić, and Lieutenant Colonel Luka Lazarević (instructor at the military academy), Major Ljuba Kostić, and General Jovan Atanackovic. Žujović submitted the English demands to the cabinet, which accepted them. The king wavered, and suggested a compromise, i.e., that "the three principal murderers retire" or that "the Skupština settle the question." Having failed to obtain the king's backing the government would have had to resign had it not been for the loan question which was before the Skupština, and the loan question temporarily overshadowed the question of the regicides.[114]

On December 2, 1905, Foreign Minister Žujović resigned. He explained in a declaration that he had taken steps toward restoration of relations with England, but had realized that the Stojanović cabinet was restricted in action on this matter. The opposition criticized the declaration on the grounds that it did not disclose the real reasons for Žujović's action, and censured Žujović for resigning without providing the Skupština with all the facts. They insisted that affairs of state must be conducted publicly and openly. The opposition demanded the government's resignation because one of its members had resigned. It warned that no change in government could be effected outside the Skupština. The government quickly explained that Žujović had promised what he could not make good, and that his resignation therefore was accepted because he was unable to honor his word.[115]

The stand taken by Žujović in his insistence on settling the issue of the regicides and the restoration of relations with England thus cost him his cabinet post. But he declared that "the renewal of friendly relations with civilized Europe, and especially with England . . . is worth a few of our ministerial portfolios."[116] After Žujović's resignation, a crisis developed at home. Some of the military garrisons in the interior were again aroused. This crisis prompted the press to demand immediate solution of the problem of the conspirators.

Needless to say, there were important leaders of both official and non-official Serbia anxious to see the matter put to a final end. They desired this action, some for reasons of patriotism and some for purely political considerations, or for reasons of professional jealousy or simply vengeance. Some were satisfied to use "legal" methods toward this end; others, as evidenced in

Novaković's "counterconspiracy," planned to use undercover pressure to eliminate the conspirators from the government.

One of the most prominent representatives of the opposition was Živojin Perić, who openly expressed doubt of the good faith of the king's murderers. He insisted that they be tried, because the affair of May 29 was contrary to the regulations of the "moral" and "positive law," and of the Criminal Code. In his opinion the declaration of the government and the Skupština on June 2, 1903, did not free those responsible for the crime from court investigation. In early 1906 the disposal of the conspirators was still undecided. Stojan Ribarac declared in the Skupština that if the government could not solve the problem it should resign.*

In 1905 so far as Serbia was concerned there was at least one bright spot on the political horizon. Russia, after her disastrous defeat in the Far East, had adopted a slightly modified policy in the Balkans. She endeavored to release herself from obligations toward Austria-Hungary with regard to the maintenance of the status quo there. Instead of favoring Bulgaria she now appeared to be favoring Serbia. There was a sudden resurgence of Russian political activity in Beograd, and the Russian minister made it known that Nikola Pašić was Russia's choice for the post of prime minister.

The prestige of the government declined because it could not deal effectively with the tasks facing it. In order to strengthen their position, the Independent Radicals made an agreement with General Sava Grujić by which he joined their party on condition that he become prime minister of the reorganized cabinet. On February 22, 1906, the Stojanović government resigned because it no longer enjoyed the confidence of the Skupština and because of obstructionist tactics by the Radicals and Populists (Narodnjaci). On March 1, 1906, Grujić became prime minister of a reorganized government consisting only of Independent Radicals. Stojanović retained for himself the Ministry of Education and Church Affairs. Colonel Vasilije Antonić, who succeeded Žujović in December, retained the Foreign Ministry portfolio. Ljubomir Stojanović in a written declaration stated that the government had resigned because the king had refused to sign the order pensioning several of the conspirators. Grujić revised the declaration and simply stated that the government resigned because of the insurmountable difficulties it had encountered. The government press organ *Odjek* announced that Grujić's version of the resignation was written without the knowledge of other members of the cabinet and that Stojanović's version was the only valid one, and the only one which was approved by all cabinet members.[117]

The Radicals and Populists relented and ceased their obstructionist policies. Nonetheless, the Grujić cabinet lasted barely a month; it resigned on April 4, 1906. The fall of the government was caused primarily by its failure to settle the regicide question, which continued as one of the principal domestic political issues and prevented restoration of diplomatic relations with England.[118]

* Vasić, pp. 209–11. The author explains Perić's interpretations of the law in this connection.

11. REVIVAL OF THE COUNTERCONSPIRACY

On September 16, 1905, after two years in prison at Požarevac, Milan Novaković was set free. Two days later he published an appeal in *Pravda* to "all patriots, friends of my ideas and those who sentenced me without having heard me." He condemned the conspirators for their activities, and "declared war" on them. On October 30 the "Society for Legal Settlement of the Conspiratorial Question" (Društvo za zakonsko rešenje zavereničkog pitanja) was founded on his initiative. At a meeting of his followers he emphasized the dangerous international isolation in which Serbia found herself, and the superior position which would result for Bulgaria in case the Macedonian Question should come up for settlement. He pointed out that instead of accepting European demands and listening to the friendly advice of the powers, the Serbian government had glorified and honored those who had enacted roles in the "barbarian tragedy." This unwise policy, Novaković added, was responsible for the "diplomatic strike," the break in relations with England, and the refusal to receive King Peter. He alleged that the tactlessness of the conspirators had caused an intolerable situation. He accused them of undermining the authority of responsible government agencies, interfering in all state affairs, and exerting all types of pressure on the government, the Skupština, and the court. They continued to harp on their "service" to the state and the people, and to seek endless awards and favors! They monopolized Beograd for themselves and their cohorts! On the day of the king's coronation in the summer of 1904, all the conspirators were decorated with the "Star of Karadjordje."[119] They were, he continued, furthering their personal welfare and enriching themselves; they were making daily scandals unequaled the world over. What apparently irritated Novaković more than anything else were those who, he said, apologized for the conspirators by arguing that the palace murder of May 29 was the people's work, that it represented a revolution, and that the people, through the Skupština, had honored the work of the conspirators and freed them of any responsibility.[120]

So far as Novaković was concerned, the June 11 (May 29, O.S.) murder was not the people's work. Four fifths of the population at the time belonged to the Radical party; not a single member of that party took part in the plot. Knowing this and fearing the people's reaction, the conspirators had at first withheld the true story of the royal murder. The assassination was obviously not a revolution. It was not an armed movement of the masses. Moreover, the Skupština possessed no right to free the conspirators. The ruler alone had the right to pardon and grant amnesty, according to Articles 50 and 51 of the Constitution. After having reviewed the situation in this manner Novaković concluded that in the best interests of the state and the nation the question of the conspirators must be settled once and for all.[121]

After the speeches of Novaković and two others, a temporary executive was chosen to head the Society for Legal Settlement of the Conspiratorial Question.* On November 22 the society decided to purchase a printing press

---

* Vasić, pp. 188–89. The committee consisted of President Popović, retired colonel; Vice-President Luka Lazarević, minister in pension; Secretary Milan Novaković; and

and publish its own journal, *Za Otadžbinu* (For Fatherland), under the editorship of Novaković. The first issue of the new publication appeared on December 10. It was supported in the struggle against the conspirators by another journal, *Narodni list* of S. Sibalić. The two papers attracted a fairly large number of readers.

The revival of the counterconspiracy found readiest response in the Kragujevac garrison. Because the Society for Legal Settlement of the Conspiratorial Question had as one of its objectives improvement of conditions in the army, it won the sympathy of some noncommissioned officers and officers at Kragujevac, where the extreme discipline and pedantry of the commanding officer, General Stepanović, were deeply resented. The noncommissioned officers wanted a reading room and a mess separate from the enlisted men, as well as a few minor changes in uniform. Some of them were still angry over the punishment of relatives and friends who had been involved in the Niš conspiracy. Altogether, their varying dissatisfactions rendered them susceptible to the appeal of counterconspiracy.[122]

On Sunday, March 12, 1906, a group of thirty noncommissioned officers met on the training grounds near Kragujevac and agreed to organize a counterconspiratorial group. Sergeant Streten Sredojević was elected president of the group. In a lengthy talk he stressed the disaffection in the army resulting from the conspiratorial question. The group agreed to extend financial support to the paper *Za Otadžbinu*. One by one the participants expressed their sympathy for and interest in the Novaković movement. Three officers were found to share their views. Sergeant Sredojević then went to Beograd to meet Novaković, from whom he no doubt received specific instructions. Upon his return he explained that he had been promised full moral support, and told his friends that the Beograd garrison was overwhelmingly behind Novaković. He said that direction for future activity would come from Beograd through Lieutenant Colonel Ljubomir Milić, commander of the Nineteenth Regiment, who had been promised the post of commandant of the Šumadija Division for participating in the movement. Sredojević warned that soon important orders would come from Beograd, and suggested that enlistments of amenable noncommissioned officers and cadets from the Noncommissioned Officers' School be speeded up.[123]

Suddenly the group was ordered to action. The order read: "Comrades, the workers' First of May is approaching . . . With their help you can free yourself from the unbearable regime. Be united with them on that day and rise in arms." Detailed instructions followed. The leaders were ordered to (1) seize at once, with the help of the socialists and troops of the garrison, the postal and telegraph offices, the railway station, and other administrative agencies; (2) imprison the divisional commandant and officers and adherents of the present regime, and in their places install opponents of the regime and

---

members Svetomir Nikolajević, minister in pension and a member of parliament; Pavle Bošković, retired general; Pavle Denić, minister in pension; Dimitrije Nikolić, retired colonel; Ljuba Jovanović, lawyer; Svetozar Djordjević, retired civil servant; Djordje Marković, retired lieutenant colonel.

their own friends (listing names), seeking, however, to avoid bloodshed in the carrying out of the assignment; (3) after having secured with the troops all ammunition stores and other military objects, proceed at once with the troops in the direction of Beograd, by way of the Niš-Beograd railway line, and stop just outside Beograd to await further instructions. The attack on Beograd was to be undertaken simultaneously by noncommissioned officers from the Niš, Valjevo, and Kruševac garrisons.[124]

Details of the final action were made public when one of the noncommissioned officers who was detained under suspicion betrayed the movement to avert a penalty. On the evening of April 17 four officers and twenty-seven noncommissioned officers were arrested and later brought to court. Sentences were pronounced on November 14, 1906, and confirmed by the Grand Military Court on January 27, 1907. Sergeant Sreten Sredojević received a twenty-year prison term and the others sentences varying from fifteen years to six months. The authorities did not then establish Novaković's connection with the Kragujevac group. In assessing the Kragujevac counterconspiracy Vasić says that it was a foolish plan. There were not enough troops at Kragujevac to stage a successful revolt.[125]

The second counterconspiracy was followed by new purges. Officers suspected as enemies of the regime were placed under surveillance or removed. On August 23, 1906, the newspaper Za Otadžbinu was confiscated. This gave Novaković the pretext of writing a pamphlet entitled Afera lista Za Otadžbinu i moja (The Affair of the Journal For Fatherland and My Own) in which he endeavored to show that the action of the Beograd police was illegal. In consequence he was placed in jail for a month for having allegedly insulted the minister of interior and the police authority. Upon his release he approached various Beograd printers with the proposal that they publish Za Otadžbinu, but none dared undertake the job. At the thirty-first meeting of the Society for Legal Settlement of the Conspiratorial Question, the members decided to disband because continuance appeared impossible. Arrangements were made for safekeeping of the seal, archives, and books. The members were freed of all obligations. Several months later, however, Novaković bought a press, and in March 1907 began publishing Za Otadžbinu. The press was seized by force on August 16, and on August 25 Novaković was imprisoned. On September 16, 1907, he and an imprisoned gendarmerie officer, Maksim Novaković, were killed under mysterious circumstances in the Beograd municipal prison. Their deaths became a subject of heated parliamentary debate when the opposition accused the government of negligence and of premeditated murder.[126]

The relations between the socialists and the Novaković movement, if such relations existed at all, as suggested by the appeal to the noncommissioned officers, have never been made clear. While a socialist deputy in the Skupština did characterize Novaković's death as "a dynastic murder," the socialists seemed opposed to the movement which he had started, and dubbed its members kontraći, or counterrevolutionary. The socialists claimed that their line of policy regarding the king was the same as that of the officer conspirators, i.e., to destroy the despotic regime of King Alexander. Moreover they hailed

the palace murder as one of the most important developments in the political
life of Serbia; it marked the turning point in the history not only of the bour-
geoisie but also in the history of the socialist workers' movement.[127]

12. THE CONSPIRATORS AND THEIR INFLUENCE

The conspirators who seized the government on June 11, 1903, gradually
relinquished it to the political parties. They remained, however, a potent
force behind the political scene. In this role of "irresponsible factors" the
conspirators contributed in part to the political instability which continued
to plague Serbia until the shocking Salonika trial of 1917.[128]

King Peter had fallen so strongly under the influence of Mašin and Popović that there were rumors that Mašin was in possession of a letter in which
Peter approved the murder of Alexander, and might possibly be blackmail-
ing the king. Under the influence of the conspirators, the former minister of
interior, who had been seriously wounded on the night of the murder, and
Alexander's private secretary were arbitrarily imprisoned. The conspirators
influenced military appointments, procurement of military supplies and credits, and in general any basic issue before the government.[129]

From the very beginning of Peter's reign, both king and politicians sought
the backing of the conspirators. Pašić was particularly noted as one who
sought their support at crucial moments. Ljubomir Stojanović alone steadfastly opposed any interference by the army in political affairs. The Radicals
opposed the so-called "irresponsible factors" only when they happened to be
against them. In the long run, however, Nikola Pašić proved to be the most
dangerous enemy the conspirators had; he was not the kind of man who could
share political power, and gradually he undermined their position and by
1907 had pushed them into the background.[130] It would be unfair to say that
all the conspirators were politically minded. Some of them simply felt a
moral responsibility for the new order and could not remain indifferent to
the partisanship and corruption which prevailed throughout the country.[131]

Besides the conspirators there were the so-called *zaveritelji*, those who
had not been participants in the conspiracy of June 11 but joined the cause
later and, like all converts, became stauncher supporters of the new order
than the conspirators themselves. They were essentially opportunists whose
aim was to ingratiate themselves with the ruling powers and thereby further
their personal interests. They spied on and discriminated against the friends
of the Obrenović house, and victimized many able officers.[132]

It would be a mistake to assume that Obrenović sympathizers had disappeared with the assassination of Alexander. A large number of higher-ranking officers did not take to the new dynasty for a long time. In January 1905
a "special mission" of these Obrenović friends went to London in search of a
suitable candidate for the Serbian throne. They offered the crown to the Duke
of Connaught, through former Serbian Minister Čedomilj Mijatović. The
friends of Obrenović apparently negotiated also with other foreign princes
and even with the illegitimate son of King Milan and Artemiza Hristić. Just
how bitter some were can be seen from the death announcement of an in-

fantry captain, in which, among other fine virtues of the deceased, it was said that he "was not a conspirator nor had he been awarded the Star of Karadjordje."[133]

For several years the conspiratorial question was a subject of lively discussion in the press, the Skupština, and even on a higher scholarly level.[134] The consensus was that the accomplishments of the conspirators were appreciated but that their continued interference in state affairs was regrettable. Živan Živanović, one of King Alexander's ministers and brother-in-law of Dragutin T. Dimitrijević-Apis, defended the conspirators in an article entitled, "Is There Crime in the Act of May 29?" which appeared in *Trgovinski glasnik* in June 1903.[135]

On May 29 (June 11), 1904, the anniversary of the assassination, the officer conspirators planned to give a dance at the Officers' Club. They used as an excuse a rumor that Queen Natalija was planning a solemn *Te Deum* (which did not take place) in the cathedral on June 11 in memory of her son. The Austrian minister and other foreign representatives decided "either to prevent the shameless exhibition or ostentatiously to leave Belgrade for the day." Much angered, Dumba told Foreign Minister Pašić that he would regard the fete as "a war dance of cannibals," and warned that if the dance took place, Peter "would certainly not be received at any European Court for years to come."[136] Whatever the reason, Pašić advised against the dance, which was postponed to June 15, the anniversary of the king's election. This incident, however, was symptomatic of the influence retained by the conspirators despite their dismissal from the Court.

They were countenanced by the Liberals and the ultra-Radicals as also by the immediate entourage of the king, by his cousin, Nenadović, and by his private secretary, Balugdžić. The king himself was particularly attached to Damjan Popović, who had brought him from Geneva and who had succeeded in gaining his confidence at once. Popović had the impudence to build a magnificent villa valued at seven thousand francs near the house occupied by the Crown Prince. As he had owned no property at all before the murders, the villa could only have been paid for by the blood money he received.[137]

The attitude of the European powers toward the conspiracy and especially toward the regicides themselves had serious effects on the international position of Serbia. The Russian press, including *Novoe Vremîa*, violently attacked Serbian neglect in removing the regicides from influential positions and warned of a possible Austro-Hungarian occupation of Serbia. It was pointed out that, even if the new dynasty had been recognized by Russia, the regicide officers had not. Beograd opposition papers such as *Narodni list* reproduced Russian and similar foreign press comments.[138] In England numerous articles appeared criticizing the situation in Serbia. In Paris a pamphlet was published entitled *Les relations entre l'Angleterre et la Serbie, par un diplomate français*, written with the intent of inducing the British to modify their attitude toward Serbia and to restore relations with that country.[139]

According to J. M. Jovanović, those of the powers who had recognized Peter,[140] himself an electee of the Skupština which had recognized the regicides, had no real basis for demanding the punishment of the regicides.[141]

The conspiratorial influence was never completely eliminated. From among the May conspirators an organization called "Unity or Death" (Ujedinjenje ili Smrt), usually known as the "Black Hand," was organized in May 1911. Like the earlier conspiracy, this one also included both officers and civilians. Its aim was to bring about unification of the Serbs, and organization members were to leave no stone unturned in working toward that sacred goal. Strict rules governed the lives of the members, who were to be totally subservient and to comply with any request asked of them. The organization could issue death warrants and make arrangements for execution or assassination. Among the principal leaders of the Black Hand was Dragutin Dimitrijević-Apis, prominent in the conspiratorial activities of 1903.[142]

There is no doubt but that the Black Hand was a powerful nefarious influence. It increased the influence the conspirators of 1903 already enjoyed in the Court, the Skupština, and in various governments. The king and some members of the Skupština and the government knew of the Black Hand, but they found it more expedient to bow to its wishes and remain silent. The armed forces were reorganized according to the wishes of the Black Hand, and it influenced foreign loans. It was active during the Balkan Wars and was largely responsible in pushing Serbia's army into northern Albania in 1912. It was involved in the assassination of Francis Ferdinand in 1914.

In 1916 Colonel Dimitrijević-Apis and a score of other officers were arrested and in June 1917 brought to trial before a court constituted in Salonika. This so-called "Salonika Affair" evoked much controversy and bitterness for the next quarter of a century. There are two interpretations of the affair: the royalist and nationalist elements condone or justify it, while the friends of those involved, left-wing writers, and many neutral observers treat it as a gross miscarriage of justice. The leaders, Dimitrijević-Apis, Major Ljubo Vulović, civilian Rade Malobabić, and scores of others were tried for organizing the Unity or Death movement, alleged to be antistate and antidynasty, for having planned to assassinate heir-apparent Alexander, and for having negotiated with Germany. According to Kaclerović, for example, these charges were trumped up and the whole affair was nothing but a final showdown between the dynasty and the conspirators. Crown Prince Alexander apparently felt that the conspirators had outgrown their usefulness and that the time had come for him to destroy their influence, especially before the dynasty, the government, and the armed forces returned to liberated Serbia. The real reason behind the affair, writes Kaclerović, was Alexander's fear for his life. He was apparently a marked man for having allegedly conducted negotiations with the enemy with the object in view of a separate peace.[143]

Sentences were pronounced on June 14, 1917. Dimitrijević-Apis, Vulović, and Malobabić were condemned to death and executed. Others were given varying prison sentences. About 180 officers were dispatched to Africa and there interned. Having ended the Black Hand, Alexander then organized the so-called "White Hand," comprising loyal and trusted officers. It was this group that enjoyed court favors during the interwar Yugoslav period.[144] Thus from 1903 until World War II there was always a question of conspiracy and conspiratorial influence in Serbian politics.

It is interesting to note that the Supreme Court of the Federal Republic of Serbia (SCFRS) in May 1953 held a retrial of Apis and his friends and, as was to be expected, found them innocent of charges of which they were accused at the Salonika trial. This has provoked a lively controversy in Yugoslav journals and scholarly publications.

In 1953 Živanović's son Milan had completed a two-volume work, *Solunski proces 1917 godine*, for publication under the auspices of the Serbian Academy of Sciences. One volume contains only the documents on the subject of the Salonika trial. The author identified Apis and the Ujedinjenje ili Smrt as a "progressive" force in Serbia's socioeconomic and political evolution and found that they were in contact with the Communists in 1917 and under the influence of the Russian Revolution. He blames Regent King Alexander for arbitrariness and brutality in staging a trial against Apis and his friends on trumped-up charges in order to eliminate a powerful opposition irreconcilable with his lust for personal power. The official spokesmen have criticized this book for want of correct historical evaluation of the Ujedinjenje ili Smrt and also took the Academy to task for having accepted it for publication.

At the retrial of Apis and his friends, staged by the SCFRS, effort was likewise made to attach "progressive" character to the Ujedinjenje ili Smrt. Lawyer Prvoslav Vasiljević, who defended Apis in the retrial, wrote several articles in which he stressed the "progressive" nature of the organization and its relations with the Serbian socialist movement. Recently, however, certain official spokesmen (Vladimir Dedijer, Branko Pavićević, Milan Bartoš) have challenged this thesis of "progressiveness," asserting that the Ujedinjenje ili Smrt was chauvinist, racist, hegemonist, militarist, and that it held negative views on the question of democratic liberties. These critics argue that the brutal methods employed by Alexander at Salonika should not be so interpreted as to give the Ujedinjenje ili Smrt a progressive character, although there were some individuals in the organization who were progressive. Two separate questions must be kept in mind, say the critics. First is the question of justice in the Salonika trial, and the second is that of ideological and historical assessment of the Ujedinjenje ili Smrt. The SCFRS, it is argued, was justified in staging the retrial which rehabilitated Apis and his friends, condemned on "invented" charges, but it had no business to assess the ideological character of the movement which not only led to the present controversy, but actually has served to detract from the Court's "objectivity." (For details on the above controversy and bibliography on the subject, see *Nova Misao*, August 1953.)

13. RELATIONS WITH ENGLAND AND THE REGICIDE QUESTION

In the autumn of 1904, after Peter's coronation, direct negotiations for recognition by Great Britain were started. On November 17, 1904, Foreign Minister Pašić had an interview with the British chargé d'affaires in Beograd, in which he outlined the Serbian position. Pašić said that he could understand the British attitude but hoped that the peace and order which existed in Serbia and the king's firm intention to rule as a constitutional monarch might influence the attitude of the British government. He emphasized the political and commercial advantages which would accrue to England by friendship with Serbia, at that time engaged in trade negotiations with several powers. Serbia, he said, was in need of friends. Austrian economic demands were heavy; and he hinted that Serbia's policy was "to find new markets for her commerce in order to lessen her dependence on Austria."[145]

The changed political conditions at home and abroad suggested in Great Britain at this time reconsideration of relations with Serbia. A realistic approach to the problem was desirable, considering the role Serbia might play in checking the German *Drang nach Osten*, and it was obvious that Serbia needed the support of a strong friendly power. Pašić chose a propitious moment, and placed his cards on the table. He explained that the construction of a railway which would link Serbia with the Adriatic was of grave importance to Serbia, and that Austria and Turkey had opposed the building of such a line. Their opposition, he believed, could be overcome with the support of a strong power. Pašić argued that even if such a line were not built with English capital, it would still serve the commercial interests of Britain. The railroad would eventually link the Adriatic with Rumania via Serbia. Pašić expressed a hope that Serbian relations with Britain would soon be renewed and promised "to do his best in bringing about a friendly settlement of the conspiratorial case."*

Nothing came of Pašić's appeal to the British. When on December 7, 1905, the Austrian and Russian governments sent the Balkan states a warning against aggressive and revolutionary activities in Macedonia (Turkey), the warning was supported by the British government in Sofia and Athens, but in the absence of regular diplomatic intercourse with Serbia no action was taken in Beograd.[146]

On December 11, 1905, the office of the British Secretary of State for Foreign Affairs passed from Lansdowne to Sir Edward Grey, and along with the office Grey inherited the Serbian question. The change had come at a time when Lansdowne himself had been brought to believe that it would be beneficial to renew relations with Serbia as soon as the occasion should present itself. On taking office, Sir Edward Grey sent to the British chargé d'affaires a copy of the Lansdowne memorandum of December 5, 1905, which specified the conditions for resumption of diplomatic relations with Serbia. In his memorandum Lansdowne advised that "it would be advantageous that His Majesty's Government should resume diplomatic relations with Serbia as soon as circumstances permit," i.e., when the Serbians had shown a desire to deal with the regicides "in such a manner as to render it possible for the King to send a representative to that capital." On another occasion he had made it clear that it would be difficult for His Majesty's government "to

---

* *B.D.*, V, No. 114 (November 17, 1904), 198. The former Serbian minister in London, Čedomilj Mijatović, a friend of Alexander Obrenović, appealed to Great Britain on several occasions for renewal of diplomatic relations with Serbia. See, for example, *The Times*, February 13, 1906.

stipulate that certain individuals should be dealt with in a specific manner, and to undertake that, when they had been so dealt with, diplomatic relations would thereupon be resumed." He pointed out that the question might arise as to the extent "to which the Serbian Government had fulfilled its promise." The officer deprived of one position might be given another the next day. He had therefore recommended that as soon as His Majesty's government was satisfied with the manner in which the Serbian government handled the regicide officers, "the King would consider the propriety of naming a representative." As matters stood, it would be for the king "to decide whether the punishment inflicted had been adequate or not."[147]

The English position outlined by Lansdowne was approved by the Liberal government of Campbell-Bannerman, and was shared also by Sir Edward Grey. Thus, the British were ready for an agreement with Serbia, provided the conspirators were cashiered. There was, however, some doubt of the sincerity of the Serbian government. Only recently, it was pointed out, one of the regicide officers—Captain Dragutin Dimitrijević—had been appointed to accompany Prince Djordje, heir to the throne, on his travels through Switzerland, upper Italy, and the Austrian seacoast.[148]

On April 11, 1906, speaking before the House of Commons, Sir Edward Grey said that the renewal of relations between Serbia and Great Britain could not be discussed "so long as the regicide officers hold official positions and influence in the Serbian Government." The British made it clear that the regicides would have to be withdrawn from their positions, without being later reinstated, before His Majesty's representative would be sent to Beograd.[149] The English chargé d'affaires was instructed to continue to negotiate with these objectives in view, but to be careful not "to commit [himself] in any way by the discussion of details."[150]

The unequivocal demands of the British once again precipitated a cabinet crisis in Beograd. General Atanacković, one of the regicides, had apparently offered to resign of his own free will "in order that his name should not appear in the same list with those of the chief regicides." He was presumably certain that "the retirement of others was only a question of two days more," an opinion shared by some individuals in usually well-informed circles.[151] After considerable hesitation, King Peter refused to sign the *ukaz* for the retirement of the regicide officers and accepted the resignation of General Grujić's cabinet on April 4, 1906. The king now faced the difficult problem of finding a political leader who could form a new government. Most of the leaders of the political parties refused to accept this responsibility unless the conspiracy question was settled first.

Austria-Hungary, involved in a commercial war with Serbia, viewed with apprehension any improvement of Anglo-Serbian relations. The British agent was quick to observe the Austrian attitude and on April 18, 1906, reported that

The two occasions during the past week on which the King's hesitation to get rid of the conspirators broadened into a definite refusal followed the return of M. Genčić, the leading civilian conspirator, from a two days' visit to Vienna and the arrival of M. Vukašin Petrović, ex-minister of finance who has lived in Austria since the marriage of King Alexander, and who is credited here with being a close friend of Count Goluchowski's, with both of whom the King had various interviews. The Austrian papers and especially the *Neue Freie Presse* have certainly spared no efforts to encourage the conspirators and to prevent the King giving way, by dwelling on the danger to the dynasty if the regicide officers were removed.[152]

The European system of pre–World War I alliances had already crystallized, and not only Austria-Hungary but all the Great Powers were becoming more and more interested in securing advantages in the Balkans. In Serbia, for example, Germany and Austria-Hungary supported the retention of the regicides, a policy opposite to that of the British, but one likely to enhance the position of the Central Powers.[153] Austria-Hungary and Germany feared possible British, French, or Italian dominance over Serbia. These countries might give Serbia sufficient financial assistance to enable her to become independent of the Central Powers; Serbia, thus supported, might serve as a buffer against Austro-Hungarian penetration toward the Vardar Valley and Salonika. "When the Austro-Serbian relations were so understood by the English representative at Beograd—it meant that the conspiracy question was ripe for solution."[154]

The Radical government initiated its negotiations with England through Italy. The Serbian foreign minister informed the British agent at Beograd through the Italian chargé d'affaires that four of the chief conspirators were ready to resign if that would satisfy British demands. The British were further informed that the Serbian government was ready to propose the immediate transfer of their minister at Berlin to London.[155] The British insisted on the removal of all six of the regicides before the question of diplomatic relations could be reopened.[156]

On May 23, 1906, Sir Edward Grey in a memorandum to the king reviewed the discussions with the Serbian government and specified what he considered should be the conditions for restoration of relations with Serbia. He pointed out that informal discussions with Serbia had taken place at intervals, and that the moment had now arrived when, "subject to the adequate punishment of the leading conspirators, and to an undertaking on the part of the Serbian government that they should not again be employed, diplomatic relations should be resumed." Grey designated the following as the principal conspirators: Colonel Popović, commanding the Division of the Danube; Colonel Mašin, acting chief of staff; Colonel Solarević, head of the military academy; General Atanacković, head of the Bureau of Decorations; Colonel Mišić, military tutor to the crown prince; Colonel Lazarević, commandant of the Beograd garrison; and Major Kostić, commandant of the palace guard. Sir Edward indicated that King Peter was disinclined to sanction the retirement of the regicides, and that he was supported in this stand by Austria-Hungary, whose leaders looked to a nullification of British influence at Beograd. Lord Grey said he had heard it reported that in return for certain commercial concessions to Austria-Hungary, the king of Serbia and the regicides were to be officially received at Vienna.[157]

On May 16, 1906, Prime Minister Pašić informed the British that Serbia was ready to retire Popović, Mašin, Mišić, Lazarević, and Kostić from army and court service, that General Atanacković had already resigned, and that Colonel Solarević had not been connected with the actual murder. He wished to know if these retirements would suffice to meet the British demands, since, in view of the elections coming in June and because of the foreign situation, Serbia was anxious to settle the regicide problem. Lord Grey indicated that "If the officers mentioned are placed on the retired list, it may be said that all the principal regicides, six in number, have resigned." He added that renewal of diplomatic relations might now be considered, although it was still necessary "before a Minister is actually appointed, to obtain an assurance that they [the regicides] will not again be employed." The recall of the regicides to service might necessitate once again the withdrawal of the British minister. In any case, Grey's memorandum to the king explained that it was desirable for political reasons to take the occasion for bringing "the matter to a satisfactory conclusion." Edward VII accepted Grey's proposal and suggested the designation of a suitable minister at Beograd.[158]

The British decision was transmitted to the Serbian government through the British ambassador at Vienna, who was "chosen as the channel of communication." To avoid ambiguity the ambassador was instructed to inform the Serbian government in writing and to mention verbally that if any of the six officers were re-employed, the British minister would be withdrawn from Beograd.[159]

On the third anniversary of the palace murders, June 11, 1906, diplomatic relations between England and Serbia were renewed. King Peter accepted[160] the resignation of the five officers, which was made public the following day. The Pašić government pensioned Popović, Mašin, Mišić, Lazarević, and Kostić.[161]

Having failed to dominate the political stage at Beograd by preventing the Anglo-Serbian *rapprochement*, the Austro-Hungarian government, through its ambassador at London, denounced as untrue a report that it had encouraged the Serbian government to retain the regicides in office and that the emperor of Austria had expressed his willingness to receive King Peter and the regicides at court. Grey acknowledged the existence of such a report but did not care to deny its veracity.[162]

After some quibbling over the content of the note to Great Britain,* the Serbian government promised that the retired regicide officers "shall never be employed in the service of the state." On the same occasion the Serbian government inquired if M. Milićević would be agreeable as Serbian minister in London. Sir E. Goschen, ambassador at Vienna, transmitted the final form

* Goschen had not been satisfied with the first Serbian communication, for it contained no promise that the officers "would not be readmitted to the Government service." Vujić, the Serbian representative at Vienna, communicated promptly with his government, and the result was a new note stating that the officers would not again be allowed to "serve in the Army." Goschen had not yet been satisfied. He had then asked, as he had previously phrased it to M. Milovanović, that the words "will never again be employed under the Government" be used. Vujić again telegraphed his government, and again the Serbian communication was corrected. *B.D.*, V, No. 127 (June 1, 1906), 145; *Borba*, p. 102.

of the Serbian note to the Foreign Office. The note was accepted as full compliance with the English demands on Serbia. The Serbian government was
most anxious to have the conspiratorial question settled before the coming
elections.[163]

Public opinion and official circles in England were almost unanimously
behind the decision to renew relations with Serbia, although some felt that
there was an insufficient guaranty that the retired officers would not be recalled. Actually, as it turned out, Serbia did stand by her promise not to
re-employ the regicides; it was not until the emergency of the Balkan Wars
that some of them were restored to military positions.[164] This, however, did
not mean that the influence of the conspirators on the Serbian government was
eliminated. In 1906 Lord Newton epitomized the feeling of many English-
men, who distrusted the Serbian pledges and regretted the "unsatisfactory
circumstance" under which diplomatic relations with Serbia were restored.
On June 22 in the House of Lords, after reviewing the various steps that had
been undertaken to effect the renewal of diplomatic relations with Serbia, he
pointed out that there were some loopholes in the Serbian decree for retirement of the regicides.[165] He declared that Section 22,[166] referred to in the
decree, was a provision by which officers who had rendered distinguished
service were allowed to retire with pensions amounting to their full salary.
Hence, it appeared that instead of being retired in "a somewhat ignominious
manner," the regicides were being allowed "to retain their present salaries as
full pensions and to leave the Army without a stain on their characters." Furthermore, Newton added, there were reports that the king had appointed two
of the officers to the position of aide-de-camp, and that in this capacity they
no doubt would come occasionally into communication with the British
minister. Then, in phraseology familiar today, Lord Newton declared that
"we have no quarrel with the Serbian nation" which is "just as much entitled
to our respect as any other nation." But he added that he did not approve
resumption of diplomatic relations with the Serbian government "under
somewhat unsatisfactory circumstances," and demanded that before the English minister was sent to Beograd the Serbian government show "better evidence of goodwill" than it had thus far demonstrated. In Lord Newton's
opinion the regicide question had been solved actually to the advantage of
the regicide officers.[167]

In replying to Lord Newton, Undersecretary of State for Foreign Affairs
Fitzmaurice explained that the British government had a precedent for suspension of diplomatic relations with Serbia in the suspension of relations with
Mexico following the death of Emperor Maximilian. Lord Fitzmaurice then
went on to say that

. . . if the duty of a country like ours is to make a clear assertion of the dignity
of the public right of Europe. . . . We ought always to be careful that, while
punishing other countries, we may not possibly be inflicting considerable injury
on our own subjects.

The policy of the Foreign Office was to obtain "acknowledgment on the
part of the Serbian Government by some public act that the crime of June

11, 1903, was not to be passed over without notice." Lord Fitzmaurice added that it would be impossible in a matter of this kind for the government "to interfere in details," and concluded that the British action "has sufficiently vindicated what we consider to be the public law affecting the case," and that because of Serbia's "very unsatisfactory condition . . . the presence of a British Minister may in itself be the means of helping towards the restoration of a more satisfactory condition of affairs."[168]

In the opinion of the Marquess of Salisbury, had England maintained normal relations with Serbia after so "heinous a crime," it would have appeared that she condoned the crime. However, Salisbury shared the views of Fitzmaurice that Great Britain had not only Serbian interests to consider but British interests as well, and that it was "of the highest importance, from a British point of view, that ordinary means of diplomatic intercourse should be resumed as soon as reasonably may be." The punishment of the regicides, he said, was not a matter with which England should concern herself very greatly. The fact is that "in consequence of the action of the British Government, and that action alone, public justice in Europe has been vindicated, and the Serbian Government have been compelled by our action publicly to admit that a great crime was committed. . . . That is a great achievement upon which the Government of this country are to be congratulated."[169]

Sir Edward Grey was asked to give answers to many questions. He was requested to explain why immediately after their retirement the regicides had been publicly entertained by the Serbian garrisons, with the assent of the Serbian government, why the regicides had been pensioned "with an increase of pay," and why some still held "important posts at the Serbian court." Grey was asked to explain whether it was "by accident or design that the date chosen for the announcement of the resumption of diplomatic relations was the anniversary of the murder of the late king and queen." Sir Edward replied that he was not aware of these matters, and would not inquire into them. Tersely he said that "The condition throughout has been that the chief regicide officers should be removed from positions in which His Majesty's Representative would be brought into relations with them. That has been done, and it is a condition of the renewal of diplomatic relations that it should be adhered to."[170]

The opposition in the House of Commons was not content and on August 2, 1906, Grey was again questioned. The questions were many and by now somewhat stereotyped. Grey was asked if he would kindly explain "what guarantees have been obtained to enable the British Minister at Belgrade to avoid coming into contact with regicides ; how the British Minister will be able to carry out his duties efficiently if he avoids all relations with regicides ; and, whether he will lay upon the table of the House the correspondence relating to the renewal of diplomatic relations between Great Britain and Serbia." Grey's reply again was brief and evasive. The assurances of the Serbian government that His Majesty's minister would not be brought into contact with regicides were sufficient, he said, and it was not necessary to lay any papers before the House.[171]

The British sent as their minister in Beograd Sir J. B. Whitehead, and the new Serbian minister to London was Dr. M. G. Milićević. The Serbian press commented favorably on the renewal of diplomatic relations. *Trgovinski glasnik* hoped that Anglo-Serbian relations would become closer than ever before and saw in the improvement of trade relations between the two countries new markets for Serbian goods. *Štampa* (August 22) also discussed future Anglo-Serbian relations and commented on the statements made to the king by the new English minister. It criticized the government for attributing the prolonged abnormal relations with England to the intrigues of certain foreign elements rather than to the actual cause—the murder of June 11, 1903. *Štampa* took a particular liking to one sentence of the English minister's speech—"I beg Your Majesty to believe that I will employ all my energies in order to obtain the confidence of Your Majesty, the Government and the Serbian nation." The editor expressed the opinion that such phrases had never been uttered before except by a few Russian ministers, who had used them deceptively![172]

It was in the interest of Great Britain to re-establish normal diplomatic relations. She obtained in Serbia a friend and ally in the Balkans, and Serbia in turn found in Britain a protector who could give moral support, and even some economic aid—all at a time when Serbia badly needed such support to strengthen her independence from Austria-Hungary. The British recognition of the Serbian regime encouraged the Netherlands to follow suit on November 19, 1906. The latter was the last of the powers to recognize Serbia, when the minister resident at Bucharest presented his credentials in the same capacity to King Peter.[173] Serbia was once again a country in good standing in the European community.

14. PAŠIĆ'S SECOND CABINET AND SERBIA'S PROBLEMS

Thus, the regicide question was finally settled and relations with England restored after the Radicals returned to power. The Radical cabinet was formed on April 17, 1906, by Nikola Pašić, who served in the dual capacity of prime minister and foreign minister. The king authorized Pašić to dismiss the Skupština and schedule new elections; the Radicals as a minority party were thereby accorded the same privilege which the Independent Radicals had received earlier, and which the Radical party had considered unparliamentary. In entrusting Pašić with the mandate to form a new government, the king authorized him to pension the leaders of the June 11 conspiracy. This was a heavy concession by the king, but without this backing Pašić could not have hoped to restore diplomatic relations with England. The election of June 11 was a decisive Radical victory. The Radicals won ninety of the one hundered sixty parliamentary seats. Success was attributed to the general failure of the Independent Radicals, the effective campaign of the Radicals, and the growing popularity of Pašić. Pašić remained in power until June 7, 1908, during which period he was in continuous dissention with two bitter and stubborn enemies—the Independent Radicals at home and Austria-Hungary abroad.

The Pašić government has to its credit settlement of the two principal political issues: restoring diplomatic relations with England, and obtaining the loan with which to buy artillery and railway equipment.

During 1906–8 Pašić concerned himself primarily with foreign relations, leaving the struggle with the opposition at home in the hands of his able colleague, Stojan Protić. This period was one of general European tension. The European alliance systems had crystallized into two opposing military blocs. The situation in the Balkans, where the Austro-Hungarian government had intensified its activities, was especially menacing. The *comitadji* (bands) in Old Serbia and Macedonia increased in number as the collapse of the Serbo-Bulgarian *rapprochement* gave way to a war of mutual extermination between Serbian and Bulgarian bands and their sympathizers. The Macedonian people were suffering heavily from the civil strife and from Turkish reprisals. Relations between the two Serbian states—Montenegro and Serbia—had worsened as Montenegrin intelligentsia educated in Beograd continued to criticize Prince Nikola. King Peter and Pašić were accused of deliberately instigating disorders in Montenegro in order to further their political aspirations as leaders of Yugoslav unification.

In Austria-Hungary the Slavs were stirred to action against German and Magyar domination. In the autumn of 1905 Croat deputies from both states of the Dual Monarchy* assembled at Fiume (Rijeka) and adopted the so-called Fiume Resolution, which was an expression of Croatian solidarity, a demonstration against the "anti-Slavic dualists," and a protest against the unpopular Khuen-Héderváry regime in Croatia—the most important Croat province in the Habsburg Empire. A few weeks later the deputies of Serbian parties from Dalmatia, Croatia, and Vojvodina assembled at Zadar (Zara) and passed the Zadar Resolution, which incorporated the Fiume Resolution. This action laid the basis for a Serbo-Croat coalition in the Austro-Hungarian monarchy and paved the way for intensified South Slav resistance to German and Magyar political and economic domination.[174]

Because of these developments and the fear that Austria-Hungary might launch an invasion of the Balkans, Pašić urged military preparedness. Likewise an independent economy and an outlet to the sea to sustain that economy became definite national objectives. Yet for the time being, the government did not abandon its endeavor to restore trade relations with Austria-Hungary.

In December 1906 the government contracted a loan in France in the amount of 95 million francs, and let its military contracts to the French firm of Schneider-Creuzot. When the loan agreement came up before the Skupština the Independent Radicals and the Populists threatened to prevent approval. Simultaneously, university students sympathizing with the opposition staged a demonstration against the government. Students favoring the Radical party countered with a demonstration of their own. The demonstrators met on Terazije Square, denounced one another, engaged in a slight scuffle in which a member of parliament was wounded, and were dispersed by police.[175]

The opposition denounced the government for placing the gun contract

* Consisting of the opposition from the Croatian Diet at Zagreb, members of the Croatian majority in the Dalmatian Provincial Diet at Zadar, members of the Croatian opposition in the Istrian Diet, and a few deputies from the Reichsrat at Vienna.

with the Schneider-Creuzot firm. Many of the opposition had felt that the Krupp gun was better. So infuriated was the opposition that during the taking of the final vote on December 12, 1906, they sang a death march in the Skupština. Such tactics naturally intensified the parliamentary crisis. On December 23, 1906, Pašić was forced to reshuffle his cabinet by changing the ministers of justice and public works.*

In January 1907 the situation at home became especially critical when the Independent Radicals and the Populists resorted to parliamentary obstruction. They accused the government of certain abuses in the elections of June 11, 1905, and singled out Stojan Protić as their chief target. All efforts to appease the opposition failed, and once again the Radicals suspected the "irresponsible elements" of being the culprits. The opposition's tactics were to split the government party by instigating a break between Pašić, whom they wished to see replaced, and the men they considered able, Miša Vujić and Milan Dj. Milovanović. Under pressure from the opposition Pašić resigned on May 27, 1907, in order to test the confidence of the Crown, as he had done earlier. Three days later by the king's request he formed a new cabinet, but this time without Stojan Protić.† The sacrifice of the latter was a gesture to placate the Independent Radicals.

In July trade discussions with Austria-Hungary were resumed, but no understanding was reached, each side holding its ground. Later, in the autumn, negotiations were once more started, but again with little success.

Other developments which contributed to political instability at home took place in 1907. On September 16 in the Beograd municipal prison, the brothers Milan and Maksim Novaković, so-called counterconspirators, were killed. The official explanation was that the guards shot them in self-defense after the prisoners had first seized guns and opened fire.[176] Their death was decried by the public, and the minister of interior and the major (Mihailo Ćerović) were directly blamed for it. Needless to say, the opposition exploited the incident and demanded the dismissal of Minister of Interior Nastas Popović, but the government refused.

In September 1907 the Great Powers handed Serbia a note in which they demanded that she put an end to the *četnik* activity in Old Serbia and Macedonia. A month later one of the bloodiest encounters yet took place between the Serbian and Bulgarian *četnici*, and consequently relations between the two countries became even more precarious.

15. DJORDJE NASTIĆ AND THE CETINJE "BOMB AFFAIR"

Nor were Serbia's relations with Montenegro cordial. The dynastic antagonism between the families of Obrenović and Petrović was replaced now by that of Karadjordjević and Petrović. This relationship between the ruling houses was in sharp contrast to the sentiments of the great majority of people of the two countries. The distrust of the Serbian government

---

* Marko Trifković replaced Milenko Vesnić, and Jovan P. Jovanović replaced Jovan Stanković.

† Protić was replaced by Nastas Petrović, a friend of Miša Vujić.

and the Crown, nurtured by Prince Nikola not without reason, was aggravated by the unstable political situation in Montenegro.

The first Montenegrin constitution, drawn up for the most part by Prince Nikola himself and adopted in 1905, was based on the Serbian Constitution of 1869. It provided for a "constitutional" but not a "parliamentary" monarchy, and as such intensified already strong opposition to the Montenegrin regime. The students educated in Beograd and in Europe formed a vociferous opposition to the prince and his government. They denounced the royal despotism and the terrorism employed by the authorities. The Montenegrin government was convinced that the opposition enjoyed the moral and material backing of official circles in Beograd. Consequently, the Montenegrin journals unsparingly attacked the Serbian leaders.

Montenegrin students and intellectuals found political collaborators in the members of the National party (Narodna stranka),* who likewise opposed the prince and the government of Lazar Tomanović, which was constituted from the prince's devotees and from members of the "conservative" True National party (Prava narodna stranka).† Eventually the opposition decided, if need be, to fight its political enemies with terrorist methods, although the "Klubaši" had declined to go to that extreme. During their studies in Russia, many of the students had learned the methods employed by the Russian narodniki and Social Revolutionaries. Some among the more radical opposition toyed with the possibility of murdering Prince Nikola. Others of the opposition made plans for the seizure of the city of Nikšić and from there the remainder of the country. Unfortunately for the young conspirators, the authorities uncovered their plan and imprisoned some of the leaders.[177]

Nevertheless, the struggle did not end. The conspirators wrote to Beograd, where they had many influential contacts in the Serbian government, especially in the War Ministry, asking for bombs to further their revolutionary activity. A similar request was sent to Ljuba Jovanović-Čupa, president of the Yugoslav Club in Beograd. The bombs were obtained from the Kragujevac ammunition factory, although it is not clear just how, and brought to Beograd, whence they were shipped to Kotor, the gathering place of the young conspirators. From Kotor the conspirators maintained contact with their sympathizers in Montenegro, and urged them to prepare for action. The proper moment for action was a source of disagreement among the conspirators. Some strongly believed the time for revolt had come, others that it had not yet come; there were still others who felt that revolution was unnecessary.

Meanwhile the news of the conspiracy once again leaked out, and the conspirators disappeared from Kotor, entrusting the bombs to Stevan Rajković, a printer. Left alone in Kotor, Rajković decided to deliver the bombs to the Ministry of Interior at Cetinje. On October 21, 1907, he reached Cetinje and betrayed the conspiracy against the prince's life. Two days later the gov-

* Often referred to as the "Klubaši" and considered to be the first Montenegrin democratic party.
† Usually referred to as the "Pravaši."

ernment officially announced that it had uncovered a conspiracy; it promptly convened a special court, and passed a special law on the basis of which the conspirators would be tried. The court was named "The Princely Court for Adjudication of Anarchist Crime." Mass imprisonments began as Rajković provided many names. In Montenegrin history the incident is referred to as the "Bomb Affair" (*bombaška afera*) [178]

Official Montenegrin journals now lashed out against the Serbian government, accusing it of having aided the Montenegrin conspiratorial movement. *Beogradske novine*, a Beograd journal known for its sympathy with the Montenegrin court, and one or two other Beograd publications as well, joined in the attack on their own government, which they too accused of having organized the Bomb Affair. The Vienna *Zeit* and certain Austrian papers welcomed the opportunity to report strained relations between the two Slavic states. Austria-Hungary exploited the situation for furtherance of her Balkan plans by encouraging the Serbo-Montenegrin dynastic rift. At Cetinje the Austro-Hungarian minister did what he could to promote the cleavage between the Serbian and Montenegrin courts, and many of the monarchy's papers, especially the semiofficial *Bosnische Post* (Sarajevo), fell in line with that policy. The fact that Prince Nikola had visited Vienna earlier in the year (May 1907), in the midst of the Austro-Serbian "Pig War," occasioned vicious rumors regarding the intentions of the prince.

The Beograd newspapers responded to Montenegrin accusations against Serbia with insults to Prince Nikola and his government. Many foreign newsmen were present at the Cetinje trials, and there were also many from the various Yugoslav provinces of Austria-Hungary and from Serbia. *Narod* of Mostar was especially critical of Nikola, the "constitutional despot."

The "Princely Court" (*Knjaževski sud*) opened in Cetinje on May 25, 1908, heard and sentenced thirty-one of the accused, and passed sentences on an additional twenty persons *in absentia*. Six of the accused were condemned to death, three given life imprisonment, and thirty-eight were meted out prison terms varying from two to twenty years. Two of the accused were freed owing to lack of evidence, and one was acquitted. Not a single one of the accused admitted that the conspirators had plotted to murder the prince, nor did they admit that the bombs were obtained with the connivance of official circles in Serbia. The government's case was based on evidence submitted by Rajković, supposedly one of the conspirators himself, and on that of Djordje Nastić, employee of the Austro-Hungarian intelligence service.

Djordje Nastić (1884–1919) was granted a state scholarship to attend schools in Mostar and Vienna (1902–3) and was the son of a man noted for his loyalty to the Austro-Hungarian monarchy. It seems that Kosta Herman, chief of the Political Section in the Bosna government, had recognized the true talents of Nastić and had him sent on a special mission to Beograd. In order to win the confidence of influential circles in Beograd, Nastić published a brochure on Jesuit activities in Bosna, entitled *Jezuiti u Bosni* (Beograd 1906). The publication contained what purported to be a series of "secret documents"—of trivial consequence and probably supplied by the Bosna authorities—regarding the Jesuit work. Corović has no doubt that

Czikann, Austro-Hungarian minister at Beograd, was fully informed about Nastić's mission, and he quotes Czikann's report (June 14, 1907) to Vienna on the subject.[179]

Nastić presented himself as a political victim of Austro-Hungarian oppression, and while masquerading as an Austrophobe he was well received in Beograd civilian and military circles and admitted into the patriotic society Slovenski Jug (Slavic South). Nastić made it a special point to establish contact with the Montenegrin students, who were bitter against the regime in Cetinje and ready to plot the assassination of Prince Nikola, and to encourage them. The prince had recently dissolved Montenegro's short-lived parliament and had thereby incurred the wrath of the opposition.

There is evidence that while in Beograd Nastić maintained contact with a Montenegrin police agent (Nika Jovićević) and posted him on the activities of the students. He likewise kept in touch with the appropriate political office of the Bosna authorities.[180] The true character of Nastić's work, however, was bound to leak out. A Serb civil servant in Vienna (Božidar Čerović) learned of Nastić's mission and felt obliged to inform some of the prominent Serbs in Bosna-Hercegovina (Vojislav Šola, Milan Rešetar, Vladimir Ćorović) about it. Through these men and through other channels, reports about Nastić were transmitted to certain responsible persons in Beograd (Stanoje Stanojević, Jovan Skerlić, Nikola Pašić). Yet despite the fact that even official circles in Beograd quickly learned of les affaires Nastić and his background, no one stood in his way, and Nastić managed to return to Bosna, where he circulated freely, crossing into Montenegro under the assumed name of Wilhelm Lange.

Upon Nastić's departure from Serbia, the Montenegrin authorities received an anonymous message from Zemun to the effect that "the shipment was sent by land and sea." The Montenegrins were baffled and could not interpret the meaning of the message until the bombs reached Cetinje and were delivered to the Ministry of Interior. The authorities in Bosna knowingly allowed the bombs to be shipped across Austrian territory.

Investigations ensued, during which Nastić appeared as the star witness at Cetinje, implicating Serbia in the Bomb Affair. He asserted that the bombs had been obtained from Kragujevac through Serbian official channels. He said that he was fully informed about the work of various organizations in Serbia, whose aim was to spread "Greater Serbian" propaganda and thereby to destroy the independent Montengrin state.

Meanwhile Vasilj Grdjić, well-known Hercegovinan Serb, succeeded in obtaining some of Nastić's papers[181] as prima facie evidence of his role as an "agent provocateur." Another prominent Serb, Atanasije Šola, was sent from Mostar to Cetinje to report on Nastić. Montenegrin Prime Minister Lazar Tomanović acknowledged the report and even corroborated it with other evidence. Moreover, repeated pleadings by Nastić for additional funds that would supposedly enable him to make further investigation of the conspiracy irritated the Montenegrins. Prince Nikola was soon fed up with Nastić and ordered him out of the country. In revenge Nastić turned against the prince and published an article in the semiofficial Wiener Allgemeine

Zeitung, charging the prince with a plan to "sell" the Croatian Serbs to Vienna. This article roused many a patriotic Slav in the Dual Monarchy. Even the great Thomas G. Masaryk was prompted to say some unkind words about Prince Nikola in the Reichstag. But after he learned who Nastić really was, Masaryk hastened to Cetinje and Beograd to find the "facts."

The privileges accorded Nastić at Beograd gave him the opportunity to collect material for his brochure *Finale* (Budapest, 1908), in which he explained how he convinced the Serbian authorities of his skill in the manufacture of bombs and talked his way into the Kragujevac arsenal. Here, he says, he became quickly disillusioned when he discovered that the manufactured bombs were not being sent to Bosna for use against Austria-Hungary, but to Montenegro instead. He said that between 1907 and 1908 the Beograd government had plotted a revolution of the South Slavs. This evidence was used at the Cetinje trial, and subsequently at the Zagreb treason trial, in an attempt to incriminate the Serbian government and show how it was plotting the destruction of the monarchy.

Nastić's role was obvious from his *Finale* and from the fact that he appeared twice as star witness against the accused Serbian patriots. If it could be shown that Serbia was conspiring against Montenegro and Austria-Hungary, then the latter, counting on the good will—if not the actual support—of Montenegro, could employ drastic measures against Serbia. The destruction of Serbian independence, or at least the annexation of Bosna and Hercegovina, was probably envisaged.[182] But the activities of Nastić and his role as *agent provocateur*, although damaging to relations between the two Serbian nations, did not bear the anticipated fruit. The leaders of the monarchy were compelled to devise new methods in dealing with the growing menace of Serbian nationalism.

The only documentary evidence Nastić could muster to implicate Serbia in the conspiracy to destroy Montenegro and Austria-Hungary was a temporary "statute" drafted by Milan Pribićević, an Austrian citizen, for the liberation of the South Slavs. It seems that Nastić might have influenced Pribićević in drafting such a statute. But even though Pribićević was a Serbian patriot and served in the Serbian army, the statute manifested republican tendencies and consequently could not have been subscribed to by the Serbian monarchy.

Finally, on Russian advice and under pressure of public opinion at home and abroad, Prince Nikola reduced two death sentences to life imprisonment. The intensity with which the political opposition was persecuted, however, did not produce political stability, and the suspicion in Beograd continued. But when Austria-Hungary annexed Bosna-Hercegovina, the dynastic feud was subordinated to more fundamental national interests, and Montenegro and Serbia stood shoulder to shoulder.[183]

16. PAŠIĆ RESIGNS

And so it went through the entire period of Pašić's tenure as foreign minister. One crisis was followed by another, and each foreign problem involved a battle of some kind with the domestic opposition. Indeed the opposition seized every opportunity to undermine Pašić and his government. When on January 27, 1908, Prince Djordje, heir to the throne, gave up his allowance, the opposition saw in this decision the nefarious work of Pašić.

A new crisis in relations with Austria occurred when, on January 28, 1908, the Austro-Hungarian foreign minister announced in the Delegations that his country had requested from the sultan permission to extend the so-called Sarajevo railway line to Kosovska Mitrovica. This Sandjak railway proposal alarmed Serbia and the Great Powers because it presaged new Austro-Hungarian expansion into the Balkans. European diplomacy was preoccupied with the problem for several months until Austria-Hungary itself decided to drop the project.[184]

In April the Austro-Hungarian minister complained to the Serbian foreign minister that Serbian schoolbooks referred to the Dual Monarchy as an enemy of the Serbs. He contrasted this situation with what he considered an exemplary attitude in his own country. Thus among other conflicts between Serbia and Austria-Hungary there now appeared "the textbook conflict."

Toward the end of March 1908 the opposition again threatened Pašić with parliamentary obstruction which would prevent the passing of the budget. They furthermore opposed the agreement the government had made for the purchase of guns; they wanted to see the commercial treaty with Austria-Hungary signed and elections scheduled. Pašić resigned on March 20, and with royal backing ten days later reorganized his cabinet (March 30) without Minister of Interior Nastas Petrović and War Minister Radomir Putnik. The latter was dropped because he had been especially criticized by the opposition over the gun question. His place was taken by General Stepa Stepanović, another brilliant soldier.[185]

Meanwhile the government dismissed the Skupština and scheduled elections for May 18. In the bitter election campaign, the Radicals accused the Independent Radicals of obstructing state affairs and thereby destroying the parliamentary system. The Independent Radicals defended themselves on the grounds that obstruction was necessary to protect the state from partisanship and from rule by an unscrupulous majority. The respective papers rehashed the old question of obstruction, the Radicals opposing it as unparliamentary, the Independent Radicals favoring it as necessary. In these interparty quarrels, the Radicals were again ably represented by their leading theoretician, Stojan Protić, who wrote a series of articles in the Radical party's *Samouprava*.[186]

The elections, after six runoffs on May 25 (*naknadni izbori*), gave the Radical party eighty-four parliamentary seats (a loss of six), the Independent Radical party forty-eight (a loss of five), the Populist (Liberal) nineteen, the Progressive seven, and the Socialist party one. The polls showed that the Populist and Progressive parties gained at the expense of the two major parties. Pašić was not pleased with the results. Not only did his party suffer an appreciable loss in popular support, but the loss was the Populist and Progressive gain, and these two parties had been considered "Austrophile."

It was doubtful whether Pašić could successfully continue as prime minister, after such a hotly contested election, as well as the opposition's parliamentary obstruction and the criticism within his own party. Even the officer conspirators had of late come to life again, openly urging the formation of a coalition government which could better deal with the shaky foreign situation, especially the complications in Bosna.[187]

Years of intensive political activity had tired Pašić. The long period as, prime minister had won him enemies even inside his party, where some fellow members considered him the principal cause of the perennial political and parliamentary conflicts. Many of his own party hoped he would relinquish the government to Miša Vujić or Milovan Dj. Milovanović, men more acceptable to the opposition. The lack of confidence within the party hurt Pašić's pride, for he now believed that the king shared the views of those who sought to replace him. Pašić thus decided to step aside and permit the formation of a government which would enjoy the confidence and co-operation of the Skupština. He resigned on June 4, 1908, but remained active politically. He now took the reins of his party more firmly in his hands. Even though he was no longer in the government, his influence remained great by virtue of his party leadership and control.

Consultations regarding the formation of a new government continued for some time. The primary aim was to effect a conciliation between the two major parties in order to organize a coalition government. Through the king's intervention an understanding was finally reached on the condition that the government formed on July 7 by Pera Velimirović (Radical) submit the budget and the trade treaty with Austria-Hungary to the Skupština before August, and that the three Independent Radicals be ready then to enter the cabinet. By way of further compromise, the Radicals abandoned their plan to modify parliamentary procedure (*skupštinski poslovnik*), while the Independent Radicals dropped their demand for new elections. Pašić and Nastas Petrović were kept out of the government because the Independent Radicals made it clear in no uncertain terms that they did not wish to work with them.[188]

By the beginning of August Velimirović had submitted to the Skupština the budget and the trade treaty, and on August 11 the three Independent Radicals joined the cabinet. The coalition government was thereby finally constituted. Obstruction ceased and the party struggle subsided. Once again there appeared to be a possibility of healing the schism between the two Radical parties, but this possibility never materialized.[189]

The Foreign Ministry passed from Pašić to Milovan Dj. Milovanović, who served in that capacity in all governments until June 18, 1912. He was one of the leading Serbian statesmen; his continued service in the Foreign Ministry gave stability and direction to Serbian foreign policy. As an intellectual Milovanović stood above Pašić, but as a party organizer Pašić had no peer. Milovanović knew politics as a science far better than did Pašić, but the latter knew far better how to apply his knowledge. Meanwhile, all groups had confidence in Milovanović. During his ministry the annexation of Bosna and Hercegovina by Austria-Hungary—a great blow to him personally and to the Serbian nation—took place. Events of a more positive nature were his alliance with Bulgaria and the preparation made for the war of liberation with Turkey in 1912.

Velimirović's cabinet fell on February 11, 1909, primarily as a result of the crisis precipitated by the Austro-Hungarian annexation of Bosna and Hercegovina. To meet the crisis, a new cabinet was formed by Stojan Novaković, chief of the Progressive party. His party had the smallest parliamentary representation, but he himself enjoyed a great reputation as scholar and statesman. His so-called "Concentration Cabinet" saw the annexation crisis to its unfortunate end.[190]

PART SIX

The Macedonian Imbroglio, 1903-8

1. THE ILINDEN UPRISING AND ITS CONSEQUENCES

THE ASSASSINS OF KING ALEXANDER CONSIDERED the promotion of Serbian national interests in Macedonia of primary importance. One of the reasons for the attack on the king in 1903 was said to have been his neglect of the "Serbian cause." It is no surprise, therefore, to find the regicides among the officers taking part in the *četnik* activities in Macedonia.[1] Whatever the relationship between the conspirators of 1903 and the *četnici*, there was after the coming of the new dynasty a marked increase in Serbian nationalist activity in Macedonia.

In the beginning of 1903, at Salonika during Delčev's absence, a decision was made by the IMRO leaders to prepare for the Ilinden uprising,* even though the people were not ready politically or materially. Delčev denounced the decision of the Central Committee of the IMRO, and at a meeting in Sofia endeavored to prevent any rash action. On his return to Macedonia he was killed by the Supremists.

Preparations for the uprising went ahead. The IMRO intensified its activities and initiated a series of terrorist acts which culminated in the fatal Ilinden insurrection in August 1903.[2] The insurgents seized most of the Bitolj† vilayet and organized what was known as the Kruševo Republic (Kruševskata republika), under the leadership of a socialist, Nikola Karev. After they had established a revolutionary council, an attempt was made to mobilize all local resources for the liberation of the rest of Macedonia.[3] The insurgents presented to the sultan and the European powers twelve articles which comprised a project of autonomy for Macedonia, Albania, Old Serbia, and Adrianople.[4]

The Macedonian insurrection elicited a great deal of interest in Beograd, where a number of meetings were held at which appeals were made for armed bands to participate in the Macedonian struggle. Volunteers, who represented for the most part *émigrés* from Old Serbia and Macedonia, were recruited with ever-increasing zeal. The Turkish minister protested against this intended violation of Turkish territory, but Foreign Minister Kaljević explained that there was little he could do about the matter "under the Serbian law," and that the purpose of "these meetings was not for the raising of bands, but merely for collecting funds and expressing sympathy for coreligionists beyond the frontier." If the government were to take measures against the bands, Kaljević added, it "would raise a degree of hostile feeling,

---

* The name is derived from St. Elijah's Day, when the uprising occurred. In 1953 Macedonians celebrated the fiftieth anniversary of the uprising, giving it a historical twist to accord with present political thinking.

† Bitola in Macedonian; Monastir in Turkish.

which [it] was not willing to face."⁵ But some of the Serbian newspapers maintained in a forthright manner that the Macedonian revolution was "not only justifiable, but [it was] the duty of every man to aid it with rifle in hand." The press, however, did not welcome Bulgarian monopoly over such a revolution, and stirred up popular resentment toward Bulgaria by describing that country's misdeeds in Macedonia and by stressing the fact that whenever the IMRO bands occupied a Macedonian village, they hoisted the Bulgarian flag. Serbs were urged to join in the Macedonian insurrection lest they lose all rights to that province. Step by step the movement for organizing Serbian bands "in aid of the Macedonian insurrection" became widespread.⁶ The St. Petersburg *Novosti* and other Russian papers declared that the time had come for Serbia "to join in the insurrection" and make her influence felt. The Serbian press, taking its cue from the Russians, wrote in similar vein. It warned the Serbian population of Macedonia against any entanglement with the Bulgarian bands, and urged them "to strike for themselves, promising that when the proper time comes they can count on Serbia."⁷ The creation of Serbian bands would permit Serbia to deal with Bulgarian elements on the basis of equal strength.

At an open air meeting at Beograd on August 30 the Macedonian Question was once again threshed out publicly.⁸ A resolution was passed to the effect that thus far all reforms intended to improve the lot of the Christian population of the Ottoman Empire had proved futile as a result of Turkish misrule, and not because of revolutionary activities by the Christians; and that because of the persecution of the Slavs in the Ottoman Empire it was the duty of the Balkan Slavs to work together and establish a common defense.* The resolution declared further that neither the sultan and the foreign powers nor the armed bands could give the Macedonians liberty and provide them with peace and order. The only way in which peace and order could be brought to Old Serbia and Macedonia was through mutual agreement among the Balkan peoples themselves.⁹ The foregoing resolution is important in that it indicated the official policy of the government, e.g., the necessity for a Balkan understanding regarding Macedonia. Serbia recognized implicitly that other Balkan states had valid claims in Macedonia, and in doing so hoped they would recognize her own national claims.

In the midst of the Macedonian turmoil, Serbia scored two unexpected diplomatic victories. After repeated Serbian protests, the Porte ordered, in September 1903, the withdrawal of its troops from the Serbian frontier. Of greater importance yet was the sultan's irade for the recognition of the Serbian nationals in Turkey.¹⁰ After six years of effort, the Porte was finally induced by General Grujić to recognize the existence of Serbian nationality within its empire. The action had wide ramifications, for hereafter the Serbs and their institutions in Macedonia would be spared "the inquisitorial activities of the Bulgarian Exarch."¹¹ Hilmi Pasha was asked to create a commis-

* Elected and authorized to carry out this resolution were Aleksandar Stojanović, publisher and president of the Skupština; Golub Janić, merchant; Jovan Jovanović, late minister of public worship; Živojin Perić, high school professor; Ljuba Stojanović, late minister of public worship; Milutin Stefanović, government cashier, retired.

sion headed by himself, which would include a Serb among its members, and which would take a census of the Serbian population and make the necessary preparations for formal recognition of Serbian nationality.[12] The Turks had hoped that the recognition of Serbian nationality would act as "a counterweight to the extension of the Bulgarian national movement." Because they lacked a national organization of their own, many Serbians had joined the Bulgarian movement. Recognition of Serbian nationality was expected by the Turks to check "this source of recruiting," and to enable the Turkish government to play Serbs and Bulgarians against each other.[13]

The Kruševo Republic collapsed in October 1903, and the forces of revolution were routed. The IMRO had made two mistakes. It overestimated the capacity of its followers to endure the struggle with the Turkish armed forces, and it relied too much on European intervention and foreign aid. According to present-day communist writers, there were also certain inherent weaknesses in the revolutionary movement. The IMRO was politically heterogeneous; there was discord at the top level over strategy and tactics. Moreover, these sources contend that the Bulgarian court camarilla through "Supremists and Exarchists" brought on the Macedonian uprising prematurely. Because Supremists and Exarchists pursued a policy which assumed that only Bulgarian armies could liberate Macedonia, they had thereby killed the people's confidence in their own ability to resist.[14]

After the disastrous Ilinden uprising the IMRO began to fall to pieces, and the Supremists with their policy of "infiltration and terror" gradually took over the IMRO, which became divided into two ideological wings.[15] One group favored "closest collaboration" with the Supreme Committee, and worked for Macedonian autonomy as a first step toward Bulgarian annexation of Macedonia. This group represented the rightist and extreme nationalist elements. The second group of the IMRO worked toward a "genuine" autonomy or independence for Macedonia, stood on the original platform of IMRO, and "tried to preserve independence" of the Supreme Committee and the Bulgarian War Office.[16] However, its "independence" was often crippled because of dependence on Bulgaria for arms and money. After World War I many of its followers became "Federalists," who advocated an autonomous Macedonia within a South Slav federation; others joined the Communist party. The rightist groups retained the name IMRO.

Turkish suppression of the insurrection was accompanied by terrible violence. The vilayet of Bitolj suffered most from the insurrection. Turkish *gendarmerie* and police nearly obliterated some of the villages and their inhabitants. Many participants in the insurrection fled to Bulgaria and Serbia, where they were sheltered and given aid. In Serbia the Circle of Serbian Sisters (Kolo Srpskih Sestara) actually maintained about two hundred refugee IMRO-ists. The government endeavored to befriend those among them who believed in Macedonian autonomy and opposed the Tsonchev-Mihailovski-Karavelov group that favored the annexation of Macedonia to Bulgaria.[17] Nikola Pašić, in a series of articles which appeared in *Ustavna Srbija*, advocated a more active Serbian policy on behalf of "our brothers in Old Serbia and Macedonia." Official statements and public discussions on the matter of "our southern regions" became almost daily occurrences. The government employed utmost care in selecting suitable diplomatic agents to serve in the Ottoman Empire. Popular interest in the future of Macedonia was greater than at any previous time. The Bulgarian historian and diplomat Toshev observes that after 1903 Serbian activities in Macedonia reached their zenith.[18]

Conditions in Macedonia after the suppression of the Ilinden uprising soon appreciably worsened. Other insurrections followed, only to be speedily quelled.[19] Small Serbian bands of *četnici* made repeated attempts to cross the Turkish frontier. Yet the Turkish minister in Beograd evidently attached little importance "to these efforts," and was satisfied that the Serbian government was "doing their best to discourage them."[20] The British chargé d'affaires in Beograd found that Serbian interest in Macedonia was prompted by "her interests in Old Serbia on the one hand, and her jealousy of any increase of Bulgarian influence on the other." He suggested that if the Turks and Albanians refrained from "a too open oppression of the inhabitants of that district," the Serbs were not likely to cause any trouble.[21] But the facts were that Serbian bands after 1903 not only invaded Macedonia with system and regularity but steadily increased in numbers and effectiveness. They were, according to Dumba, "on the defensive against the Bulgarian bands in Macedonia. In Serbia it was impossible to avoid furnishing oppressed co-nationals with arms and sometimes even sending armed bands across the border for their protection."[22] Similarly, the activities of the so-called societies for the aid and assistance of the "downtrodden brothers"* continued to expand both in size and scope.[23]

2. MACEDONIAN REFORMS AND THE SERBIAN ATTITUDE

After the Ilinden insurrection, the foreign ministers of Austria-Hungary and Russia busied themselves in preparing at Mürzsteg (October 1903) a new scheme of reforms for Macedonia. Representatives of the two powers "most vitally interested" in Balkan affairs agreed that Austro-Hungarian and Russian civil agents be appointed as assistants to Hilmi Pasha and that several specific reforms be carried out. These included the reorganization of the *gendarmerie* by officers chosen from the armies of all five of the Great Powers; the rearrangement of administrative districts to conform to ethnic groupings; provision for various improvements in judicial administration; and, finally, certain financial dispositions which were intended to aid those who had suffered damage and loss during suppression of the insurrection.[24]

Serbia welcomed the Mürzsteg reform program but did not approve of the potent position Austria-Hungary and Russia occupied in its application. The Serbian government favored inclusion of the Balkan states in the administration of reforms as the best guaranty that the reforms would be correctly applied. Otherwise the Serbian government was quite skeptical about the success of the reforms, and hoped that the Macedonian and other Balkan problems would not be settled outside a general European congress.[25]

* Especially active were the Circle of Serbian Sisters (*Kolo Srpskih Sestra*) and the Society for Collection of Aid (*Društvo za prikupljanje pomoći*).

The Mürzsteg reforms furthered for Serbia the immediate objective of curbing Greek and Bulgarian nationalist and religious activities in Macedonia. Serbia found it expedient hereafter to promote actively the extension of the reforms to Old Serbia, and eventually planned to request from the Porte a renewal of the Patriarchate of Peć and organization of Serbian parishes into eparchies subordinated to Serbian bishops. The inhabitants of Old Serbia presented several petitions to the inspector general and to Russo-Austrian agents, in which they asked for reforms and complained of persecution.[26] In supporting the Albanian element against the Serbian and, as we shall see below, by excluding Old Serbia from the reforms, Austria-Hungary had hoped to extend her own political and economic control over the region. Such a policy made Austrian relations with Serbia worse, since additional encroachments in the Balkans by Austria would have been detrimental to the national interests of Serbia.

After 1903 the Serbs emphasized "political and economic" rather than "educational and religious" work in Macedonia, and their policy was one of peaceful activity in the "southern regions" in order to obviate any possible excuse for the monarchy's military intervention. There was much complaining among certain Serbian nationalist circles that work in Macedonia and Old Serbia had to be concealed from the Foreign Ministry.[27] Even Minister Dumba noted that Serbia was primarily interested in maintenance of "the conservative *status quo* policy" with the aim of protecting Old Serbia from "Bulgarian incursions." This policy involved "a more or less active support of *comitadji* bands; and a more or less public constitution of committees" charged with the collection of money for Macedonian aid. The money apparently came in "very slowly."[28]

After the Mürzsteg reform scheme, which established Austro-Russian spheres of influence in the Balkans, the Serbian government next evolved a policy of espousing co-operation among the Balkan nations based on the principle of "the Balkans for the Balkan peoples." The Serbs opposed any insurrection in European Turkey until the three Balkan powers (Bulgaria, Greece, and Serbia) should agree on a common policy, since otherwise there was danger of foreign intervention which would not serve the interests of the Balkan peoples. The Serbian government felt that an understanding with Bulgaria on Macedonia might eventually provide a just solution for the complicated problem. If an understanding with Bulgaria was not possible, then some agreement with those of the Macedonian revolutionaries who were least subservient to the Bulgarian government might be considered.[29]

In a circular of December 2, 1903, to its diplomatic agents abroad, the Serbian Foreign Office defined the official policy on Macedonia and Old Serbia as follows:

> Serbia sets great store on peace in the Balkan Peninsula, for she is greatly in need of it today, but she sets much greater store on her own existence, which would remain unimperiled only if the position of Old Serbia and Macedonia were improved by means of far-reaching and effective reforms, which would make impossible either a one-sided settlement of the Macedonian Question on the lines of the Bulgarian nationalist claims, or an extension of the occupation on the lines

of the ambitions to which the Vienna-Budapest press gives frequent expression in an unequivocal fashion.[30]

The circular laid emphasis on the necessity of a Balkan *rapprochement*. It stated that the three Balkan Slav states should rid themselves "of the historical atavism" which caused rivalry among them and should instead seek mutual understanding. Their mutual rivalry paralyzed their strength, while united efforts, the circular stated, would guarantee "improvement of the miserable situation of their kinsmen in Turkey," and would prevent foreign aggression. The circular stated that the Balkan states should renounce their claims to disputed provinces in Turkey and support the application of "the most widespread and practical reforms possible," respecting the nationality rights of all concerned.[31]

In January 1904 the government instructed consular agents in Turkey to turn their attention to strengthening the sympathy of the Slavic population for Serbia, to serve as spokesmen and defenders of the Slavic inhabitants in Turkey, and to observe closely and report on the reform work of the Russian and Austrian civil agents and the officers of the *gendarmerie*.[32]

The Serbian government considered Article III as one of the most important provisions of the Mürzsteg Agreement; it provided among other things for the territorial division of administrative units on ethnic lines.[33] In Beograd Article III was interpreted as tantamount to a designation of the territories which each of the Balkan states might in the future rightfully claim as its own. That recognition meant the ultimate partition of Macedonia, an eventuality which the Serbs favored throughout the pre–World War I period.

Once the Porte accepted the Mürzsteg Agreement, Austria-Hungary sought to exclude the western part of the vilayet of Kosovo (the sandjaks of Peć [Ipek], Plevlja, Priština, Prizren, Sjenica, Novi Pazar [Novi Bazar]), from reforms, and demanded that the reforms in the eastern part of the vilayet of Kosovo (districts of Kačanik, Kumanovo, Kratovo, Palanka, Skoplje) be exclusively entrusted to her *gendarmerie* officers. Austria-Hungary, therefore, strongly opposed the proposal that she share with Russia the reform work in the western part of the Kosovo vilayet.[34] The policy of Austrian diplomacy was in sharp contrast to the emperor's declaration before the Delegations on December 16, 1903, that the reform action would be undertaken "without any selfish motives."[35] The Russian minister in Beograd [Muraviev] saw in the Austrian demands "the first consequence of Russian reverses in the war with Japan," and was fully cognizant of what the Austrian policy would mean to Serbia. On March 4 Pašić instructed the Serbian minister in Constantinople to request Zinoviev to oppose the Austrian demand. But, writes Ćorović, the Russians, unable after the Far Eastern fiasco "to oppose" Austria-Hungary, pretended "to trust" her. The Russians consequently agreed to the exclusion of reforms from the western part of the Kosovo vilayet for "the time being only."[36]

On February 12, however, Lamsdorff had assured Novaković that the reform project would include the entire Kosovo vilayet and that the Austrian officers would not be charged with the work in that vilayet.[37] Subsequently

Zinoviev hinted to Simić that Serbia should not broach the subject to other powers because such action would be considered "a breach of confidence" in Russia. On February 25, 1904, Lamsdorff, while urging Serbia to rely exclusively on Russia's protection, reiterated that Austrian officers would not be entrusted with the reform work in the Kosovo vilayet. Assured by the Russians, Pašić was in a position to inform the legations in Rome, Sofia, and Constantinople that for the time being the government would take no further action. Serbian suspicion that Russia and Austria-Hungary had concluded a secret agreement on Macedonia was dispelled by the French, who informed Serbia that Russian policy in the Balkans was in complete harmony with that of Great Britain, Italy, and France. The Serbian government next approached Italy regarding the Kosovo vilayet, because this power too opposed Austrian demands regarding that region. The Montenegrin prince had also appealed to Victor Emmanuel to oppose the demand of Austria-Hungary. It was in this connection that Italy once again urged the establishment of a Balkan bloc against any future Austrian expansion.[38]

The Serbs meanwhile had suggested that French and Italian officers be entrusted with the reform work in the vilayet of Kosovo, but Vienna was in no position to support such a proposal. Indeed, it was after prolonged negotiations that Austria-Hungary even agreed to entrust the reform work in the Bitolj vilayet to Italian officers.[39] The Serbs interpreted the exclusion of reforms from the western part of the vilayet of Kosovo—roughly Old Serbia—to mean that Austria would retain an unhindered position in promoting Albanian nationalism in that area to the detriment of the Serbs. When the reform region should be eventually reorganized according to Article III of the Mürzsteg Agreement, which envisaged "the fairer grouping of the various nationalities," the Serbs might be deprived of the western Kosovo vilayet permanently.[40] Italian General de Georgis noted moreover that the Austro-Hungarian *gendarmerie* officers were more interested in the study of the terrain and correction of their maps than in the reforms.[41] Dumba, who found the Serbian reaction quite normal, diligently posted his government on all phases of the reform problem.[42] The Austrian explanation of the policy was that exclusion of the western portion of the Kosovo vilayet from reform was only temporary and was necessary because the Albanians would revolt against the introduction of reforms in that district.[43]

The Porte was seemingly more inclined to the Serbian than the Austrian policy regarding the western Kosovo vilayet and suggested that reforms might well be extended to that district, particularly to the mixed Serbo-Albanian sections as suggested by Serbia as early as 1902. Goluchowski cautioned the Serbian minister, on March 2, 1904, that this Turkish offer was not sincere, but merely a maneuver to obstruct the whole reform program.

The efforts of Serbia to extend the reforms to the western part of the vilayet of Kosovo and to prevent Austria-Hungary from acquiring the right to administer reforms in the eastern part of the vilayet failed. Neither of the objectives was achieved: the western part of the vilayet of Kosovo was excluded, and Austria-Hungary, despite Serbian protests, was charged with the reforms in the eastern districts (part of Macedonia) of Kačanik, Kumanovo, Kratovo, Palanka, and Skoplje.[44] Under Russian pressure, however, the Austrians finally agreed that in the western part of the vilayet of Kosovo "reliable" Turkish *gendarmerie* officers would be used.[45]

The Austrian victory in the matter of reforms was considered the "greatest" since the occupation of Bosna and Hercegovina in 1878. The fact that Austria-Hungary succeeded in excluding the Sandjak* and the western part of the Kosovo vilayet from the reforms signified her determination to keep these areas free from any other foreign influence. There was, of course, some legal basis for her action, as she could claim that the Sandjak and Kosovo areas "to beyond Mitrovica" were entrusted to her by the Congress of Berlin.[46] Such events as the founding of a Catholic church by Francis Joseph in Skoplje, consecrated on August 18, 1902, were not without significance.[47] It was feared that Austria-Hungary, entrusted with execution of the reforms in the territory which separated Serbia from Montenegro, would forever alienate that stretch of land from the Serbian nation and prevent the possible union of Serbia and Montenegro. The Serbs further observed that the *kaza* of Kačanik—almost homogeneously Albanian—was brought under the reform program and assigned to Austria-Hungary on her request. Only strategic considerations could have explained the Austrian interest in Kačanik, as the Kačanik Pass controls the entrance into Old Serbia.[48]

In addition to the military and political advantages she secured from the reform program, Austria-Hungary lost no time in building schools and churches in Albania to serve as centers of propaganda and sources of Austria-sponsored Albanian nationalism.[49] The Albanians were allowed to resume and intensify their terrorist activities against the Serbian element; they murdered Serb nationals and stole their property and cattle. The Albanian League, renewed a few years back, usurped local authority.[50] Thus Austria-Hungary, which in the time of King Milan had favored Serbian "southern expansion," now opposed it, and her recent activities suggested the possibility of further territorial expansion in the Balkans. Indeed, the Serbs had many reasons to expect a new Austrian drive into the Balkans. Since 1901 there had been talk of building a Bosna-Mitrovica railway. The Albanian disturbances and anti-Serb activities were at least in part instigated by Austria-Hungary. The Austrian flirtations with Bulgaria, and her obvious designs to surround Serbia with "occupied districts," "spheres of influence," and "allies," all spelled one and the same thing, i.e., activation of the *Drang nach Südosten*.[51]

The Austro-Serbian conflict "consisted in which would keep the other from Macedonia." According to Slobodan Jovanović, the Dual Monarchy failed to see that she "could only hope to expand in the Balkans in the name of 'the Yugoslav idea'." So long as she oppressed her own South Slav subjects, her Balkan policy was bound to assume an imperialistic aspect.[52]

On February 29, 1904, the Porte was formally informed by Austria-Hungary and Russia that reforms would be excluded "at present" from the western districts of the Kosovo and Bitolj vilayets. This decision was appar-

* Sandjak of Novi Pazar.

ently approved by the other Great Powers, although somewhat reluctantly by Italy. The Russian and Austrian governments, however, declared on February 29 that if Turkish officers in the areas excluded from reforms failed in their duties they would be replaced by foreign officers. This declaration was not sufficiently unequivocal to satisfy the Serbs, and the Porte, on March 17, still insisted that reforms be extended to all vilayets. On March 2 Goluchowski promised Vujić that the reforms would be extended in the future to those districts (Peć, Priština, and Prizren) which were not purely Albanian (the area southwest of Peć and Scutari), but this promise was not kept.[53]

The Serbian requests that reforms be extended also to the Sandjak of Novi Pazar encountered firm opposition on the part of the monarchy. On March 23 Goluchowski told Vujić that the Sandjak had been assigned to Austria-Hungary for military occupation by the Congress of Berlin, and that it was agreed at Mürzsteg to exclude the Sandjak from reforms.[54] Lamsdorff, on the other hand, assured Novaković that no such decision regarding the Sandjak was made, although precise information regarding the agreement to exclude the Sandjak of Novi Pazar from the reforms had also come to the attention of a French diplomatic agent.[55] At a later date Lamsdorff promised Novaković once again that in the future the reforms would be extended to the western districts of the vilayet of Kosovo, but Novaković on this same occasion got the impression that Lamsdorff recognized the exclusive position of Austria-Hungary in the Sandjak of Novi Pazar.[56] The French government had likewise turned down the Serbian request that the Sandjak of Novi Pazar be included in the area of the reforms. So far as the Sandjak was concerned, the Austro-Hungarian government was sure that its military forces in the Sandjak were doing all that was necessary in the way of improving conditions.[57] Fully cognizant of the rights of the Dual Monarchy in the Sandjak under the Treaty of Berlin, the Serbs nevertheless advanced a rather tenuous theory that these rights were no longer valid because by a special convention with Turkey, signed in 1879, the monarchy had agreed to restrict her military garrisons to three cities: Plevlja, Prijepolje, and Priboj. The Italian government and some foreign diplomats were ready to support Serbia's position. Having herself become weary of the new Austro-Hungarian designs in the Balkans, Italy was prepared to back any formula that might prevent territorial aggrandizement in the Balkans by the Dual Monarchy.[58]

3. THE SERBIAN *ČETNIK* MOVEMENT

The conflict with Austria-Hungary was but one side of the Macedonian Question; there were also perennial conflicts with the Bulgarian government. The Serbs were, after the Ilinden fiasco, content to accept a Macedonian autonomy in which they would enjoy racial equality with Bulgaria. A group of the IMRO followers were receptive to this thesis. Failure of the Ilinden insurrection in 1903 and Turkish reprisals had induced some Macedonian groups, especially those in the regions of Bitolj, Ohrid, and Debar, to adopt the line of Serbo-Bulgarian amity. After the Ilinden disaster many pro-Bulgarian *četnici* (or *comitadji*) who were unable to escape to Bulgaria found refuge in Serbia. They were quartered in several of the larger cities (Beograd, Niš, Kragujevac, Požarevac, and Šabac) and lived in military fashion. The most active among them was a law student named Matej Gerov. Some of these Bulgarian *četnici* altered their previous anti-Serbian attitude and came to accept the formula of Serbo-Bulgarian co-operation.[59] In 1904, however, Tsonchev's "Supremists" had complete control over the IMRO, and this precluded, for the time being, the possibility of any co-operation with Serbia.

To arrest the growth of Serbian influence, the IMRO intensified terrorist activities against the Serbs and those who sought their protection. The outbreak of fresh Serbo-Bulgarian violence in Macedonia came, ironically enough, at the very moment when the governments of Bulgaria and Serbia were conducting secret negotiations toward a treaty of alliance and an agreement on partition of Macedonia. In fact some of the bitterest battles between the IMRO bands and Serbian *četnici* were fought in the period between Prince Ferdinand's visit in Niš in May 1904 and King Peter's return visit to Sofia in October of the same year. The resurgence of Bulgarian terrorism was allegedly ordered by the so-called Bulgarian commercial agency (consulate) at Salonika and the educational section of the exarchate. One of the principal aims of the Bulgarian-controlled IMRO was to compel the Macedonians to recognize the exarchate, and many did so in order that their lives and property might be spared. The new conflicts between the Serbian *četnici* and the IMRO bands inflamed the smoldering press war between Sofia and Beograd.[60]

Toward the end of 1904 the IMRO, under Damian Gruev, attempted to "liberate" Poreč from Serb control. Gruev was wounded in the bloody encounter and captured by the Serbian *četnici* of Micko Krstić. When his wounds healed he was allowed to return to Sofia after promising to work toward Serbo-Bulgarian co-operation in Macedonia, on a basis of complete equality. Gruev reached Sofia in the winter of 1904 and in fact submitted the Serbian proposal for consideration to the IMRO Congress which had assembled at the Rila monastery, and over which he presided. The congress rejected the proposal on the ground that the IMRO was the only group that had the right to work for Macedonian liberation and could not permit any other revolutionary organization to share in that sacred mission.[61] Unable to achieve an equal position with Bulgaria in Macedonia, the Serbian government began to take a more genuine interest in Macedonian revolutionary work.

Before 1904–5, official circles in Beograd had for the most part discouraged the *četnik* action in Macedonia on the assumption that it would only add to a general turmoil which might precipitate foreign intervention, and that such action would expose the inhabitants to reprisals by the Turks and Bulgarians. Nonetheless some small and poorly equipped bands did, from time to time, cross the Turkish border, only to be slaughtered. Gradually there crystallized in Macedonia and Old Serbia a resistance movement against the Turks and the activities of the Bulgarian bands. "Secret bands" were organized here and there, operating without interconnection or a co-ordinated plan.

Such bands, dedicated to Serbian nationalism, had existed in Macedonia long before 1903.*

Milorad Godjevac, impressed by the success of the Bulgarian agents and *četnici* in converting the Macedonians to Bulgarian nationalism, proposed a similar plan of action by Serbia. In 1902 a group of Serbian nationalists, among them Godjevac and Luka Ćelović, organized the Executive Committee of the *četnik* organization. For a time Ćelović's own home served as headquarters, and he himself gave generous sums from his very considerable savings to the organization. A "Committee" (Komitski odbor) was organized at Vranje with branches at Leskovac and Niš. Because it hoped for friendly relations with Bulgaria, the Serbian government for a time discouraged this private action. But educators and teachers who suffered at the hands of the IMRO encouraged armed resistance and organized a *četa* (band) in March 1904 in the village of Poreč. The first sworn *četa,* led by an old *četnik,* Micko Sokolović-Pavlovski, captured Damian Gruev, chief of the Bitolj region and member of the Executive Committee of the IMRO in Sofia, popularly known as the "King of Macedonia" (Kral na Makedoniata).[62] The first *četa* organized outside Macedonia and led by Andjelko Aleksić entered Macedonia in 1903 and was completely wiped out by the IMRO in May 1904. The movement in favor of the *četnik* operations, despite setbacks in the field, gained support, and by the winter of 1904–5 the number of *četnici* in Macedonia and Old Serbia constituted "a small army." Young nationalists from various Serbian regions, including Austria-Hungary, flocked to Beograd to serve in the *čete.*[63]

The bands were trained at Beograd, Vranje, Leskovac, and Niš, and then dispatched to Macedonia by way of Vranje and Mrdare to areas of operation independent of one another. Two principal theaters of operation were the Skoplje and Bitolj regions. In each region there were a number of local "Serbian defense" committees. The *četnici* were usually clothed in ordinary peasant garb, carried various kinds of rifles and bombs, and were on the whole well trained. The *čete* were under military discipline, and those commanded by regular army officers were subject to war regulations.[64] The *četnici* fought against regular Turkish forces only when compelled to do so. The duty of the *četnici* was to protect Serb conationals from Turkish oppression and denationalization, to which they were being subjected by Bulgarian agents, and to "Serbianize" as many Macedonians as possible in order to justify future claims on Macedonian territory. In this way Serbian policy differed little, if any, from that pursued by the Bulgarian government. Serbian *četnik* activities in Macedonia had a difficult start, but gradually, as the bands increased in number, they were able not only to hold their own but also to dislodge the Bulgarian-controlled IMRO bands from several districts in Macedonia.

4. "THE BALKANS FOR THE BALKAN PEOPLES"

During the nineteenth century Serbo-Bulgarian union had often been discussed by thinkers and statesmen of both nations. South Slav patriots

---

* *Južna Srbija,* pp. 157–58. The author describes earlier operations by Serb-orientated *četnici* and gives the names of the principal leaders.

dreamed of a Yugoslav state that would stretch from the "peak of the Triglav to the Black Sea." At the beginning of 1867 a group of Bulgarian *émigrés* in Russia, Rumania, and Serbia, convinced that only by alliance with Serbia could they free their own people from the Turks, approached the Serbian government with this project in mind. A treaty was drafted on April 5, 1867, which provided for the "brotherly unification of Serbs and Bulgars into a single Yugoslav kingdom" under the hereditary rule of the Serbian prince. Unfortunately, the untimely death of Prince Mihailo (May 29, 1868) prevented the execution of the treaty.[65]

In 1897 Bulgarian Premier Stoilov, harassed and worried by the Greco-Turkish war, proposed a treaty with the Serbian government under Djordje Simić, which accepted the proposal, on the advice of Russia, and the first Serbo-Bulgarian political treaty was concluded on February 19, 1897.[66] This was followed by a commercial treaty signed on March 6, 1897.[67] In accordance with the treaty the two parties agreed to maintain the status quo in the Balkans and to act in concert on all questions concerning their conationals in Turkey. They furthermore agreed not to obstruct each other's national, religious, and educational activities in the Ottoman Empire,[68] and to invite Prince Nikola of Montenegro to participate in the treaty. Russia was the only great power informed of the full text of a treaty which unfortunately brought no lasting results. The return of King Milan to Serbia in the same year, and the change in Serbian foreign policy resulting therefrom, precluded the possibility of sincere Serbo-Bulgarian co-operation. The Treaty of 1897 (*Ugodba*) remained, as one writer put it, but an empty expression of the desire of Serbian Radicals and Bulgarian Russophiles.[69]

After 1903 once again there was talk of mutual understanding and co-operation between the three Slavic states in the Balkans. Grujić and Montenegrin Foreign Minister Gavro Vuković met in September 1903 to discuss the Balkan situation, which they considered "catastrophic both for our people in Turkey and for the two Serbian states."[70] On January 17, 1904, on orders from Prince Nikola, Foreign Minister Vuković approached Premier Grujić with a proposal for an agreement between their two countries for co-operation in the Balkans. Vuković referred to recent Austrian activities, such as the militarization of Boka Kotorska and the frontier of Hercegovina, and felt that an agreement with Serbia was most urgent. Failing to reach an agreement, the two countries, said Vuković, would shirk their sacred responsibility to the Serbian people. The Serbian government accepted the Montenegrin overture and on February 10, 1904, proposed preliminary discussion on three points: that the two rulers would undertake to work in agreement and co-operate on the defense of the Serbian people and the furtherance of its interests; that they would accept the reform program of the Great Powers in European Turkey; and, should the reform program fail, the two rulers would adopt a position that would best serve the interests of the Serbian people.[71]

On February 10, 1904, the Montenegrin government accepted the Serbian proposal for an agreement, which meant that the two states would resist jointly any enemy action directed against either of them.[72] The negotiations between Montenegro and Serbia were the beginning of a broader scheme of

Balkan understanding which was to include Bulgaria, Greece, and possibly Turkey.

Before 1903 the Porte, under repeated pressure from the great powers, had made occasional concessions to the Balkan states in matters concerning religion and education. After 1903 the Porte sought understanding with the Balkan states. In 1904 relations with Greece were improved appreciably. Rumania was given some rights and favors in Macedonia by Turkey as a step toward friendly relations with that country.[73] In February 1904 the conviction prevailed in Constantinople that Austria-Hungary would at any moment invade Old Serbia. Some Turk officials, like Sali Pasha, who was deputy to the vali in Skoplje, urged united Balkan action against any Austro-Hungarian expansion. The sultan himself offered an alliance to Serbia and Montenegro twice in the course of 1904. In December he spoke to the Montenegrin minister of "the necessity for an understanding between Turkey, Serbia, and Montenegro for defense against the common enemy."[74] He also sounded out the Bulgarian government with the same object in mind.

The discussion between the Serbian states and Turkey did not materialize into an alliance, as a result of Russian interference in Beograd and because Turkey was assured by Germany that she should expect no unfriendly action from Austria-Hungary.[75]

During 1904–6 the Montenegrin prince on several occasions urged an understanding between Serbia, Montenegro, and Bulgaria. When Prince Ferdinand visited Cetinje in 1904, Nikola suggested that they work together as "eternal and permanent friends." He complained that the Bulgarians were not as sincere in dealing with him as they were in dealing with the Serbs, and he hoped the Serbs might be more reasonable in their territorial claims. Nikola expressed similar ideas to Bulgarian Minister Toshev on October 17, 1905, and said that "if our brother Serbs would be more modest in their demands there would be no special obstacle to reaching a lasting understanding."[76] The prince ridiculed the Serbian proposal for division of Macedonia into areas destined for annexation by the several Balkan states, and urged first of all an understanding among the three countries which might provide a basis for a broader Balkan alliance. The Russians, said he, "instead of strengthening the Slavic nations in the Balkans, go off to be defeated by the Japanese, and leave the Austrians and Italians to intrigue and sow discord among the Slavs."[77]

On October 30 Nikola invited Toshev for a discussion, and again suggested an agreement between the three Slavic states, to which Greece would be added. The prince proposed a meeting of the three Slav rulers somewhere on the Riviera. He would go to Rome to visit his daughter, he said, and from there would sail on his yacht to the Riviera, "where all three of us can meet: your prince, King Peter, and I." The prince added:

> To tell you the truth, my hope rests only in Prince Ferdinand, and should I agree with him, then old Nikola will discuss matters more firmly with Beograd . . . Turkey will view our position differently. With 300,000 Bulgarian, 200,000 Serbian, and 50,000 Montenegrin bayonets we shall represent a force that will kill any appetite our enemies might possess. Turkey will seek an understanding

with us under conditions which we shall dictate. The first of these conditions will be autonomy for Macedonia. There will then be no reason for Europe to interfere in Balkan affairs.[78]

In his discussion with Toshev, Nikola left the impression that he was laboring to make his son, Mirko, ruler of an autonomous Macedonia and possibly *mbret* (king) of Albania.

Accordingly, early in November 1905 Prince Nikola transmitted via Toshev a personal letter to Prince Ferdinand, repeating his plea for understanding among the three Slavic states and proposing a meeting. Ferdinand delayed his reply, and kept Toshev waiting in Sofia. A few weeks later Nikola's letter was published by the *Frankfurter Zeitung*. Toshev was unable to explain this indiscretion to Ferdinand, who was much angered by it. After three months Ferdinand decided to decline Nikola's invitation on the grounds that it was "untimely" and ordered Toshev back to Cetinje with a letter to that effect. Nikola showed no haste in receiving Toshev, and when he did finally receive him on February 15, 1906, he could not conceal his disappointment in the communication from Ferdinand.[79]

Prince Nikola, however, did not cease promoting a Balkan understanding. On October 22, 1906, he remarked to Toshev that peaceful work aimed toward solution of the Macedonian Question was unrealistic. He now opposed the idea of autonomy for Macedonia and suggested that the Macedonian problem be settled by arms. The eleventh hour was approaching, he said, and "if we are prepared and in agreement, each will be satisfied, each of us will gain something."[80] Thus more than once in the course of 1905 and 1906 Nikola urged a Bulgaro-Montenegrin alliance, but neither the Serbo-Montenegrin nor the Bulgaro-Montenegrin agreement materialized.[81]

Meanwhile Bulgaria had come to realize that the Macedonian problem could not be solved to her advantage by a revolution or a unilateral action. She thus resolved to adopt a policy of mutual accord with the Balkan states,[82] although Russia at the time discouraged Serbo-Bulgarian negotiations for fear that Austria-Hungary might seize them as a pretext for some undesirable action. The leading representatives of the Bulgarian-orientated Macedonian revolutionaries, General Tsonchev and Boris Sarafov, visited Beograd in December 1903 with a view toward an understanding between Serbia and Bulgaria.[83] In Bulgaria General Savov and Danev apparently favored this policy. The latter told the recently appointed Serbian minister, Jovan M. Jovanović, that Austria was their real enemy, and that she should be feared and not Turkey. The minister reported, on February 13, that the newly designated Bulgarian chargé d'affaires in Beograd hinted that he was setting out on a special mission, and added that the Bulgarians had at last come to realize that in case of disorders the same fate awaited Macedonia that had befallen Bosna.[84]

The Bulgarian government suspected Austria of plotting to take advantage of Russia's troubles in the Far East by occupying "the northern districts of Macedonia." For this reason the Bulgarians started treaty negotiations with Turkey and Serbia almost simultaneously. The agreement with Turkey, concluded on April 8, 1904, would, it was believed, deprive that power of a pretext for an attack on Bulgaria.

According to the Turko-Bulgarian agreement the Bulgarians promised "to prevent the formation of bands in their territory, to punish those who, after committing crimes in Turkey, took refuge in Bulgaria, and to prevent the sending of arms and explosives into Turkey." In return Turkey undertook "to carry out the Mürzsteg reforms, to grant a general amnesty to political offenders, to readmit refugees who during the past two years had fled to Bulgaria, and to restore their possessions." Other serious points of difference were to be examined by a special commission and settled to mutual satisfaction. Neither party to the agreement was sincere, and after a few months relations between them deteriorated again.[85]

5. SERBO-BULGARIAN *RAPPROCHEMENT*, 1904–5

On January 18, 1904, in an audience granted the Bulgarian attaché, H. G. Hesapchiev, King Peter expressed a strong desire for an understanding with Bulgaria.[86] Hesapchiev promptly transmitted Peter's sentiments to Sofia, and was authorized on January 31 to open preliminary discussions with Serbia with a view toward conclusion of a treaty of alliance and a military convention. On February 11 Hesapchiev had his first meeting with Nikola Pašić, who asked for concrete proposals by the Bulgarian government. Three weeks later Hesapchiev received detailed instructions, in the foreign minister's handwriting, so as to keep the discussions as secret as possible. The Bulgarian minister at Cetinje, Dimiter Rizov, was instructed to join Hesapchiev in Beograd for the formal discussions. The Serbs were represented at the conference begun on March 7 by Sava Grujić and Nikola Pašić.

Despite the fact that their interests were basically at variance, both sides made concessions, and an agreement was successfully reached. A Treaty of Alliance and a Treaty of Friendship were signed on March 30,[87] and a Final Protocol on the following day. After ratification, the treaties were exchanged in Sofia on April 29, 1904.[88]

As was to be expected, the question of Macedonia provided the principal stumbling block during the three weeks of negotiation. The Bulgarians proposed that the two states maintain peace, prevent foreign encroachment on Macedonia, support the reform project, and agree on what policy to adopt if the reform project should fail. They advocated the autonomy or independence of Macedonia.

Pašić, who had originally opposed creation of "still another Slavic state and nationality [Macedonian] in the Balkans," changed his position after the foreign powers adopted the Mürzsteg reform project; he was now ready to accept a separate Macedonia, provided it was not created at Serbia's expense. That is, he opposed the inclusion of the vilayet of Kosovo into Macedonia, which he wished to see go to Serbia and Montenegro if Turkey collapsed. By the same token, Pašić was ready to see the territory from the Mesta to the mouth of the Maritsa and possibly even the vilayet of Adrianople go to Bulgaria. According to Pašić, the vilayets of Salonika and Bitolj (Monastir) would constitute Macedonia, an autonomous region in which the Serbs and Bulgarians should enjoy equality. Autonomous Macedonia would be in a customs union with Serbia, and Salonika was to serve as a free port for Serbian exports and imports. Pašić reasoned that Old Serbia (vilayet of Kosovo) would compensate Serbia for Bulgaria's union with Eastern Rumelia and Greece's gain in Crete.[89]

The Bulgarians opposed the separation of the so-called Old Serbia from Macedonia because, among other reasons, it would be difficult to draw a boundary line. They wanted the question of Old Serbia left out of the negotiations; it would, they opined, resolve itself naturally in a few years. But Pašić insisted that before negotiations were continued the Bulgarians would have to agree that Old Serbia was not to be considered a constituent part of Macedonia.

The delimitation of the Macedonian territory proved to be a crucial problem. The Bulgarians stretched Macedonia to include almost all of Old Serbia, and limited the so-called Old Serbia to the *kaza* of Priština. The Serbs, equally stubborn, stretched Old Serbia and restricted Macedonia. After much debate, the Bulgarian delegates accepted the Serbian position, and the first article of the Treaty of Alliance stipulated that "Macedonia and Old Serbia" would include the vilayets of Salonika, Bitolj, and Kosovo. In principle, therefore, the Bulgarians agreed to the existence of "Old Serbia." The Final Protocol of March 31 further stipulated that the vilayet of Kosovo, referred to in Article I of the Treaty of Alliance, would include the Sandjak of Novi Pazar, at the time under Austro-Hungarian military occupation.[90]

The relationship of Montenegro and Russia to the Serbo-Bulgarian alliance seriously occupied the minds of the delegates. The Bulgarian delegates were anxious for a complete understanding among the Balkan Slavs, with Russia to be so informed, for they were sure of the concurrence of both Prince Ferdinand and the Russian tsar, who had earlier urged an agreement among the three Slavic states in the Balkans. In any case, Bulgaria's Hesapchiev was warned by the Russian representative at Beograd, Muraviev, that the "Serbs would consult Russia before they entered into any agreement with Bulgaria."[91] Pašić believed Russia would not oppose a defensive agreement between Bulgaria and Serbia, except perhaps certain details in the treaty and possibly the reference to the principle "the Balkans for the Balkan peoples." But so long as Russia's policy continued to be one of maintaining the status quo in the Balkans, Pašić believed it unlikely that Russia would approve an offensive alliance between Serbia and Bulgaria. Hesapchiev suggested that parts of the treaty likely to be repugnant to Russia be withheld from her. Since a Serbo-Bulgarian attack on the Ottoman Empire was contemplated only if the projected reforms in Macedonia failed, Hesapchiev suggested that the provision of the treaty providing for this contingency be kept secret. Pašić concurred and, ironically enough, suggested that Turkey might be admitted to the first portion of the agreement, which was defensive in character.[92]

Responsible individuals in Bulgaria and Serbia were convinced that no permanent reforms could be enforced in Turkey, that the reform scheme would prove but an additional source of trouble, and that, in the end, the whole Macedonian problem would have to be solved by the use of force. Hence it was necessary that any agreement between Serbia and Bulgaria should provide for such an eventuality, especially since both states viewed with grave apprehension Austro-Hungarian activities in Macedonia.

To convince the Serbs of their sincerity, the Bulgarians found it necessary to explain their concurrent talks in Constantinople. These talks, they said, came as a result of pressure from Macedonians living in Bulgaria, as Bulgaria's only motive was to prevent possible Turkish attack. Needless to say, suspicious Beograd saw in the discussions at Constantinople the desire of Bulgaria to settle the Macedonian Question to her own advantage by dealing directly with the Turks. Whatever the real Bulgarian objectives, negotiations with the Turks failed, allegedly because the Turks insisted that before they entered into any agreement Bulgarian activities must cease in Macedonia.[93] The Serbian minister in Sofia reported on April 30 that he could obtain no reliable information on the reported Turko-Bulgarian Military Convention, but that its existence was likely.[94]

For fear of an Austrian move, the Serbian government meanwhile had sent a special emissary to St. Petersburg to sound out the Russian government on the various Balkan questions. There were reports that the Dual Monarchy was making military preparations, that Russia had agreed to permit Austro-Hungarian troops to cross Serbia, and that if the Serbs cooperated, they would be given a part of Old Serbia. For some months there were rumors of an impending Austro-Hungarian military move in the Balkans, and there were hints that tended to substantiate the rumors. As a matter of fact, the Marquess of Lansdowne found it necessary to ask the Austrian ambassador, Count Mensdorff, if there was any truth in the rumor that "military preparations on a large scale were proceeding in Austria." Count Mensdorff would only say that he had heard reports "to that effect," but could not say whether they were true.[95]

As early as April 9, 1903, *Danzers Armee-Zeitung*, an influential Austrian military journal, discussed the possibility of an Austro-Hungarian descent into the valleys of the Vardar and the Drin, and on April 30 it hinted at possible Austrian action in case of the partition of Turkey. On May 7 the same journal suggested that Austria-Hungary should be entrusted with the role of pacifying Macedonia and Albania, and that if reforms failed, the Austrian army might be dispatched thither and partially supplied through "friendly Serbia." Similar suggestions appeared in the July 2 and August 6 issues, in which it was proposed that the Kosovo Plain serve as the principal base of operations, and that Mitrovica be taken and fortified "before the outbreak of hostilities." A military convention with Serbia was suggested because that country controlled the main communication artery from Beograd to Niš. In October and December *Danzers Armee-Zeitung* again advised action in Macedonia and Albania in order to follow "the natural line of monarchy's expansion."[96]

Many in Beograd interpreted the articles appearing in *Danzers Armee-Zeitung* as the official Austrian line of policy, especially since some of the articles were written by top-ranking and influential officers. During those trying days the Serbs were isolated and could not expect diplomatic support even from Russia. In September 1904 the Russian consul in Skoplje, Razumovski, complained to his Serbian colleague, Mihailo Ristić, that he was instructed not to go into the vilayet unless accompanied by the Austrian consul, and to co-operate closely with him.[97]

A statement made by Goluchowski on September 18–19, 1903, seemed to have justified Serbia's apprehensions; he said that he would "never allow the creation of a Greater Serbia or a Greater Montenegro" or "of Constantinople passing to Russia." Any of these developments would make it impossible "to govern Austria," because "the centrifugal Slav elements would tear her to pieces." He declared that "rather than allow either of these eventualities, Austria would appeal to the sword."[98] If the existing situation in the Balkans could not be maintained, Goluchowski explained that "Turkey must gradually 'as slowly as possible' be replaced by a system of autonomous states." Bulgaria, Rumania, and Greece would be allowed considerable territorial expansion, but Serbia would have to remain "weak" and Montenegro "little." An independent Albania was also envisaged.[99] The Austrian ambassador in Berlin, Count Szögyény, told Prince Lichnowsky, in March 1904, that Vienna would tolerate Bulgarian expansion, "though not aid it," but would not tolerate any expansion by Serbia.[100]

Serbia was not the only power that feared Austrian action at this time. Italy and France considered the Austrian attitude a warlike one. In February 1904 France sent a note to Vienna warning against any unilateral action in the Balkans. Goluchowski replied that no such action was contemplated, and in April 1904 assured Tittoni that Austria-Hungary was not planning on further territorial expansion.[101] Be that as it may, Tittoni promised Serbian Minister Milovanović that Italy would not recognize any changes in the Balkans which violated the Treaty of Berlin, unless such changes were agreed upon at a conference of the signatories. Tittoni also said he would insist that the Balkan powers be admitted to such a conference, and he later made a similar declaration in the Italian Parliament. The French ambassador in Rome, Camille Barrère, told Milovanović that the French would insist that no great power be allowed territorial aggrandizement in the Balkans.[102]

The Italian foreign minister was genuinely perturbed over the reports of possible Austro-Hungarian action in the Balkans. He told the Serbian minister that those reports were "unfortunately well founded."[103] On February 22, Bulgarian Premier Petrov said to the Serbian minister that on the basis of reports he received from Salonika and Skoplje it was Austria-Hungary that encouraged recent Albanian disturbances. The Serbian government received similar reports from Rome as well.[104] The French consul in Skoplje, Choublier, expressed open fear that Austria might occupy Old Serbia and Macedonia. At the same time the Serbs complained that the Austrian consul, Parra, through secret channels read all communications to and from the local Serbian consul.

The German states were apparently annoyed with the frequent Italian remonstrances. The German ambassador in Rome, Count Monts, felt that

Italy was following a line that would lead to war.[105] Bülow found it necessary to suppress the talk of an Austrian war with Italy, Serbia, and Rumania—talk which was widespread among "the fiery Magyars and restless general staff people" of Austria-Hungary.[106]

Official Austrian assurances that there would be no new conquests served to slacken the tension in European diplomatic circles. But that did not mean that Austria had definitely relinquished her expansionist policy in the Balkans. Austrian assurances were not enough to dispel the suspicion which she had built up. Consequently the idea of Balkan unity and a concerted Balkan effort to check Austrian expansion began to gain support in many prominent circles. Milovanović was one of the most outspoken exponents of that formula; he was sure there was no other effective way of handling the Austrian threat.[107] On March 18, 1904, Signor Avarna, the Italian ambassador at Vienna, reported that Austria-Hungary could not have been ignorant of the genuine hostility of the Radical party, which reflected the general sentiment of the Serbian kingdom. He then added that

the attempts made, for the last two months, by Serbia to come to an accord with Bulgaria in anticipation of future eventualities in the Balkans certainly provoke lively observations from the Austro-Hungarian representative at Beograd. But they are considered here, at least outwardly, with some indifference; since . . . Austria-Hungary knows full well that the rivalry existing between Serbia and Bulgaria, and their conflicting national aspirations, make the practical execution of such an accord unattainable.[108]

Avarna's observation might have been exaggerated somewhat for there were ample indications that Austria-Hungary feared a Serbo-Bulgaro-Montenegrin *rapprochement* and sought to keep the Balkan states apart.

6. THE RUSSIAN ATTITUDE

The Serbian special emissary who had been sent to St. Petersburg had meanwhile made inquiries of responsible representatives of the Imperial government regarding the position that the Russians would take in case of an Austrian invasion of Turkey through the Sandjak of Novi Pazar or through Serbia. Pašić's views regarding the Balkan question were contained in a letter of instruction he had drafted on March 14 for the minister in St. Petersburg, but which he possibly never dispatched.[109] In this letter he spoke of Austrian activities and military preparations along the Serbian frontier, and of rumors about the impending Austrian invasion of Macedonia through Serbia. He spoke of a reported agreement between Austria-Hungary and Russia, according to which Serbia would be obliged to permit passage of Austrian troops over Serbian territories. If Serbia co-operated voluntarily she was to be compensated with a part of Old Serbia.

Pašić felt it of utmost importance that the Serbian representative in Russia verify these various reports and ascertain Russia's policy. More concretely, Pašić desired to know if Serbia could rely on Russian military support should Austria invade Turkey through the Sandjak or through Serbia. If Russia for one reason or another was unable or unwilling to come to Serbia's assistance, Pašić wanted to know if Russia would object to an agreement between Austria-Hungary and Serbia that would offer Serbia territorial compensation, i.e., Old Serbia. Would Russia object to an agreement among the Balkan states for common resistance to Austro-Hungarian expansion into the Balkans? If Bulgarian occupation of Macedonia was opposed by the united efforts of the other Balkan states, including Turkey, what attitude would Russia take? These were some of the questions the Serbian minister was instructed to ask Count Lamsdorff.

Pašić finally added that "the best policy for us and for the Slavs as a whole would be that of the maintenance of peace at all costs and the preparation for defense should some European power attempt to take advantage of Russia's difficulties in the Far East." In line with this policy Pašić found that an understanding between Serbia and Bulgaria would be indispensable, but that it would not be achieved without Russian backing.

It was to Russia's interest, Pašić said, to prevent the inter-Balkan squabbles and to promote a Balkan *rapprochement*. "Time was precious," he said, because "Austria-Hungary might at any moment advance 'beyond Mitrovica,' and if that should occur, Serbia's hopes for independent statehood would vanish and Austria would become the master of the Balkans." Pašić advised the Russians not to appease Austria-Hungary in the Balkans, and to consult with Italy, France, and Great Britain, in whom they would find "powerful support" against Austria-Hungary's expansionism.[110]

The Serbs did not expect complete satisfaction from the Russians, who were still feeling their way in Beograd. The nature of the Russian attitude toward Serbia at this time has been a controversial subject. Some writers say the Russian policy regarding Serbia was one of secondary importance until Minister Hartwig arrived in Beograd in 1909. Before Hartwig's arrival, Russia played her Balkan policy with Bulgarian cards, and Serbia, "like a drumstick on a drum, was used mainly to support Russo-Bulgarian interests."[111] Many prominent Russians, such as Paul Miliûkov, the historian and statesman, believed that a strong Bulgaria would best serve Russia's interests in the Balkans, and for that reason pushed Bulgarian rather than Serbian national claims in the Balkans. "The annexation of Bosna and Hercegovina ended this policy" and brought Serbia into favor with Imperial Russia.[112] This characterization of Russia's policy toward Serbia is somewhat exaggerated. It is true that in 1904 there were in Russia many "Bulgarophile" statesmen and diplomats, but their influence on foreign policy was by no means preponderant.[113]

7. THE AUSTRIAN ATTITUDE

Even if Russia had sympathized with Serbia in early 1904 she was in no position to commit herself wholeheartedly to the Balkan problems. Pašić knew this and proceeded to explore various other possibilities which might bring his country security. In 1904 on different occasions he sought agreements with Bulgaria, Turkey, and Austria-Hungary. Because the greatest threat to Serbia's security came from Austria-Hungary, he considered an understanding with Bulgaria first on his agenda. Rumors of Austrian troop concentrations in Bosna, and the reorganization of the Austrian military command especially worried him. There were reports about suspicious activities of Austrian monitors on the Danube, and about the certainty that Austria-Hungary would exploit the opportunity offered by the Russo-Japanese war to push toward Salonika.

According to the Austrian minister, these rumors were all groundless. He writes that his country was determined "on continuing the conservative policy of reform in Macedonia jointly with Russia." He claims to have pacified Pašić and "induced him to publish an article in the semiofficial newspaper *Samouprava* which allayed the worst of the panic." Although the "reserve" maintained by the Russian, Gubastov, did not help matters very much, Dumba writes that he preferred Gubastov's policy to the "intrigues carried on by Charykov and the chargé d'affaires, Muraviev."[114]

The extent to which Dumba had succeeded "in pacifying" Pašić is hard to determine, but we do suddenly discover Pašić seeking an agreement with Austria-Hungary at the same time that discussions with Bulgaria were in progress. Serbia's friendship was obviously to go to the highest bidder, the country that offered the greatest benefits to Serbia's national aspirations. Dumba writes that

> In the course of the spring and summer of 1904 he [Pašić] broached the subject of his wish for a closer cooperation with the Habsburg Monarchy no less than three times. On each occasion he began with the assurance that he knew that Serbia had nothing to hope for in the west. The occupation of Bosna-Hercegovina had been arranged by the Great Powers in accordance with our desires and only depended upon us.
>
> Serbia's future lay in the south. If Austria-Hungary would bring about extension of the measures for the protection of the Serbs against the Albanians to the vilayets of Peć, Prizren, and Priština, and would promise Serbia that in the distant future when Macedonia was partitioned on the basis of nationalities such districts as were inhabited by a definite Serb majority should be given to the Kingdom of Serbia, he on his part would promise loyally to support our *status quo* policy of reform as against Turkey and even to arrange for an Austrophile Party to arise in Serbia!

Dumba says further that, contrary to his own wishes, he was unable "to follow up these suggestions," since his government was anxious above all "to confirm the entente with Russia; and any philanderings with a Balkan Power might have disturbed it."[115]

The Austrian minister, cognizant of the Bulgaro-Serbian *rapprochement*, questioned Pašić about it. He learned that the discussions between Serbia and Bulgaria centered on a fiscal union "as a precursor no doubt to a complete trade and customs union." Dumba warned that the economic discussions between the two Balkan states were "incompatible" with Austro-Hungarian commercial interests and its position "as the most favored nation in Bulgaria." Pašić explained that he had no desire "to tamper" with the Austro-Hungarian commercial treaty, and hinted at the possibility of "opening up larger districts for agricultural production by including Bulgaria." He favored "as far-reaching a union as possible" between Serbia and Bulgaria. For the present, however, he desired to come to an understanding with Austria on economic questions, which would prepare the ground for "a closer political *rapprochement* and for the elimination of the numerous causes of friction with Bulgaria."[116]

At the end of May, Pašić gave Dumba his "solemn assurance that he had made no political agreement with Bulgaria" regarding Macedonia, that Serbia would continue to adhere to the policy of status quo in the Balkans, and that she was hoping for an improvement of the lot of her conationals in Macedonia through the Mürzsteg reform program. The king's private secretary, however, told Dumba that delimitation of Bulgarian and Serbian spheres of interest in Macedonia had been a subject of discussion during the negotiations.[117]

8. THE SERBO-BULGARIAN TREATIES OF 1904

The two treaties with Bulgaria—the Treaty of Friendship and the Treaty of Alliance—were signed on March 30 (April 12, N.S.), and ratified and exchanged on April 29, 1904. The Final Protocol was signed on March 31 (April 13), 1904.[118] The Treaty of Friendship, dealing with cultural and economic matters, embodied principles and questions to be dealt with in subsequent treaties and conventions. The two states agreed (I) to permit free import of each other's products, maintain the same customs policy, and prepare for an eventual customs union (*Zollverein*); (II) to facilitate mutual trade exchange and transit by reducing freight and passenger rates; (III) to equalize their telegraph and postal rates and to introduce the Cyrillic alphabet into their telegraphic communications; (IV) to remove all restrictions on free travel by their respective citizens; (V) to conclude a judicial convention, enforce court decisions, and surrender criminals (*du droit commun*) and military runaways; and finally, (VI) to conclude a monetary convention for the establishment of the free circulation of their currencies and thereby facilitate trade exchange between their respective citizens. The agreement was to be made public only after consultations between the two states and was to go into force upon its ratification. The treaty could be terminated by mutual concurrence of the two allied governments.

The Treaty of Alliance consisted of a preamble and eight articles. The preamble stated that the two governments were "guided by the principle of 'the Balkans for the Balkan peoples,' and were imbued with a desire to safeguard the peace and security of their people, to preserve the territorial status quo on the Balkan peninsula, and to improve the conditions of their conationals in the Ottoman Empire." The two states agreed: (I) on the utility of the Mürzsteg reform scheme for the vilayets of Salonika, Bitolj, and Kosovo (Macedonia and Old Serbia), and on the advisability of striving for extension of the reforms to the vilayet of Adrianople, and of seeking an amelioration of the lot of their conationals; (II) to use every effort to maintain peace in the Balkans, and to defend themselves jointly with all the means in their power against any encroachment on their territorial integrity or national independence, from whatever quarter; (III) to oppose jointly any hostile act toward or occupation of any of the above-mentioned four vilayets;

(IV) to conclude in connection with Articles II and III a special military convention, which would cover all possible eventualities; (V) to prepare for full solidarity among the Balkan Slavs and to create favorable conditions for a direct understanding between Serbia and Montenegro, and when the question of Albania should arise, to support a solution favorable to the interests of Montenegro; (VI) to treat and decide in concert all questions which in content or spirit fell within the treaty; (VII) to submit to the Russian tsar for final arbitration all controversial questions, and in case the tsar failed to make a decision, to submit them to the Permanent Court of Arbitration at The Hague. Finally, it was agreed (VIII) that the Treaty of Alliance would remain secret but might be communicated to another power if the two governments so agreed. In five years the treaty might be revised if the signatories found it necessary. The treaty would go into force upon its ratification.

The concluding protocol declared that the Treaty of Friendship, which contained the provisions of a cultural and economic character, might be made public under specific stipulations. The Treaty of Alliance, which contained political and military provisions, would remain secret. The phrase "to conduct the same customs policies" in Article I of the Treaty of Friendship meant "so far as the existing trade treaties of the two states permit." A supplement to Article III of the Treaty of Friendship was added, to the effect that the two states would in due time take joint steps with the Russian government with the view of establishing direct telegraphic communications between Russia and Bulgaria—if possible, in the Cyrillic alphabet.

The protocol likewise explained some portions of the Treaty of Alliance. The vilayet of Kosovo (Article I) was understood to include the Sandjak of Novi Pazar. A supplement to Article I explained that the two powers would strive for establishment of mutual tolerance between their conationals in the Ottoman Empire. The territory of Albania (Article V) was defined as that embracing the vilayets of Scutari (Skadar) and Ioannina.

Finally, the protocol stated that the treaties be written in both Bulgarian and Serbian, that after ratification the original copies be kept in the private archives of King Peter and Prince Ferdinand, and that a copy of the Treaty of Friendship should be deposited in the archives of the respective ministries of Foreign Affairs. The treaties were ratified and exchanged on April 29, 1904, in Sofia. In due time the Serbo-Bulgarian agreements were transmitted to the Russian government and to the Montenegrin prince.[119]

Thus the first concrete step had been taken toward the establishment of a Serbo-Bulgarian political union and an eventual *Zollverein* between the two countries.

9. SERBO-BULGARIAN RELATIONS FOLLOWING THE TREATIES

The frequent meetings between King Peter and Prince Ferdinand of Bulgaria were the cause of many rumors.* The first meeting took place at

* Many of the Skupština deputies were perturbed especially because Foreign Minister Pašić was secretive about his discussions with the Bulgarians. See for example interpellations and discussions regarding relations with Bulgaria, *N.S.,* I (1903-4), 322 ff.

the railway depot at Niš on May 15, 1904, when Peter induced Ferdinand, who was passing through, to stop off for a few hours.

The discussions in Belgrade had not then got to the stage when this interview might have led to the conclusion of any binding agreement. The impatience of the two rulers in this case outran events. King Peter's wish to make a display, his desire to greet at least a non-sovereign prince on Serbian soil, possibly curiosity on the part of Ferdinand, conspired to make of the Niš interview a sensational and surprising affair.

The King, who loved display, was accompanied by three ministers as well as by generals and aids-de-camp who were only there to create a brilliant background. There was neither time nor occasion for a political conference at that moment, as I was assured by eyewitnesses, and even the toasts exchanged were distinctly on the chilly side and contained no reference to a political *rapprochement*.[120]

This surprising development was closely observed by the foreign representatives. They knew of the negotiations between Serbia and Bulgaria but did not know their nature and scope. The French minister at Beograd reported that at Niš the two rulers exchanged views on the Balkan situation and discussed the policy to be pursued in case Austria-Hungary as a result of Russia's embarrassment in the Far East should descend on Salonika.[121] The Italians were pleased over the Serbo-Bulgarian *rapprochement*. Foreign Minister Tittoni wrote to Chargé d'Affaires Romano Avezzana in Beograd that "these accords, which are destined to cement further the economic relations between the states and to eliminate occasions for future friction in their reciprocal relations, are elements and guaranties of peace and . . . in the general interest of the powers concerned in Balkan questions. Thus, for our part, we cannot but be pleased at the good intention of which these negotiations give evidence."[122] Although not aware of the exact nature of the agreements between Serbia and Bulgaria, Avezzana expressed to Pašić in the name of the Italian government "the pleasure which it had caused and the hope that other accords, such as that of a tariff union, would follow." Pašić admitted that such a union was being considered, but pointed out the insuperable difficulties which obstructed its final realization.[123] In Rome at the same time, Tittoni expressed to Serbian Minister Milovanović his satisfaction at the Serbo-Bulgarian *rapprochement*. Avezzana reported in some detail King Peter's meeting on May 15 at Niš with Prince Ferdinand, and noted that the two rulers, accompanied by their respective ministers, seemed highly pleased with their conversations. No written engagements were undertaken, he said, but formal assurances for common action in the maintenance of peace in the Balkans were exchanged.[124]

Friendly relations between the sovereigns of the two Balkan states were manifested once more on June 18, 1904, when, upon returning to his own country, Ferdinand again passed through Beograd and had another interview with Peter in the presence of Pašić. "Both sovereigns were affectionately embarrassed when the king climbed into the princely car and accompanied the prince up to Rešnik, a few kilometers away from the Serbian capital."[125] The Far Eastern situation and the question of military credits before the Austro-Hungarian Delegation also tended to bring the Slavic Balkan states together.[126] On October 17, 1904, King Peter, accompanied by Grujić and Pašić, arrived in Sofia.[127] He was received by Prince Ferdinand, the cabinet, and several prominent citizens. Before his arrival there a semiofficial announcement was issued at Beograd and Niš in which the activity of the revolutionary bands in Macedonia was denounced, and assurances made that the governments of Sofia and Beograd, with the aid of the Great Powers administering the reforms, would seek an end to their crimes.[128] The reception at Sofia was unusually magnificent, calculated to show the identity of interests between the two peoples, as well as the military preparedness of Bulgaria. A gala dinnner was held at the court, and a brilliant ball at the military academy. Many toasts were drunk in the name of the "necessity for intimate and brotherly unity." On October 18 a huge military parade was staged in Sofia by the local garrison, after which Peter returned to Beograd.[129] Needless to say, the *comitadji* bands in Bulgaria and opponents of the Russophile policy regarded all these new developments with disgust.

The French minister at Sofia was quite certain that nothing very important had transpired there, that the discussion was relative only to tariff modification, that the need for a *rapprochement* was merely pointed out in passing, and that simple assurances of good will were exchanged. He was sure that Macedonia was not discussed, since "the Bulgarians consider Macedonia as their home and do not want anyone to interfere."[130] General Petrov of Bulgaria made a public announcement that Peter's trip had no political significance,[131] but agents of Austria-Hungary and Rumania had learned in June from reliable "Bulgarian sources" that Serbia and Bulgaria at least had plans for a customs union.[132]

Nikola Pašić kept the treaty with Bulgaria in the greatest secrecy. The cabinet members knew only that part of the agreement which dealt with cultural and economic matters and which was discussed in cabinet meetings. But before the year 1904 expired, the existence of the secret treaty had become known.[133] Who was responsible for divulging the secret? Both sides accused each other of betrayal of confidence and the question remains one of controversy. The Serbian side of the story is that Bulgaria was never sincere about the treaty, and that she never for a moment abandoned her objective of eliminating Serbian influence in Macedonia. The Serbs alleged that Bulgarian bands were in touch with Austrian agents all the while. The Macedonian leaders, Boris Sarafov and P. N. Daskalov, were said to have been assured by the Austrian agent, Müller, that his government did not object to an autonomous Macedonia or a "Greater" Bulgaria, but that it definitely opposed partition of Macedonia and the slightest territorial aggrandizement by Serbia.[134]

Damian Gruev, captured by Serbian *četnici*, purportedly admitted that the Austro-Hungarian consul in Bitolj had advised the Bulgarians "to prevent Serbian penetration of the Kičevo district." The Serbs accused Bulgarian representative Toshev of posting the Austrian vice-consul in Bitolj on the movement of the Serbian irregulars. Late in September the Beograd press reported a number of acts of violence perpetrated by the Bulgarian bands on the Serbian populace, although the Bulgarian Foreign Ministry issued a statement repudiating the charges.[135] Thus hope for co-operation and friendship anticipated from the secret treaty with Bulgaria disappeared into thin air. This is not to imply that Serbian leaders were sacrosanct in their dealings with the Bulgarians; the Serbs contributed to the revival of Macedonian anarchy.

The Serbian government had apparently accepted the cultural and economic portion of the treaty with certain reservations, fearing that the customs union might induce Austria-Hungary to curb Serbian livestock exports. Some members of the Serbian government, including Finance Minister Lazar Paču, found that Article I of the Treaty of Friendship, referring to the *Zollverein*, expressed only "the principle toward which it was necessary to strive," and that Article I required further study. Pašić worked two whole days (June 22–23) to formulate the official Serbian attitude, which was that

Article I should not be so interpreted as to expect either state to sacrifice its vital interests and risk economic and financial collapse. The idea was not to allow the treaty to lapse, nor does it involve the principle of the most favored nation clause. The treaty directs the two states to work gradually and as far as possible without injury to their interests in the direction of uniform financial regulations and for preparation of the ground for a customs union.[136]

Pašić felt that the two states should move toward a customs union "cautiously and carefully," in order to avert any perilous crises. The first step, he said, was to make tariffs uniform in the two countries. The Serbian tariff system was the more modern, and Pašić thought that it was a better model than the Bulgarian ad valorem customs tariff. Consequently, he suggested that Bulgaria should be the one to make changes, so that both countries might have the same classification of articles and the same tariff rates.[137]

Moreover, the Serbs recommended, in reference to Austria and the difficulties which she could make in the way of exporting livestock from Serbia, that Bulgaria join as soon as possible the circle of powers mutually bound by veterinary laws and agreements. In conclusion Pašić remarked:

It would be necessary to take up regulation of monopolies and sales taxes in order that both states have the same monopolies and sales taxes on the same items and at the same level, because otherwise one can hardly think of a customs union.[138]

On July 7 the Bulgarian government agreed that the texts of the treaties be communicated to Prince Nikola of Montenegro on the same day by the Serbian and Bulgarian ministers at Cetinje, neither of the ministers being allowed to see the contents. The Russian government was informed of the texts of the treaties through its representatives at Sofia and Beograd on September 15, together with the Serbian reservations about the customs union which were approved by Bulgaria.[139]

10. THE BALUGDŽIĆ AFFAIR

On December 16, 1904, Prince Ferdinand had a half-hour meeting with King Peter at the Beograd railway station. Three days later the *Neue Freie*

Presse published a telegraphic dispatch from Beograd which purported to contain the essence of the discussions between the two rulers.* The report was so accurate that it could have come only from someone close to the Serbian king. Suspicion was cast on Balugdžić, who served in the dual capacity of Peter's secretary and correspondent of the *Neue Freie Presse*.

The evidence suggested that Peter might have deliberately passed on the information; the Bulgarian prince was angered by this disclosure and was particularly incensed by a reference to his "two-faced Macedonian policy." On December 21 he dispatched the clipping from the *Neue Freie Presse* to Hesapchiev, together with a note to the effect that hereafter he would have "not a shadow of confidence in the Serbian government, not an atom of desire for a new meeting. With what took place [the Serbs] have themselves cut the thread which linked us."[140] Hesapchiev complained to Pašić, who was apologetic, but did not resort to the drastic step of dismissing Balugdžić. It was only when Balugdžić began to criticize Pašić through the use of the press that he was summoned to court and sentenced to a year's imprisonment. But the slippery Balugdžić succeeded in fleeing to Austria without serving his sentence.[141]

Thus by early 1905 the chances for a lasting understanding between Bulgaria and Serbia had diminished. The Serbian consul in Skoplje obtained documentary evidence of co-operation between the Austrian consul, Parra, and the Bulgarian bands. The Bulgarian premier, Racha Petrov, told the Serbian minister in Sofia, on January 28, 1905, that the Austrians had indicated on many occasions that they had no objection to Bulgarian activity in Macedonia and would be ready to support the Bulgarian cause. Petrov admitted that the IMRO had contact with the Austrians.[142] Another Bulgarian, Danailo Rizov, admitted also that there existed a permanent liaison between Bulgarian agents and the Austrian consulate. The Austrian civil agent, said Rizov, was thoroughly informed of the IMRO activities.[143] The Russian consul at Skoplje, Belaev, noted that the Austro-Hungarian consul and officers opposed the Serbs and were "always exclusively behind the Bulgarians."[144]

Yet despite the Balugdžić incident and conflicts in Macedonia, diplomatic relations between Bulgaria and Serbia were sufficiently correct to allow the negotiation of a trade treaty a few months after Peter's visit to Sofia.[145] The delegates were chosen and discussions initiated at Beograd in the beginning of March 1905. The Bulgarians favored immediate conclusion of a customs union, whereas the Serbian delegates held to the reservations their government had stipulated in the Treaty of Friendship. For the Serbs, the customs union was to be the goal toward which "it would be necessary to strive" but not a means immediately practicable. The Bulgarians, as we mentioned earlier, had accepted these Serbian reservations, but on this occasion pressed for the customs union. In the end, the Serbian government agreed to negotiate concerning the customs union, but solely "as a test" (*za opit*), to see what obstacles there would be in reaching such an agreement.[146]

---

* *N.F.P.*, Nr. 14486 (December 20, 1904), p. 12.

Meanwhile, the Grujić-Pašić cabinet was replaced by that of Ljuba Stojanović and his Independent Radicals. The new cabinet agreed to sign the already drafted agreement for a customs union, provided it was not submitted to the respective parliaments for ratification but that it remain in the archives and serve as a historical document which might be utilized under more favorable conditions in the distant future.[147] A customs union agreed upon on June 22, 1905, was to go into effect March 1, 1906, and expire on March 1, 1917, when it would be replaced "by a common tariff schedule for both countries."[148] The agreement was to remain a secret arrangement; it was accepted by Serbia with the reservation that it not go into effect until possible modifications of the text were made as a result of new trade treaties to be concluded with certain other states.[149] It was believed that both states would have by March 1, 1906, successfully concluded their treaties with Austria-Hungary.

Disregarding its promise the Bulgarian government suddenly decided, "for somewhat questionable motives," to submit the customs agreement with Serbia to the Sobranie.* The Sobranie approved the agreement by acclamation on December 20, 1905. Once the news reached Austria-Hungary, she promptly closed her borders to Serbian livestock. The press of the monarchy attacked both Serbia and Bulgaria, charging that the customs agreement was directed against her. Bulgaria was reminded that the Treaty of Berlin did not grant her the right to conclude customs unions.[150] The Austro-Hungarian attitude regarding the Serbo-Bulgarian Customs Union and the crisis it caused in Serbian relations with Austria-Hungary will be discussed in a later chapter.

The brief period of Serbo-Bulgarian diplomatic cordiality ended in 1905, but the idea of a Balkan union persisted. For the most part, the Bulgarians continued a policy aimed toward Macedonian autonomy, while the Serbs and Greeks sought the division of Macedonia into "spheres of influence." Intrigues and band warfare continued; Beograd still feared an Austro-Hungarian invasion of Macedonia, especially after learning that the monarchy's agents were in contact with the Bulgarian guerrilla bands and organizations. The Serbian minister at Sofia reported that Vienna had solicited Bulgarian disinterestedness in the affairs of the Sandjak of Skoplje (Úsküb). In return, Bulgaria was promised territory in the eastern part of the three European vilayets.[151]

The Italian minister in Beograd complained to his German colleague that "Austria was systematically working to make conditions in the Balkans bad and was the intellectual originator of the attacks of Bulgarian bands on the Serbian population."[152] In response to the complaints of the Italian minister,

---

* According to Jovan M. Jovanović, Bulgaria submitted to the Sobranie this "archival document without practical significance" with the intention of frightening Turkey (*Borba*, p. 90). The official Bulgarian explanation was that they wished to ratify the agreement before the existing treaty with Serbia expired on January 1, 1906 (Helmreich, p. 7). Iaranov says that the agreement failed because of Austro-Hungarian opposition and because Serbia was not in earnest about it but merely wished to use it as pressure on Austria-Hungary (Iaranov, *Stopanskata politika na Bŭlgariĭa*, pp. 167–68).

Germany's Chancellor von Bülow on October 26, 1904, told his minister at Beograd there was no evidence that Austria-Hungary was planning an invasion of Turkish territory in the direction of Salonika, but that her "self-preservation" required prevention of an alliance of the Balkan Slavs.[153] Taking advantage of the new anti-Austrian campaign in Serbia, a group of Hungarian statesmen spent several "mysterious" hours in Beograd, where apparently they promised to resist the monarchy's aggressive policy toward Macedonia.[154] However, there was some speculation at this time that Germany was encouraging Hungarian agitation in an effort somehow to supplant Austrian influence in the Balkans. Considerable significance was attached to the German emperor's felicitations to King Peter on his name day.[155]

In Macedonia meanwhile conditions went from bad to worse. The reform scheme lacked genuine backing from both the Great Powers and the Balkan states. In February 1905 Austria and Russia demanded that the Balkan states prohibit recruiting of guerrilla bands in their territories.[156] On April 10, 1905, Vienna protested to Serbia against the activity of the četnik bands in Macedonia, which might prompt the Bulgarians "to incite the Albanians" to fresh massacres of the Serbs and compel the monarchy "against its wishes" to dispatch its troops into the area.[157] Several weeks later, in July 1905, the Beograd press screamed over the Albanian massacres of Serbs in Old Serbia and suggested that Austria-Hungary was behind them.

Serbian Foreign Minister Žujović regretted what he considered Bulgarian lack of interest for common action in Macedonia. A joint stand by Bulgaria and Serbia was especially desired in face of the protests by the powers, who blamed the Balkan states for the excesses in Macedonia.[158] The Bulgarian government hesitated to associate itself with Serbia in any joint action which might be interpreted to mean that it recognized Serbian interests in Macedonia. In April 1905 a major conflict between Serbian and Bulgarian guerrilla bands in Macedonia took place.[159] But after 1903 Bulgarian influence waned in Macedonia, and by 1906 this became a matter of serious concern to the Bulgarian government, being openly discussed in the Sobranie.[160]

11. RELATIONS WITH ITALY

The international situation of Serbia during 1904 and 1905 was, to say the least, most unenviable. The pressure on Serbia by Austria-Hungary increased as Russia, faced with internal and foreign troubles, absented herself from the Balkans. But in the absence of Russia the Serbs saw the possibility of using Italy as a counterweight against Austria-Hungary. Relations with Italy had been very cordial for some time, and the Italian king called King Peter his *"beau-frère."*[161] The French minister noted growing Italian influence at Beograd:

The Balkan states for which Austria planned servitude or absorption were drawing closer together; Bulgaria had come to an agreement with Turkey; the king of Serbia had, under the auspices of the prince of Montenegro, established closer ties with Prince Ferdinand. In a word, a spontaneous movement for *rapprochement* had begun among these nations. To offset any Austrian attempt to profit by the Russian reverses the Balkan countries were looking toward Rome. Together they were trying to push the Italian government into seizing the political initiative in support of the maintenance of the status quo. One could see at work here the capable personality of the Serbian minister, M. Milovanović, who had won over political circles in Rome.[162]

Milovanović did indeed exert great pressure on Italy to seize the political initiative in the Balkans. On December 29, 1904, and again on January 21, 1905, Milovanović sent to the Foreign Office long reports on his discussions with Tittoni and with foreign diplomats in Rome. He spoke of Italian determination to stop any future Austrian expansion, but saw in the Serbo-Bulgarian understanding the best safeguard against Austria-Hungary. Tittoni declared himself against "any underhand policy such as might be contrary to the Triplice," though he did not think that intimacy between the Balkan states should embitter relations between Vienna and Beograd. He summarized his government's policy as follows:

In these conditions Italy, who is utterly opposed to any territorial occupation, and aims, at the present political moment, at a loyal maintenance of the status quo, becomes the natural ally of the tendencies and forces, however variously induced, which indirectly co-operate to this end; and therefore I regard with approval the more intimate union that has grown up between Serbia, Bulgaria, and Montenegro.[163]

In the course of 1903 Tittoni had on several occasions told Milovanović that his government desired to see an agreement between the Balkan states, particularly between Serbia and Montenegro. For this reason and also from his own conviction, Milovanović frequently recommended the policy of *rapprochement* between the Balkan states. Tittoni had apparently urged the same course of policy to Bulgarian Minister Minchovich in Rome.[164]

At the beginning of 1905 Pašić inquired of the Italian government whether it would back Bulgaria and Serbia should they resist an Austro-Hungarian drive to Salonika. Italian backing, he reasoned, would induce all the Balkan powers, including Turkey, to join in a united front. Pašić was no fool; he was not unaware of the fact that Italy's opposition to Austro-Hungarian expansion in the Balkans sprang only from the fact that Italy had no share in it. It was likely that in supporting Serbo-Bulgarian understanding, Italy wished "to force Austria into an agreement" at the expense of the Balkan states.[165]

On one occasion when he was angered by Italian claims of certain Macedonian districts for the Albanians, Pašić cried out, "By God, we shall fight anyone who attempts to take those lands, even if it be our brother by birth. If our struggle with Austria is a difficult one, it will not be so difficult with the Italians. Let Italy know that when the time comes for dividing us and breaking the Balkan peninsula to pieces, we shall prefer to be swallowed up by Austria rather than by any other country." He went on to urge Italy to co-operate with the Balkan peoples, since otherwise no one except the Germanic powers stood to gain in the Balkans. "If we cannot remain free," he said, "then we shall join our enslaved brothers and share their fate until better days come. In that way we shall at least become a unified mass of some ten to twenty million people stretching from Trieste to Salonika."[166]

Pasıc particularly resented Tittoni's statement in the Chamber of Deputies on May 12, 1905, that after the administrative reform of Macedonia was carried out "those districts which are of a prevailingly Albanian character and are today added to the Macedonian vilayets will have to be restored to Albania proper." This would have meant the inclusion of Peć and Prizren, two cities so very prominent in Serbian history, into Albania. Pašić then posed a question: "Is it not better to defend ourselves jointly with Turkey from enemies who are supposedly coming to help us, but in reality aim to steal our home?"[167]

On July 8, 1905, *Danzers Armee Zeitung* was at it again. It warned that if Serbia did not peacefully co-operate with Austria-Hungary if the latter undertook operations in the Balkans, then Serbia should be treated as an enemy and the monarchy should "raise [her] already drawn sword against [Serbia]." That would result in war with Serbia and temporary postponement of the Macedonian Question. After Serbia was annihilated the monarchy should undertake "a further offensive against Macedonia." The same journal again referred to a possible creation of "Greater Bulgaria," including a major portion of Macedonia, of an independent Albania, and of absorption of Serbia and Montenegro by Austria-Hungary. Incorporation of the two neighboring states, it was argued, represented a forward step in "historical development"—the unification of peoples "speaking a common tongue."[168] Such unification would bring all South Slavs under the Austro-Hungarian Crown, an idea subsequently toyed with by Conrad von Hötzendorff, chief of the general staff.

To make certain that the ethnic ratio of peoples and districts claimed by Serbia remained intact, the Serbian government contemplated sending a note to the signatories of the Treaty of Berlin, with a demand that they guarantee the integrity of all regions subject to the reforms. The government was primarily interested in acquiring undisputed future possession of Old Serbia (the vilayet of Kosovo). The first step was to insist on extension of the reforms to the whole Kosovo vilayet, originally excluded from the reforms, at Austria-Hungary's insistence. Should the powers reorganize the reform region into ethnic districts, Serbia planned to ask permission to annex Old Serbia. Meanwhile, the cabinet of Pašić fell and was succeeded by the cabinet of Independent Radicals under Ljubomir Stojanović.

The new government decided on a more cautious policy regarding Old Serbia, fearing that if Serbia asked extension of the reforms to, and future annexation of, Old Serbia, Austria-Hungary might counter with a request that the predominantly Albanian part of the Kosovo vilayet be added to Albania, probably even before reforms were extended to the Kosovo vilayet.[169]

The Italians promptly inquired if the change of government in Beograd affected Serbia's foreign policy, especially with regard to Bulgaria. The Italian minister at Beograd, Marquis Guiccioli, had been instructed to work on the Serbo-Bulgarian understanding.[170] Because of parliamentary elections scheduled for July 10, 1905, the government of the Independent Radicals was unable to give an immediate response to Italy, or to Bulgaria, which had also been concerned by the change at Beograd. Prime Minister Ljubomir Stojanović promised that if the elections came out in the government's favor, his action would be governed by Serbian interests; he warned, however, that despite a strong desire for co-operation, if there were no real basis for common action, his government would not concern itself with empty formulas.[171] In the parliamentary elections the government of the Independent Radicals received a majority of only one vote, in spite of which the party decided to rule as long as it could.

In August 1905 Serbian diplomats abroad were called home for consultation on the country's foreign relations.[172] Many specific issues were discussed, such as the text of a note to the powers stating Serbian grievances with regard to conditions in Old Serbia and Macedonia. It was suggested that the Serbian government enter into negotiations with the Albanians, preferably with Catholics, for the purpose of ending Albanian attacks on the Serbs. Besides the Macedonian Question, the diplomats discussed all other phases of foreign relations. The conferees decided that a concordat with the Holy See should be concluded in order to weaken separatist tendencies caused by religious differences among the Yugoslavs, thereby depriving Austria-Hungary of further opportunity for sowing discord between the Catholic Croats and the Orthodox Serbs.[173]

Other problems discussed at the conference included a possible *rapprochement* with Bulgaria, a proposed treaty of alliance with Rumania and Greece, relations with Turkey, and King Peter's projected journey to St. Petersburg. With reference to the recent visit to Beograd of the Hungarian statesmen, the Serbian government decided that it could not favor either member of the Dual Monarchy—Hungary or Austria. It was agreed that in case Serbia's national security should be menaced, the government would have to depend for support on Italy and France because relations with Great Britain had not yet been restored and Russia was preoccupied in the Far East.[174]

12. THE BALKAN TURMOIL CONTINUES

After Balugdzıc indiscreetly allowed the subject of the discussion between Peter and Ferdinand to leak out, relations between Serbia and Bulgaria deteriorated. In a *pro memoria* on Serbo-Bulgarian relations prepared by the Bulgarian government, Pašić was held primarily responsible for the new conflict between Serbians and Bulgarians in Macedonia. The Serbian government rejected the accusation and pointed out that it was in fact Pašić who had striven for Serbo-Bulgarian *rapprochement*. Foreign diplomats were warned by the Serbs to read the Bulgarian *pro memoria* with reservations.[175]

The successors of Pašić retained his policy of friendship with Bulgaria, and the Stojanović government declared that its policy rested on the principle of "the Balkans for the Balkan peoples." Leaving aside the question of Macedonian autonomy, on which no real agreement was possible, the government planned to insist on the extension of the Mürzsteg program of reforms to include Old Serbia and the vilayet of Adrianople. In this connection it hoped to obtain Rumanian backing.

The conditions in Old Serbia were so bad that emigration had markedly increased during the first half of 1905. Simić, minister at Sofia, was convinced at this time that the lamentable conditions in Old Serbia were largely caused by Austro-Hungarian intrigues. The Serbian government called the attention of the powers to the sorry state of affairs in Old Serbia and Macedonia, and warned the Porte that the Albanians in Old Serbia were serving Austrian interests.[176] On September 8, 1905, the Albanians attacked a Serbian frontier station (Ugljarski Krš) on the Serbian side of the border and murdered several officials. A week later the Serbian government informed the Austrian Foreign Office of this renewed Albanian lawlessness; Goluchowski replied that he would instruct his ambassador in Constantinople to request the Porte to establish order.[177] The Serbs tried to persuade Sofia to make a joint appeal to the powers for an extension of the Mürzsteg program of reforms to include the Kosovo and Adrianople vilayets, and for a guaranty of the integrity of the reform region in European Turkey. The Bulgarians agreed in principle with the idea of appealing to the powers but declined to appeal jointly with Serbia, in order to avoid action that might be construed as recognition of Serbia's "equal right" to Macedonia.[178]

In his speech from the throne in November 1905, King Peter reiterated his desire to maintain friendly relations with Austria-Hungary and Russia. His general outline of foreign policy was accepted by the Skupština, but it reminded the monarch of the losses in prestige and the human sacrifices on the "southern borders" as a result of "unjustifiable attacks by foreigners." It declared that in Macedonia and Old Serbia the very existence of the Serbian people was at stake. To improve conditions in those regions, the Skupština asked for extension of the Macedonian reforms to other regions inhabited by Serbs hitherto not included—the vilayet of Kosovo.

The Mürzsteg scheme of reforms brought no improvement in Turkey. On November 15, 1905, the Great Powers warned the Balkan states not to obstruct the work of the reforms and for the last time demanded Turkey's acceptance of the financial reforms.[179] On December 8 the Serbian government replied that its position as well as that of Serbs living in Turkey would be made easier if the reforms were extended to the mixed Serbian-Albanian districts. Although some foreign representatives, including Buchanan, English minister in Sofia, found the Serbian proposal well founded, it was not adopted because of Austrian opposition.[180] It was not until the naval demonstration by the powers on November 27 that Turkey gave in and the sultan finally accepted the financial reforms on December 23, 1905.[181]

The speed with which Austria acted in connection with the financial reforms precipitated new suspicions. Tittoni told Milovanović that "there existed in Vienna a very strong current in favor of seeking an excuse to intervene in the Balkans and that, although he did not believe this current would prevail, it was nevertheless necessary to be prepared for any contingencies." French Prime Minister Rouvier told the Serbian minister in Paris, Vesnić, he had the impression that "one of the powers would not be unwilling to mix more openly and more actively in the affairs of European Turkey, but that this ought certainly to be prevented."[182]

In early December 1905 Russia and Austria-Hungary sent notes to Serbia, Bulgaria, and Greece, blaming them for the failure of reforms and requesting them to use their influence in ending disturbances in the "three vilayets," and in exchange promising to endeavor seriously to improve the lot of the Christians. The two powers warned the Balkan states that they were determined, if need be, to use force in order to maintain the status quo in the Balkans.[183]

Foreign Minister Jovan Žujović in a conversation with foreign representatives stated that if the status of Turkish territory was in any way altered Serbia would "change her attitude of peaceful reserve." The German minister found this statement too strong and advised Žujović to put the idea in a milder form so as not to arouse Austria. Žujović retorted that should Austria-Hungary obtain a mandate for "the pacification" of Old Serbia and Macedonia, that would serve as a signal for "a general revolution" in those provinces. In Žujović's opinion the Balkan states alone were capable of peacefully settling the Macedonian Question, and he added that if Serbia alone, or jointly with Montenegro, was charged with the administration of Old Serbia, order would soon be established there.[184] On December 16, 1905, Žujović told the Russian and Austrian ministers that Serbia would protest against any new changes in "present relations between the states and nationalities in the Balkans" and that Serbia would seek to restore the balance of power which had been "on several occasions altered to the detriment of the Serbian people."[185]

Once again the Serbs turned to the Bulgarians for a joint *démarche* to the powers, which would manifest the solidarity of their interests and aspirations.[186] The Bulgarian foreign minister, General Petrov, and the Serbian minister at Sofia, Simić, agreed on three points that should be included in the *démarche*. Serbia and Bulgaria would reject responsibility for conditions in Macedonia, which were to be blamed, not on rivalry and conflicts between the Balkan nationalities, but on the incompetence of the Ottoman administration. They would then declare that they did not menace the status quo. Finally, the two Balkan states would make it known that they had accepted the Mürzsteg program of reforms as the starting point for further action. Despite this preliminary agreement, the Bulgarian government again failed to conclude the negotiation and thereby associate itself with Serbia in the joint demands to the powers.[187]

The latest reforms in European Turkey accomplished as little as did the earlier ones. In 1907 the IMRO, although weakened by internal strife, was accused of preparing a new uprising in Macedonia that might prompt intervention of the powers. In anticipation of the uprising, the leaders of Serb and Greek organizations countered with preparations of their own.[188] The manifestations of Serbo-Bulgarian friendliness in 1904–5 had given way to open hostility by 1907–8. Under Austro-Hungarian pressure, the customs treaty with Bulgaria had been canceled. Serbia, therefore, lost all the privileges that had been granted her by the treaty, and traffic through the Bulgarian ports of Burgas and Varna was rapidly reduced.[189] Attacks against Serbia in the Bulgarian press became more frequent. General Savov, the

Bulgarian minister of war, in a conversation with the Italian military attaché at Beograd, went so far as to threaten Serbia with war.[190]

In early October 1907 Austria-Hungary and Russia sent a *note verbale* to Serbia, Greece, and Bulgaria. The note concerned the interpretation of Article III of the Mürzsteg program which was supported by France, Germany, Great Britain, and Italy. The article was interpreted to mean that as soon as order was restored in the reform region, the Ottomans would be requested to undertake an administrative rearrangement which should be based on the distribution of nationalities. The powers warned the Balkan governments that this administrative rearrangement did not imply a possible partition of European Turkey among the Balkan states, or the setting aside of areas which could rightfully be claimed as irredenta by the several states.[191] The two powers stressed that the principal objective of the administrative reorganization was the establishment of a more efficacious system, together with reduction of the amount of work done by the local administrative officials. The Balkan states were told that the terrorist activity of their bands would not be allowed to influence the ethnic delimitation of the new administrative subdivisions, which would be accomplished on the basis of the *status quo ante* and after thorough independent investigations.[192]

The Serbian government objected to the suggestion that the administrative delimitation would be carried out on the basis of the *status quo ante*, because the reform region comprised not only Macedonia in its geographical or historical sense but also embraced a part of Old Serbia. It was further pointed out that ethnic areas were in a state of constant flux caused by the changing numbers of various nationalities in them. The Serbian government reiterated its old contention that the reforms be extended to the sandjaks of the Kosovo vilayet. They observed that in these sandjaks the lot of the Christians was far worse than in other vilayets. Since the Great Powers had decided to institute reforms in Macedonia and part of Old Serbia, the Serbs saw no reason why reforms should be excluded from the remaining sandjaks of Old Serbia, which constituted the "cradle of the original Serbian state."[193]

In February 1907 the British requested the Serbian government to prevent bands of guerrillas from crossing into Old Serbia and Macedonia,[194] alleging that such bands were led by Serbian officers.[195] The Serbs replied that were they to place troops on the frontier in order to prevent the passage of the bands, the Turks would reinforce their frontier troops and thereby bring additional hardships to Serbian villages in Turkish territory.[196] The government denied that it was subsidizing the bands, and asserted that they were financed by private subscription which could not be prevented. It added that nearly half the population of Beograd, among them many well-to-do citizens, were of Old Serbian extraction and subsidized the bands because of their keen interest in their native land. The officers who led these bands, according to the Serbian government, were either in the reserve or on furlough and had obtained permission to leave the kingdom of Serbia.

The Bulgarians believed that the Turkish government, which closely followed the intra-Balkan rivalry and band warfare, chose for reasons of expediency to support Greek and Serbian elements against the Bulgarians.[197]

This seemed plausible because at the beginning of 1907 relations between Greece and Turkey had improved as a result of the latter's concessions regarding Crete. As Turkey began once again to develop aggressive designs toward Bulgaria, rumors began circulating that Turkey and Serbia had concluded a verbal understanding under which, in case of a war between Bulgaria and Turkey, Serbia would attack Bulgaria. Montenegro was believed also to have been included in this agreement.[198] The appointment of the Serbian Archimandrite Sava as vicar of the Veles-Debar eparchy lent credence to a possible Serbo-Turkish *rapprochement*. The distrust between Serbia and Bulgaria, however, was mutual. Serbia suspected that Bulgaria and Austria-Hungary had reached an understanding to incite anarchy in Macedonia which would serve as a pretext for decisive action against Turkey to the detriment of Serbia.

Relations between the two Balkan states deteriorated, especially during the first half of 1907, when Dr. D. Stanchov became foreign minister of Bulgaria.[199] The Serbs saw in Stanchov a close confidant of Prince Ferdinand and a devoted partisan of a Bulgaro-Austrian collaboration. Serbian suspicion seemed justified when the Bulgarian government renounced the customs treaty which had given Serbia certain trade privileges and concessions, such as those pertaining to livestock transit through the ports of Varna and Burgas. This action was obviously a reprisal for the recent activities of the Serbian *četnici* in Macedonia.[200] In the course of 1907 both Bulgaria and Austria had complained of Serbian and Greek band activity in Macedonia, accusing them of obstructing the reforms and of harming innocent citizenry. Bulgaria further denounced Serbian activity in Macedonia in a special memorandum addressed to the powers. Meanwhile the London Balkan Committee urged a European conference to solve the Macedonian problem, and appealed to the Balkan governments to find a solution to the Macedonian Question acceptable to all interested parties.

In August of 1907 both the Beograd and the Vranje branches of the Macedonian Committee were dissolved, and they were not reconstituted. At least two reasons for this action are apparent—the resignation of the president of the Macedonian Committee, General Nikola Stepanović, and the lack of funds. The failure to reconstitute the committee may perhaps be also explained by the desire of the government to comply with the often-repeated advice of the Great Powers.[201] It must be noted, however, that there was a private Macedonian Committee functioning independently of the Serbian government and without official subsidy.[202]

The projected reforms for European Turkey not only failed to take effect but from October 1903, when the reforms were first announced, until the Young Turk revolt in the summer of 1908 conditions in Macedonia became progressively worse and band warfare correspondingly increased. The year 1906 was crucial so far as the reform program was concerned. In that year the new foreign ministers of Austria-Hungary and Russia, Baron Alois von Lexa Aehrenthal and Alexander Izvolsky respectively, initiated for their two countries a more energetic Balkan policy.

The position of the Ottoman sultan had weakened. Relations between

Greece and Bulgaria were strained as a result of Bulgarian pogroms against the Greeks in Bulgaria and warfare between their respective bands in the Salonika vilayet. Recognition of the Rumanian nationality in Macedonia and the opening of the Aroumanian schools and churches precipitated the conflict between some Kutsovlachs and the Greeks.[203] On February 11, 1907, the Albanians attacked the towns of Novi Pazar and Gnjilane, and in the course of the next three months committed a series of other outrages.[204] The Russian ambassador, Zinoviev, admitted to the Serbian diplomatic agent, Živojin Balugdžić, that conditions in Old Serbia were "desperate" and that they could not be improved without reforms, but he added that the Austrians refused to hear of it. The Italian ambassador at Constantinople, Imperiali, hesitated to discuss the question any longer with the Austrian representative because it was "disagreeable to Austria-Hungary." The British consul at Salonika sympathized with the Serbs and condemned the Austrian attitude, and the British minister in Beograd on several occasions suggested to Forgách, his Austrian colleague, that the Serbs had some justification for complaining. On one occasion Zinoviev exclaimed that the whole situation was "a misfortune" because "nobody dares to offend Austria-Hungary." He advised the Serbs to address themselves directly to Vienna.[205]

Pašić took Zinoviev's suggestion and on September 7 promised Aehrenthal that the Serbian government would not meddle in the question of Bosna, which it considered definitely settled, and after several other Austrophile gestures elaborated on the Serbian special interest in Old Serbia to which he hoped reforms would be extended. Presumably Pašić hoped to return to Milan's policy of sacrificing Bosna for Austrian support of Serbian "southern expansion." Nothing came from this direct approach. Austrian policy in regard to Old Serbia remained unchanged, and in the autumn of 1907 the Serbs again found it necessary to complain to Vienna about the Albanian activities.[206] The Serbs and Russians requested the Porte to send troops to the Peć district in order to re-establish order. Zinoviev at the same time was unable to obtain the co-operation of the Austrian ambassador. The Albanian disturbances continued through the spring of 1908.[207]

In face of the extremely critical situation in Macedonia during 1907, the powers concerned themselves with the extension and enforcement of reforms. On an English suggestion, Austria and Russia prepared a set of judicial reforms, although they vied with each other in their mutual suspicions. Izvolsky was astounded, in the latter part of the autumn, when the tsar showed him a confidential message from Constantinople which suggested that Austria would not press for the judicial reforms if the sultan granted her a railway concession in the Sandjak of Novi Pazar.[208] To the sultan the new reforms seemed but a further infringement on his sovereign rights; he ordered his own system of judicial reforms, and appeared to ignore those of the European powers.

13. THE SERBIAN *ČETNIK* ACTIVITY

In February 1907 the English requested the Serb government to put a stop to the entry of *četnici* into Turkey, lest the conflicts between them and the Bulgarian bands precipitate war between Serbia and Bulgaria. The Serbs replied that they "could not prevent [their people] from defending themselves against attacks by foreign bands." They suggested that the "band warfare" would end only if the Bulgarians agreed to it; they explained that they had invited the Bulgarian government to co-operate in ending the conflict in Macedonia, and that the Bulgarians failed to respond.[209]

In April 1907 the English representative at Beograd still found it difficult to ascertain the extent to which the Serbian government aided the bands. Retired and pensioned officers, it was believed, made trips to the south and worked with the revolutionary committee at Beograd. In November 1906 the Skupština had voted a credit of 300,000 dinars for aid under parliamentary supervision to sufferers in Old Serbia and Macedonia. Subsequently an additional amount was appropriated in the nature of "secret credit" for "extraordinary expenses and the defense of national interests."[210] These appropriations corroborated the allegation that the government itself was implicated in the "band warfare," yet these figures did not suggest large-scale operations in Macedonia. Other government resources and private funds were indubitably used, but with "effective discretion." Most Serbian sources, however, seem to agree that 1906 was the most significant year in the Serbian četnik activity. In many sectors the četnici succeeded in checking the infiltration of Bulgarian bands and thereby "staked out" Serbian territorial claims in Macedonia and Old Serbia.

On November 14, 1907, the Bulgarian government once again called the attention of the Great Powers to the deplorable Macedonian situation which they attributed to the machinations of the Greeks and Serbs. Such a situation, it stated, could not but evoke Bulgarian reprisals, and the Bulgarians, consequently, ought not to be held responsible for fighting in self-defense.[211] The apparent success of the Serbian bands increased the tension between Beograd and Sofia, and caused political repercussions in Bulgaria.

At the end of 1907 and the beginning of January 1908 the Serbian četnici were at odds over the tactics to be employed in Macedonia. One group, led by Bogdan Radenković, favored a plan by which the četnik operations would be directed from Beograd. Another group, supported by the Metropolitan Vićentije of Skoplje, favored independent četnik action, supported financially by sympathizers in Beograd. The dispute over tactics destroyed discipline in the field and some of the leaders (vojvoda) operated without supervision or co-ordination. On February 5, 1908, one Alimpije Marjanović (Lazar Mladenović) was sent to investigate the situation in the field and mend the schism. He and Radenković drew up a "constitution" for the entire territory of Macedonia and Old Serbia, defining the duties and rights of the četnici. Marjanović returned to Vranje, organized a band, and on February 25 was designated leader of the entire četnik organization. He restored discipline and order and purged the unruly leaders. Within a month he succeeded in establishing full authority over the organization. He then reorganized the village čete (groups) and defined the rights of each regional vojvoda.

The Serbian četnici now extended their activities southward toward Ovče Polje and eastward in order to eliminate the vestiges of Bulgarian control.

The *četnici* had established two secret avenues of entering Macedonia—Stracin for Kumanovo and Brodac for Palanka. The *četnici* had just gained momentum when the Young Turk revolution broke out in the summer of 1908.[212]

14. ON THE EVE OF THE YOUNG TURK REVOLUTION

In the beginning of 1908 the Porte turned a deaf ear to suggestions by the European powers for a renewal of their mandates administering the reforms. The Ottomans could now effectively evade such questions because they enjoyed the unequivocal support of Germany and Austria-Hungary. The sultan proposed that the administration of reforms be placed entirely under Ottoman control. This plan, he said, would eliminate conflicts among the powers, preserve the prestige and sovereignty of Turkey, and at the same time maintain continuity of the reforms. It was by now apparent that the European reforms in European Turkey had failed. The turmoil in Macedonia continued unabated; there was an increase in the numbers and in the activity of bands of all nationalities, including the Turkish and Rumanian. The Serbs urged some of the powers to open consulates in Peć in order to serve as possible restraints on Albanian activity. Izvolsky and Charykov accepted the proposal and promised to support it. Russian initial enthusiasm toned down as the Turks and the powers opposed the idea.[213]

The Macedonian problem became even more complex when in February 1908 Aehrenthal explained *inter alia* before the Delegations that it was necessary for Austria-Hungary, being a Balkan power by virtue of her control of Bosna, to have a Balkan railway policy. Despite his assurances of peaceful intentions, the Serbs and most of the European powers could see nothing more in Aehrenthal's plan than a renewed Austro-Hungarian expansion into the Balkans.[214]

Austria-Hungary continued systematically to work toward keeping Serbia and Bulgaria from an agreement concerning Macedonia, which was hardly possible in 1908. In the beginning of 1908 the Liberal Bulgarian cabinet of Dr. P. Gudev was replaced by the Democratic cabinet of Alexander Malinov, which as far as Beograd was concerned meant that "Bulgaria would continue to ply the Austrian waters."[215]

At about the same time Toshev replaced Rizov as Bulgarian minister at Beograd. The latter's position had become untenable after the failure of the 1904–5 agreements. The Radicals were not enthusiastic, to say the least, over the new appointment. One of the Skupština deputies demanded an explanation of why the government had agreed to accept a "Serb-eater" as Bulgarian minister at Beograd.[216] On February 20 Toshev presented his credentials at an official audience with King Peter. Toshev tells how certain prominent and responsible Serbs pressed him to work for an understanding between Serbia and Bulgaria. This, he says, got to be the "usual topic of conversation at every gathering." The Serbian minister at Sofia, Simić, likewise urged a *rapprochement*, and so did Sergeev, the Russian minister plenipotentiary at Beograd, who acted in line with the official policy of St. Petersburg, which was desirous of curbing the Germanic expansion. France, England, and Italy also showed a predilection toward Balkan union. From the Serbian standpoint, an agreement with Bulgaria at this time could prevent eventual Austro-Bulgarian co-operation and would enhance Serbia's prestige with the Yugoslavs in Austria-Hungary. But Toshev saw in these Serbian overtures an ulterior motive aimed to facilitate the solution of the Macedonian problem at Bulgaria's expense.[217]

As the situation in Macedonia grew steadily more chaotic, the powers again initiated discussions with the Ottomans over the merits of the various reforms. On February 13, 1908, the Macedonian Question was a subject of discussion in the British Parliament. The consensus was that something had to be done to stop the anarchy in Macedonia and to prevent its spread to the rest of the Balkans. Undersecretary for Foreign Affairs Fitzmaurice declared that it might be necessary to place an independent Christian governor over the disputed region. This statement alarmed the Turks and worried Austria-Hungary.[218]

A few weeks earlier when England, backed by Russia and France, had requested the extension of the Mürzsteg reforms, Baron Aehrenthal declared before the Hungarian Delegation that to abandon the Mürzsteg program and place a governor general in Macedonia would lead to dangerous developments. He said that it was not possible to enlarge the *gendarmerie*, and that in the final analysis the movement of the bands must be stopped by the Turkish authorities themselves.[219] The Italian foreign minister, on February 27, in the parliament stressed the need for an enlargement of the *gendarmerie*. On February 29 Sir Edward Grey announced that he had proposed to the powers a plan for the settlement of the Macedonian problem. According to Sir Edward's plan, the *gendarmerie* would be enlarged and officered by Europeans, who hitherto had served only as instructors, the civil agents and financial advisers would be attached to the supreme governor as part of the government, Turkish troops would be reduced, the Great Powers would guarantee territorial integrity of Macedonia, and administration of reforms would be entrusted to a governor designated by the sultan with the approval of the powers. The British plan suggested autonomy resembling that provided for Eastern Rumelia in 1878, but not a single power accepted this suggestion without reservations. Germany and Austria rejected it outright. Russia offered a counterplan which differed from the British plan in that it provided for maintenance of the status quo. Italy and France accepted the change from the dual Austro-Russian control to general European control, as proposed by Russia, as well as the *gendarmerie* reform and the organization of field guards for the protection of the peasantry.[220]

Under the pretext of intensifying the reforms, the sultan issued on February 28 an irade renewing the mandates of the civil agents. At the same time Abdul Hamid, irritated by the European interferences, instigated the Albanians to oppose the Sandjak railway and any new measures which might be brought up in that connection.

On March 27 there was a huge meeting at Sofia, representing all Macedonian societies, welcoming Sir Edward Grey's proposal to designate a governor general in Macedonia. Sir Edward's proposal meant autonomy, and that solution for the Macedonian problem was quite acceptable to the Bulgarians, who believed it to be a first step toward Bulgarian annexation of Macedonia. The Serbs, Greeks, and Turks, according to Toshev, were less enthusiastic about Grey's proposal than were the Bulgarians.

Not to be outdone by England, the Russians proposed, on March 14, that the supreme inspector should continue in the same capacity as before, i.e., that he could not be dismissed without the approval of the powers. They proposed furthermore that the members of the finance commission be given additional controls, and that the powers support in Constantinople a program of judicial reform.[221] The English opposed the Russian proposal. To their way of thinking, the designation of a governor general was a most fundamental question, and on March 27 Grey expressed surprise that the Russians should reject a proposal which offered reduction of Turkish military garrisons in Macedonia and a collective European guaranty in the region.[222]

On April 5 Izvolsky admitted in the Russian Duma that nothing positive had been accomplished in Macedonia, and that the judicial reform project, "worked out together with Austria-Hungary," had encountered unexpected difficulties. He explained that he did not immediately agree with the English reform project and that he had offered his own counterproject. Said he: "We must avoid doing anything which the sultan might construe as infringement on his sovereign rights. We must know that measures such as the designation of a governor general would mean for the sultan the political loss of Macedonia." Ultimately England agreed to withdraw her proposal for a governor general and for the reduction of Turkish forces in Macedonia. Meanwhile, Izvolski warned the people of Macedonia that Russia's policy was to maintain peace in the Balkans and not to precipitate an armed conflict.[223]

In Austria-Hungary, there were rumors of an impending Serbo-Bulgarian understanding under Russian protectorship. They were probably officially disseminated to alarm the sultan, whose troubles had increased in May when an uprising occurred on the island of Saros. In July 1908 Abdul Hamid dispatched Munir Pasha to various Balkan capitals to undermine any possible *rapprochement* between these powers. In Beograd, Munir expressed sympathy with the construction of a Danube-Adriatic line as an answer to Aehrenthal's Sandjak railway, and hinted at the existence of cordial relations between Turkey and Serbia. In order to cause dissension in the Balkans, the Austrians exaggerated the importance of Munir's visit to Beograd and alluded to a possible military agreement between Serbia and Turkey.[224] On several occasions, the Austrian minister plenipotentiary at Beograd, Forgách, suggested to his Bulgarian colleague that it might be wise for Bulgaria to attack Serbia while the latter was still unprepared. Toshev was assured that Russia at the moment could do no harm, while the two German states would support the cause of Bulgaria.

To dispel any suspicion in Sofia with regard to Munir's visit, the Serbian foreign minister, Dr. Milovanović, told Toshev on July 5 that Munir's visit was a farce, and that if he should broach the subject of combining against Bulgaria he would be flatly denied an opportunity to treat such questions.

Instead Milovanović promised to work toward an agreement with Bulgaria because the existing situation required just this action. Milovanović at the same time condemned the *četnik* activity in Macedonia and said that failure on the part of Bulgaria and Serbia to reach an agreement would mean the continued murdering of the "innocent people of Macedonia," a tragedy which could not but help the cause of their common enemies.[225]

Needless to say, the reforms made little improvement in Macedonia, and the Serbian and Bulgarian *četnici*, Greek *andarte*, and the Turkish army and *bashibazouks* were fighting it out at the expense of the local inhabitants. England, growing increasingly apprehensive over the German Near East policy, decided to take a somewhat firmer stand in Macedonia. In Russia likewise there existed strong dissatisfaction with the government's policy in the Balkans. New and more effective reforms in Macedonia were demanded to safeguard and protect the interests of the Slav population. Under this pressure the Russian government decided to propose new measures for Macedonia.

On May 28, 1908, King Edward of England and Tsar Nicholas II of Russia met at Reval. Out of this meeting came, on May 30, a special communiqué announcing an agreement on the Macedonian Question which had been under discussion between the two governments for some time past. The agreement was the Izvolsky-Hardinge reform project for the establishment of an autonomous administration in Macedonia.[226] It was a detailed plan for the pacification of Macedonia, combining the best features of the former plans of Russia and England.[227] The two powers planned to secure the agreement of the other powers before they announced their project. At the same time, however, Izvolsky sought secretly to reach an understanding with Aehrenthal.

On June 19 Izvolsky sent a secret memorandum to Aehrenthal on the subject of Balkan policy, including the questions of the Dardanelles and the annexation of Bosna-Hercegovina. Aehrenthal promptly informed the Turks of the Russian query. This, together with the recent Anglo-Russian understanding at Reval, induced the sultan to resist even more determinedly any new infringement on his sovereignty. On July 23, 1908, the Young Turk revolution gave an answer to the Reval agreement. The revolution broke out just at the time when Munir Pasha and the Ottoman minister, Fethy Pasha, were being received in audience by King Peter.[228]

The Young Turks were at first successful; they restored a constitutional regime in the Ottoman Empire by putting into force the Constitution of 1876. On July 24 an imperial irade was sent to the governors of the provinces, instructing them to hold the necessary elections for the Chamber of Deputies. Freedom of the press was granted and a general amnesty was declared for all political exiles and refugees. The sultan agreed to govern in accordance with the principles of the Constitution. A new cabinet was formed in which Kiamil Pasha was the grand vizier. The Committee of Union and Progress acted as a vigilance committee,[229] sending its agents to every corner of the Empire. Corrupt governors and officials, and those upon whom any suspicion rested, were immediately dismissed. The reform of European Turkey had now started from within.

The revolution brought an end to the reforms imposed upon Turkey by the European powers, who began withdrawing their reform agents. As soon as the reform *gendarmerie* was removed from the countryside, armed bands descended from the hills into the cities. These events in Turkey ruined Bulgaria's plan for an autonomous Macedonia, and Bulgaria therefore adopted a cool and hostile attitude toward the Young Turk administration. Serbia, on the other hand, found it in her interest to delay the inevitable collapse of the Ottoman Empire.[230] Relations between Serbia and Bulgaria remained antagonistic, with no hope for improvement until the two states agreed on the future disposition of Macedonia and Old Serbia.

M. Pašić was in favor of co-operating with Bulgaria for common aims, and of deferring the discussion of the rights of the two nations in the expected inheritance until it should actually fall due, but his intentions were frustrated by the uncompromising claim of the Bulgarians to the whole of the territory awarded to them by the Treaty of San Stefano.[231]

According to Nikola Pašić, the Serbian government was so sure of the justice of its claim that it would be willing to accept the decision of an ethnographical commission which should draw the frontier line between Serbs and Bulgars in Macedonia. Of course, he said, the frontier could not be a very definite one, because the two nationalities, "being closely akin, 'mixed on meeting as liquids do'," but he assumed that an impartial commission could draw a fairly equitable line.[232]

A few months after the Young Turk revolution, the Serbian government was forced to divert its attention from Macedonia to Bosna-Hercegovina. The feeling aroused by Austro-Hungarian annexation of Bosna-Hercegovina was so intense that the Macedonian problem was, for a time, overshadowed by this more immediate threat from Habsburg imperialism.

PART SEVEN

Economic Emancipation

IN THE COURSE OF THE NINETEENTH CENTURY, Serbian commercial relations were governed by tariffs based upon treaties drawn up by the Ottoman Empire and Austria-Hungary in accordance with the Treaty of Požarevac (Passarowicz) of 1718.[1] These arrangements set out low import duties on Austrian goods,[2] and remained binding for Serbia despite various efforts to provide the country with an independent economic system. Prince Miloš (1817–39, 1859–60) attempted to evolve a tariff system for Serbia in 1819, but the real foundation for the development of Serbian commerce was laid in 1830,[3] when the Ottoman Empire recognized Serbia's autonomy.[4]

Serbia, however, remained within the Ottoman economic unit; her attempt to establish an autonomous customs tariff in 1843 was opposed by Austria,[5] which insisted that the differential rate she enjoyed in Serbia under the arrangements with the Ottoman Empire remain unchanged.[6] The Austro-Ottoman Treaty of 1862, approving the new Turkish importation tax of 8 percent, provided for the maintenance in Serbia and other Balkan states of the *status quo actuel*.[7] Article 28 of the Treaty of Paris of 1856 guaranteed economic autonomy for Serbia,[8] and gave Prince Mihailo a legal basis for the enactment of an autonomous tariff law in 1864.[9]

After the Treaty of San Stefano, marking the end of the Russo-Turkish War, 1877–78, Serbia turned to Austria-Hungary for political and economic succor. Foreign Minister Jovan Ristić acted with "diplomatic reservations" and "hidden intentions," but Prince Milan dealt "directly, sincerely and naïvely."[10] Before the Congress of Berlin assembled in June 1878, the Serbian and Austrian foreign ministers had held several informal discussions in Vienna and Berlin on relations between their two countries. At the Congress Ristić endeavored to secure Austrian backing for Serbian claims to territories—primarily Pirot and Vranje—won in the recent war, but lost by the Treaty of San Stefano. The Austro-Hungarian foreign minister, Count Andrássy, promised his country's support for Serbia, on condition that Serbia renounce her claims in the Sandjak of Novi Pazar, considered by Austria-Hungary as her sphere of influence, and that Serbia enter into a general economic agreement with Austria-Hungary.[11]

Having no other choice at the time, Serbia readily accepted the demands regarding the Sandjak of Novi Pazar. She was more vitally concerned about the second of Andrássy's stipulations, the economic agreement promised by Andrássy, which Ristić reluctantly agreed to accept in order to secure Austrian backing at the Congress.[12] On July 8, 1878, Andrássy and Ristić signed an economic agreement, after considerable bickering over its final form.[13] The agreement opened up a new era in Serbo-Austrian relations; Serbia became closely integrated into the Austro-Hungarian economic system. The agreement concerned three questions : railways, trade, and regulation of the Iron Gate, the bottleneck in Danube navigation. Serbia agreed to construct within three years a railway line from Beograd to Niš, which would eventually join the Salonika line at Vranje, and the Constantinople line at Pirot. The railway would be operated by the Society of the Ottoman Railways, but the project was later limited by the Treaty of Berlin to only those territories Serbia had acquired in the recent war. Austria-Hungary promised to link her own railway system with that of Serbia at Beograd, and to support Serbia so far as possible in obtaining similar connections at Vranje and Pirot.[14]

The two countries agreed to conclude a trade agreement or a customs union immediately after the Congress of Berlin. They further agreed that Austria-Hungary would have the sole right to regulate the Iron Gate on the Danube ; Serbia agreed to allow Austria-Hungary to have "temporary" use of the Serbian bank of the Danube for this purpose.

While at first glance the agreement seemed an arrangement disadvantageous to Serbia, some writers see nothing especially extraordinary about it. Serbia had to build railways sooner or later. The only question at the time was whether Serbia could allow the heavy financial drain on her meager resources. The conclusion of the trade agreement with Austria-Hungary was certainly more desirable than the Turko-Austrian customs agreements, which were still binding for Serbia. Neither did the agreement for Austro-Hungarian regulation of the Iron Gate (Djerdap) carry with it anything especially repugnant. Serbia could not manage the affair financially ; why then refuse that right to Austria-Hungary ?[15]

Austria-Hungary meanwhile supported Serbian claims at the Congress of Berlin. Yet despite this service the Treaty of Berlin put Serbia into a very precarious position, both economically and politically. It is true that Serbian territory was increased and that she was declared an independent state, but Articles XXV and XXXVII placed this enlarged Serbia at the mercy of her stronger neighbor, Austria-Hungary. The latter was entrusted with the provisional occupation and administration of Bosna and Hercegovina and the military occupation of the Sandjak of Novi Pazar. Serbia was consequently surrounded by Austria-Hungary on three sides.

On June 24, 1878, the Skupština assembled at Kragujevac to consider the terms of the Treaty of Berlin and the Ristić-Andrássy economic agreement with Austria-Hungary. After a long talk by Ristić, at a secret session, both were approved.[16] It now remained for Serbia and Austria to negotiate detailed agreements on railway and trade. Serbia wished to make the trade agreement first and then the railway agreement. Trade was of far greater importance for Serbia. Moreover, Serbia feared she could not at the moment assume the heavy debt resulting from railway building. Austria-Hungary, on the other hand, took the reverse stand. She insisted that the trade agreement should follow the railway agreement. The Serbian government ultimately acquiesced, but on condition that Turkey and Bulgaria be included in the railway discussions.[17] The Treaty of Berlin did envisage such a quadruple agreement, and so did the Ristić-Andrássy understanding of 1878. Obviously it was to the advantage of both states to link up the Serbian railways with those of Bulgaria and Turkey.

By inclusion of Turkey and Bulgaria in the discussions, Serbia hoped she might secure better over-all conditions for construction of the railways. Serbia feared that so long as her railways were not connected with those of Bulgaria and Turkey (Constantinople and Salonika) they would serve only Austrian economic interests; Serbian exports would still be directed to Austrian markets exclusively. Serbia was also much concerned about the three-year period envisaged by the Ristić-Andrássy agreement, within which she would have to construct the railways. If Turkey and Bulgaria agreed to construct their lines within three years, and failed to do so, then perhaps Serbia might with justification delay her part of the bargain also.

Austria-Hungary insisted that an Austro-Serbian railway agreement must precede the quadruple discussions, and Serbia had to agree to a bilateral railway agreement first. However, having once accepted the idea of bilateral agreement, the Serbs proposed temporary postponement of the construction of the lines from Niš to Pirot and from Niš to Vranje, which would link her system of railways with those of Bulgaria and Turkey. These two connections from Niš would be of little value to Serbia so long as their Bulgarian and Turkish extensions were not built.[18] A compromise was finally reached, according to which Serbia promised to build within three years the line from Beograd to Niš, with an extension to Vranje. Prince Milan was so anxious to reach a railway agreement in order to proceed with trade negotiations that he was ready to accept virtually any proposal made by Austria-Hungary. The Railway Convention was signed on March 28, 1880, and in May of the same year submitted to the Skupština for ratification.[19]

There was considerable parliamentary opposition to the government's acceptance of the Railway Convention. The opposition insisted that the trade agreement should have preceded the one on the railways because of the urgent need for establishment of a normal and stable economy. The opposition spokesmen contended that until a trade treaty was concluded with Austria-Hungary the Serbian railways would serve only Austrian interests, and that country would remain Serbia's only economic outlet.

Ristić was as aware as anyone else of Austrian economic aspirations, but he felt that Serbia could be economically independent only if she obtained an outlet to the sea, and that the Beograd-Vranje railway would make it possible eventually to reach the sea at Salonika.[20] He also argued that it was to the interest of Austria-Hungary and Turkey to connect Serbian railways at Vranje with those of Turkey; it was, he believed, only a matter of time until that would be done. The railway bridge which was to be built over the Sava especially aroused the opposition. The frontier between the two states would be the middle of the bridge. The train could not stop for loading and unloading at that point; it was therefore agreed that the Austrian railway administration be extended across the bridge into the Beograd station. This was interpreted by some as outright infringement on Serbian territorial integrity, although the arrangement was not unusual in railway conventions. Finally, however, the Railway Convention was ratified by the Skupština;

next on the agenda was the signing of the trade treaty—a document of great importance for the understanding of future Austro-Serbian trade and economic relations.

1. THE AUSTRO-SERBIAN TRADE TREATY OF 1881

The Serbian government was ready to sign a trade treaty with Austria-Hungary, but not a customs union. In a customs union the more developed Austro-Hungarian industry would tend to prevent Serbian industrial development. Moreover, there was danger that a customs union might be but a step toward a political union. So far as Austria-Hungary was concerned, the trade treaty was not urgent; she could impose any customs she wished on Serbian imports. Serbia, on the other hand, could not impose more than 3 percent on Austrian imports. Not only did Austria-Hungary prolong trade discussions, but she even applied restraints on Serbian imports. In November 1878 she stopped imports of Serbian horned cattle on pretense of an infectious disease, which did exist but was not extensive. On January 1, 1879, Austria-Hungary introduced a new customs tariff, which was detrimental to Serbian trade. The customs on hogs, constituting 41 percent of the total Serbian export, was raised from 1.05 silver florins to 2 gold florins, an increase which caused an economic crisis in Serbia and caused merchants to put pressure on the government to conclude a trade agreement with Austria-Hungary as soon as possible. But all efforts to initiate trade discussions with Austria-Hungary were in vain; the latter insisted that the Railway Convention be agreed upon first.[21]

The unhappy economic situation and the possibility of a customs war with Austria-Hungary induced the Serbian government in 1879 to conclude provisional trade agreements with England, Italy, Russia, Switzerland, and Belgium. These agreements were based on the principle of the most-favored-nation. Because no Serbian exports were sent to these countries, the agreements were of greater political than economic import. The Treaty of Berlin gave Serbia the right to make separate trade agreements. Until then the trade agreements, including capitulations signed by Turkey, were equally binding for Serbia, a "vassal" of Turkey. Article XXXVII of the Treaty of Berlin specified that until Serbia concluded trade agreements with other states, she was to retain "the actual conditions of commercial intercourse."

Until the conclusion of new agreements, nothing will be changed in Serbia in regard to the actual conditions of the commercial intercourse of the Principality with foreign countries.

No transit duties shall be levied on goods passing through Serbia.

The immunities and privileges of foreign subjects, as well as the rights of Consular jurisdiction and protection, as at present existing, shall remain in full force so long as they shall not have been modified by mutual consent between the Principality and the Powers concerned.[22]

Consequently, the primary object of the treaties concluded in 1879 had been "the establishment of formal right to independent customs policy."

On January 26, 1880, a permanent trade agreement was signed with

England, and once again the importance was political rather than economic, because Serbian exports could already flow freely to "free trade" England. The true import of the agreement lay in the fact that England became the first power to renounce the capitulations which had allowed her citizens under the arrangements with the Ottoman Empire special privileges in Serbia. Moreover, it was hoped the agreement with England, concluded on a basis of full equality, would strengthen Serbia's bargaining position with Austria-Hungary. The Serbian hopes did not materialize. Austria-Hungary was displeased with her neighbor's independent attitude and became even more intransigent in her demands.[23]

Formal trade discussions with Austria-Hungary finally began in June 1880. Austria-Hungary demanded from Serbia in the name of the most-favored-nation clause the same concessions which had been made to England. She claimed the most-favored-nation treatment on the basis of an agreement signed with Turkey in 1862. With her reference to the Treaty of 1862 Austria-Hungary injected in the trade discussions a legalistic question. The Serbian government replied that it was not bound by the Treaty of Berlin to retain in force Turkish trade treaties, but merely "the actual conditions of commercial intercourse," that is, existing tariff rates. The Treaty of 1862 did establish the tariff rate that Serbia could impose on Austrian products, but Serbia had pursued an autonomous tariff policy since 1856, and in 1864 had actually established an autonomous tariff system. Austria made no objections at that time, and Serbia retained her own tariff system. Thus Serbia did not in practice strictly abide by the Treaty of 1862, and Austria had never taken exception to it. Jovanović says that actually on one occasion in 1874 Count Andrássy admitted that the Treaty of 1862 had never applied to Serbia.[24]

In the final analysis, the controversy boiled down to whether or not Austria-Hungary should continue after the Treaty of Berlin to enjoy "most-favored-nation" treatment. The most-favored-nation clause was recognized by the agreement of 1862, but the Treaty of Berlin was not explicit on this point. The Treaty of Berlin spoke of "existing conditions of commercial intercourse." What conditions did it mean? Those of the Treaty of 1862, or those of the Serbian customs tariff of 1864?

The trade discussions were therefore stalemated. Serbia was willing to accord "most-favored" treatment to Austria-Hungary, but expected the same in return. Austria-Hungary, on the other hand, held that she already enjoyed that status, and on September 18, 1880, in what amounted to an ultimatum, threatened economic repressions unless Serbia recognized the Austro-Hungarian position. Haymerle demanded that Ristić make a declaration renouncing the economic independence of Serbia, which Ristić refused. The effect of such a dictatorial attitude was to strengthen rather than vitiate the antagonism of Ristić, who was moved to risk a customs war on Austria-Hungary, if need be. A customs war, he said, would come and go, but economic independence, once lost, would not be easily regained. The hardships brought by a customs war on Serbia would be heavy, but not so heavy as to cause a grave national crisis, for consumer demand for imports was not well developed; producers alone would suffer.[25]

Should there be a customs war, the Ristić government felt that Serbia would require the support of one of the Great Powers. At first it was thought that Russia might be this power, and a Serbo-Russian trade treaty was proposed. But Russia declined the proposal, and England, having shifted her Balkan policy after the Congress of Berlin, came to Serbia's assistance. Pursuant to a policy of opposing Austro-Hungarian economic expansion in the Balkans, Lord Salisbury concluded a trade treaty with Serbia. The English minister encouraged Serbia to risk a customs war with Austria-Hungary, saying that if it came he would urge his government to influence the Porte to give Serbia a railway connection at Vranje—for Serbian exports via Salonika. The English policy was even friendlier when in 1880 Gladstone—a friend of the Balkan Christians—came to power.

The Serbian government believed that even if the customs war came it would be of short duration, because Austria-Hungary would not wish to lose Serbian markets permanently; trade negotiations would necessarily be renewed after a time and would then probably be conducted on a basis of equality. The two principal classes in Serbia—agrarians and merchants—feared the consequences of a customs war. Only craftsmen and intellectuals favored it, and these two groups were so negligible that the Ristić government would find it necessary to resign.[26]

Meanwhile Prince Milan prepared to make a pilgrimage to Vienna. Before doing so, he wished to have the railway agreement with Austria-Hungary settled. The agreement was therefore signed on March 28, 1880. On June 14, 1880, Prince Milan left Serbia and during a lengthy stay in Austria-Hungary had discussions—much to the discomfiture of Ristić—with Francis Joseph, Haymerle, and Baron Benjamin von Kállay. Upon his return to Serbia he once again tried to prevail on Ristić to accept the Austrian demands. Ristić refused and tendered his cabinet's resignation on October 14.[27]

The new cabinet, constituted of Progressives under the leadership of Milan Pirocanac, inherited the task of completing trade discussions with Austria. On October 29 the government recognized the validity of the agreement of 1862, and gave Austria-Hungary the right of most-favored-nation without reciprocity. Unlike the Ristić government, the new cabinet was not protectionist. It held that Serbia's most important economic objective should be to secure Austrian markets and a low customs tariff for Serbian agrarian and livestock exports. The treaty was finally signed on April 24, and went into force on June 5, 1881.[28]

The trade treaty with Austria-Hungary was intended to pave the way for a customs union. As it was, the treaty stood somewhere between an ordinary trade treaty and a customs union. Special customs relations were established by giving the border-traffic arrangements broader application. Normally, a ten-kilometer zone on both sides of the frontier is designated as a zone in which trade is either free of customs or under a very low tariff. The purpose is to protect border areas which are by their very nature disposed to mutual trade. The Treaty of 1881 provided special customs tariffs for border traffic, but in a way applicable to the entire country. So, for example, all trade in hogs, regardless of origin, enjoyed the same customs rate. Instead of applying special customs to border traffic, special duties were laid on certain categories of products. These favors granted to Austria were not given to any other power. The most-favored-nation principle did not apply to border traffic, and consequently other powers could not expect the same kind of treatment.[29]

The low tariff and favors in border traffic which Austria-Hungary sought and obtained covered articles which could be produced in Serbia with little capital and technical equipment. This was just the kind of industry that Serbia might have developed, for there was certainly no serious danger that Serbia might develop heavy industry. The obvious policy of Austria-Hungary was to prevent the development of light industry in Serbia, encouraging that country to develop an exclusively agrarian and raw materials economy. Therefore, considerable concessions were granted to Serbian agrarian produce. The principal exports—oxen, hogs, dry prunes, prune jam, skins— were placed on a special list governing border-traffic favors. Grain, also an important Serbian export, was not listed in this category; however its export to Austria was free. Subsequently Austria did impose customs on grain, but even then the rates on Serbian grain were the lowest.[30] By these various provisions Austria-Hungary was able virtually to monopolize Serbian trade. The establishment of a customs union appeared only a matter of time.

Concurrently with the trade treaty, the two powers signed a Veterinary Convention which applied only to horned cattle and did not cover hogs. Austria-Hungary could deny the importation of horned cattle only under conditions stipulated in the convention. But she could stop the importation of hogs any time she felt like doing so. The convention, for example, permitted Austria-Hungary to close the borders to those animals which were diseased, and to those suspected of disease as well.[31] The latter proved to be a particularly flexible clause, and Austria-Hungary did not hesitate to exercise it whenever she could make political capital from the action.

To prevent Serbia from circumventing the treaty by burdening the imports with a variety of domestic imposts, Austria-Hungary caused the treaty to specify that Serbia was not permitted to tax products of foreign origin higher than the same type of goods produced in Serbia and that the goods not produced in Serbia were duty-free. However, when the need did arise the Serbian government did not hesitate to rid itself of the limitations of the treaty in quest of new sources of income.[32]

On October 31, 1886, by an amendment to the law of June 14, 1884, the Serbian government was responsible for the first serious infringement of the provisions of the trade treaty. The rate of turn-over tax on shops handling manufactured goods, predominantly imports, was established at 5 percent, while the rate on those handling raw materials, exports for the most part, was established at 1 percent. In 1888 the turn-over tax on shops handling manufactured goods was raised to 7 percent. Thus, in addition to the established customs and other taxes on imported goods which were permitted by the treaty, an additional 7 percent of turn-over tax was imposed. By the time the Treaty of 1881 expired, this turn-over tax exceeded in amount the entire customs revenue of Serbia. Austria-Hungary realized that the violation of the treaty had been forced on Serbia by circumstances, and, because the

Austrophile Progressives dominated the political scene in Serbia, it was felt unwise for the empire to do anything that might undermine its prestige. Meanwhile the turn-over tax remained in force and became in fact an integral part of the Serbian customs policy.[33]

The Austrians seemingly feared, furthermore, that Serbia might establish monopolies on articles which concerned Austria-Hungary vitally—sugar, paper, matches, and other items. Consequently the treaty had restricted the Serbian government to the establishment of monopoly rights over three items only: tobacco, salt, and explosive powder.[34]

If the Treaty of 1881 limited the economic development of Serbia, it did carry within it some political importance. The treaty abolished the old privileges Austria-Hungary had enjoyed in Serbia through her agreements with Turkey, and the Consular Convention, which was signed simultaneously, abolished capitulations.[35] Yet all these advantages were more theoretical than real. In June 1881 Serbia signed a Secret Convention with Austria-Hungary, by virtue of which she became almost a political appendage of the neighboring monarchy.

2. THE AUSTRO-SERBIAN SECRET CONVENTION

The trade treaty with Austria-Hungary was followed by a political agreement embodied in the Secret Convention of June 28, 1881, contracted for a period of ten years.[36] The convention was renewed in 1889 before Milan's abdication, but was allowed to expire in 1899. The return of King Milan to Serbia in that year meant that the convention, to all intents and purposes, was still in force. The secrecy of the convention was closely guarded. Besides Milan, only three or four political leaders knew about it. The convention was in a sense a corollary to the "Dreikaiserbund" signed on June 18, 1881, some ten days earlier. The "Bund" contained at least two provisions affecting Serbia—the Russian agreement to the annexation of Bosna-Hercegovina by Austria-Hungary, and the latter's promise not to oppose the unification of Bulgaria and Eastern Rumelia. Once again Austria-Hungary and Russia divided the Balkans into spheres of influence! So long as she was permitted to extend her influence in the eastern portion of the Balkans, Russia was willing to sacrifice Serbia and her national claims to Austria-Hungary.

Milan was convinced that his country's destiny was bound up with Austria, and was therefore ready to sign the Secret Convention. One of the basic aims of the convention was to curb Serbian influences and activities in Bosna-Hercegovina. Article II of the convention expressly stated that Serbia would "not permit any political, religious, or other intrigue to be directed from her territory against the Austro-Hungarian monarchy, including Bosna, Hercegovina, and the Sandjak of Novi Pazar." Austria undertook similar obligations "with regard to Serbia and her dynasty, the maintenance and strengthening of which she will support with all her influence. . . . If Austria feared Serbian penetration into Bosna, Prince Milan feared Karadjordjević penetration into Serbia."[37] Austria further promised "if the Prince of Serbia should deem it necessary, in the interest of His dynasty and of His country, to take in behalf of Himself and of His descendants the title of King,

Austria-Hungary will recognize this title . . . and will use her influence to secure recognition for it on the part of the other Powers" (Article III). She also promised that "if, as a result of a combination of circumstances whose development is not to be foreseen at present, Serbia were in a position to make territorial acquisitions in the direction of her southern frontiers (with the exception of the Sandjak of Novi Pazar), Austria-Hungary will not oppose herself thereto, and will use her influence with the other Powers for the purpose of winning them over to an attitude favorable to Serbia" (Article VII).[38]

To establish her role as virtual protector over Serbia, Austria-Hungary sought control over Serbian foreign policy. Thus, Article IV of the convention bound Serbia neither to "negotiate nor conclude any political treaty with another Government," and not to admit to her territory a foreign armed force, regardless of type, "without a previous understanding with Austria-Hungary." Finally, it was agreed that

If Austria-Hungary should be threatened with war or find herself at war with one or more other Powers, Serbia will observe a friendly neutrality . . . and will accord to [Austria-Hungary] all possible facilities, in conformity with their close friendship and the spirit of this Treaty. Austria-Hungary assumes the same obligation towards Serbia.

The Secret Convention was formally signed at Beograd; Foreign Minister Mijatović and Austrian Minister Baron de Herbert represented their respective countries.[39]

Prince Milan consulted only three of his ministers in connection with the convention. Others knew nothing about it. Stojan Novaković did not know of it until twelve years later, when its existence leaked out. Piroćanac and Garašanin did not see the text of the convention until after it was signed. Neither was satisfied with it, and in protest they resigned. The prince was abroad at the time and the cabinet crisis lasted for several weeks. An acceptable formula was found which ended the crisis. The Foreign Ministry was transferred from Mijatović to Piroćanac so as to put an end to the prince's direct control of foreign policy. Also as part of this formula Piroćanac was sent to Vienna to persuade Benjamin von Kállay, deputy to the foreign minister, to give a new interpretation to Article IV, which was the portion of the convention most resented by Piroćanac and Garašanin.

Piroćanac feared that by Article IV Serbia would lose the right to conclude independent political agreements, an occurrence which would be tantamount to a recognition of Austrian protectorate. As a result of their discussions, Piroćanac and Kállay signed in Beograd, on October 25, 1881, a declaration to the effect that

Article IV cannot impair the right of Serbia to negotiate and to conclude treaties, even of a political nature, with another Government. It implies for Serbia no other engagement than that of not negotiating and of not concluding any political treaty which would be contrary to the spirit and the tenor of the said secret Treaty.[40]

The Piroćanac-Kállay Declaration satisfied Piroćanac but otherwise had only paper significance, because on October 24, 1881, Prince Milan had sent to Kállay a personal declaration in which he condemned Piroćanac's action and of his "own free will" promised to "assume the formal engagement on My honor and in My quality as Prince of Serbia, not to enter into any nego-tiations whatsoever relative to any kind of a political treaty between Serbia and a third state without communication with and previous consent of Aus-tria-Hungary."[41] Piroćanac did not know of this letter when Kállay agreed to sign the declaration.

That Milan's promise prevailed can be seen from "everything that oc-curred in Serbia between 1881 and 1906."[42] In the field of economy Serbia regulated her relations with other countries only "through her commercial treaty with Austria-Hungary," which was accompanied by navigation, veter-inary, and nationality conventions, and certain articles of "the Turkish capit-ulations."[43]

3. THE TRADE TREATY OF 1892

A new trade treaty with Austria-Hungary was signed on June 28, 1892. The Radicals, who came to power under Nikola Pašić in February 1891, wished for economic independence from Austria-Hungary, but because that policy at the time was impossible of realization, they signed the new treaty, which did not differ essentially from the one they had opposed.[44]

The principal Serbian export was still livestock. The most accessible markets were those of Hungary, both because of geographic proximity and because of existing railway connections. To ship the livestock via Salonika to Marseilles and other Mediterranean and Western ports was certainly far less practical. Serbia could not free herself from Austria-Hungary until she should begin to export slaughtered meats in place of livestock. An attempt by Kosta Taušanović, a Radical leader and able economist, to build a large slaughterhouse with the aid of English capital was not very successful. In 1892, when the time came for trade negotiations with Austria-Hungary, Serbia was still in pretty much the same position relative to Austria that she had held in 1881. Indeed, Jovanović says there was even less opportunity for a break with Austria-Hungary in 1892 than there had been in 1881. Serbia had meanwhile incurred a heavy state debt, which required annual pay-ments of 20 million dinars in gold. These obligations could not be met if Serbia suddenly lost the markets of Austria-Hungary.[45]

The principal aim of the Radical government was the same as that of the Progressive government in 1881—to obtain from Austria-Hungary the most favorable customs tariff possible for Serbian livestock and agrarian products. In the new treaty, as in the old, particularly favorable rates for border traf-fic were granted Serbia on agrarian products and livestock, regardless of whether the products came from the border area or some other area. The whole system of the first trade treaty remained in force. Serbia was directed for an additional eleven years to produce raw materials, selling them to Austria-Hungary and in return obtaining manufactured goods.[46]

Austria's privileged position extended to a virtual monopoly on all grains, on dried prunes and prune preserves without sugar, on oxen, honey, and a certain type of *šlivovica* (only on the border of Bosna), and on wine in barrels from the Timok, Krajina, Kruševac, Morava, and Toplica regions. Under the new treaty, hogs, however, were not accorded the favored-customs treatment. The reason for this was that Austria-Hungary had reduced her customs rate on hogs for other countries as well as Serbia, and also because there was no possibility of competition for Serbian hogs from any quarter except Hungary.[47]

With the exception of grain, the customs rate for all articles within the border traffic remained the same as it had been under the Treaty of 1881. Several additional districts were extended the privileges of border traffic in wines, even though most of these did not border on the monarchy. The agreement of 1892 differed from that of 1881 in that it included an established differential customs rate under border traffic. The rates were appreciably higher than those of 1881 and were more favorable to Serbia.[48]

The new Veterinary Convention stipulated with added clarity the circumstances under which Austria-Hungary could close her borders to Serbian livestock. By the earlier convention, Austria-Hungary had been able to close the borders on mere suspicion of disease, whereas, according to the new convention, the disease had to be proved to exist. The convention listed measures each of the signatories should take to prevent the spread of livestock diseases, although for practical purposes these specifications affected only Serbia. No longer were Hungarian veterinarians permitted to come to Serbian soil, but they examined the livestock in Hungary; hence Austria-Hungary could still, if she so wished, close the frontiers without adequate reason.[49] In 1895, less than two years after the treaty was signed, Austria-Hungary forbade importation of Serbian hogs to and through Hungarian territory for a period of several months.[50]

Because the Treaty of 1881 by its very nature and intent had prevented full development of Serbian crafts and industry, the state initiated a system of concessions to private industry in order to encourage industrial expansion within the limits permitted. And because private industry could not by law obtain the right of monopoly, the Serbian government granted other types of privilege, such as freedom from customs and taxes. The Treaty of 1892 imposed certain restrictions on such concessions to native industry by the Serbian government.[51]

The principal benefit which the agreement of 1892 brought to Serbia concerned finance. "In financial matters the new agreement emancipated Serbia from the surveillance and control of Austria-Hungary." New sources were opened for Serbian state revenue, and the customs revenue was increased by 50 percent.[52] The customs duty based on value was replaced by a duty based on weight. Serbia was permitted to have four additional monopolies: petroleum, cigarette paper, matches, and alcohol. The turn-over tax, hitherto merely tolerated, was legalized. According to the 1881 agreement Serbia could impose a consumption tax only on goods produced in Serbia; this clause had incurred too much controversy over interpretation. Article X of the agreement of 1892 permitted a consumption tax to be imposed on certain goods not produced in Serbia.[53]

In 1892 Austria-Hungary could neither seek nor accept from Serbia privileges favoring her products on Serbian markets over those of other foreign countries. The new policy for international trade was governed by the Austro-Hungarian agreement with Germany, which allowed the former to secure for herself a privileged customs position only if the same privilege were accorded Germany. For this reason, in the Treaty of 1892 Austrian imports into Serbia no longer enjoyed the so-called differential tariff which had been concealed under cover of border-traffic regulation. Instead, Austrian imports were given a favorable customs tariff. This did not alter in essence the favorable position enjoyed in Serbia by Austro-Hungarian industry.[54]

The principal criticism in the Skupština of the Treaty of 1892 was that the customs rates on Serbian grain exports to Austria-Hungary were raised, especially those on wheat and rye. This made for keener competition on Austrian markets between the local products of the monarchy and those of Serbia. The Austro-Hungarian customs policy on grain was cleverly devised to meet the divergent economic interests of the monarchy. Hungarian agrarian interests were protected from the flood of cheaper foreign grains, and at the same time, in order not to discourage development of the growing Hungarian flour industry, "the type of grain necessary to that industry was permitted to enter free of all duties."[55]

The Treaty of 1892, like that of 1881, was intended to prepare the way for a possible customs union. Both treaties favored trade between Austria-Hungary and Serbia by means of a frontier traffic "wherein the goods were exempted from customs-taxes." Until 1906 Serbia regulated her activity in international commerce only though her trade treaty with Austria-Hungary. Practically all imported goods came from Austria-Hungary, and 90 percent of Serbia's exports were sold in markets at Vienna and Budapest. When King Milan abdicated (March 6, 1889), Serbia was some 400 million francs in debt. From 1864 to 1884 Serbia's commerce grew from 33 million francs to 90 million francs; but in the next twenty years, 1884 to 1904, which may be taken as the period of Obrenović subservience to Austria-Hungary, her commerce rose only from 90 million francs to 127 million francs. In the period of subjection to Austria-Hungary, from 1881 to 1900, Serbia was forced to take out nineteen loans which amounted to about 456,997,000 francs,* and the budget deficit in 1900 amounted to 62,359,758 dinars.[56]

The Austro-Hungarian economic domination deprived Serbia of an opportunity for full economic development. Production was limited to such items as fruit, cattle, and cereals. The almost exclusive control by the Habsburg monarchy of Serbian foreign trade and the monopoly of Serbian "credit, railway traffic, the tariffs of river navigation on the Danube and the Sava," served to isolate Serbia from trading relations with other European states.[57] Moreover, Serbia was geographically in the economic orbit of Austria-Hungary. She was a landlocked state; her closest sea outlet was at Salonika on

---

* The Serbian dinar was equal to one franc.

the Aegean, but the railway thither had to traverse hazardous and bandit-infested Macedonia. A more dependable Danube river route would take commerce to the Black Sea, away from its natural direction. In view of these conditions and under normal circumstances the lion's share of Serbian foreign trade would quite naturally remain with Austria-Hungary.

Nationalistic manifestations of one kind or another during the cabinet of Stojan Novaković (1895–96) irritated Austria-Hungary, until once again the frontiers were closed against the importation of Serbian hogs. Such arbitrary action induced Novaković and his sympathizers to think of freeing Serbia once and for all from the economic dominance of Austria-Hungary. One means to this end was to be the building of modern slaughterhouses for Serbian livestock, because slaughtered and packed meats might be shipped longer distances. Simultaneously Serbia would develop a specialized industry and no longer depend exclusively on near-by Austro-Hungarian markets. After the demise of the Novaković cabinet, this policy of striving toward an independent economy was not relinquished; in 1898 the Serbian Company for the Slaughter and Packing of Livestock was founded. From the time it came into existence until 1901, it achieved a steady increase in the production of slaughtered and packed meat. In the first year of its operation the company exported 1,425,000 kilograms of meat and in 1901, 6,014,000 kilograms. The largest quantity of meats went to England, lesser quantities to France and the French possessions in North Africa. The results of the new industry proved conclusively that development of the meat industry could find for Serbia new markets and free her from Austro-Hungarian domination.[58]

In the last decade of the nineteenth century, Serbian economists and statesmen were busy studying ways in which their country might establish economic independence. An impressive amount of published material on the subject appeared. Some authorities alleged that despite the geographic proximity of Austria-Hungary, Serbia could find for all three of its principal export commodities—cereals, livestock, dried prunes—other equally good markets. Some even held the extreme view that Austria-Hungary was more dependent on Serbia than the latter was on the former, and that a commercial war with Austria-Hungary would be a blessing for Serbia because she would be forced to develop her natural resources and economic potentialities independently. Eventually, it was believed, Austria-Hungary would not only lose Serbian raw materials but would also lose the Serbian market for her industrial exports. A group of prominent men urged the construction of appropriate industrial facilities and a search for new trade outlets before the trade treaty with Austria expired in December 1903. When Austria-Hungary should be brought to realize that Serbia could do without her, then, it was believed, she would cease treating Serbia as a backward area fit only for economic exploitation.[59]

Even if Serbia were eventually to succeed in her independent economic policy, it was unlikely that Austria-Hungary would stand idle during the period of transition. When, at about the turn of the century, Serbia began to develop an independent line of policy, Austria-Hungary started considering countermeasures. In 1902 the Austro-Hungarian Joint Delegation voted

75 million crowns for construction of the railroad from Sarajevo to Mitrovica, which would, so it seemed at the time, establish a direct connection between the monarchy and the line running between Salonika and Constantinople, without crossing Serbia.[60] The Russian war minister, General Kuropatkin, saw in this plan the nefarious influence of the Germans, who wished to obtain "a connection between Hamburg, Berlin, and Bagdad."[61] The Sarajevo-Mitrovica line, via the Sandjak and the Kosovo Plain, had been talked of first in 1900, and had instantly evoked Serbian opposition. It was believed that the line would enhance the political influence of the Dual Monarchy in the territories Serbia hoped some day to annex. As a countermeasure Serbia considered at the time her earlier plan of a southern Russia-Rumania-Serbia railway connection with the Adriatic through Turkish territory. This line would give Serbia a direct route to the sea for her exports and at the same time would facilitate the extension of Serbian influence on the Kosovo Plain and in other Turkish-held territories.[62] Again in 1902 Austria-Hungary proposed the immediate construction of the Sarajevo-Mitrovica line, despite German opposition made on the grounds that it might "cause further unrest in the Balkans." Count Goluchowski and Francis Joseph, during Count Lamsdorff's visit to Vienna in late 1902, discussed the Sarajevo-Mitrovica line, and Lamsdorff seemed to have been favorably disposed, but gave the Austrians to understand that he could give a definite answer only after consultation with the tsar.[63] Zinoviev was convinced that the tsar would not consent to the idea and would insist on the status quo in the Balkans.[64]

In order to gain as much economic independence from Austria-Hungary as possible, Serbia began searching for new outlets for her exports. On May 27, 1902, Serbia concluded a trade treaty with Turkey, which besides arranging for the trade exchange between the two countries provided Serbia with a favorable railway transit. The latter facilitated Serbia's commerce through Salonika and also served thereby to increase state revenue because of greater use of the Beograd-Ristovac line.[65] The government explored at the time other possible routes as well: through the Bulgarian ports of Varna and Burgas, and the route by way of the Danube.

Nationalism was gaining momentum in Serbia. Economic and political emancipation from Austria-Hungary became the watchword of Serbian nationalists. To some the principle "the Balkans for the Balkan peoples" appeared to be the only solution of the Balkan problem and the only lasting basis for peace in the Near East.[66] By the crucial year of 1903 the Austrian policy of controlling Serbia economically and politically was encountering strong resistance; it was working against historical forces.

4. AUSTRO-SERBIAN TRADE RELATIONS AFTER 1903

Economic relations between Austria-Hungary and Serbia from 1903 onward underwent a profound change. This was the result of the nationalist policy of the new regime and the new dynasty. The Grujić government of 1903 proposed a far-reaching economic program: reorganization of trade in answer to the needs of the over-all national economy, search for new foreign markets, improvement of shipping facilities via Salonika and the Danube, and conclusion of new and more favorable trade treaties with foreign powers. The government further proposed improvement of communications and transportation facilities. It planned, through additional taxes, to raise funds for the construction of railways that would connect the eastern parts of the country with the western and with the main railway artery of the Morava basin. A society was organized to obtain foreign capital for the construction of the railways. Finally, the government proposed numerous technical and reclamation projects in order to raise the productive capacity of the country.[67]

In preparation for negotiation of the new trade treaties, the Grujić cabinet submitted to the Skupština on October 13, 1903, a general customs tariff law which leaned toward protectionism. Some of the newspapers, such as *Trgovinski glasnik* and *Ustavna Serbia*, had persistently urged adoption of an autonomous customs law before the trade treaty with Austria-Hungary expired.[68] This law passed the Skupština in March 1904.[69]

One of the most urgent tasks before the Grujić cabinet was the stabilization of finances. The government was able to meet in part the current and temporary debts through the loan obtained in 1902 but realized only at this time. Additional loans had to be made for the construction of railways and the modernization of the army. Inability to solve the financial problems, coupled with multitudinous other difficulties—the "conspiratorial question," the "diplomatic strike" of the powers, the political bickering at home—forced General Grujić to resign on February 2, 1904. Stojan Protić, a Radical stalwart, refused the royal mandate to form a new cabinet, and on February 8 Grujić was reappointed premier.

Grujić's second cabinet included a number of men who were to influence the course of Serbia's economic as well as political development for a generation. The Foreign Ministry went to Nikola Pašić (Radical), who laid the basis for the foreign policy that remained unaltered until 1918. The Ministry of Finance was entrusted to Dr. Lazar Paču (Radical), under whose wise administration the country not only averted bankruptcy but in a short time, despite many insurmountable difficulties, became financially solvent. In 1903 Serbia had a budgetary deficit of 11.5 million dinars, whereas in the succeeding two years she had a surplus of 6.5 million and 4.5 million dinars, respectively.

During 1903–4 Serbia avoided rash economic and political action because, being isolated, she was in no position to cause even the slightest irritation to Austria-Hungary. As a matter of fact, in the spring and summer of 1904 Nikola Pašić broached at least three times the subject of closer co-operation with Austria-Hungary.[70]

At first glance, Pašić's policy seemed strange, in view of his determined Russophilism during the Obrenović rule. Now that the Obrenović dynasty was gone he seemingly adopted their policy of pro-Habsburg foreign orientation. But there was an ulterior motive behind his action. His attempts to establish close co-operation with Austria-Hungary came in the spring and summer of 1904, a time in which Russia was preoccupied with the Japanese war and Austria-Hungary dominated Balkan affairs. Without Russian backing, Pašić did not dare pursue a policy inimical to Austria-Hungary.[71]

What is even more important is that Pašić strove simultaneously for Austro-Hungarian friendship and Bulgarian alliance. In fact, he managed to sign a customs union with Bulgaria which was to prepare the ground for political union. With Bulgarian help, he hoped to check any possible Austrian penetration of the Balkans. With Austrian help, he hoped to obtain a part of Macedonia which Bulgaria claimed in entirety.[72] Pašić's negotiations with Austria-Hungary were definitely motivated by expediency, but the alliance with Bulgaria was in harmony with his ideology and with the country's national interests.

5. DISPUTE OVER THE SERBO-BULGARIAN CUSTOMS UNION

The trade treaty between Austria-Hungary and Serbia expired in early 1905 and was twice provisionally extended, once to the end of 1905 and once again to March 14, 1906. It was agreed that during this provisional arrangement a new Austro-Serbian treaty would be concluded. The treaty was unfortunately not agreed upon until 1908, and during the prolonged trade discussions relations between Serbia and Austria-Hungary were ruptured, causing the "Pig War." The reasons for the break in traditional economic relations between the two countries were many. The new economic policy of the Dual Monarchy was governed by the conflicting needs of her agrarian and industrial regions—Hungary and Austria, her economic relations with Germany, and her over-all political policy in the Balkans, especially that of regaining full control of Serbia. The policy of the Serbian government after 1903 was aimed at emancipating the country from economic and political domination by Austria-Hungary. Serbia had recently adopted an autonomous customs system on the basis of which the treaty with Germany had already been concluded.[73]

When negotiations for a new trade treaty were started the Austrian demands were great, but Serbia was in a more favorable position for negotiation than she had been when the Secret Convention was in operation. Austria-Hungary proposed a treaty which would deprive Serbia of most of the earlier favors she had enjoyed for the goods she exported to Austria, and at the same time would provide preferential rating for Austrian industrial products in Serbia. In addition, Austria made certain additional demands, such as monopoly on state contracts, before she would sign a new treaty. Serbia found these latter demands especially repugnant and considered the Austrian attitude incompatible with the usual practice between two independent states. The rejection of her demands by Serbia caused Austria-Hungary to become even firmer with Serbia. The two states prepared for a showdown.

Fresh trade treaties, based on the new Serbian tariff law, would, it was believed, strengthen Serbia in dealing with Austria-Hungary.[74] Consequently the government began secret negotiations for new treaties with some of the European states. When the Stojanović cabinet, during 1905, sounded out a number of states with regard to treaties, the Bulgarian government was one of the first to respond. This was a short-lived period of good will between Beograd and Sofia, when the leaders of the two countries tried to bring about an economic and political understanding between their two nations. In 1904

Bulgaria had renounced all trade treaties and had planned negotiations for a set of treaties based on a new customs tariff.[75] Serbian negotiations with Bulgaria were successful and a customs treaty was signed on June 22, 1905, to go into force on March 1, 1906. The treaty consisted of nineteen articles. The document was kept secret until December 20, 1905, when the Bulgarian government, without previous consultation with the Serbian government, as had been specified by the agreement, submitted it to the Sobranie, which ratified it by acclamation.[76]

The terms of the Serbo-Bulgarian customs treaty were of some importance. In order that the two states might come into closer economic relationship the agreement provided for the establishment of a customs union. However, they were to retain their own tariffs until March 1, 1917, and during that time could conclude separate commercial treaties with foreign states. The agreement also provided for exchange of goods free of duty, excepting those goods regulated by special provisions, and for free flow of interstate commerce except under extraordinary military and hygienic conditions. The two governments were to introduce as far as possible identical customs laws and other regulations, and employ no discrimination against each other's goods. They furthermore agreed to co-operate toward the improvement of their mutual trade and industry, permit citizens of one country freely to work and live in the territory of the other, and make available to one another their respective rail, water, and other transportation facilities. The treaty specified the subsequent conclusion of consular and monetary conventions, intended to embrace their existing territories as well as any additional territory that might in the future belong to them. Finally, it was agreed that the economic agreement should go into force on March 1, 1906, and run to March 1, 1917, when it would be succeeded by the Customs Union (Zollverein).[77] Many Serb patriots contended that the Serbo-Bulgarian Customs Union would serve as a possible prelude to a political union, which would lead to the exclusion of foreign interference, particularly that of Austria-Hungary, from the Balkans.[78]

The treaty with Bulgaria secured for Serbia additional markets and an export route. The trade exchange between these two states was not expected to become very vital, since they produced and sold the same type of goods; more important was the transit through Bulgarian seaports, whence Serbian goods could be shipped to foreign markets.

Any Balkan combination potentially dangerous to the existence of Turkey and Austria-Hungary was not likely to be ignored by these two empires. On January 25, 1906, the Porte protested against the Serbo-Bulgarian customs agreement.[79] Upon receipt of the news of the agreement, the Turko-Serbian trade talks at Constantinople were promptly suspended, and the Porte sent a note to Bulgaria protesting the latter's agreement with Serbia on the grounds that it was a violation of the terms of the Treaty of Berlin.[80] But Turkey, whose complaint was more justifiable than Austria's in view of her position as a suzerain state vis-à-vis Bulgaria, was less arrogant than Austria-Hungary, and merely requested Bulgaria to change those provisions of the treaty which were not in Turkey's interest, and those changes were effected.[81] The Vienna government, which similarly appreciated the significance of the Serbo-Bulgarian *rapprochement*, reacted as promptly.[82] According to Pašić,

Austria was evidently anxious to show Europe that Serbia lay in her power. In this she has been bitterly deceived. Serbia may be weaker than Austria, but she has nevertheless her dignity as a State. Austria does not wish to see the solidarity of the Balkan countries, and this explains her conduct in the question of the customs union.[83]

When the news of the Serbo-Bulgarian agreement reached Vienna, the trade discussions with Serbia were at once ended. On January 5 Count Goluchowski told Serbian Minister M. Vujić and Serbian delegates M. Milovanović and M. Popović that Austria-Hungary could not recognize the Serbo-Bulgarian Customs Union and therefore could not continue trade discussions which were then in progress. Goluchowski warned the Serbian delegates that Bulgaria was dishonest in her dealings with Serbia and that Bulgaria as a vassal state could not enter into agreements which violated the Treaty of Berlin. The Serbian explanation was that the treaty with Bulgaria was signed "conditionally" to allow for modifications in the text in accordance with the "new treaty" to be concluded between Serbia and Austria-Hungary. Goluchowski ignored this explanation and demanded to know if Serbia was prepared to abandon the treaty with Bulgaria as preliminary to the resumption of negotiations with Austria-Hungary. The Serbs refused to withdraw from a treaty "already signed" with Bulgaria, whatever the importance, for one "not yet signed" with Austria-Hungary. They found that it was quite sufficient on the part of their government when signing the treaty with Bulgaria to have secured "a free hand" to modify or reject the treaty should the conclusion of the treaty with Austria-Hungary demand such action.[84]

Count Goluchowski was somewhat annoyed by the fact that the two Balkan states kept their agreement secret, and contended that Serbia had wished to use the secret treaty as a means of pressure on Austria-Hungary. Serbia apparently had kept the treaty with Bulgaria secret pending negotiations with Austria-Hungary because, Ćorović alleges, it would have been difficult to alter a published text of the treaty, if such alterations were necessary, as a result of the new Serbo-Austrian trade treaty.[85]

On January 11 Count Goluchowski notified Minister von Czikann that negotiations with Serbia would not be resumed until the government received a complete copy of the Serbo-Bulgarian agreement, and until Serbia withdrew from the agreement and gave written assurances that it would not be submitted to the Skupština for ratification.[86]

The Vienna press was severe in its criticism of the new Balkan development. *Zeit* wrote, "Bulgaria has committed suicide; by her action she has renounced the customs treaty with Turkey, concluded in 1899, while Serbia in desiring a customs union with Bulgaria will suffocate in her own swine-fat for abandoning the Veterinary Convention with Hungary."[87] *Fremdenblatt* indicated that Austria-Hungary would not allow any changes affecting her economic relations with Bulgaria, which were based on the most-favored-nation treatment and guaranteed as such by the Treaty of Berlin.[88] The *Neue Freie Presse* of January 3, 1906, wrote that the Customs Union was "a challenge to Austria-Hungary, for Serbia's commerce gravitates toward Austria-Hungary . . . The Customs Union is an economic farce . . . But the conclusion of such an agreement is a symptom of the endless agitation and ambition prevailing amongst the Balkan States, of the continual scheming and intriguing, which neither Austria-Hungary nor even Russia will be able long to pass over in silence." On the following day the same paper threatened that the monarchy would "most energetically" strike a blow (*den Gegenstoss*) at "the pretended customs union between Serbia and Bulgaria," not by breaking off diplomatic relations, "but on quite a different ground, where it would have its effect." Serbia was reminded that she was dependent on Austro-Hungarian markets, and that these markets might no longer be available. On January 5 the *Neue Freie Presse* reminded King Peter that "the Obrenović rulers saw that Serbia must look to Austria-Hungary's good will, if she did not wish to be crushed . . . between that power and Russia." The paper added that the proximity of Austria, whose gunboats on the Danube were within sight of Beograd, represented a permanent warning that Serbia needed Austria's friendship. The question of the customs union involved, according to the *Neue Freie Presse*, "the raising of the entire Balkan question. It would be a shameful act if a rash Balkan intrigue were to jeopardize the peace of Europe . . . This Serbo-Bulgarian Customs Union, in itself meaningless . . . cannot be concluded without the opposition of Austria-Hungary, and that might produce dire consequences for Serbia."[89]

The principal Hungarian newspapers (*Pester Lloyd, Pesti Hirlap, Az Ujság*), on the other hand, were critical of their government's policy regarding Serbia, and a large segment of the Slavic press, together with some representatives to the parliaments of the monarchy, sympathized with the cause of Serbia. The Czech *Národní Listy*, for example, attacked the government for its so-called "repressive measures" toward Serbia.[90] The question of Serbo-Austrian trade became the subject of polemics among professional economists. The consensus of the Austrian economists was that Serbia could not exist without Austro-Hungarian markets. Where else, one of them asked, could Serbia sell her agricultural produce?[91] The press of England, France, and Belgium favored Serbia in her conflict with the neighboring giant. The London *Times* of January 6, 1906, commented that "Whatever in the long run be the outcome of these negotiations, it is clearly understood here that the conclusion of the treaty is in itself of great political significance and that it does not mean an increase of Austro-Hungarian influence in the Balkans."

The British informed the Serbian government that they considered the Austrian demands on Serbia not in line with the usual "stipulations in commercial understandings between independent states."[92] This same idea was conveyed by Edward Grey to the Austrian ambassador in London.

The foreign envoys in Vienna, especially the German, Russian, French, and Italian, were surprised at such a display of "an irritability by the Ballplatz which was based not merely on economic but also on political grounds." The French envoy reported that Count Goluchowski would not resume commercial negotiations with Serbia unless that country first sacrificed her agreement with Bulgaria. Goluchowski apparently had told the same thing to Bulgarian Minister Sarafov, who replied that Bulgaria would not give up her treaty with Serbia.[93]

In Beograd ministers of Italy, France, and England on different occasions approved the Serbian attitude, and by doing so encouraged her to resist the excessive demands of Austria-Hungary.[94] Rumanian Minister Take Jonescu advised Serbia to stand firm in spite of any temporary losses she might suffer.[95]

Serbia found it difficult to comply with the rather stiff Austro-Hungarian note. If she were to withdraw from the Customs Union, she ran the risk of jeopardizing her relations with Bulgaria, the improvement of which the government cherished greatly. Furthermore, Serbia seemed to be required to void her agreement with Bulgaria without knowing what kind of treaty Austria-Hungary had in store for her. In reply to the Austro-Hungarian note of January 11, the Serbian government stated on January 13 that it could not give a written promise,[96] but repeated that it would not submit the agreement with Bulgaria to the Skupština before the trade treaty with Austria-Hungary was concluded. The prime minister stressed the flexible nature of the treaty, which permitted many possible modifications. He explained that it was of local character and not directed against any foreign power and that it could be changed "if necessary" in accordance with the terms of the new treaty with Austria-Hungary.[97] The Serbian government expressed readiness to modify any provisions of the treaty with Bulgaria which Austria-Hungary considered offensive, and in this connection transmitted to Vienna a copy of the Serbo-Bulgarian treaty.[98]

Austria-Hungary found Serbia's note "vague" and inadequate, a palliative which merely added to the existing "difficulties and misunderstandings."[99] On January 18 the Austrian government repeated its demands, and a few days later Serbia reiterated its earlier answer.[100]

Austria-Hungary, in no mood for bargaining, insisted simply that the treaty with Bulgaria had to be terminated at once. The more intransigent officials and a segment of the Austrian press wished for a prompt application of repressive measures against Serbia, and the government obliged.[101] Goluchowski met with the Hungarian prime minister to discuss the type of steps to be taken.[102] Serbian delegates were meanwhile recalled from Vienna.[103] On January 22 all imports from Serbia were stopped. The monarchy once again "discovered" an infectious disease in Serbian livestock, and on the basis of Article VII of the Veterinary Convention closed her borders to them.[104] This action, to say the least, was quite irregular but by no means novel. The monarchy, as pointed out earlier, had resorted to such tactics several times before.[105] The rupture in economic relations started the commercial war—or "Pig War"—in which "the little Serbian David" refused "to capitulate before the Austro-Hungarian Goliath."[106] The opinion prevalent in Austro-Hungarian circles was that the "closing of the frontier has never failed in its effect upon the Serbian government" and that Serbia, therefore, was sure to submit to the will of the monarchy. An Austrian agent in Beograd explained that the only concern of the Serbian peasant was to obtain a good price for his produce. When that became impossible Serbia would drop her intransigence within a month. Some Serbs were also convinced of the effectiveness of the Austrian repressive measures. Pro-Obrenović Vukašin Petrović, for example, had advised Austria-Hungary to adopt the strong-arm method in hope of precipitating a crisis in Serbia that would bring an Austrophile government to power.[107]

The situation was so serious that many in Serbia, as stated previously, feared Austro-Hungarian military action to force Serbia into submission.[108] There was some justification for Serbian apprehension. On January 18, 1906, *Danzers Armee-Zeitung* reported on "the military character of the frontier with Serbia" just in case "our monarchy should find itself at war with Serbia."[109]

In Serbia the immediate repercussions of the Austro-Hungarian attitude brought the political opposition solidly behind the government. Nikola Pašić, then in the opposition, protested against what he called the monarchy's disregard of Serbia's rights as an independent state. He congratulated the government for its stand in rejecting the Austro-Hungarian ultimatums. Stojan Novaković, also of the opposition, criticized the monarchy for its unfair and inhuman treatment of Serbia. Vojislav Veljković denounced the policy of the Dual Monarchy as one contrary to the spirit and the letter of international law, according to which all powers were equal, regardless of their size. The Skupština, after lengthy deliberations, unanimously approved the government's refusal to accept Austro-Hungarian demands. The Serbian government promptly reacted on the monarchy's economic reprisals by prohibiting the import and transit of sugar and alcohol produced in Austria-Hungary.[110]

The Russian and Italian ministers in Beograd told their Austrian colleague that his country's demands on Serbia were unjust, and urged a conciliatory policy. The French, Italian, and English ambassadors in Vienna spoke in similar language to the Serbian minister and to Count Goluchowski. The attitudes of the Russian and German representatives were seemingly less outspoken, although many German officials felt that Goluchowski's methods in dealing with Serbia were "tactless" and ill advised. Italian minister Guiccioli, whom Albertini describes as "a pronounced Slavophil," wrote to his Foreign Office on February 18 that his assignment in Beograd was a difficult one, that is, to "favor the independence of the Balkan States and their ties of mutual friendship" and yet to act "in accord with Austria-Hungary." He noted that Austria-Hungary's "sole purpose" was "to crush all aspirations to independence" of Serbia and "to hinder the formation of any bond of solidarity between the peoples of one kin." He assured the Foreign Office that he had thus far acted in conformity with his instructions and that he had done his best "to reconcile these incompatibles and to avert mischief," although he was not certain that this untenable situation could continue.[111]

The pressure of public opinion from both the Slavic and Hungarian opposition, as well as Serbian refusal to compromise, influenced Count Goluchowski to adopt a somewhat conciliatory position a few days after the formal rupture of economic relations.[112] Previously he had taken exception to the secrecy of the Serbo-Bulgarian Customs Treaty, but now having seen the text he realized that his initial fears were not justified. He presently concentrated on breaking the Serbo-Bulgarian *rapprochement* by emphasizing alleged insincerity on the part of the Bulgarians. Goluchowski quoted the Bulgarian Racha Petrov as having purportedly said that he attached little importance to the treaty with Serbia, and that only after Bulgaria failed to obtain from the Austro-Hungarian government the treatment accorded Serbia in the matter of veterinary regulations did Bulgaria announce the Customs Treaty without prior consultation with Serbia.[113] Thus, according to Ćorović, Goluchowski, after failing to destroy the Serbo-Bulgarian Customs Treaty openly and by threats, had decided to accomplish that objective by sowing discord between Serbia and Bulgaria.

In early February of 1906 Goluchowski and Francis Joseph told the Serbian minister on separate occasions that it was to the mutual benefit of the two countries to resume normal trade relations and advised that the Serbs make the first move toward reopening negotiations.[114] The Serbs accepted this overture and announced their readiness to accept the Austrian demands. The prearranged plan required that the Austrian government stipulate the provisions of the Serbo-Bulgarian Customs Treaty it wished to see changed, and Serbia would then oblige in so doing.[115]

The list of proposed changes was transmitted to Serbia on February 16, 1906. Austria-Hungary wanted Article I worded so that it would assure her of the most-favored-nation treatment; otherwise, she alleged, the Article was in violation of international law. Article II, which exempted Bulgarian goods from all duties, also violated, according to her, international law and the principle of the most-favored-nation treatment, and she demanded appropriate modifications. Austria-Hungary requested that the treaty with Bulgaria should not be called a customs union. She wanted the last portion of Article III altered and the second paragraph of Article VII eliminated. These items concerned privileges on railroads, waterways, and roads which the signatories promised each other, but which Austria-Hungary found inconsistent with Article X of the Quadruple Railway Convention, signed in 1883 (by Serbia, Turkey, Bulgaria, and herself), unless her citizens were granted identical privileges. Austria-Hungary demanded also that Article XIV be replaced by the corresponding provision from the Serbo-Bulgarian Treaty of 1897. The latter change would deprive Serbian and Bulgarian contractors of priority in state contracts, and all contractors would enjoy the same privileges. Finally, Austria-Hungary demanded that "in accordance with the international convention concerning the most-favored-nation clause, all the special privileges contained in the treaty with Bulgaria should be extended also to Austria-Hungary on the basis of her commercial treaty with Serbia."[116] In the final analysis, Austria-Hungary refused to recognize the Serbo-Bulgarian agreement as a customs union, and insisted in the name of the most-favored-nation clause on privileges equal to those Serbia gave Bulgaria.

If the Customs Union could not be completely voided, then the monarchy's object was "to pervert" it. According to Count Goluchowski, the document signed between Serbia and Bulgaria was not in any event a true customs union. "For if in truth it were, it would be bound to exclude other contracting states from the facilities mutually agreed upon under the terms of the treaty, and therefore necessarily to exclude also the recognition of Austria-Hungary's right of application of the most-favored-nation clause."[117]

The Serbian government approached Bulgaria, informed her of the Austrian demands, and asked for consent to alter the text of the Customs Treaty. The Bulgarian government, according to Ćorović, appreciated the Serbian difficulties but explained that for its part the changes in the text of the treaty could not be made "without legislative action," because the treaty had already been invested with the force of law. Nonetheless, the Bulgarian attitude was sufficiently reassuring to permit the Serbian government to inform Vienna on February 23 that it would make the requested changes in the treaty with Bulgaria, adding, however, that due to the special nature of the Austro-Hungarian economic position, Serbia could not adopt an identical attitude with regard to Austria-Hungary and Bulgaria; she could not, in other words, give Austria-Hungary the special privileges which Serbia and Bulgaria had granted each other in the customs union treaty.[118] More specifically, on February 24, 1906, the Serbian government explained that a treaty between Serbia and Bulgaria—the two agrarian states—could not possibly injure Austrian economic interests, i.e., industrial exports. Nevertheless, the Serbian government expressed its willingness to see Articles I and II altered. In respect to Articles IX, XII, and XIV, however, the Serbs held that changes were not necessary, and that in any case they would not stand in the way of restoring normal relations.[119] Needless to say, the changes made in the Customs Treaty with Bulgaria, even though forced upon Serbia by Austria-Hungary, spelled an unhappy omen. After a brief period of cordiality, relations between the two Balkan states began to deteriorate.

On March 3, 1906, Serbia and Austria-Hungary agreed to a provisional trade arrangement based on the most-favored-nation principle. They agreed to suspend repressive measures against each other's trade and to enforce the provisions of the existing Veterinary Convention. Serbia agreed to give Austrian goods the same treatment they had had on February 28, that is, before the trade treaty expired. The temporary accord on trade was put in force simultaneously by the two governments, and was to remain in force "until further notice."[120] These temporary accommodations were apparently not satisfactory. As a matter of fact, on March 12, 1906, the *Times* reported that

Austria-Hungary not only continued to exclude Serbian live-stock of all descriptions, but applies the autonomous tariff to Serbian agricultural produce, the duties hitherto imposed being in some cases quadrupled or even sextupled. On the other hand, pending the settlement, a large amount of Austrian merchandise destined for Serbia was waiting at Semlin and other stations near the frontier, where some 800 loaded wagons stand in the sidings.[121]

How did the Serbian public react to the Austro-Serbian conflict? There was widespread approval of the government's policy. One writer compared the situation with the Austro-Rumanian conflict that had taken place a few years before, and concluded that "we should not fear commercial war with Austria-Hungary. Only the Austro-Hungarian manufacturers should fear it."[122] *Delo* warned that "the commercial war would be better than any caricature of a commercial treaty . . . which would retard our work toward emancipation."[123] Patriotic fervor spread throughout the country ; practically all political parties of consequence were united on this issue. Meetings, discussions, and conferences were held in order to urge the government to take a firm stand. The following resolution was passed at a mass meeting in Beograd :

The assembled merchants accept the Customs Union with Bulgaria as a measure of mutual defence for political and economic interests. We are firmly opposed to the idea of bargaining away the friendly relations with the Balkan states, as well as to any effort from whatever quarter directed toward suspension of the treaty with Bulgaria as a price for the agreement with Austria. We desire good and friendly relations on a sound basis . . . We protest against the closing of the frontiers, as an act in violation of the existing treaty, and urge enforcement of similar measures against the importation of Austrian goods when the treaty expires.[124]

In face of the existing conflict with Serbia, the two parts of the Dual Monarchy united on common action despite their differences of opinion regarding trade relations with Serbia. M. Wekerle, Hungarian prime minister, in acknowledging the measures taken by the Austro-Hungarian joint government, declared that "We have to be in harmony with the other half of the monarchy and approve the measures taken toward Serbia."[125] On April 5, 1906, the Austro-Hungarian government stipulated in the form of a declaration four conditions under which a trade agreement with Serbia would be possible : a simplification of the tariff system, a revision of the text of the tariff so as to obtain clear principles governing taxation, a fixing of the future tariff quota, and a guaranty that in the state contracts Austro-Hungarian products of equal price and quality should be given the same treatment as those produced by other European states. The contracts obviously referred to armament, railway materials, and salt.[126]

The Serbian government agreed to give Austro-Hungarian products the same treatment it gave others, but explained that pending gun contracts would be placed with a firm recommended by a military commission.[127] In an interview given to the *Politische Korrespondenz* Prime Minister Sava Grujić said :

The Austro-Hungarian action in regard to the contract question is contrary to the international law in force for trade between two independent states. The demands which Military Attaché Pomiankowski made for Austria-Hungary in connection with the gun question could be put only before a satrapy and not before a sovereign state.

Grujić personally stressed the fact that nothing could be done about the gun contract until the commission made its report. The military commission, he said, would secretly vote for what it considered the best guns.[128]

The stalemate in trade discussions with Austria-Hungary and the regicide controversy with England caused the fall of Grujić's cabinet on April 17, 1906. The new cabinet under Nikola Pašić, made up from the Radical party, continued the commercial war with Austria-Hungary, but succeeded in restoring diplomatic relations with England and settling the regicide question.

6. THE LOAN AND GUN QUESTIONS

The provisional trade arrangement between Serbia and Austria-Hungary, agreed upon in March 1906, had left several problems unsolved. At first the question of the Serbo-Bulgarian Customs Union appeared as the principal stumbling block in the path of successful commercial negotiations between Serbia and Austria-Hungary. That question was resolved and a provisional trade agreement was made possible. When discussions for a permanent treaty were reopened, the principal controversy centered on the so-called "loan and gun questions." Since the time of Alexander Obrenović, Serbia had planned to equip her armies with rapid firing artillery. This plan was taken up more seriously after Alexander's death and remained on the agenda of all cabinets that followed. After 1904, furthermore, various Serbian governments had been carrying on negotiations for a loan that would provide funds for modern armaments and the construction of railways. The two principal political parties agreed that a new foreign loan should be obtained in order to meet payments and, if possible, reduce the huge national debt inherited from the Obrenović rulers. Furthermore, without a loan, construction of railways, modernization of the army, location of new markets, and general economic improvement were believed impossible.

In the spring of 1904 the Grujić cabinet prepared to negotiate in Paris a loan of from 30 to 40 million francs. A group of French and German financiers was willing to provide the money. Austria-Hungary, to whom Serbia was already deeply indebted, was intentionally excluded from participation in the projected loan.[129] There was strong opposition to the proposed loan, precipitating a parliamentary crisis lasting several days. King Peter stepped in himself and tried to reconcile the two Radical parties. The government was obliged to drop the proposed loan. Grujić resigned on November 19, 1904, and the king invited Nikola Pašić, noted politician and statesman, to form a cabinet. On November 27, 1904, Pašić came up with a cabinet constituted exclusively of Radicals. Pašić tackled the loan question with vigor, but, like his predecessor, he encountered opposition on this and other current issues—the conspiratorial question and the matter of Bulgarian policy complicating further an already complex situation.

The Dual Monarchy insisted that Serbia should place her state orders for military material with Austrian industries, particularly with the Škoda works. Her military attaché in Beograd was instructed on December 27, 1904, that the success "in the gun question" was absolutely necessary, and that no other foreign power should be permitted to compete with Austria-Hungary in the matter of armaments.[130]

For Serbia the question of arms was one of great importance. These arms had to be superior to, or at least as good as, those recently obtained by Bulgaria. The guns obtained from Škoda in May 1903 had proved most unsatisfactory. More careful selection from various European gun models was the only wise thing to do. The Serbian government wished to pursue a financial and military policy in the best national interests, despite multifarious pressures from Austria-Hungary. As a matter of fact, these pressures and the talk of possible Austrian invasion of the Balkans convinced the Serbs that they should not buy Austro-Hungarian guns. Pašić resented the arrogance of the Vienna government and the variety of pressures used to coerce Serbia into submission.

There is reason to believe that the Pašić government had never intended to consider Austrian guns but only those produced by the Krupp (German) and Schneider (French) firms. Because Bulgaria ordered Schneider guns, and because in 1904 she was considered a possible ally, it was felt that Serbia ought to have similar equipment. Škoda products were included among the models to be tested by a military commission only under strenuous insistence by Austria-Hungary. As indicated earlier, the Pašić government had formed a commission of military experts to test the guns of several firms and to determine which of the guns should be ordered.[131]

When the new government opened negotiations for the loan on October 25, 1904, Minister of Finance Lazar Paču was approached by a representative of Wiener Bankverein, who was authorized to offer Serbia a 30-million-dinar loan on the security of the Serbian railways, "on condition that all military supplies should be obtained from Austria." He further proposed that the Serbian state railways "be sold to a limited liability company with a capital of 20 million dinars, in which [Wiener Bankverein] would in all probability be well represented. The staffs of the Serbian railway service would continue, in the main, in their posts, with the exception of the higher officials, who would be brought from the monarchy 'for the purpose of supervision.' "[132]

In an audience with the king on December 14, Dumba said, in recommending Škoda's tender, that "the Serbian attitude regarding the artillery order and the loan was 'a touchstone and a kind of barometer' of her attitude toward Austria-Hungary." Three days earlier the Austrian military attaché, Joseph Pomiankowsky, had been even more explicit during his conversation with War Minister R. Putnik.[133]

Throughout the whole of 1905 the government concerned itself with the loan and gun questions. In January 1905 the artillery commission, which had been designated to select the firms whose military equipment the state might consider buying, agreed on Saint Chamond and Le Creusot of France, Krupp and Erhard of Germany, and Škoda of Austria-Hungary. The king approved the products of these firms, and the Skupština allocated 300,000 francs for the purpose of testing the various models of guns.[134]

The guns designated for testing did not arrive in Serbia until April 1905, as the Dual Monarchy refused to permit the transit of foreign munitions across her territory to Serbia. After the guns arrived, testing and administrative rigmarole required days before any decision could be reached. While the guns were being tested the government was busy negotiating a loan in France, and on May 8, 1905, made an agreement for a loan of 110 million francs at 4½ percent interest.[135]

French financiers were willing to make the loan to Serbia. However, they wished for a short-term loan because of the uncertainty which then prevailed "on the money market as a result of the long duration of the Russo-Japanese War." They were no less interested in the Serbian order for big guns than were the Austrians. They were willing to leave small arms, munitions, and railway materials to other countries "participating in the loan."[136]

On April 4 Dumba protested against what seemed Serbia's abandonment of the idea of testing the guns and presented a demand that 40 percent of the Serbian orders should be given to Austria-Hungary as compensation for her loss. Pašić refused to be intimidated. He explained that arrangements had already been made "with the syndicated banks," reserving 60 percent of the state contracts for Austrian and German industries, equally divided, and 40 percent for those of France. The French minister in Beograd had similarly informed Dumba on March 1.[137]

Parliamentary opposition to the agreement was very strong because the loan bore heavy obligations and a high rate of interest. A special session of the Skupština was called for May 8, 1905, but in face of the situation in the Skupština the loan agreement was not raised at all. With little chance of success, the government of Pašić resigned. On May 16, 1905, Ljubomir Stojanović, leader of the minority Independent Radical party, formed the cabinet. The Skupština adjourned on May 17, leaving the loan question undecided.

During their campaign for the July 10, 1905, elections, the Independent Radicals criticized Pašić on a score of issues but particularly for the 110-million-franc loan contracted on conditions damaging to the best interests of the state. For this and other reasons the Independent Radicals elected eighty-one of the total one hundred sixty parliamentary seats.[138] Since this represented a bare majority, the future of the Independent Radical cabinet under Stojanović was not bright, and the cabinet of necessity chose a cautious, almost bipartisan policy. The cabinet remained in power during eleven months of continued parliamentary reverses. It turned down the loan arranged for in France by the Radicals, and proceeded, despite strong opposition, to find a smaller loan in which Austrian capital would participate.

Arrangements for the loan were agreed upon on November 4, 1905, nominally in Brussels with an international syndicate, but in fact in Beograd with a representative of the Austrian Bankverein and associated financial group. The loan amounted to 70 million francs and was, on paper at least, more favorable than the one concluded by Pašić. The loan was to be issued at 84.5 percent, as against 83.5 in the case of Pašić's French loan. But, Ćorović writes, the former involved such conditions as "the right of option," and carried no guaranty that Serbian securities would be quoted on the stock exchanges of the monarchy, as the Serbian government had asked.[139] According to Ćorović, furthermore, the loan was calculated with a view toward securing Serbian state contracts. Indeed, in a note on November 2 the

Austrian government demanded that Serbia make a written promise, in connection with the loan agreement, that she would place her state orders with Austrian firms. The Austrian note, however, arrived after the loan negotiations had been completed.[140]

The Stojanović loan was considered an Austrian victory, and to keep it that way the monarchy's Foreign Office on November 10 issued instructions to the press to ignore the loan and to minimize the importance of advantages Austria-Hungary received therefrom. Meanwhile the Serbian government was ready to honor the loan agreement and was prepared to "reopen the gun question." On September 21, 1905, a new committee of military experts was sent abroad to visit various factories and examine and test the different gun models. Simultaneously the official press began preparing the public to think of the guns not as a political question but as one of economics.[141]

The loan agreed upon by the Stojanović cabinet came to naught when Austria-Hungary learned of the Serbo-Bulgarian Customs Union in December 1905 and in reprisal suspended trade discussions.[142] This diplomatic conflict between Austria-Hungary and Serbia occurred at a moment when many prominent people in Serbia, including King Peter, were ready for a conciliatory policy vis-à-vis the monarchy. Milovanović explained that the Serbian policy toward Austria-Hungary was not aggressive and that agreement could be reached easily if Austria-Hungary wished. Vujić suggested that Austria-Hungary should abandon her old policy of secret agreements with the king for an "open policy" of agreements with the constitutionally established governments of Serbia. Even some foreigners noted Serbia's conciliatory gestures. In October 1905 the Italian ambassador in Vienna, Duke Avarna, remarked to Milovanović that he believed the new Serbian government "had been drawn into the Austrian orbit." Milovanović countered by explaining that his government would seek to dispel Austro-Hungarian suspicion of Serbia as Serbia becomes convinced that Austria-Hungary was not "planning new conquests or occupations in the Balkan Peninsula."[143]

After vigorous Austro-Hungarian protests against the Serbo-Bulgarian Customs Union and suspension of trade discussions with Serbia, the conciliatory mood of Beograd disappeared. The Serbian government lost interest in the Austrian loan, which in any case had been opposed in important Serbian political circles. Hereafter all Serbian groups were united against Austro-Hungarian pressure. Radicals and Independent Radicals stood firm on the subject of artillery orders. Only General Sava Grujić believed that some concessions might still be made to Austria-Hungary and artillery orders placed with Škoda.[144] The Independent Radicals were unable to settle the relations with Austria-Hungary and resigned on February 22, 1906. The Stojanović cabinet was succeeded by another Independent Radical one under Sava Grujić—which remained in power less than a month. The Radicals under Nikola Pašić returned to power on April 17, this time to stay.

Serbia took the position that the twelve-year trade treaty under discussion was a question separate from the military and state contracts. The trade treaty concerned the basic economic requirements of the two countries, and the special contracts served only the momentary need. Rationalization of this kind made no impression on Goluchowski, who on April 5 demanded that Austro-Hungarian products of equal price and quality should not be excluded from consideration in Serbian state contracts—military contracts and salt for the most part.[145]

Goluchowski was apparently falsely informed that the military commission had actually voted in favor of Škoda products, and for that reason he insisted that Serbia could not reject the Austrian products for purely financial and political reasons. In his opinion Austria-Hungary, having offered generous concessions to Serbian agrarian produce, deserved reciprocal treatment. Major Pomiankowski in a conversation with Premier Grujić shared Goluchowski's views. The Serbs denied that the military commission favored Škoda products and held that trade concessions offered to Austria-Hungary were, contrary to Goluchowski's assertion, much greater than those Austria-Hungary offered Serbia.[146] The fact that Serbia was willing to place her railway and certain other state contracts with Austria-Hungary was not enough; what Austria-Hungary wanted was the contract for guns.

In an audience with King Peter on April 8, the day before the bids for guns were to open, Austrian Minister Czikann demanded that under no condition should Škoda products be excluded from consideration and that the king should personally see to that. Somewhat more diplomatically Goluchowski told Vujić on April 25 that the monarchy's products should "in principle" be given a priority, "all other things being equal." Goluchowski concluded, "We, of course, are not in a position to demand that any particular order should be placed with Austria-Hungary but we shall certainly determine the extent of the concessions under the new commercial treaty by the extent to which the state contracts now under discussion are given to Austria-Hungary."[147]

Czikann was instructed to inform Pašić that the gun question was "still" very much a part of the commercial treaty. The war minister instructed Major Pomiankowski to explain that Austrian demands on Serbia were based on the following: Pašić's earlier promise that he would buy guns from Austria-Hungary, the decision of the military commission, which had found Škoda equipment better than Schneider but inferior to Krupp models, and the fact that certain other contracts should go to Austria-Hungary because they involved lower prices. The Serbs replied that in the matter of guns their government would abide strictly by the recommendations of the military commission; that French and German guns must be included among the models to be tested, because Serbia's loan was to come from those countries; that Austria-Hungary had already been promised a large share of Serbian state contracts; and, finally, that even if Pašić had made promises they were not binding on the military commission.[148] Thus Austria-Hungary insisted the gun contracts were a part of the general trade treaty and that the two questions must be treated simultaneously. Serbia was equally determined in expounding its interpretation that the gun question was not part of the trade treaty.

Under pressure from Austria-Hungary Serbia finally consented to order part of her guns (mountain artillery) from Austria-Hungary. This partial concession did not satisfy official circles in Austria-Hungary, which continued to accuse Nikola Pašić of deliberately refusing to purchase Austrian equipment, although purportedly superior to that offered by other powers. Most contemporary and later Serbian sources, however, insisted that the gun tests definitely showed that Austrian gun models were inferior to other models.[149] The military commission in its final report gave the highest score to the Schneider guns.[150] But the *Times* (London) reported on April 12, 1906 that

Serbia had been negotiating with various French, German, and Austro-Hungarian firms for some time past with a view to the placing of orders for several batteries of field guns. The Austrian Škoda guns proved on trial to be better than most and cheaper than any of the weapons tested in the presence of a perambulating commission of Serbian officers, but the Serbian government still hesitates to place its orders in Austria.

According to Ćorović, the ten-member military commission voted six to four in favor of one Krupp model against the comparable Schneider model, and seven to three in favor of another Schneider model. The business transaction with the Krupp company was not possible because company representatives insisted on being given either a complete order or in sharing the order with Škoda. Krupp refused under any conditon to share the contract for guns with Schneider. Since none of the Škoda products was recommended by the commission, the Serbian government was in no position to comply with the Krupp requests.[151]

The poor showing of the Škoda models was not surprising ; the Austrian officials knew as a result of earlier tests held in Austria-Hungary that Škoda guns were inferior.[152] Despite the results of the tests, the Austro-Hungarian government in a note to Serbia on May 16, 1906, refused to withdraw its demands regarding the guns and made it clear that trade negotiations would not be opened nor the provisional trade arrangement extended until "the promise" of Pašić was carried out. On the next day Pašić denied ever having promised to purchase guns in Austria-Hungary, and that come what may he would abide by the decision of the commission.[153] There is lack of concrete evidence to the effect that Pašić promised to buy guns from Austria-Hungary. On June 13, 1905, Dumba reported that Pašić declined a promise in writing and Pomiankowski reported on June 18 that Pašić was too "indefinite and even 'negative' on the gun question."[154]

When at last Austria-Hungary learned with certainty that the Škoda guns did not pass the military commission's test, she stopped insisting that her guns be tested. Instead, on May 22, Czikann informed Pašić that Austria-Hungary could not consider final the findings of the military commission. This apparent inconsistency was but a face-saving device. On May 28 F. Kossuth, the Hungarian minister of national economy, told Vujić that Goluchowski could not give way on the question of guns and suggested that Serbia compromise on the artillery question. Similarly, on June 26 Czikann told

Pašić that after such prolonged discussions Austria-Hungary found it absolutely necessary not only to espouse "the cause of her artillery manufacturers," but to satisfy them.[155]

As pointed out earlier, responsible factors of the monarchy were cognizant of the low quality of Škoda products. Dumba admitted that the first battery of Škoda field artillery guns delivered to Serbia in the time of Alexander was of inferior quality. But apparently his orders were to do his utmost to obtain for Škoda a contract of from fifty to sixty batteries. Škoda, he relates, had long been in difficulties; it owed 4 million crowns to the Österreichischen Kreditanstalt, and was told that no further credit would be extended. The guns supplied by Škoda for Austria's coastal and other defenses were insufficient to keep the works going. At the court ball in Vienna, he was told by the emperor, the archduke, and Count Goluchowski that they wanted him to see the contract through.[156]

Ćorović is quite certain that it was this financial difficulty of Škoda that explained the determination of the monarchy's diplomacy, which was bent on forcing Serbia to purchase all her required guns from Škoda. The gun trade, he says, was necessary to save the industry. The Serbian minister in Vienna explained the pressure for contracts as also being due to the fact that the archduke had investments in Škoda. He further learned that the emperor had personally promised the Škoda firm that they would get some of the Serbian contracts.[157]

7. THE IMPASSE

The general narrative of Serbo-Austrian economic relations has been interrupted to give unified treatment to the historically important loan question and gun controversy. It remains now to pick up this narrative from June 1906 in order to relate those two questions to the over-all pattern of Serbo-Austrian economic relations. Serbia, as we noted earlier, insisted on her right to purchase guns and ammunition wherever and whenever national interest required. Yet she promised repeatedly to buy from Austria other industrial products in the value of 26 million dinars, and possibly more, should the Serbian railways be extended.[158] At the same time the government demanded from Austria-Hungary a most-favored-nation treatment and the right to export to that country during the period of the provisional agreement —until the end of the year—a specified number of various types of livestock.[159]

Serbia approved in general the Austrian provisional plan for resumption of economic relations, provided Austria-Hungary honored a series of specific conditions. These were: that the points on which a provisional agreement was reached should not prejudice the future discussion regarding the terms of the regular trade treaty; that since the special tariff would be effective only for the duration of the provisional agreement, the changes in the Serbo-German treaty requested by Austria-Hungary should be delayed; that because the general tariff system was a law, and there existed no special law regarding the provisional regulation of economic relations, the Serbian government had no legal power to alter the existing situation without legislative action; and finally, that the three-month limit of the provisional agreement could not be accepted, principally because of the nature of the Serbian livestock exports, which could not be altered within such a short period of time. The short-term agreement would favor Austrian industrial exports, and the Serbian government, therefore, desired that the provisional short-term agreement be extended until the end of the year, or until a new treaty should be concluded.[160]

Meanwhile on June 17, acting on the recommendation of its own and Germany's ministers at Beograd, the Austro-Hungarian government informed Serbia that it would extend the provisional trade arrangement then in operation for a period of only three additional months, beginning June 22, if Serbia would lower her import tariff on certain specified Austrian goods. Before this "Provisorium" should go into effect, however, Serbia was expected to give a written promise that she would not take any steps toward procurement of guns and other state contracts that might be prejudicial to Austria-Hungary. Without this promise, the monarchy threatened to suspend the existing *modus vivendi*; and, in case the "Provisorium" should be extended, Austria-Hungary reserved the right to terminate it if Serbia failed to comply with the agreed conditions.[161]

Speaking before the Skupština on July 31, Pašić declared that "On all other questions we can come to an agreement provided there is good will on both sides, but on this question which involves our honor and the right to self-determination, we cannot agree."[162] He requested an immediate report from the military commission, and permission to publish a Blue Book on trade negotiations with Austria-Hungary, which the Skupština unanimously approved. The appearance of the Blue Book, covering negotiations from March 3 to July 24, 1906, elicited a severe attack on Serbia by the Austro-Hungarian press.[163] Vienna was obviously unhappy over the Serbian decision to issue the Blue Book. The Serbian envoy was told that publication of such a book would "only aggravate mutual relations," and that, moreover, the Austrian note of April 5 on the question of the guns was a confidential communication.[164]

In the final analysis, the demands of Austria-Hungary virtually meant that all Serbian governments were to be bound in such a manner that in purchasing supplies for the state they should automatically give Austro-Hungarian manufactures preference over those of other nations. Austria-Hungary demanded also a certain share in the provision of loans to Serbia and such state contracts as that for rock salt, then held by Rumania.[165] Austria demanded preferential treatment for her guns, which, it claimed, were quite as good as those of Krupp or Schneider, and offered on better financial terms; Serbia's rejection of the Austrian bid for the gun contracts was regarded as discrimination, and when Serbia refused to make a written promise to this Austria retaliated promptly: no contract for guns, no trade treaty.

The line taken by Serbia was that the trade treaty and the state contracts were separate questions, wherefore the Serbian government resented the assumed dependency of one on the other. According to a British agent in Beograd,

This is all the more understandable as Serbia has no guarantee that the permission to export her cattle to Austria will not be stopped whenever Austria wishes to force a certain course of action on this country, and, bearing in mind former outbreaks of political swine fever, the public is not disposed to purchase a doubtful treaty, at the further cost of the freedom of Serbia to place her orders where she will.[166]

In a note of September 30, 1906, the Serbian government stated that it could not grant priority in state contracts to any one government, since that would be incompatible with the principles of "self-determination" and "free competition." Such practice was inconsistent with the usual standards and the principle of the most-favored-nation.[167] *Neues Wiener Tagblatt* responded with a statement, no doubt inspired by Goluchowski, that Austria-Hungary had acted hitherto with tact and courtesy toward the settlement of economic affairs with Serbia, but now that Beograd had provoked "a trial of strength," they would get just that.[168]

For Serbia an order of Austrian guns would have increased dependence on the monarchy, would mean acquisition of inferior equipment, and in view of possible troubles in European Turkey and a conflict with Austria-Hungary rising therefrom, it would have been a mistaken military policy. If the Škoda factory had supplied Serbian state contracts, Austria-Hungary would have had valuable military data on Serbian arms and military equipment. Lončarević assesses the Serbian attitude at the time in the following manner:

A forced order to Škoda's would not only look like a tribute which Serbia was bound to pay to Austro-Hungarian industries, but would also involve a still greater danger, namely that Serbia, in arming her fighting forces, might give herself over to the mercy of the very Power by which alone her independence was seriously threatened.[169]

The Serbian proposals for new trade contained a relatively high tariff rate on cereals, a reduced quota of livestock, increased import duty on fresh meats, and exclusion of the Veterinary Convention. But the crux of the conflict with Austria-Hungary did not involve these conditions, which were less favorable than those the monarchy enjoyed under previous agreements with Serbia, but the gun question. As was pointed out earlier, Serbia agreed to purchase 26 million dinars worth of state supplies from Austria-Hungary, and yet even that was not an adequate substitute for the guns. Whenever Serbia refused to be subjected, Austria resorted to economic reprisals.

A few veterinary surgeons on the frontier inspected the Serbian swine, found them suffering from sundry diseases, and forbade their export across Austrian territories.

The moment the economy treaty was signed, the learned veterinaries suddenly discovered that the Serbian swine were again quite healthy.[170]

Austria-Hungary was anxious that relations with Serbia should improve before diplomatic intercourse between Serbia and England was restored. The support of England would strengthen Serbia's international position and make her less compliant.[171] She also feared that England, France, and Italy might devise a way of assisting Serbia economically and financially in order to check Austrian expansion plans in the Balkans. Austria-Hungary was thus compelled to gain control of Serbian economic and political life with great dispatch. In this project, the monarchy apparently had German backing. During his recent visit to Vienna, Kaiser Wilhelm had referred to Serbia as "a bone in the throat which must be got rid of."[172]

Some believed that Pašić, in order to satisfy discontented elements at home, wanted deliberately to encourage the prevailing hostility to Austria by making the latter appear a demoniacal power poised to swallow Serbia. His method, some observers believed, was to undermine the prestige of Austria by making offers which "while reasonable from the Serbian point of view, were certain of being rejected at Vienna." In any case, Pašić had a choice of one of two possible alternatives: he might accept the Austrian *diktat* and thereby reduce Serbia to a mere puppet, or he might rebuff Austria and assert Serbia's independence. The latter course of action was obviously more costly for the immediate future, but in the long run it would give the country many economic and political advantages.[173]

The failure of Goluchowski's policy regarding Serbia caused his fall. On October 21, 1906, he was succeeded by Baron Alois von Aehrenthal.[174] Vujić cautioned his government that Goluchowski's fall did not entail a basic change in the monarchy's attitude toward Serbia. On the contrary, he said, the court and the military party placed even "higher hopes on Baron von Aehrenthal." Both Vujić and Vesnić warned that Aehrenthal was more "cunning" than Goluchowski and that he could not be trusted.[175] Goluchowski's successor was convinced that the policy "of making Serbia politically and economically dependent," by exerting economic pressure on her and of closing the frontiers had "lost somewhat of its sharpness."[176] Aehrenthal also believed that it was inadvisable to treat together the gun question and the trade treaty.[177] Marquis Palavicini, ambassador in Constantinople, likewise was critical of the former chief's policy and in this matter agreed with Aehrenthal.[178]

On November 7, 1906, after months of wrangling with the monarchy, the Serbian government placed its gun contract with the French firm of Schneider-Creusot. The order consisted of sixty quick-firing field and twenty-five mountain batteries. On November 12 Paču agreed on a loan with a group of Franco-Swiss financiers in Geneva in the amount of 95 million francs at 4½ percent interest, to be issued at 90 percent of the nominal value. The government had to assume additional costs, bringing the issue down to 86 percent, which was only slightly less than the costs envisaged by the previous loan project.[179] But when the loan agreement came up before the Skupština, the opposition (Independent Radicals and Populists) threatened by obstruction to prevent its passing. They disapproved of the Schneider-Creusot contract; many apparently believed that the Krupp models were better.

Because of the parliamentary stalemate in Serbia the financiers of Vienna and representatives of Škoda still hoped to prevail upon Serbia to turn over to Škoda a part of the order placed with the Schneider firm. French Premier

Clemenceau was requested to influence the Serbian government toward such a decision. The offer of mediation between the Serbian and Austrian governments by French Foreign Minister Pichon, on January 16, 1907, came too late. The Skupština had already voted that the gun contracts should be placed with Schneider.[180]

8. POLITICAL REPERCUSSIONS IN THE MONARCHY

The conflict with Serbia touched off political and ideological squabbles in the "ramshackle" Empire. It gave an opportunity for the heterogeneous national and social elements to voice their own opinions and sentiments on the official policy regarding Serbia. Discussion of trade relations with Serbia was often on the agenda in the legislatures. The Magyar part of the empire had one set of conditions which should govern trade with Serbia, and the German part of the Empire another. The two states of the Dual Monarchy were in constant economic conflict; the struggle between the agrarian barons of Hungary and the big industrialists of Austria found a focal point.

This conflict between the two parts of the monarchy—Austria and Hungary—was of course, one of the many centrifugal forces at work disturbing an equilibrium which had only recently been reached. Hungary had remained a separate economic unit in the monarchy until the middle of the nineteenth century.[181] In 1850 the Austro-Hungarian Customs Union was established by an imperial decree and was confirmed by the Ausgleich of 1867.[182] Trade relations between the two states of the monarchy were to be examined from time to time. The Ausgleich stipulated that Austria and Hungary would form a customs union, surrounded by a uniform tariff frontier. There was to be between them no customs frontier and no dues were to be levied on commerce.[183] But by about 1890 the difference between the economy of the industrial and the nonindustrial parts of the monarchy had become conspicuous. Hungarian dependence on Austria for industrialized goods began to lessen because of industrial development.[184] Moreover, an opportunity offered for the agrarian aristocracy "to raise their rents by increasing the price of grains through the help of tariff protection." The big landed interests were anxious to maintain high duties on the import of grains, in order to keep the domestic price at a high level.[185] The policy of the landed oligarchy directed against the import of livestock from the Balkan states was even more catastrophic, causing a permanent customs conflict between the monarchy and Rumania and Serbia. Jászi asserts that the Austro-Hungarian Customs Union

From 1850 until 1900 was a free-trade organization, at least in the sense that it did not make the bread of the masses more expensive. After 1900, and especially after 1907, this feature of free trade ceased to exist.[186]

From the year 1897, when the commercial Ausgleich expired, economic relations between the two states were regulated by a provisional agreement, ordered by the emperor in accordance with the constitution.[187] The so-called Szell formula of 1899 (Article XXX) gave Hungary the right to operate as a separate customs territory if no agreement with Austria was reached by the end of 1902. In the absence of such a new agreement, however, no trade treaty could be concluded binding the whole of Austria-Hungary beyond the year 1907. The economic relations of Austria-Hungary with other nations in the meantime were to be regulated by the principle of reciprocity.[188] Finally, in 1906, a new tariff was introduced which provided prohibitive duties on certain foreign agricultural products which had previously gone free of duty. This tariff facilitated re-establishment of economic relations between Austria and Hungary by renewal of the Customs Union of 1907.[189] In 1907 the Ausgleich was extended for ten years; negotiations for renewal were begun in January 1916 and terminated on February 24, 1917, but the Dual Monarchy collapsed before the new agreement could be submitted to the parliaments.[190]

Still another fact which should be noted is that Austria-Hungary, by virtue of her treaty with Germany, concluded in 1892, was placed, so to speak, in the German economic system. Accordingly, Austro-Serbian commercial relations were to a certain degree governed by the Austro-German treaty. The economic position of the monarchy required that any new trade treaty with Serbia must provide fewer concessions to Serbian agriculture and livestock. Besides the economic interests which clashed, there were also the interests of Austro-Hungarian diplomacy. The agrarians demanded protection for their products, the industrialists sought wider markets for manufactured goods, and diplomacy groped for the fulfillment of its objectives in the Balkans. The last two, of course, complemented each other. These various interests were represented by determined spokesmen in the parliaments of the Dual Monarchy.

A typical agrarian, Deputy Klieman, denounced the Serbian trade treaty as a product of the scheming Austrian industrialists and "the government's Oriental policy." In his opinion, the treaty was injurious to Imperial commercial interests, and he cited the fact that the monarchy had "an active commercial balance of 37 million crowns with Turkey, but a passive commercial balance of 22 million crowns with Serbia."[191] Dr. Ellenbogan, speaking on behalf of the Social Democrats, opposed in principle "all duties on the necessities of life,"[192] and therefore he opposed the protection on agricultural goods which was sought by the agrarians. In response to his Social Democratic colleague, Deputy Prasak queried, "Tell me, my dear friend, where the lot of a worker is better—where necessities of life are cheap, or where they are expensive?" He then added his own version of how the trade treaties were formulated:

Gentlemen, our trade treaties are not the work of the Ministry of Agriculture or the Ministry of Commerce; they are the work of Goluchowski and those of his kind. Consequently they will not be made to satisfy the needs of agriculture, industry, crafts, etc., but they will be made to suit the minister of foreign affairs.[193]

Deputy Schuhmeier challenged agrarian theorizing, citing facts and figures on how the rising prices on meats had led to an increasing slaughter of horses year after year, and said "the consumption of horse meat at home for the year 1904 amounted to approximately 26,000 horses."[194] He said that a common man could hardly afford to buy good meat and was compelled to eat horseflesh. But while Deputy Zimmer held that workers and peasants did not have to eat meat,[195] Deputy Plass urged war against the importation of Serbian swine.[196]

Deputy Schraffl, in a well-documented speech, explained that Serbia would not place her loan with Austria-Hungary, nor would she buy locomotives and railway materials from her, because "our industry can expect Serbian contracts only when Serbia is given concessions on her agricultural produce."[197] Deputy Iro reasoned that after the conclusion of the German-Austrian trade treaty, with high customs tariff on agricultural products, only one possibility remained for Austria, namely, "completely to close our frontier to livestock imports from the Balkan lands."[198] "Gentlemen," said Deputy Zuleger, "I speak to you as a German farmer; we do not fear the Serbian army, but we must fear Serbian oxen and swine."[199] Finally, Dr. Chiari took up a neutral position, maintaining that the endeavor to conclude a new and more favorable commercial treaty was justified, and he saw no justification in terminating the Serbian treaty à tout prix, for the time being.[200]

These bits of evidence amply illustrate the diversity of interests and purposes among the various elements in the monarchy. Such a situation deprived the policy makers of united popular backing. In Serbia, on the other hand, the government on the whole enjoyed popular support, a fact which explains the nation's readiness to endure the hardships of the trade war with Austria-Hungary.

The soundness of Austro-Hungarian policy regarding Serbia was debated long after the "Pig War" had ended. One author observes that Goluchowski's activities had done much to develop Serbophobia in Austria-Hungary and Austrophobia in Serbia.[201] Count Ottokar Czernin, the foreign minister, stated in the Upper House on July 27, 1913, that

We did not find the strength to crush Serbia and Montenegro or the greatness to enlist them as our friends. We did not prevent their military development, but economically and commercially, by a policy of pin-pricks, we drove them to desperation. We closed our frontiers to them and all we have achieved thereby is that they have grown strong, they hate us, and for all that [they are] not afraid of us.[202]

9. SEARCH FOR NEW MARKETS

Any success Serbia might achieve in her conflict with Austria-Hungary depended on the support she could obtain from other powers. She searched for friends and new markets. Within a few months Serbia had signed a number of trade treaties and entered into advantageous agreements with certain French, Italian, Rumanian, and Bulgarian steamship and transportation companies. Railway transit to Salonika and a loading zone in its harbor were secured from Turkey,[203] despite warnings from Austria-Hungary that "they looked upon this as an abandoning to some extent of [Turkish] neutrality."[204] A commission was appointed to investigate the possibilities of new trade routes and markets.[205] Trial shipments of cattle and swine were sent to Egypt, Italy, Malta, and Greece.[206] These proved very satisfactory and accounted in no small part for Serbia's ability to endure the hardships caused by the tariff war with Austria-Hungary.

Enthusiasm ran high in nationalist circles. Many patriots were ready to give themselves to the service of the government and the nation. *Trgovinski glasnik* reported on each phase of the commercial struggle with Austria-Hungary, and especially on each victorious round in the battle. One of the most dramatic episodes was the accidental discovery of Egyptian markets for Serbian livestock. At the time of the break with Austria-Hungary, a Serbian officer, convalescing in one of the Egyptian resorts, on his own initiative explored the possibilities of Egyptian markets and found them suitable to Serbian exports. Arrangements were eventually made for the first Serbian export of cattle to Egypt. *Trgovinski glasnik*, on October 1, 1906, reported that a first shipment of ninety-six head of cattle was going from Salonika to Alexandria, to reach there on October 7; and all the details about the ship, route, and markets were given.[207] Four days later, on October 4, *Trgovinski glasnik* reported that the shipment had reached Alexandria three days ahead of schedule, as though emphasizing the speed with which Serbia was emancipating herself from the Austro-Hungarian monarchy.[208] The paper listed those who were involved in the first shipment—merchants, buyers, shippers, and others—honoring them as if they were soldiers distinguished on the field of battle. Serbia meanwhile opened a commercial agency in Alexandria, and in 1907 established diplomatic representation at Cairo. Serbian statistics on the exports to Egypt are not very precise because some shipments, due to a peculiar legal status of that country, were credited to Turkey. In any event, at least three thousand head of cattle were sent to Egypt in 1907, and in each of the subsequent two years nearly five thousand. Sheep were also exported to Egypt, and interestingly enough, about five thousand head of hogs were exported to Muslim Egypt in 1907. During the "Pig War," according to one estimate, about 15 percent of the entire number of sheep and goats exported went to Egypt.[209]

Aware of the dire consequences that might result from economic war with Austria, the Serbian government had taken precautionary steps. The trade treaty with Germany which had been signed on December 29, 1904,[210] guaranteed freedom of commerce and communication for both states, privileges and rights for their respective citizens identical with those of a most-favored-nation, and free exchange of goods except when defense, hygiene, or public security was involved. The treaty was to remain in force until December 31, 1917. Treaty negotiations with Germany had come at the invitation of that power, and the fact that the German negotiations preceded those with Austria-Hungary antagonized the Vienna government. The trade treaty between Serbia and Germany displeased Austria-Hungary, and Dumba was prompted to remark that Serbian exports to Germany would have to cross Austria-Hungary. On the other hand, Kaiser Wilhelm expressed satisfaction, on January 22, 1905, that Austrian intimidation did not frighten the Serbs.[211] The Serbian envoy, Mihailo Milićević, in Berlin, was told that the German government was wiser than Austria-Hungary in dealing with the Balkan states, taking full cognizance of their susceptibilities.[212] The Austro-Hungarian press criticized the Serbian treaty with Germany on general principles and because certain special concessions had been made to Germany. The *Neue Freie Presse* warned Serbia that she depended on Austria more than Austria did on her.[213]

In the course of 1906—thanks to Russian, French, and Italian assistance and to her able ministers of national economy, Milorad Drašković and Kosta Stojanović—Serbia managed to find outlets for a considerable part of her foreign trade, so that the amount of damage to her trade caused by the closure of Austrian borders was, within less than a year, appreciably reduced.

A trade treaty with Montenegro was concluded on January 1, 1905, providing for most-favored-nation treatment. The treaty was ratified on April 2, 1907.[214] A similar treaty was signed with Turkey on May 5, 1906, the most important provision of which concerned Serbian transit trade.

Serbian exports and imports were to pass through Salonika free of duty; and, in order to facilitate the trade in cattle, the Serbian government was allowed to rent part of the harbor and an adjacent piece of land. In return for these privileges and the concessions granted her on the Turkish railways, Serbia reduced her customs tariff in favor of certain Turkish goods.[215]

A trade treaty with France was signed early in January 1906 and ratified on October 12; it specified the most-favored-nation treatment on all import, export, and transit goods.[216] In February 1907 a treaty was signed with Russia, to be in force for a period of ten years or until renounced. This treaty granted to Serbia special traffic facilities on the Danube and on Russian railways.[217] A treaty with Switzerland was signed on February 1, 1907,[218] and two days later there followed one with Great Britain.[219] A treaty with Belgium, concluded on April 11, 1907, provided most-favored-nation treatment in regard to transit and specified the maximum duties to be levied on Belgian goods entering Serbia.[220] Similar treaties were signed with Sweden, Portugal, and Rumania. The treaty with Italy conventionalized duties with respect to certain Serbian goods, such as cattle, pigs, and cereals.[221]

The Austro-Hungarian press continued its attacks on Serbia. This inimical attitude came obviously not only as a result of Serbian independence, demonstrated by the Serbo-Bulgarian Customs Treaty, but also because of Serbia's improved relations with England, her friendship for Russia, and the accelerated activity of the Yugoslavs in Austria-Hungary and Turkey. Control of Serbia became increasingly more vital to Austria-Hungary in her effort to restrain this South Slav nationalism, to keep Serbia from figuring as the Yugoslav "Piedmont," and last but by no means least, to keep Serbia from falling into the orbit of the Franco-Russian entente.

In early 1907 Pašić paid a visit to Aehrenthal and without showing any signs of an intent to appease expressed hope for the renewal of trade negotiations on the basis *do ut des*.[222] On February 8, 1907, the Serbian government renewed its offer to place state orders to the amount of 26 million dinars with Austro-Hungarian firms, if quality and prices were the same as those quoted by other firms. The Serbs kept their promise of giving an Austrian firm a contract for rifles and a Hungarian firm a contract for railway cars. This latest gesture was not necessarily a sign of defeat but a desire to end the conflict with Austria-Hungary on a satisfactory basis of agreement. Serbia had agreed to take advantage of the Provisorium, which specified that she employ all efforts toward restoring normal trade relations with Austria-Hungary.[223]

Aehrenthal tentatively promised to resume negotiations on March 10, but internal politics in Serbia complicated the situation.[224] On May 27 Pašić resigned because of parliamentary obstruction by the Independent Radicals. Three days later he withdrew his resignation and reorganized the cabinet. On June 29 the Skupština, by a vote of seventy-four to thirty-six, authorized the government to conclude a provisional treaty with Austria-Hungary, to be in force until December 31, 1907.[225] A delegation was sent to Vienna to initiate negotiations, which progressed slowly and soon reached an impasse. On September 7 Pašić paid a visit to Aehrenthal, after which negotiations were resumed in Vienna on October 24, 1907. Serbia was represented in the negotiations by Laza Paču, her minister of finance. On March 14, 1908, an agreement was finally reached, "pending the decision of the Austrian and Hungarian parliaments."[226]

The treaty was accompanied by special notes from the Austrian foreign minister, explaining its various provisions and stressing the quantity of Serbian livestock export to Austria-Hungary, and in its essence actually restored many of the privileges the Dual Monarchy had enjoyed earlier under the Veterinary Convention. Serbian exports to Austria were limited to 35,000 head of horned cattle and 70,000 swine slaughtered prior to export. The treaty found many opponents, and long parliamentary debates over it ensued in both Austria-Hungary and Serbia. On March 10, 1908, Pašić again resigned and ten days later once again formed a cabinet. The king authorized him to dismiss the Skupština and to schedule new elections, which were held on May 18; as had been anticipated, the Radicals polled the majority of votes, although they had lost six parliamentary seats. Dissention within his own ranks and apparent loss in popularity caused the resignation of Pašić on June 4. Finally, after a prolonged crisis, an Old Radical, Pera Velimirović, formed on July 20 a cabinet into which Milovan Milovanović, the minister at Rome, entered as foreign minister; but parliamentary debates on the treaty continued. On August 6 Mika Popović, minister of economy, delivered a two-hour speech stressing the distinct advantages secured by this latest treaty as compared with previous treaties, and the new foreign minister joined him in urging approval of the instrument. The treaty finally passed the Skupština on August 13, 1908.

The Austrian and Hungarian parliaments, however, refused to ratify the treaty. The agrarian spokesmen suggested that Serbian produce would still provide serious competition, although the import of live animals was forbidden and only a small quantity of slaughtered cattle and swine permitted. The new Serbian duties on Austrian merchandise were lower than those of the general Serbian tariff, but less favorable than those in force before the economic conflict. Although failing of ratification the treaty was put into force provisionally on September 1, 1908, by the Austro-Hungarian government. The Provisorium was not renewed because of the stubborn opposition of the agrarians of the monarchy, and when it expired on March 31, 1909, the tariff war was resumed.

The tariff war between Serbia and Austria-Hungary continued for an additional two years. Finally, in the spring of 1910, the two governments agreed to resume trade negotiations, which were officially begun on July 16. A new treaty was concluded on July 27, 1910. The most important difference between the new treaty and the treaty of March 1908 was the reduction of the livestock quota allowed in Austro-Hungarian imports—the number of oxen was reduced from 35,000 to 15,000 and the number of swine from 70,000 to 50,000. The Skupština ratified the treaty on November 30, 1910, the Austro-Hungarian parliament on January 24, 1911, and it went into effect June 23, 1911.[227] By that time the economic crisis had been passed and a new foundation for the native economy firmly laid. Serbia had freed herself from Austrian economic domination.

10. THE VICTORY

It was widely believed that the abnormal trade relations in 1905 and the sudden trade disruption with Austria-Hungary in 1906 would cause a complete economic collapse in Serbia. Such an expectation appeared natural because during the past thirty years or so Serbia had traded almost exclusively with Austria-Hungary. For the five-year period preceding 1906 Austria-Hungary had supplied 53.35 percent of Serbia's imports and absorbed 83.66 percent of Serbia's exports. With the loss of Austro-Hungarian markets, the consensus was that Serbia would lose from 48 to 50 million dinars on her exports, owing to inability to locate new markets. Yet after one year of conflict with Austria-Hungary it was clear that this assumption was inaccurate, and that Austrian trade was not absolutely indispensable to Serbia. The high-minimum tariff rates of Austria-Hungary not only did not stop Serbian exports but, as it turned out, Serbian exports increased in quantity over those of the preceding years.[228] By 1907 Serbian exports already exceeded by a surplus of 9,873,548 dinars those of 1902, the best export year. After the lapse of the treaty with Austria-Hungary between 1906 and 1909, average annual exports exceeded those of the treaty period "by a surplus of 29 million dinars."[229]

Figures show that Serbian trade dropped slightly at the beginning of the conflict with Austria-Hungary, but that it rose rapidly thereafter. The first year of the tariff war showed a marked drop in both exports and imports. Exports to Austria-Hungary dropped from 64,712,406 dinars in 1905 to 30,032,477 in 1906. Imports during the corresponding period fell from 33,375,501 dinars to 22,206,498 dinars.[230] Trade with other countries, including England, France, and Turkey, had also declined in 1905–6. The goods of these countries, which came under the rates of duty provided by the tariff annexed to the Austro-Serbian treaty, which expired in 1906, were thereafter subjected to the rates of the new Serbian general customs tariff. The rates of the new tariff, which was put into force in March 1906, were high and thereby the importation of certain goods was discouraged.[231]

The second year (1906–7) of the tariff war showed an increase in total imports and exports, indicating that Serbia had crossed a major hurdle in her struggle for economic emancipation from Austria-Hungary. The total amount of Serbian imports in 1907 amounted to 70,583,327 dinars—an increase of 26,254,685 over the preceding year. Total exports were 81,491,262 dinars—an increase of 9,887,164 dinars.[232] Imports from Austria-Hungary in 1907 showed an increase of 3,393,448 dinars over imports in 1906. Imports from most other countries increased, except those from Russia and Bulgaria, and especially from Germany, which had been the first to conclude a trade treaty with Serbia on the basis of the new tariff law. *Trgovinski glasnik* considered the Serbian trade treaty with Germany

far more dangerous and injurious to Austro-Hungarian trade interests than even our agreement with Bulgaria. And yet, Austria-Hungary did not even consider a commercial war with Serbia because of our treaty with Germany, but with the usual grumbling and opposition accepted it as a *fait accompli*.[233]

The following table[234] shows Serbian imports in 1906 and 1907 in value of dinars:

Country	1906	1907
Austria-Hungary	22,206,498	25,599,946
Germany	9,732,722	20,320,391
England and colonies	4,562,906	10,220,270
Italy	936,721	2,299,488
France	1,142,623	2,428,603
Holland	226,510	1,121,605
Turkey	1,845,881	3,326,512

During the corresponding period there was a drop in exports to Austria-Hungary, which was more than counterbalanced by increased exports to Germany and a few other countries. The following table [235] shows Serbian exports in 1906 and 1907, valued in dinars:

Country	1906	1907
Austria-Hungary	30,032,477	12,932,380
Germany	19,053,882	32,925,623
Italy	572,319	4,898,867
Russia	151,650	3,133,719
Belgium	6,259,929	13,010,853

The Austro-Serbian commercial war continued until September 14, when the treaty that had been signed at Vienna on March 14 was put into force provisionally. Because of this, improved trade relations and increase in trade exchange with Austria-Hungary were noted in 1908 over 1907. Exports rose from 12,932,380 dinars in 1907 to 21,501,402 dinars in 1908. The figure was still far short of the average annual exports to Austria-Hungary in the years immediately preceding the tariff war. Imports rose from 25,599,945 dinars in 1907 to 32,151,945 dinars in 1908,[236] nearly the amount of imports in 1905. Exports to Germany decreased from 32,925,623 dinars in 1907 to 14,018,977 dinars in 1908, but imports increased by 1,041,056 dinars—from 20,320,391 in 1907 to 21,361,347 in 1908. Total exports in 1908 amounted to

77,749,078 dinars, representing an appreciable drop from 81,491,262 dinars recorded in 1907. English exports to Serbia decreased from 10,220,270 dinars in 1907 to 8,803,350 in 1908, particularly in textiles and machinery.

By the provisional treaty of 1908, Serbia did not seek so much to secure markets for her agricultural exports as to obtain the right of transit through Austria-Hungary. Exports and imports from beyond Austria "were very often entered under Austria-Hungary owing to their being imported and exported by way of Fiume and Trieste, from which places they were forwarded to their ultimate destination with a fresh Austro-Hungarian bill of lading."[237] This accounts in part for the sudden increases in the figures representing Austro-Serbian trade in 1908. A closer examination of the statistical data on Serbian trade would undoubtedly show that the official figures given did not always portray the exact volume of trade.

The tariff war resulted in damage to Austria-Hungary. The Serbian customs tariff that came into force on March 1, 1906, increased the duties on foodstuffs and on manufactured goods, while most raw materials for manufacture were still admitted free. That situation, and the ensuing tariff war with Serbia, caused in Austria-Hungary a general increase in prices, particularly on foodstuffs. The result was a rise in the cost of living.[238] The drop in importation of cattle and cereals led to an increased consumption of horseflesh. Austrian imports of sheep and pigs from England trebled, as an effect of the quarrel with Serbia.[239] Austro-Hungarian trade was further affected in 1908–9 by the Serbian and Turkish boycott of Austrian manufacturers during the crisis caused by the annexation of Bosna and Hercegovina.[240]

Economic conditions in Serbia after the initial setback showed steady improvement. Revenue from the monopolies enabled the government to contract on favorable terms a loan of 95 million francs. There was an important increase in revenue obtained from customs duties provided by the new tariff. The former tariff, dating from 1893, had imposed rather moderate customs duties, and a surtax of 7 percent ad valorem, under the heading of sales tax, had been levied on all imported goods. The new tariff incorporated this tax with the customs duties, and rates on imports were further increased to counterbalance the loss to the treasury caused by the virtual abolition of export duties. The reductions conceded in the various trade treaties of 1907 did not go below the former conventional rate plus *obrt* (turn-over tax),[241] in any single instance.

At the beginning of the customs war, the country had faced almost insurmountable problems in trying to find new markets and new outlets for her exports, and for a time Serbia experienced a grave crisis. But in the end, her efforts in this direction were crowned with success. Through Salonika and Sulina Serbia found new markets in Asia Minor, Egypt, Greece, Italy, France, and Spain. She found the means for direct communication with Belgium, England, Sweden, and Norway without passing through Austria-Hungary. In the course of the struggle, Serbia "was sustained by all our actual friends and especially by Italy," and aided by France from 1906 to 1912 "in everything concerning loans and credits." For the time being, Germany was the country which profited the most commercially from the Austro-Serbian conflict, largely because hers was the first commercial treaty to be signed by Serbia on the basis of the autonomous tariff law, and because of Germany's proximity and accessibility to the transportation system of Central Europe. By 1908 Serbia had surmounted the major hurdle in her struggle for economic emancipation from Austria-Hungary. She entered "a period of political and financial revival; the state budgets were balanced with surpluses."[242]

The customs war caused a complete change in the ratio of trade with individual foreign powers. Instead of controlling 90 percent of Serbia's trade, Austria now enjoyed but 30 percent, and trade with other powers increased proportionately.[243]

The customs war forced Serbia to improve her export products both in quality and quantity. The length of export routes necessitated, for example, a transformation in the articles of commerce; raw materials were replaced by semimanufactured goods; live cattle were replaced by fresh and salted meats and animal products of various sorts. The customs war obliged livestock breeders

to abandon the exportation of live cattle and to devote themselves to the industry and preparation of half-manufactured exportation articles. Slaughter houses, factories, steam-mills, etc., were created, cereals were replaced by flour, live cattle by fresh meat, salt-meat, etc.

In this way Serbia avoided "gravitating exclusively towards the Austro-Hungarian markets, for the transformed products could choose longer ways towards distant markets." The table [244] below shows fluctuations of export products in millions of francs from 1906 to 1908:

Product	1906	1907	1908
Cattle	18.3	3.6	7
Cereals	22	31	27.7
Fruit	15.1	22	15
Animal products	15.6	10	16

Whereas before 1906 the low tariff on industrial goods from Austria-Hungary had precluded industrial development in Serbia, after 1906 Serbian industry developed steadily. Similarly, the exemption of customs duties on cereals and other Serbian raw materials in the frontier zone had previously permitted these items to flow freely into Austria-Hungary for milling purposes, thus preventing the development of that industry in Serbia; now raw materials were kept within Serbian territory, and processed there.

The Veterinary Convention, which had been signed on September 30, 1882, and prolonged by the Trade Treaty of 1892, had prevented the normal and methodical breeding of Serbian cattle. Export of better breeds of cattle was often prohibited under pretexts such as pest and disease. Such prohibition occurred in 1882–83, 1884, 1890, 1894, 1896, 1898, 1901, 1902, and 1906. This situation, as well as official neglect, accounted for the inferior quality of Serbian livestock products. Seventy thousand head of cattle exported by Serbia in 1905 equaled in weight half that number of Western European cattle. A Hungarian delegate during trade discussions in 1905 was said to have remarked that he would have been ashamed had his country produced "such small cows as those produced in Serbia." Austria bought the Serbian cattle for her cities and poverty-stricken areas, such as Galicia, and exported her own better cattle to Germany.[245]

The trade relations with Austria-Hungary established in 1911 safeguarded certain essential elements of Serbian industrial development and gave Serbia "the liberty to take measures with regard to all questions of national economy. Serbian navigation, veterinary supervision, and the traffic with other Balkan and European states" were no longer subjected to Austro-Hungarian control.[246]

The results of the "Pig War" show that the Austro-Hungarian policy of crushing Serbia's every attempt at independence which interfered with the monarchy's political ambition was a failure.[247] The ancient Austrian method of bringing economic pressure to bear on Serbia in order to force her into political submission was at last nullified. The policy of considering Serbia only as a *quantité négligeable* or *quantité méprisable* was outdated.[248] Goluchowski's economic policy regarding Serbia could no longer be followed.[249]

Resolved on regaining her dominant role in Beograd, Austria-Hungary resorted in 1908 to new tactics. The first of these steps appeared on January 27, 1908, when Aehrenthal, in his exposé to the Hungarian Delegation, announced his government's intention of linking the existing railway of Bosna through the Sandjak of Novi Pazar with the Mitrovica-Salonika line. Such a development would, among other things, definitely separate Serbia from Montenegro, preventing their union and depriving Serbia of an Adriatic outlet. The railway project was followed by an elaborate smear campaign against the Serbo-Croat Coalition in Austria-Hungary and against the kingdom of Serbia. Austria-Hungary staged two trials of persons charged with treason at Zagreb and Vienna, in which she implicated Serbia, with the aim of compromising the Serbian government. Finally, in October 1908, Austria-Hungary announced the annexation to the monarchy of Bosna and Hercegovina, an event which nearly precipitated a world war and represented a heavy blow to the national aspirations of Serbia and Montenegro.

PART EIGHT

The Danube-Adriatic Railway

AT THE BEGINNING OF THE REIGN OF KING MILAN (1868–89), a proposal had been made to connect Serbia with the sea by a Danube-Adriatic railway line from Radujevac via Niš to reach the Adriatic Sea somewhere in the vicinity of Lake Scutari. The railway line was to be linked with the system of Rumania and Russia (probably at Odessa), thereby giving those two countries also an Adriatic outlet. The exact terminus of the railway was uncertain; it was to be either San Giovanni di Medua or Antivari.[1] Toward the close of the century, once again there was talk of the Danube-Adriatic railway. Serbia and Russia worked confidentially on the project and took steps to forward its execution in 1897 and 1901. There were several possible routes for this railway. According to the Serbian plan, the line would go from Prahovo with a bridge connection to Gruja, the nearest Rumanian city, via Negotin–Gramada–Niš–Doljevac (261 kilometers), thence through the valley of the Kosančica to Mrdare–Podujevac–Priština–Prizren–San Giovanni di Medua.[2] The suggested line would avoid the Sandjak of Novi Pazar, in which Austria-Hungary garrisoned her troops, and would cross territory in which Turkey was undisputed master.

The Rumanian government was approached on the subject of a Danube-Adriatic line sometime in 1898. Various preliminary agreements were reached and preparations for the construction of the Danube bridge between Kladovo and Turnu Severin were initiated. But the railway plan was abandoned as Rumania lost interest in the project, probably as a result of Austrian pressure as well as the belief that it would provide undesirable competition to her Black Sea commerce. Other reasons as well caused the project to be abandoned; technical problems, building costs, and absence of a definite plan as to location of the terminal. Rumania was not wholeheartedly behind the project, because she felt the line would benefit Serbia more than it would Rumania. Then there was disagreement on the gauge of the railway, the Serbs apparently favoring the narrow and the Rumanians the standard gauge. Negotiations with Rumania collapsed entirely in 1899 and were not reopened until 1907.[3]

Austria-Hungary was cold toward the Serbian projected Adriatic railway, fearing that it might make Serbia economically independent. She suspected Serbian action, even though at the time construction was proposed the Serbian government was in the secure hands of Vladan Djordjević and King Milan.[4] To strengthen her stranglehold on Serbia, Austria-Hungary in November 1900 advanced a plan for construction of the so-called Bosna *Ostbahn*—the Sarajevo-Mitrovica railway[5]—and by winter of 1902 was ready to proceed with arrangements for its construction.[6] Germany discouraged the project, fearing new troubles in the Balkans,[7] and Russia, who saw in it an Austro-German drive to Bagdad, was opposed to the whole idea.[8]

Needless to say, the projected Vienna-Constantinople railway through Bosna and the Sandjak of Novi Pazar much alarmed certain patriots in Serbia. Nikola Pašić was prompted to arouse the Serbian public by a series of articles in the Radical party organ *Zakonitost* (1900–1901). To prevent the encirclement of Serbia by Austria-Hungary, he suggested an energetic diplomatic opposition by the Great Powers and the construction of the Danube-Adriatic railway, a line of international importance, which would neutralize the Austro-Hungarian Sandjak-Constantinople railroad.[9]

The Serbian railway scheme elicited more interest in Europe than any other of the several proposed Balkan railway projects. The Serbs were in earnest about the whole thing and were looking for suitable investors. The Russians, Italians, and French promised to support the Serbian project at Constantinople. Italy and France vied with each other for the lion's share of the financing and construction of the Danube-Adriatic line. Théophile Delcassé refused joint Italo-French operations and hoped to persuade the Turks to grant the French interests an exclusive concession. This Italo-French rivalry ended when the Porte categorically refused to authorize the construction of the projected Serbian Adriatic line.[10]

At one time in 1902 the Turks favored the Serbian line crossing Turkish territory (Kosovo), or some such line (Salonika-Bitolj-Adriatic), as a means of checking the railway scheme of Austria-Hungary. The Turks dropped the idea when Austria-Hungary, under Russian pressure and Serbian and Montenegrin protests, postponed the Sarajevo-Mitrovica project.[11] On the other hand, the Russians, because of their commitments to Austria-Hungary, and the political instability in Serbia, were half-hearted about the Danube-Adriatic railway even though they had originally contributed a million francs toward the project. Count Lamsdorff saw no good reason for fresh squabbles with Turkey and Austria-Hungary over a Balkan railway, and practical Count Witte, the noted minister of finance, saw no great advantage to Russia in a Danube-Adriatic railway.[12] Italy alone had shown serious interest in the Serbian project, but she too failed to exert much effort toward its realization.[13]

It was not until after 1905, following the outbreak of the customs war with Austria-Hungary, that serious attention was given the Danube-Adriatic railway. Indeed, the customs war proved how vital to Serbia was the railway, which could give direct access to the sea. Trade via the Danube to the Black Sea followed a circuitous route. Shipment by way of Salonika involved a risk resulting from Turkey's fickle moods and the prevailing chaos in Macedonia. Furthermore, the railway to Salonika was for the most part controlled by Austrian and German capital.[14] The Serbian government had hoped to form an international syndicate, without Austro-Hungarian or German participation, to provide funds for the Adriatic railway construction.

1. THE SANDJAK RAILWAY

For strategic and political reasons essentially, the Crown council in November 1900 approved a plan to construct what came to be known as the Sandjak railway. The two parliaments of the monarchy approved the plan in 1902. Before broaching the subject in Constantinople, Foreign Minister Goluchowski consulted with Berlin, but to his astonishment found no unequivocal support in that quarter. He was advised in Berlin to secure Russian backing to silence whatever Balkan opposition might develop.[15]

During his visit to Vienna in December 1902 Count Lamsdorff encountered an Austrian query regarding the Russian attitude to a Sandjak railway. Emperor Francis Joseph found it expedient to talk with Lamsdorff in person. The Russian was told of the great cultural and economic advantages that would come from such a railway and was asked if his country would support the project in Constantinople.[16] Lamsdorff took the same negative position that the Russians manifested in 1900, and Goluchowski found no alternative but to drop the project for the time being.[17]

That the Austrian government was serious about its railway scheme can be seen from the fact that the parliaments in 1902 had appropriated funds for its construction.[18] The railway program called for a two-pronged extension of the existing line from Sarajevo. One spur would link Sarajevo with the Adriatic and the other—the eastern one—with Uvac and Vardište on the Serbian frontier. From here, at some future date and under a more favorable international situation, it would be extended to Mitrovica and the Aegean. The Sarajevo-Uvac line was constructed despite considerable topographic obstacles.[19]

The completion of the *Ostbahn*—Sarajevo-Uvac railway—and the reports regarding various proposals for a trans-Balkan railway prompted the Austro-Hungarian government to revive its Sandjak railway project.[20] The engineers made a study of the terrain and recommended two possible routes from the border of Bosna to Mitrovica: one by way of Priboj and Prijepolje and the other by way of Sjenica and Novi Pazar.[21] This Sandjak railway, when completed, would have been 180 kilometers longer than the existing Beograd-Niš line. The projected line would have also been handicapped by the fact that the shipment of goods would have required loading and unloading from standard- to narrow-gauge systems. It was, therefore, apparent that the railway was planned more to serve military and strategic purposes than economic. It would afford Austria-Hungary an outlet on the Aegean by circumventing Serbian territory, and would further minimize the importance of any railways that Serbia might build. The monarchy's position vis-à-vis Old Serbia, Macedonia, and Albania would have been strengthened and facilities provided for possible future expansion.[22] But the alarm incited in Serbia and Montenegro by the Sandjak railway proposal, coupled with the Russian opposition and German indifference, induced the Austro-Hungarian government to postpone the whole thing for the time being. Similarly, the plan of the Serbian Danube-Adriatic railway was temporarily dropped as a result of pressing internal problems caused by the assassination of King Alexander.

2. SERBIA REVIVES THE DANUBE-ADRIATIC RAILWAY PROJECT

In 1905 the Serbian government activated its interest in the Danube-Adriatic railway, and during the autumn of 1906 there were widespread rumors about the project. On November 17 *Pester Lloyd* discussed it at some length. It was speculated that the visit to Beograd of the Turkish ambassador to Paris, Munir Bey, was connected with the railway project. There was talk of a Turkish railway crossing the Kosovo Plain and Albania to the Adriatic, a railway which would be linked with the Serbian system. The Austrian Legation in December 1906 suspected that financial arrangements for the new railway had already been made, and that the funds would be supplied by a Franco-Italian syndicate. Aehrenthal, in consequence prepared for counteraction. Baron Marschall, the German ambassador in Constantinople, wrote that Austria-Hungary

. . . would strongly oppose the Ulcinj-Niš railway line, because it might end the political and economic preponderance which she hitherto exerted . . . in Serbia. Besides, such a railway would be looked upon in Vienna as an Italian-Serbian-Montenegrin maneuver calculated to weaken Austria-Hungary's political position not only in Serbia, but also in Albania and Macedonia.[23]

The Adriatic railway line which was planned in 1905 would have started at Prahovo on the Danube (with a link to the Rumanian system at Craiova by a bridge over the Danube) and go by way of Zaječar, Knjaževac, and Niš (here it would meet the Beograd- Salonika/Constantinople line), thence through Prokuplje and Kuršumlija to the Turkish border. From this point on its course had not been definitely decided upon, although many believed the best route would be by way of Priština and Prizren[24] to San Giovanni di Medua as the likely terminus on the Adriatic. The Rumanians informed the Serbian government on December 15, 1906, that they would not negotiate regarding the Danube-Adriatic line until completion of the Serbian section of the line from the Danube to the Turkish frontier.[25] Prince Nikola of Montenegro insisted that the Adriatic line should not circumvent his state; he wanted the terminus of the line on the Montenegrin coast. In his view an Albanian port was never likely to become part of "Greater Serbia." He argued that a line to Antivari would be shorter in that it would cross only one hundred kilometers of Turkish territory. The prince suggested that the Montenegrin section of the Danube-Adriatic line (the "Montenegrin Line") should run from Rožaj via Berane, Andrijevica, Nikšić, and Podgorica to Antivari on the Adriatic. It would connect with the Turkish line at Mitrovica and with the Serbian near Kuršumlija, whence it would proceed to Niš, where it would be joined to the Serbian-Rumanian line. The total length of the line was estimated at four hundred kilometers and construction costs at 120 million francs.[26] In the spring of 1907 Prince Nikola warned that if the Danube-Adriatic railway did not pass through Montenegro his country would be politically and economically doomed. The railway, he said, would enable the country to develop; it would supply employment for his subjects at home and thereby check the ever-increasing emigration to America. In order to have his "Montenegrin line" realized, he sought the backing of the Great Powers.[27]

The Serbian railway scheme called for the outlet at San Giovanni di Medua and not at Antivari for the simple reason that the Serbs wished to avoid the maritime police supervision to which Austria-Hungary was entitled by Article XXIX of the Treaty of Berlin. The Montenegrins, however, saw in it a deliberate attempt by Serbia to circumvent Montenegro. The Serbs were apparently willing to see a branch line constructed to Antivari, but insisted on San Giovanni as the principal terminus. They could not explain their position publicly lest they provide Austrian diplomacy with an argument against Serbia.

The question of extension of the Serbian railway project through Turkish territory was beset with political complications. A number of tentative offers had been made to the Serbian government for extension of the railway project. In July 1906 a group known as the Anglo-Serbian Syndicate offered to form a company for its construction, if the Serbian government would guarantee "five percent interest on the invested capital and grant certain rights to mines and forests along the line." The offer was not considered. Later in the year Alfred Stead devoted some time to the matter, "sending two experienced engineers to inspect the Timok Valley section, where between Knjaževac and Niš the greatest difficulties are anticipated." He negotiated with Emile Erlanger and Co., of London and Paris, with a view to financial support, the condition being that the Serbian government "should guarantee interest on the capital expended on the Serbian section." A definite offer for the construction of the line had apparently also been made by a German firm, and quite possibly by various other groups as well. In view of the serious intention of building the railway, the Serbian government had decided that a short extension of the narrow-gauge line from Paraćin to Zaječar "should be built with full-sized bridges and tunnels, in order that it may eventually be utilized as a portion of the Timok Valley line."[28]

3. AUSTRO-HUNGARIAN COUNTERACTION

To counter the Serbian railway scheme, Aehrenthal advanced various plans and proposals of his own. In a conversation with the German representative at Vienna he alluded to the possibility of connecting the Serbian and Austrian railways at Višegrad, a project which would enable Serbia to reach the Adriatic on the Dalmatian coast by way of Sarajevo and Metković. In case this plan materialized, he said, Austria-Hungary could build the Priboj-Mitrovica link through the Sandjak of Novi Pazar.[29] He actually urged the Serbian government to connect its own railway network with the Austrian Vardište-Sarajevo-Metković line via Užice and Stalać, and when the Bugojno-Arzano line was completed, it might even be possible for Serbia to reach the Adriatic at Split.[30] Had Serbia accepted this proposal, the monarchy would have been successful in keeping Serbia from the Kosovo Plain and Albania, and Serbian traffic would have been routed through Austrian territory to an Austrian port. It should also be pointed out that the Varadište-Sarajevo-Metković line was to have been narrow gauge and could not have adequately served a large volume of traffic.

Meanwhile both the Austrians and the Germans exerted pressure on the Porte against Serbia's railway proposal. The German Foreign Office considered it unwise for the sultan to permit construction of a Danube-Adriatic railway.[31] Furthermore Aehrenthal was at this time perfecting the former Sandjak railway project and preparing to spring it into the open. In December 1906 the German ambassador in Vienna warned his home office that Austria might soon request from Turkey the concession to build the Sandjak railway and would ask for German backing in Constantinople.[32] The German government apparently did not oppose the idea at this time, although it left it up to Austria to initiate negotiations with the Porte.[33] Informal requests by Austria for German backing brought no tangible results.[34]

In February 1907 Aehrenthal called a conference at Vienna for the examination of various Balkan railway schemes:[35] the linking of the railways of Bosna and Serbia; the construction of the Sandjak of Novi Pazar railway; and the possible construction of the San Giovanni di Medua–Scutari line. Also discussed was a Bulgarian proposal to link Kûstendil to Skoplje, a project backed by Austria and the board of the Oriental Railway Company, since the proposed railway would facilitate traffic on the company's Skoplje-Salonika line.[36] In March 1907 Austria-Hungary requested German backing in Constantinople toward securing Ottoman permission for the construction of the Uvac-Mitrovica line—the Sandjak railway.[37] During his subsequent visit in Berlin (April 30 to May 4, 1907), Aehrenthal further discussed the Sandjak railway, and was promised German backing in Constantinople, although Aehrenthal was reminded that Germany did not wish to irritate the sultan and risk losing his friendship.[38] The Germans at the same time dampened Aehrenthal's railway scheme by pointing out many of the technical problems that Austria-Hungary would face in building the Sandjak railway.[39]

On December 14, 1907, Aehrenthal told Marschall, German ambassador in Constantinople, that he would in the near future request the Sandjak railway concession from the sultan and that he expected German assistance.[40] Whatever the details that transpired between the two foreign offices, Aehrenthal seemed certain that he would enjoy full German backing when he did finally announce his railway scheme. There is no evidence that the Germans knew any more about Aehrenthal's plans than what Aehrenthal told Marschall.[41] William II claimed that he was surprised by Aehrenthal's announcement.[42] Nor was the German government informed of the steps that Aehrenthal planned to take.[43] Seemingly, Aehrenthal wanted to prove to the world that he was independent of Germany.[44]

Izvolsky likewise indicated he had not known of Aehrenthal's plans, although in October 1907 he discussed with Aehrenthal various problems, including the Straits.[45] However, a report did reach Izvolsky about Aehrenthal's alleged discussion with the Porte on the subject of the Sandjak railway. Not until several days before his famous exposé did Aehrenthal notify Russia of his pet project.[46] When informed, Izvolsky apparently protested but in a friendly and mild manner, as he anticipated no vigorous Slavic indignation.[47]

France, similarly informed a few days earlier, even promised to support Aehrenthal's proposal at Constantinople.[48] England, on the other hand, flatly refused to accord Austria-Hungary such backing.[49] Before the exposé the Italian ambassador was also advised of the impending proposal.[50]

The Austro-Hungarian government formally requested the Sandjak railway concession in Constantinople on December 27, 1907, and the sultan seemed then favorably disposed.[51] The grand vizier similarly saw no danger in the Austro-Hungarian project and agreed with it.[52] Aehrenthal assured the sultan that the monarchy's Balkan policy was a peaceful one and minimized the military importance of "the narrow and mountainous Sandjak." On September 7, 1907, however, in a confidential memorandum, Aehrenthal had minimized the economic importance of the Sandjak and stressed its political value.[53]

Finally, in a speech before the Hungarian Delegation on January 27, 1908, Aehrenthal, assured of success in Constantinople, expounded his plan for the Sandjak railway. Said he:

The line from Uvac to Mitrovica will unquestionably have to be kept as part of the communications policy, for it not only brings the railway system of Bosna into connection with the system of communications of the neighboring states, but also opens for us, generally speaking, new prospects for our communications policy. On the completion of the connection between the railway systems of Bosna and Turkey, it will be possible for trade from the monarchy, by the direct route through Sarajevo, to gravitate toward the Aegean and Mediterranean seas. We hope, that is, that a connection will speedily be effected between the Turkish and the Greek railways at Larissa. In this way a direct Vienna-Budapest-Sarajevo-Athens-Piraeus line will be established. This would be the shortest route from Central Europe to Egypt and India.[54]

In concluding, Aehrenthal said, "We are at the gates of the Orient, where numerous difficult problems need to be solved. Our voice will be heard only if we are strong and united."[55] Aided by the Germans, the Austrians were successful in prevailing upon the sultan to issue an irade, on January 31, 1908, giving the Austro-Hungarian government a concession for the Sandjak railway[56]

4. DIPLOMATIC DISCUSSIONS REGARDING SERBIA'S PROJECT

The "Pig War" and the reports about the Sandjak railway served to convince Serbia of the absolute necessity for a Danube-Adriatic line free from Austro-Hungarian control. No time was lost in Beograd on the preparation and perfection of such a plan. It was decided after some deliberation that the Adriatic railway should be standard gauge. Discussions were initiated with Turkey and Rumania; London, Paris, Rome, and St. Petersburg were all requested to back the Serbian railway project in Constantinople.[57] Italy and France were favorably disposed to the project. The Italian government requested the British to support the Serbian project in Constantinople. In March 1907 Ambassador San Giuliano spoke to Lord Grey about it. Milovanović reported that Grey was well disposed toward the Serbian project and had told San Giuliano that he would

immediately give the necessary instructions to the British ambassador in Constantinople to act together with the Italian ambassador in raising the question at the Porte, as soon as it should be presented in such a concrete form as to give prospects of its successful settlement.

Because he anticipated Turkish and Austro-Hungarian opposition, Grey suggested that the ground first be prepared in order to assure success of the project. The British Foreign Office officially chose for the moment not to support any railway project when it appeared that all the schemes for Macedonian reforms were being dropped.[58] Yet, a few weeks later, the British offered to make no objections to the Serbian railway, since it favored improvement of communications in general, although they realized that the Serbian project more directly interested certain other powers which were Serbia's neighbors. Lord Grey refused to take any definite action without first knowing the attitude of the Porte and the other powers.[59]

The Italian ambassador in Constantinople, Marquis Imperiali, advised Serbian Chargé d'Affaires Živojin Balugdžić that Serbia should urge Russia, hitherto somewhat cautious, to back the Serbian railway despite "scruples" which bound her to Austria-Hungary.[60] Weeks later, on April 21, the Russian ambassador in Constantinople, Zinoviev, told Serbian Minister Jaša Nenadović that the Serbian railway plan was not realizable, due to the attitudes of Turkey and Austria-Hungary. On June 27 Izvolsky stated to the Serbian minister Dimitrije Popović, that because the Serbian railway was "vague" Russia could not support it.[61] He said that construction of the Serbian railway would be difficult for physical reasons and lack of capital.[62] But if the Russian policy was not one of unconditional support of the Serbian project, that did not mean that Russia would permit any measure which would increase Austrian and German influence in the Balkans.[63]

The Italians showed the greatest interest in the Serbian railway; they urged the Serbian government to push their plan ahead while there was a chance of Turkish approval. On July 8 the Italian government instructed its minister in Bucharest to support the Serbian overtures to the Rumanian government relative to the Danube-Adriatic railway. The minister was instructed to undertake this task only "if he was certain of success."[64]

Other Balkan states could not view with indifference the projected Serbian railway, which would alter the economic and political situation in the Balkans. During his visit in Berlin and Vienna, Bulgaria's prime minister, D. Stanchov, submitted his country's plan for the railway from Kiûstendil via Skoplje to the Adriatic,[65] which had been suggested some years ago. Indeed the Bulgarian government had discussed this line with the Porte on several occasions since 1904. The Italian government had already spoken of the Antivari-Scutari line as still another Balkan line.[66]

5. TURKO-SERBIAN DISCUSSIONS

Early in 1907 relations between Serbia and Turkey were especially cordial. The Porte was concerned over the latest activities of the Bulgarians. The visits by the Bulgarian prime minister, D. Stanchov, to Vienna, Berlin, and St. Petersburg, the support given to Bulgaria by Austria-Hungary, and an apparent *rapprochement* between Bulgaria and Rumania, encouraged by Austria-Hungary, were developments which disturbed the Turks,[67] and drew them closer to Serbia.

In February Munir Pasha delivered to King Peter a private letter from the sultan in which he presumably expressed a wish for intimate and friendly relations with Serbia. The Serb leaders hesitated to enter into any entanglements with the Turks that might involve Serbia in war with Bulgaria. But, on the other hand, they saw that an agreement with Turkey might prevent any aggressive action by Bulgaria, and Pašić took the liberty of stipulating Serbia's conditions for such an agreement:[68] maintenance of the status quo in the Balkans; Turkey's promise of aid if Bulgaria attacked Serbia, or if Bulgaria invaded Macedonia; Serbia should mobilize her forces if Bulgaria entered Thrace; Serbia would oppose Austria-Hungary's invasion of Turkey by way of Serbia, unless such action by Austria-Hungary was sanctioned by the powers; the two countries would co-operate on the question of Bosna-Hercegovina with a view toward effecting the evacuation of the Austro-Hungarian army and bringing about an administrative autonomy in the provinces under the sovereignty of the sultan; and the population in the two provinces would be given the right of self-determination. In order to popularize a treaty with Turkey in Serbia, Pašić hoped to obtain from Turkey: recognition of Serbian nationality on full equality with the Greek; concessions for the Danube-Adriatic railway; restoration of the Peć Patriarchate; and finally, a Turkish promise that concessions for the Sarajevo-Mitrovica and Kйustendil-Skoplje railway lines would not be granted to Austria-Hungary without Serbian concurrence.[69]

The Turks found the Serbian demands to be quite exorbitant. There was no point in entering into an agreement with Serbia so long as the latter was not obliged to attack Bulgaria, if Turkey and Bulgaria found themselves at war. After an audience with the sultan on April 20, the Serbian minister was of the impression that the Turks had not been sincere about the agreement with Serbia but merely wished to appear friendly in order to intimidate Bulgaria.[70] Soon the Turks took a definite and firm stand against the Serbian railway. The grand vizier told the Austrian ambassador that the Porte "could never" support such a scheme because it was "too dangerous for herself." Similarly, on March 13, Fethy Pasha said to the Austrian minister in Beograd that the Porte opposed the Serbian railway project. The Serbs could do very little thereafter, and on April 25 Pašić sent instructions to the minister in Constantinople not to ask for the railway concession for the time being but to keep it on the agenda and also to work on the appointment of a Serb as metropolitan in the Veles-Debar See.[71]

6. THE BULGARIAN RAILWAY PROJECT

The new Austrian minister to Beograd, Count Forgách, had been given instructions on July 6, 1907, to have a conciliatory attitude and "good will" in his dealings with the ministers of the Serbian government, but always as "a representative of a great power to a small state that is in grave difficulties."[72] But actually the Ballplatz showed neither retreat nor conciliation, and continued to back the Bulgarian and Greek railway projects but not the Serbian. The Bulgarian government hoped with the backing of the monarchy to secure from the Porte a concession for the construction of the Kйustendil-Kumanovo line, which would link Sofia with Skoplje and

Salonika, before the completion of the Serbian Adriatic railway. The latter, in the minds of Bulgarian statesmen, was expected to be detrimental to the Bulgarian economy and to delay, and possibly prevent, the connection of the Bulgarian and Rumanian railways by a bridge at Sistova.[73]

Stanchov felt that the Serbian Adriatic railway would be harmful to Bulgaria's interests in Macedonia, and since it would also be in conflict with the interests of Austria-Hungary, there was, he believed, basis for co-operation between the two powers. In exchange for Austria-Hungary's support at Constantinople, the Bulgarians promised to guarantee Austria-Hungary's economic and political interests in the Balkans.* The Bulgarians had also requested Austria-Hungary to encourage Rumania not to join her railways with the Serbian (Gruja-Prahovo), but instead to join the Bulgarian railways (Calafat-Vidin). In this connection the Bulgarians also directly approached the Rumanian government. However, the Rumanians assured the Serbian minister at Bucharest, M. Ristić, that a railway connection with Bulgaria was out of the question.[74]

The sultan refused to authorize the Bulgarian railway despite the backing of Austria-Hungary.[75] The Bulgarian government had requested the railway concession on several occasions during 1907 and each time it was turned down. The request for the alternative railway line concession which would have linked Bulgaria by way of Seres to the Aegean Sea was likewise refused. A similar fate befell the projected Greek railway connecting Larissa and Platamona with Salonika.[76] Instead of granting railway concessions to their neighbors, the Turks began talking of their own railway, Dzhumaîa-Seres-Orfani.[77]

7. AEHRENTHAL'S PRESSURE ON MONTENEGRO

After his exposé, Aehrenthal addressed a memorandum to Montenegro in which he reminded King Nikola that in accordance with Article XXIX of the Treaty of Berlin Austria-Hungary enjoyed the right to build a railway from the Austrian frontier via Bar to Scutari, or some other point in Albania. Such a railway or road was to be entirely controlled by Austria-Hungary, although Montenegro would be expected to provide a certain number of employees and guarantee the security of communication. Aehrenthal alluded to a previous agreement with Montenegro on the subject.

The Montenegrin government replied that Article XXIX did not grant Austria-Hungary the right to build railways in the newly acquired Montenegrin coastal region.† It claimed that right for Montenegro, which was obliged "to come to an understanding with the neighboring monarchy when it decided to build the road or railway in that district." The Montenegrin government declared that it had made no other separate agreement with

---

* Stanchov made similar promises earlier when, on December 6, 1906, he told Count Turne, Austrian minister in Sofia, that Bulgaria "would certainly undertake nothing that would be in the least against [Austro-Hungarian] interests." *Odnosi*, p. 107.

† Article XXIX: "Le Monténégro devra s'entendre avec l'Autriche-Hongrie sur le droit de construire et d'entretenir à travers le nouveau territorie monténégrin un route et un chemin de fer. Une entière liberté de communication sera assurée sur ces voies."

Austria-Hungary, and that no such agreement could have existed in violation of "the provisions of the Treaty of Berlin." The Montenegrin premier, Lazar Tomanović, was annoyed by the aggressive and arrogant attitude of the Austrian representative, Baron Khun, who treated the Montenegrin ministers "as if Montenegro were an Austrian province."[78]

The Austrian railway demand on Montenegro evoked much speculation. Did Austria-Hungary contemplate penetration of Albania from the sea-coast as she had from land? There was much opposition to the monarchy's aggressive tactics in Montenegro. Finally, under pressure from several foreign powers, Aehrenthal first softened and later abandoned his demand on Montenegro.

8. EUROPEAN AND SERBIAN REACTION TO AEHRENTHAL'S ANNOUNCEMENT

The Aehrenthal statement before the Hungarian Delegation caused a good deal of concern in various European foreign offices. The blow was especially felt in Beograd. While the Serbs were still in the negotiating stage of their scheme, Austria had not only obtained the Turkish concession for the Sandjak railway but had acquired the capital for the costs of construction, and was requesting permission to survey the terrain over which the line would be built.

German Ambassador Marschall was instructed to back the Austrian project on pretense that it would further Balkan trade and facilitate "pacification" of Macedonia.[79] Although Aehrenthal's pressure on the judicial reforms had somewhat irritated the Turks,[80] the grand vizier found that his country stood to gain more than it would lose by co-operating with Vienna and therefore recommended to a ministerial council approval of the Austrian request.[81] On January 31 the sultan issued an irade granting Austria-Hungary the requested railway concession. The representative of the Turkish government and the Austrian-controlled Oriental Railways Company were authorized to undertake a study of the Uvac-Mitrovica line—the Sandjak railway.[82]

Beograd was especially alarmed. Austrian Minister Forgách noted that Aehrenthal's announcement was "a severe blow for Serbia," and that Serbia's "eventual connection with the sea, through Bosna," would not be adequate compensation. He added that the plan destroyed the dream "so dear to the Yugoslav fancy," of a trans-Balkan railway which "would not touch upon [Austro-Hungarian] territory."[83]

The Serbian government now pushed forward more determinedly its own plans for a Danube-Adriatic railway, supported by Russia and Italy,[84] while the Austrian railway project encountered opposition from the Great Powers. To Serbia the Sandjak line signified near disaster; the construction of such a line would, it was believed, prevent possible union between Serbia and Montenegro, and the two Serbian states would have been prevented from ever inheriting parts of Macedonia and Old Serbia. Some Serbs attached such significance to the Sandjak railway that they felt the Danube-Adriatic railway could be no more than a partial compensation:

Baron Aehrenthal has presented an important political question by demanding on one hand the connection of Sarajevo with Mitrovica and on the other the connection of Kotor with Scutari via the Montenegrin seacoast. It cannot be assumed that the Great Powers—Russia, Italy and France—will go beyond their present action. The Danube-Adriatic railway is not even good politics. Something else must be sought . . . revision of the Treaty of Berlin, division of Macedonia, autonomy for the Rumelian vilayets, etc. All these are solutions that might now be discussed, because the Danube-Adriatic railway cannot and should not be sufficient compensation for the Uvac-Mitrovica line.[85]

In Paris the Austro-Hungarian ambassador, Count Khevenhüller, spread the news that Serbia had been notified before Aehrenthal's announcement about the Sandjak railway plan, and that she had agreed to it. This softening policy extended to Cetinje as well, the Austrian offering the prince various things, including guns, if he would consent to the Sandjak railway.[86] On instructions from his home office, Forgách declared on February 8 that in asking for the Sandjak railway concession Austria-Hungary had no other interest than

to facilitate communications and bring the East into closer contact with the West; that [Austria-Hungary] had nothing against Serbia's seeking any other lines of communication; and that she would help Serbia's national interests.[87]

Pašić suspected that the statement by Forgách was but "a palliative for our appeasement."[88] The supposed Austrian willingness to see the Serbian railway built was not sincere and, as subsequent events showed, it was intended merely as a diplomatic maneuver. The Serbian ministers at London (Milovan Milovanović), St. Petersburg (Dimitrije Popović), Constantinople (J. Nenadović), and Paris (M. Vesnić) spontaneously cautioned the Foreign Office not to take too seriously recent Austrian overtures.[89]

On February 23 Forgách again offered Pašić an outlet on the Dalmatian coast, intending to show the world that the monarchy was not selfish but magnanimous and that this time Austria-Hungary was ready to extend financial backing. In his instruction to Forgách on February 25, Aehrenthal frankly admitted that the aforementioned project was intended to make Serbia's Danube-Adriatic project superfluous; he was ready to extend Serbia financial support toward construction of her share of the line via Austrian territory to the Adriatic. Pašić declined the Austrian offer and continued to work on the Danube-Adriatic railway through Turkish territory.[90] He believed that Austria-Hungary resorted to dilatory tactics in order first to secure the Sandjak line and then to concentrate on defeating the Danube-Adriatic project.

The Russian government took the position that the Sandjak railway scheme would upset the status quo in the Balkans and, therefore, would violate the Austro-Russian agreements of 1897 and 1903.[91] On February 14 Izvolsky told the German ambassador, Count Pourtalès, that Aehrenthal's plan would "greatly increase the unrest seething among the Balkan peoples," and added, "C'est une bombe qu'il m'a jetée entre les jambes."[92] While noncommittal regarding the Serbian railway project prior to Aehrenthal's announcement, the Russians now came out openly for it. Izvolsky promised the Serbian minister in St. Petersburg that the Russians would support it at Constantinople and in Paris, where a financial syndicate would be formed. He said the same thing to the Italian ambassador. Izvolsky advised the Serbs to make their action "coincide" with Austria's, and he planned to recommend that the same Turkish commission charged with the investigation of the Sandjak line be authorized to investigate the Adriatic line. Charykov, then assistant to Izvolsky, explained to the Serbian minister that the completion of the two railway lines simultaneously would neutralize any economic advantages that one line might secure over the other. Consequently, he said, they should be worked on simultaneously.[93] The Russians apparently advised the Austrians that both railways be supported at the same time. The latter explained that because of their special right to the Sandjak, in accordance with the Treaty of Berlin, they saw no reason why the two railway plans should be put "into one international pot" (*in einen internationalen Topf zu werfen*).[94]

The Russian ambassador in London, Count Benckendorff, frankly told his German colleague that the Sandjak railway was "not in the spirit of the Russo-Austrian agreement," and went on to say:

The Pan-Slav idea in Russia will gain ground because of this latest move on the part of Austria. The Slav Balkan nations, especially Serbia, are perturbed . . . the accord of the Great Powers in Constantinople is imperiled. The sultan's resistance to the powers will be strengthened. Everything that has been accomplished by the reforms will be undone, because Austria cannot on the one hand beg for concessions and on the other present notes demanding reforms in the seriousness of which the sultan no longer believes. There is now a danger of the situation becoming again what it was before the Balkan agreement, when Austria and Russia stood glaring at each other *comme des chiens de faience.*[95]

The tsar himself, in a special audience, made a long complaint about Aehrenthal's recent action. The Russian policy was to avoid throwing the Porte "still further into the arms of Austria and Germany" and allow them a privileged position in the Balkans to the detriment of the Slavs.[96] *Novoe Vremîa* published an article arguing that

This Austrian plan has for its ultimate aim the Germanization of the Near East, and the whole project is the creation of a great Eastern German Railway to the Mediterranean, advantageous only to Germany and Austria-Hungary and dangerous to everyone else. Baron Aehrenthal is apparently living in the moon, and has forgotten that besides Turks and Greeks in the Balkans, there are millions of Slavs.[97]

The British ambassador in St. Petersburg, A. Nicolson, reported on February 18 that certain Russian circles believed that in regard to the Sandjak railway Austria-Hungary was backed by Germany in accordance with a prearranged plan.[98] *Rossiîa*, in a leading article on February 19, explained that even if Austria-Hungary felt justified in undertaking the Sandjak scheme on the basis of the Treaty of Berlin, her unilateral action in the matter was in violation of the agreements of 1897 and 1903, and one that could not but imperil the reform work in European Turkey.[99] Zinoviev told the German ambassador in Constantinople, on February 25, that Austria's action was *"mauvais procédé"* and that after it the Austro-Russian agreement ceased to exist.[100] Sir Charles Hardinge remarked to the Serbian minister in London that the Mürzsteg Agreement "had obviously taken ill."[101]

To appease the Italians, who felt betrayed like the Russians, Aehrenthal expressed willingness to see the Italians build the Montenegrin port of Bar (Antivari) and the Bar-Virpazar railway. He also offered concessions to Italian navigation on Lake Scutari, where the Italians already enjoyed certain rights. An Italian syndicate was authorized in 1905 to construct and operate a narrow-gauge railway from Bar to Virpazar, and Compagnia di Antivari was similarly given the right to improve harbor facilities in Antivari and provide steamer service on Lake Scutari.[102] These inconsequential offers could not satisfy the Italians, who complained that as an ally of Austria-Hungary they should have been informed of the Sandjak project before its announcement.[103] The Austrians insisted that they had consulted with Italy,[104] but the Italian ambassador in Vienna, Duke Avarna, told the Serbian minister, on February 3, 1908, that "Baron von Aehrenthal had said nothing to him about it."[105]

Whatever the facts, the Italians had accepted reluctantly the Austrian railway project as a *fait accompli*, and then threw their full support behind the Serbian project. In a speech before the Italian parliament on March 11, Foreign Minister Tittoni stressed the economic advantages that Italy might expect from the Adriatic railway and declared that Italy must protest against Austria-Hungary's railway monopoly in the Balkans. Furthermore, Italy held that various political treaties and undertakings did not exclude full freedom of movement in the sphere of economic interests,[106] and that while remaining faithful to her treaty obligations she chose to support the Serbian railway plan as one that best suited the needs of the Italian economy.*

Aehrenthal argued that the Sandjak railway did not come under the scope of the Mürzsteg Agreement, and that in any case the Sandjak line was but a natural development of commerce. The proposed line would not disturb the status quo in the Balkans, the maintenance of which was agreed upon under the Mürzsteg Agreement, but would strengthen trade relations with the Balkan states. It was very important to Austria-Hungary, according to Aehrenthal, to facilitate her exports by providing better trade routes.[107]

At last, on March 13, the Serbian government sent a note to Turkey in which it requested a concession for the Danube-Adriatic railway. Two days later a note was dispatched to Vienna asking for support in Constantinople, according to the promise of February 8. Aehrenthal explained that he could not support the Adriatic railway until he was informed of the route and until Serbia made clear her position regarding the Adriatic outlet via Bosna. Pašić countered that he would accept the connection through Bosna to the Adriatic but not if Serbia had to sacrifice her own project. Among other things he

---

* He further stated that "one thing only could we reasonably demand, that, just as she [Austria-Hungary] wished to construct the railway which most benefited her own commerce, Italy, with the other Powers and the Balkan States, would be free to construct those railways which they held to be most apt to benefit and intensify their own commerce." Tommaso Tittoni, *Italy's Foreign and Colonial Policy*, p. 98.

said that Serbia's line was to be standard gauge, and, as such, it would be of far greater economic importance than the narrow-gauge line through Bosna. He finally reminded Aehrenthal of the existing trade difficulties with Austria-Hungary, and asked how anyone could expect Serbia to sacrifice her own project for one controlled by Austria-Hungary.[108]

Germany shared Aehrenthal's view that the Sandjak railway did not violate the Treaty of Berlin, in that it was an economic project and therefore did not come under the scope of the Mürzsteg Agreement. The German spokesmen believed that the railway would improve economic conditions in the Balkans and facilitate pacification of Macedonia. Serbia was told that Germany in general favored the construction of railways in the Balkans but would not support any one project because she might be asked at some later date to lend support to a rival project "to which our support could not consistently be given."[109]

Excepting the statements of its diplomatic representatives in Constantinople and Beograd, the French government repeatedly expressed willingness to help the Serbian railway project, promising to use its influence in organizing a syndicate for its construction as soon as possible. Cambon, the French ambassador in London, felt that Russia should be persuaded to be the one to raise the question of the Adriatic railway in Constantinople and otherwise to support the construction of that railway.[110] Thus Serbia was sure of the backing of at least three powers—Russia, Italy, and France. Rumania also promised to support the Serbian railway. The Rumanian minister, Sturdza, told the Serbian minister, M. Rakić, on February 14, that construction of the bridge over the Danube at Kladovo might begin at once.[111]

On March 3 in the form of an answer to Aehrenthal's exposé the Russian Foreign Office issued a circular in which the Danube-Adriatic railway was warmly recommended in the name of equality and as an aid in the economic development of the Balkan nations.[112] The Russian position on the Balkan railways was clearly defined in the memorandum communicated to the English on March 3, 1908:

> The Russian Government had always felt a keen interest in the economic development of the Balkan States and their inhabitants, and they were consequently of the opinion that the construction of railways, linking up the different parts of the Peninsula and affording them free access to the surrounding seas, would contribute to the peaceful progress of the countries in question.
> In these circumstances, the Russian Government acceded to a request of the Serbian Government that the Russian Ambassador at Constantinople should support a project for a line opening up communication between the Danube and the Adriatic Sea, and instructions have been issued accordingly. Moreover, the Russian Government, being convinced that it would be easy to coordinate and conciliate on the spot the various interests concerned, would view in a manner equally favorable other railway projects which might be put forward by the respective Balkan States, and would offer them diplomatic support of a similar character.[113]

The Italian minister of foreign affairs had accepted the Russian circular respecting the Balkan railways.[114] The Italian government immediately thereafter had sent instructions to its ambassador at Constantinople to support the Serbian railway scheme, and Signor Tittoni hoped that Great Britain would do the same. Tittoni felt that the railway would benefit Macedonia and might therefore fall within the general framework of Macedonian reforms.[115] The Italian government asked the French Foreign Office to obtain English support for an international syndicate for construction of the Serbian railway. It was proposed that England, Russia, Italy, and Serbia each raise 15 percent, and France 40 percent of the capital.[116]

The French government supported the Serbian railway ostensibly on the grounds that construction of new railways in European Turkey would contribute to the general welfare and security. On French request the British authorized their ambassador at Constantinople, Sir Nicholas O'Conor, to discuss the question of the Serbian railway with his Russian, French, and Italian colleagues, but he was not to take part in soliciting the Porte for a concession for a Serbian line, as the French requested. Moreover, Sir Nicholas was instructed, as confirmed in a memorandum to the Russian ambassador, not to take any action in support of the Serbian scheme at Constantinople until some proposals for effective Macedonian reforms were made. Otherwise the Foreign Office shared the views of the Russian government as to the benefits of railways in the Balkan peninsula, and, though unwilling to support the Serbian railway at Constantinople, expressed sympathy for it and the hope of seeing it realized "simultaneously with the Austrian railway project."[117]

Great Britain was the only power which refrained from joining on behalf of Serbia's railway scheme. She had condemned the Austro-Hungarian unilateral action which destroyed the Macedonian reform program and found that she could not well support Russia's stand, which she felt was similar in character. Yet the British informed the Serbian minister in London, on February 20, that "they fully understood the [Serbian] proposal and its import for the complete emancipation of Serbia."[118]

In a communication to the Serbian government on February 21, the British explained that while they had no objection to either the Serbian or the Austrian plan, they could not support either one at the moment when the powers were contemplating persuading the Turkish government to accept the introduction of new and "very important reforms."[119]

The British defined their position on the Balkan railways in the following words:

. . . that if satisfactory proposals for reform were put forward, and effectively pressed upon the Ottoman Government, His Majesty's Government would then be prepared to use their influence at Constantinople to represent that, if the Novi Pazar scheme were sanctioned, the Danube-Adriatic project should also be agreed to.[120]

Sir Edward Grey explained that the British attitude toward these railway projects was

and should be, one of benevolent neutrality. Some of them are rival schemes. I see no reason why we should take in hand to oppose one in order to favor another. We are favorable to any railway development which is likely to promote general trade and develop the country, and, therefore, so far as that particular point is concerned, taken by itself and on its merits, I do not see that we are very greatly concerned.[121]

Russia, Italy, and France were critical of the English policy on the grounds that construction of Balkan railways would contribute to rather than undermine the reform work and the establishment of security in European Turkey.[122]

Meanwhile, Izvolsky showed momentary retreat which, Ćorović believes, was a result of the British "neutrality" in the matter of railways. On February 22, to the astonishment of the Serbian minister, Izvolsky declared that the railway was not Russia's business and that Russia would not take the initiative in the question, but "would only help [Serbia] in [her] work."[123] This way, he said, he would not, like Aehrenthal, incur the wrath of Europe. For a time he refused to allow the participation of Russian capital in the syndicate for construction of the Serbian railway. But this was only a passing mood; Izvolsky again took up the support of the Serbian railway and by the investment of Russian capital encouraged the participation of French and English capital.[124]

Germany remained loyal to her neighbor and ally; she stood behind Austria-Hungary. The Germans were interested in the Sandjak railway for political, military, and financial reasons; there were indications that the Sandjak railway was to have been financed by the Deutsche Bank, which had financed the Bagdad railway.[125]

Secretary of State Schoen had informed the Russian representative that all railway projects in the Balkans would contribute to peace, and that for this reason Germany was "ready to accept" the idea of the Serbian project.[126] On February 21 Schoen assured the Serbian minister of Germany's support, because, he said, Germany had always favored "the development of a communications system in the Balkans."[127]

But it is one thing to support a Serbian railway and still another to support the Serbian project. Various ramifications of the Serbian and Austrian railway schemes were obviously discussed between Vienna and Berlin on a close and intimate basis. When Aehrenthal informed Berlin that Austria-Hungary appreciated Serbia's need for an Adriatic outlet but hoped that he might persuade Serbia to choose a line more agreeable to Austria-Hungary, one connecting the railways of Serbia and Bosna with an Austrian port, the Germans quickly backed this formula. The German government was certain that Russia would accept the idea of a Serbian railway connection through Austrian territory because Russia's only interest was to get for Serbia "a railway connection with the Adriatic."[128] On March 12 Schoen backtracked from his earlier statement and told the Serbian minister that Germany could not support the Serbian project until she agreed with Austria-Hungary. He said that Germany did not have as much interest as other powers "in exerting her influence in favor of the Serbian plan," and alluded to a possible Serbian railway connection with the Adriatic through Bosna.[129] When the time came, on March 17, to back the Serbian request in Constantinople for the Danube-Adriatic railway concession, only the Russian, French, and Italian ambassadors did so.[130]

If Germany and Austria-Hungary stood together on the Balkan question, the doubtful partner of the Triple Alliance, Italy, was consistently at variance with them. On March 6 Baron von Marschall, German ambassador in Constantinople, cautioned that Italy ought not to be ignored, since that might put the Alliance in jeopardy.[131] The Italian government complained against Germany's failure to support "vital Italian interests" where "the specific interests of Germany" were not compromised. Similar Italian representations were made in Vienna. Rome believed the support of Turkish resistance by Germany and Austria-Hungary would "immediately imperil the existence of the Triple Alliance."[132] Meanwhile, Tittoni took the question of the Serbian railway seriously; he suggested demonstration of naval force to compel Turkey to make concessions for the Danube-Adriatic line.

The determined stand of Italy and Russia against the Sandjak railway and in favor of Serbia's railway scheme produced a diplomatic stalemate. On April 3 Schoen reiterated to Miloš Bogićević, Serbian chargé d'affaires, that Germany "was following the [Serbian] project with much sympathy" and was willing "to support any railway plans in the Balkan peninsula, as nothing but good could come of them." This time, Schoen added, Serbian views "regarding the connection through Bosna were comprehensible."[133] Similarly, on April 7 Aehrenthal told the Serbian minister that he was well disposed to the Serbian line, that railways in Turkey would contribute to the peace and welfare of the people, but that he was not in a position to support the railway. Minister Forgách was so sure that the Serbian railway had so many obstacles before it could be realized that he advised that the Serbian line should not be attacked publicly.[134]

On February 27 the Porte was informed that Austria-Hungary would back concessions for such railway lines which "either Turkey herself might consider necessary, or the monarchy might be asked to support by a third state." In this way Vienna would reserve the right to pass on various railway proposals; she might suppress the lines she did not approve, or prevent their construction unless on financial or other terms favorable to Austria-Hungary. The Italian government, quite distrustful of Austrian aims, announced that it could not be indifferent to the financing of the Adriatic railway, and that it hoped Austria-Hungary would not obstruct formation of a company in which Italy would be strongly represented. The sultan told the Serbian minister that he "would formally grant" Serbia railway concessions when Austria-Hungary "showed less touchiness about it."[135] But Aehrenthal was not intimidated either by the Italian remonstrances or the sultan's displeasure. He told the German ambassador, on May 18, that he would not "blindly" back every railway scheme in the Balkans, the Serbs and Italians notwithstanding.[136]

9. BÜLOW AND THE KAISER SEEK A RAILWAY SETTLEMENT

In deference to Russia and Italy, Germany acted less brusquely than Austria-Hungary, and pretended not to be resolutely behind Vienna. Bülow had apparently assured Tittoni, on April 12, that neither Germany nor Austria-Hungary would work against either the Adriatic railway or Italy's legitimate interests in the Balkans within the limits of the territorial status quo and preservation of Turkish independence. He warned Italy to abstain from "over-hasty insistence." Tittoni agreed to delay bringing up the railway question in Constantinople, and on April 13 suggested the Serbs do the same.[137] The reason for this Italian decision, in part at least, was attributed to the fact that the Ottoman Bank, principal negotiator in the floating of the railway syndicate, refused the French and Italians the representation they expected. The Bank insisted on retaining for itself 50 percent of the capital and offered Italy 30 percent. It was only after prolonged negotiations that a ratio of participation in the financing was established: France 45 percent, Italy 35 percent, Russia 15 percent, and Serbia 5 percent.[138]

The growing Italian defection and Austrian annoyance to the sultan gave Germany serious concern. In April 1908 the kaiser and Bülow toured Italy attempting to sooth the Italians, and then visited Corfu. The kaiser took it upon himself to mediate with the Porte, and recommended to Turkan Pasha, who was sent to welcome him, that the sultan grant the permit for an Adriatic railway. The kaiser subsequently noted that Vienna "must" support Serbia's scheme in Constantinople and that the German and Austrian ambassadors should act together on the matter.[139] This he believed would tend to preserve the Austro-Russian agreement. On May 16 the Serbian minister in Berlin was told that the question of the Adriatic railway would now be settled favorably for Serbia because Germany and Austria-Hungary had joined the other powers in support of it.[140] The Russians, who took the kaiser's move as *"une généreuse démarche,"* insisted on open support by Vienna.[141]

What exactly transpired in the discussions between Austria and Germany is difficult to ascertain. One thing was clear, and that was that Austria was not yet ready to approve unconditionally the Serbian Adriatic railway. Aehrenthal appeared to have given in to the kaiser and had agreed to support the Serbian and Bulgarian railway projects, but at the same time hoped to limit this support by asking the Porte to issue an irade permitting only the tracing of the Serbian line.[142] Once driven to compromise, Aehrenthal chose to limit his concession as much as possible. Through his initiative it was decided in Vienna and St. Petersburg to ask Turkish concession for the Serbian railway, but only for that portion of the line from Mrdare to Štimlje, and not all the way to the sea. Just how it came about that Vienna and St. Petersburg should agree on such an idea is not clear to this author. Needless to say, Serbia was astonished, and protested against this partial concession, but St. Petersburg cautioned that the grant represented only the first stage of the negotiation. The Italians and French opposed this proposal, and so did the Ottoman Bank for financial reasons.[143] Sir Charles Hardinge told the Serbian minister, on May 21, that "this limit could only be in the interests of Austria-Hungary, and in no event in [Serbian] interests."[144]

Austrian diplomacy seemingly hoped to divide the Adriatic railway into sections, causing thereby endless difficulties by negotiating separately over each section, and thus enabling Austria-Hungary to control Serbia as long as possible. Aehrenthal told Tschirschky, on May 4, that Austria-Hungary could not support a "primarily" Serbian railway, nor Serbian objectives in the

Balkans, unless Serbia first changed her policy toward Austria-Hungary.[145]

After German mediation and the compromise proposal, the Turks pretended to agree to the concession of Mrdare-Štimlje, but, like Austria-Hungary, they did so hoping that they might be able to scuttle the Adriatic railway by prolonging its completion. On June 4 the grand vizier told the Serbian minister that he considered the question of the issuance of the irade settled, and told the Russian and French ambassadors that preliminary work would start "as soon as the required means were secured."[146]

10. THE RAILWAY FEVER SUBSIDES

Organization of a syndicate for the construction of the Serbian railway with Russian, French, Italian, and Serbian participation was begun at Rome. Each government guaranteed proportionally the interest on the capital figure of 68 million francs at 3.5 percent.[147] The English were apparently in favor of the plan and instructed their ambassador in Constantinople to act accordingly.[148] By an arrangement agreed on in June 1908 the French were to supply most of the capital for the construction of the Adriatic railway from the Serbian border to the Adriatic; the Italians were alloted the financing of the port construction on the Adriatic. Russian, Serbian, and British interests were represented in each case.[149]

On June 20 the Serbian government announced that it would give up the concession for the Danube-Adriatic railway in favor of the French-controlled Salonika-Constantinople Railway Company. The Russians welcomed this change in tactics. The Turkish authorities meanwhile procrastinated. They urged the company to leave the survey until the next year. After the Macedonian reforms came to an end, the British and the Russian envoys in Constantinople pressed the Turks to stop delaying and to issue the irade for the Serbian railway, but the Turks had at the moment a more pressing problem—the Young Turk revolution.[150]

On the Austro-Hungarian side, plans for the Sandjak railway were drawn up and preliminary work started. Construction, however, was delayed. In the memorandum which he drew up on August 9, 1908, Aehrenthal said:

The preventing of a pan-Slav coalition along our southern frontier can . . . hardly be secured by the occupation or annexation of the Sandjak. But even if we are able, by intervention in the Sandjak, to keep Serbia and Montenegro permanently apart, we should still not have attained the main objective . . . to make our southern frontiers secure in case Turkey in Europe breaks up.

We shall not obtain these secure frontiers until we decide to grasp the nettle firmly and make a final end of the pan-Slav dream.

Antagonism between Bulgaria and Serbia is already today a factor that can be reckoned with; in Bulgaria the conviction prevails that the road to Macedonia must lead over the body of the Serbian state, and it is certain that the most violent strife will break out between Serbia and Bulgaria for the possession of Skoplje.

If we take Bulgaria's side in this conflict and favor the creation of a Great Bulgaria at the expense of Serbia, the necessary preparation will have been made, and in the moment of a favorable European constellation, we can lay our hands on the rest of Serbia.

Then we should have the secure frontiers of which I have spoken above: and Albania will become independent under our aegis, a Montenegro with which we maintain friendly relations, and a Great Bulgaria which is indebted to us.[151]

After the annexation of Bosnia and Hercegovina in October 1908, Austria-Hungary evacuated the Sandjak of Novi Pazar and abandoned the Sandjak railway project. At the same time the annexation crisis, extending from October 1908 to March 1909, convinced the Serbian government even more of the urgency of the Adriatic railway which had been approved by the powers. For a time it seemed there was a feeling that the powers would go out of their way to satisfy Serbia regarding her railway proposal as a kind of compensation for the loss of Bosnia-Hercegovina. A company (*Jonction Salonique–Constantinople*) was organized for the construction of the railway from Mrdare to San Giovanni di Medua. The French, Italian, and Russian governments backed the company in Constantinople, and the Porte gave permission for the construction of the railway on September 3, 1909.[152]

The Russians were particularly active in support of the Serbian project. Ambassador Charykov at Constantinople was primarily instrumental in securing the Porte's permission. Izvolsky discussed the Serbian railway project with Tittoni at their meeting in Racconigi (October 1909) and he had also assured Rifaat Pasha, the Turkish foreign minister, that the Adriatic railway was intended to serve both Serbia and Turkey. On October 27, 1909, two Russian engineers were sent to Old Serbia to survey the line and they were joined at Salonika by a Turkish officer.

The Young Turks meanwhile changed their attitude toward the Serbian railway project and proceeded to obstruct the work of the Russian engineers. In the vicinity of Peć, in December 1909, an attempt was made to kill the Russian engineers. The Russians saw in this a deliberate plot by "some foreign power" and withdrew their officers from the area. There is some indication that Austria-Hungary might have encouraged the Turks to use whatever methods possible in delaying the construction of the Adriatic railway.[153]

The new position taken by the Young Turks was that they would support the idea of the Adriatic railway so long as it was not under foreign control. They also suggested changes in the route proposed by the Serbian government. Instead of a direct link between Prizren and the port of San Giovanni di Medua, the Turks proposed a line Prizren-Debar-San Giovanni di Medua. This circuitous line would be longer than that proposed by the Serbs and would perforce be slower in expediting the Serbian shipments to the Adriatic port.

Resorting to delaying tactics of one sort or another the Turks succeeded in postponing the construction of the Adriatic railway until July 29, 1911. An agreement was then signed with the *Jonction Salonique–Constantinople* for the construction of the line via Debar despite protests from Austria-Hungary and Germany. When the engineers in April 1912 once again arrived on the terrain to survey the projected line and begin work, the political situation in the Balkans had markedly changed its complexion. The Albanian uprising and the wars that followed prevented construction of the railway.[154] In 1953 the Beograd-Uleinj line was at last begun.

Conclusion

IN RETROSPECT, ONE CAN DISCERN IN SERBIA AFTER 1878 two distinct political camps that might be conveniently identified as Austrophiles and Russophiles. Both were influenced by contemporary political and economic thought in Western Europe, but they held divergent views regarding their country's foreign orientation. The former were the backers of the Progressive party, which in 1898 ceased to exist as a party but remained an ideological inspiration. The two typical leaders of the Progressive party were Milan Piroćanac and Čedomilj Mijatović. Piroćanac was a convinced subscriber to Western liberalism and a profound admirer of Western culture, and was of the conviction that sound politics required a close relation between Serbia and Austria-Hungary. Only with Austrian help could Serbia, he believed, curb Russian influence in the Balkans. In the eyes of Mijatović, the Russians represented retarded civilization and a semi-barbarian state threatening the main streams of European culture and political and economic development. King Milan was committed to this camp and was its principal source of strength.

The Russophiles, also loosely defined, were those who followed the Radical party and to a lesser degree were the followers of the Liberal party led by Jovan Ristić. The Radical party derived its ideology from the West, but its leaders were strongly influenced by the Russian exiles in Switzerland, ranging from anarchist Bakunin to Socialists of every color. Many were also influenced by the Russian *narodniki*. As time passed, the Radical party became less socialist and republican and more nationalist and monarchist. It continued to vaunt itself as a peasant party, but too often sacrificed the interests of the peasants. It claimed to be a true defender of "constitutional government" and yet consistently compromised with forces of reaction. Its leaders saw in Russia a bulwark for the future of all Slavdom, a champion against the traditional Slavic enemies—the Germans and the Turks. This conviction was all the more important since Serbia stood in the way of the *Drang nach Osten*, and therefore her dreams of national development could be realized only with Russian backing.

As time passed the power of the Radical party grew and that of the Progressive and Liberal parties declined. Correspondingly, Austro-Hungarian influence had begun to wane and Russian influence to grow in Beograd. But neither foreign power had full confidence in the last Obrenović ruler. In the later period of his reign King Alexander had to resort to dependence on the Radicals, whom he did not fully trust, in spite of a series of concessions made to them from 1900 to 1902. As one would expect, the Russians backed the Radicals and the Austrians opposed them. The Radicals demanded full control of the government as the opposition against the king increased.

Unwanted at home and abroad, Alexander ruled his last year with the aid of court favorites. The return to personal rule by the king intensified the opposition against the Crown. The general instability of Serbia hampered normal economic, political, and cultural development. The unpopular royal regime brought the country to the verge of ruin. Dissatisfaction was widespread and permeated all social strata. A conspiracy against the king was organized—an essentially military movement. Despite general displeasure with the state of affairs, the political leaders sought to ameliorate the situation by compromising with the Crown. By early 1903 opposition to the king reached revolutionary strength. The disturbances in March 1903 were precipitated by a handful of young progressive intellectuals and workers. Even more radical demonstrators demanded an end to royal tyranny and the establishment of a republic. Recent communist historians refer to the March Demonstration as "the first political conflict between the proletariat and the government."

The repercussions of the March troubles were far reaching. The ruthlessness of the *gendarmerie*, which, acting on government orders, crushed the rebellious masses, intensified the opposition to the Crown and the Cincar-Marković cabinet. The army, which had refused to shoot at the March demonstrators, was subjected to a purge. Anti-Obrenović elements were tracked down. In the face of these developments, the military conspirators decided upon final action. On June 11 they forced the palace and murdered the king and queen.

The military conspiracy was essentially apolitical. It lacked a coherent political program and seemed devoid of any ideological persuasion. By virtue of its secretiveness it was unable to generate mass appeal and command a large following. Nor did it represent the entire Officers' Corps which it alleged to represent. The most that could be said for the conspirators was that they were anti–Alexander Obrenović, and that they sought to eliminate the Obrenović dynasty by doing away with the heirless king. What would then follow was seemingly not clear in the minds of the conspirators. The bulk of them did agree that the return of the Karadjordjević dynasty would best serve the national interests, but a few meek voices were courageous enough to suggest the establishment of a republic. A republic would certainly have invited Austro-Hungarian and Russian intervention. Hence monarchy was chosen as the most expedient form of government. Neither Austria nor Russia was expected to reject Peter Karadjordjević as Serbia's new king, and for that reason, and because of his popularity, he was chosen to succeed Alexander. Thus the palace attack, when it did come, was not a complete revolution in any true sense. Nothing was basically altered. The palace murders were followed by purges, but no changes in government and social structure were effected. The state apparatus remained as it was. Simply, one government and dynasty replaced the other. But the new regime abode more strictly by constitutional and parliamentary practices. The new king had no desire to violate his oath and establish a personal rule.

At the outset, in 1903, the new regime was beset by many difficult problems. The new dynasty, which came to power as a result of the conspiracy, had first of all to obtain European recognition. It was months and even years before all principal members of the European community recognized King Peter. Because of the instability at home and the pressure from without, the regime endeavored not to identify itself with any single great power, although through the Radical party and Peter himself, Russian influence in Beograd was in the ascendancy. The regicide question was a serious problem both internally and in Serbian foreign relations. The "counterconspiratorial" movement came into existence directed against the regicides. The powers intervened in the internal affairs of Serbia, seeking to compel the latter to remove the regicides who held prominent positions in the government and the court, and staged a "diplomatic strike," excluding Peter from the European royal fraternity, and breaking off diplomatic relations. The power most determined to see justice done in Serbia was England; she withheld her recognition of the new regime until the promise to remove the objectionable regicides from important government positions had been given.

England was by and large satisfied with the removal of the regicides, but the latter continued to influence political events in Serbia. The same officers that murdered Alexander Obrenović in 1903 were behind the organization called "Unity or Death" (Black Hand) in 1911. They were also active during the Balkan Wars and were implicated in the assassination of Archduke Francis Ferdinand in 1914. Prince Alexander Karadjordjević, whose dynasty was put on the throne by the conspirators, was primarily responsible for the conviction of the Black Hand leaders in the Salonika trial of 1917. They had apparently outlived their usefulness and presented a threat to his political aspirations. To counteract the Black Hand, the Prince organized his devotees into the White Hand. The result was the continuation of conspiratorial influence until World War II. The question of the Salonika trial and the Black Hand, astonishingly enough, suddenly popped up in 1953 but this time in an entirely new political setting. The Communist government of Serbia held a retrial of those convicted at Salonika, and they were found innocent, as was to have been expected. This recent affair has led to heated controversy among the historians, publicists, and former conspirators, as to whether or not the Black Hand was a "progressive movement." There is indication that the ghost of the 1903 conspiracy and its successor, the Black Hand, still hovers in the background of Yugoslav politics.

The cabinets after 1903 extended civil liberties and democratic freedoms. Despite many irregularities in connection with the elections and otherwise, the king and the political leaders did not on the whole transgress constitutional bounds. A constitutional monarchy had come to Serbia at last. To be sure, there was opposition to the established regime from right and left. Some pro-Obrenović and Austrophile elements continued to cause difficulties, and the Socialists howled about the exploitation and political persecution of the workers.

Republicanism and socialism, the origins of which can be vaguely traced to the first half of the nineteenth century, received impetus after 1903. The workers now had the opportunity to organize themselves politically, and through mushrooming syndicates they were able more effectively to defend their class interests. But so long as the dynasty was identified with national interests and retained the popular backing, the chances of any appreciable republican and Socialist success were very slight indeed. Serbia had first to achieve national unification before she could embark on an internal socioeconomic transformation. Yet the new regime gave opportunity for expression to the antimonarchical movements, which crystallized into going concerns. Despite the squabbles which accompanied the break in Socialist ranks in 1903, the Socialists succeeded in electing a deputy or two in several of the subsequent parliaments.

The change of the dynasty in 1903 brought acceleration of nationalistic activities at home and abroad and gave vent to rapidly growing Yugoslavism. Some Yugoslav historians say that one of the reasons for the collapse of Obrenović rule was Alexander's neglect of the "national interests" at home and in the provinces still under foreign yoke. The Serbian nationalist activities in Old Serbia and Macedonia lagged. Bosna-Hercegovina and other neighboring provinces of the Habsburg Empire were left to the will of the foreign rulers. To pursue a genuine national policy required above all else an emancipation from Austria-Hungary's influence. The conflict with the latter power in Macedonia, the Albanian attacks on the Serbs, and the "Pig War" were all manifestations of that struggle for emancipation, and the period after 1903 can be characterized as one of growing Austro-Serbian tension. Scores of newspapers and journals and societies, in Serbia and in provinces of Austria-Hungary, cautiously but persistently furthered the cause of Yugoslav unity, a unity that could be effected only through Austro-Hungarian state collapse.

The hoped-for *rapprochement* with Bulgaria and Montenegro was never realized. The conflicting interests of the three Slavic nations were nurtured by Austria-Hungary as a policy to prevent the creation of a Slavic bloc on her southern frontiers. The unfortunate fratricidal warfare between various Balkan bands reflected the irreconcilable nationalisms of the time. They all claimed Macedonia, a possible vacuum when Turkey should recede into Asia, as their irredenta. It was a vicious circle. One nation forced another to act, lest the power equilibrium in the Balkans be upset. In 1904 the Secret Treaty with Bulgaria on the division of Macedonia into spheres of influence did not materialize, and was probably never concluded in earnest. The Turks played one faction against the other, and Austria, Russia, and Italy viewed each other's activities with apprehension, supporting their respective satellites in the field of banditry. If the record of the Balkan states is unenviable, that of the Great Powers is not much better, least of all that of Austria-Hungary, which was to no small degree responsible for the Albanian terror over the Serbian nationals, a policy deliberately calculated to displace Serbian influence in Old Serbia.

The governments and ruling houses of Montenegro and Serbia were unable to cement friendly political relations. The union of the two states was not yet possible, not only because particular forces were still strong but also because expansionist interests of the countries conflicted in the Sandjak of Novi Pazar, Old Serbia, and Bosna. Yet one observation can be safely asserted, and that is that Serbia had forged far ahead of Montenegro as the leader in the Yugoslav struggle for national liberation.

The Entente Cordiale (1904) between England and France, which strengthened the Russo-French alliance, isolated Germany, which now began to support Austria-Hungary and her aggressive policy in the Balkans. During Russia's preoccupation in the Far East in 1904–5, Austria-Hungary brought every conceivable pressure to bear in a futile effort to reassert herself in Beograd, and worked against Serbian national interests in Old Serbia and Macedonia. When the trade treaty between Serbia and Austria-Hungary expired in 1904, Austria returned to her ancient tactics in dealing with Serbia. She attached political conditions to purely commercial transactions, such as the demand that Serbian state contracts be placed with Austro-Hungarian firms. Such arrogance on the part of the Dual Monarchy evoked an outburst of national pride and popular resistance to any compromise. The break in trade relations with Austria-Hungary led to the "Pig War" and ultimately to a Serbian victory in the form of economic emancipation from Austria-Hungary. However, Serbia continued to depend on foreign financial assistance; France replaced Austria-Hungary in this sphere and became the principal lender to Serbia and the founder of the Franco-Serbian Bank. French credits gave impetus to Serbian commerce and industry.

The results of the "Pig War" were far reaching. New markets and trade routes were found. Austria-Hungary, which had previously controlled 90 percent of the trade, controlled only 30 percent of Serbian trade after the customs war. The Western powers and the Balkan states increased their trade with Serbia. After 1904 commercial relations with foreign powers were regulated by the autonomous tariff law enacted by the Skupština. The character of trade changed. Trade relations with Rumania, Turkey, Bulgaria, and Greece, previously of no importance, were now close and continued to improve. Navigation and railroad facilities of the Balkan states began to play a more important role in Serbian foreign trade. The progress achieved through economic emancipation from Austria-Hungary was self-evident. Statistics point to that conclusion in all divisions of the country's economy. In general, there was large expansion of all productive forces. Yet all this did not mean that sacrifices by Serbia and her peasantry were negligible in the early stages of the "Pig War." The peasant always suffered when Austria-Hungary chose to prohibit imports of Serbian cattle, and after 1881 she did that often for political reasons. "The peasant paid the cost of the customs war in 1906–7, and of the Bosna-Hercegovina crisis which followed in 1908–9."[1] The livestock economy was still preponderant in the country and any restrictions on livestock exports caused hardships on the peasantry. Yet in the complete absence of any kind of organization of peasant credit, the peasants were forced to shift from livestock to agriculture and thereby save their land. When it became necessary to ship wheat by a somewhat circuitous route via Braila, the peasant defrayed the costs of transport by virtue of accepting lower prices for his wheat.[2]

The "Pig War" stimulated industrial development in Serbia. From 1900 to 1910 the number of industrial enterprises increased from 153 to 465. The value of industrial production in the same period increased sevenfold. Progress was achieved principally in light industry—sugar, textiles, meat, and leather. As was to be expected, many of the industrial installations were built by foreign capital, which found cheap labor in Serbia. The growth of industry and general economic development affected the social structure of Serbia. The traditional differentiation between the social strata, especially between villagers and city folk, became more pronounced. The number of industrial workers increased. Likewise, as the crafts increased, especially the bigger workshops, the number of skilled workmen increased. In the villages there were signs which warned of future trouble; the number of families without land was growing. Correspondingly, the number of well-to-do peasants grew also.

Then came the crucial year of 1908. Relations with Bulgaria were tense. Those with Russia had strengthened. The Macedonian reforms had collapsed. Austria-Hungary startled the world with a proposal for the Sandjak of Novi Pazar railway that would separate Montenegro from Serbia forever and bring the Dual Monarchy close to her ultimate aim—realization of the *Drang nach Südosten* (Salonika). The negotiations in foreign capitals over the Austrian proposal and various Balkan counterproposals, including Serbia's Danube-Adriatic railway, occupied the next few months in Serbian foreign relations. Meanwhile new and more vigorous Macedonian reforms were being contemplated by England and Russia. In June 1908 the Young Turk revolution terminated all efforts at reforms and brought to a close the first period of Karadjordjević rule. The first phase of the policy initiated in 1903 ended; Serbia had sailed safely through many a storm, gained in international importance, developed a democratic system of government, and consolidated national resistance to foreign imperialism.

Notes, Bibliography, and Index

Notes

Notes to Part One

[1] On the projected match with a German princess and other plans to marry King Alexander, see *Vl. Al. Ob.*, III, 1–2, and Stojan Novaković, *Dvadeset godina ustavne politike, 1883–1903*, pp. 200–211. For the factual data in these introductory pages the author is especially indebted to Professor Jovanović, *op. cit.*, and the following: Dragiša Vasić, *Devesto treća;* Živan Živanović, *Politička istorija Srbije, 1897–1903*, IV.

[2] V. Čubrilović and V. Ćorović, *Srbija od 1858 do 1903*, pp. 172–73, 191; *Vl. Al. Ob.*, III, 1–2.

[3] C. Mijatovich, *A Royal Tragedy*, pp. 120–21.

[4] *Ibid.*

[5] *Ibid.*, p. 121.

[6] *Ibid.*, pp. 123–24; Novaković, p. 209.

[7] Mijatovich, pp. 120–23.

[8] *Vl. Al. Ob.*, III, 2–3.

[9] Mijatovich, p. 123.

[10] General Dimitrije Cincar-Marković was designated acting supreme commandant of the army during Milan's absence (*Srpske novine*, June 9, 1901).

[11] Mijatovich, p. 130; Živanović, IV, 193–234. The author devotes an entire chapter to what he calls "suspicious signs on the eve of the marriage," in which he lists several incidents from 1899 to 1900 that hinted at the king's decision to marry Draga Mašin.

[12] Mijatovich, pp. 83–84.

[13] *Ibid.*, p. 85.

[14] *Ibid.*, p. 86.

[15] *Ibid.*, pp. 87, 141.

[16] Novaković, pp. 207–8.

[17] Quoted in Mijatovich, p. 91.

[18] *Ibid.*, pp. 87–91, 141.

[19] *Ibid.*, p. 88.

[20] *Vl. Al. Ob.*, III, 27. The author quotes some of the letters.

[21] *Ibid.*, pp. 29–32.

[22] *Ibid.*, p. 33.

[23] Mijatovich, pp. 94–96.

[24] Pera Todorović, leader of the Radical party, tells in his memoirs (*Ogledalo,* IV–V, Nos. 58–63, 1904) how the Russians reacted to Milan's return to Serbia on October 19, 1897, and how they insisted that Milan must leave the country.

[25] Mijatovich, pp. 102–3.

[26] *Ibid.*, pp. 104–5.

[27] *Ibid.*, pp. 65–67.

[28] Živanović, pp. 107–14. Some historians say Milan himself was responsible for the plot. See Djurdje Jelenić, *Nova Srbija i Jugoslavija*, pp. 213, 472; Mijatovich, p. 67.

[29] Mijatovich, pp. 68–69.

[30] *Ibid.*, p. 70.

[31] Lazar Stanojević, "Jedna nedovoljno poznata strana naše novije istorije," *Letopis Matice Srpske; Vl. Al. Ob.*, III, 33–34.

[32] Mijatovich, p. 71.

[33] *Ibid.*, p. 73.

[34] *Ibid.*, p. 74.

[35] Pera Todorović, *Ogledalo*, Nos. 63–70, 1904; Mijatovich, pp. 75–78. Mijatovich says that everywhere in Beograd the impression at the time was that "the marriage of Alexander with Draga was the work of the Russian policy."

36 *Vl. Al. Ob.*, III, 3; Mijatovich, pp. 131–32.

37 Mijatovich, pp. 131–32.

38 Živanović, IV, 200–201, gives the complete text of the cabinet's letter of resignation.

39 *Vl. Al. Ob.*, III, 3.

40 Mijatovich, p. 133.

41 Živanović, IV, 210.

42 *Vl. Al. Ob.*, III, 4–7; Mijatovich, p. 143; Živanović, IV, 203.

43 Živanović, IV, 204.

44 *Ibid.*, p. 205.

45 Mijatovich, pp. 141–42.

46 *Ibid.*

47 Mijatovich, pp. 135–37; Vladan Djordjević, *Kraj jedne dinastije,* pp. 559–88; Živanović, IV, 210.

48 Živanović, IV, 206; *Vl. Al. Ob.*, III, 9.

49 Živanović, IV, 206; Mijatovich, p. 144.

50 Mijatovich, pp. 145–47.

51 Živanović, IV, 206–9.

52 *Vl. Al. Ob.*, III, 35.

53 Mijatovich, p. 145; Živanović, IV, 207, 211.

54 Mijatovich, p. 149; Živanović, IV, 228.

55 *Vl. Al. Ob.*, III, 10.

56 Živanović, IV, 212–14.

57 *Srpske novine,* July 9, 1900.

58 *Vl. Al. Ob.*, III, 11–12.

59 *Ibid.*, p. 13.

60 Živanović, IV, 221.

61 *Vl. Al. Ob.*, III, 14–15.

62 Djordjević, III, 642.

63 *Vl. Al. Ob.*, III, 16–18; Antonije Antić, *Politika,* October 27, 1926; Živanović, IV, 219–20.

64 *Vl. Al. Ob.*, III, 19–21.

65 *Ibid.*, p. 24.

66 Mijatovich, p. 147; *Srpske novine,* July 14, 1900; Živanović, IV, 221–22; *Srpske novine,* July 18, 1900.

67 Mijatovich, p. 148.

68 See for example the article entitled "After the King's Proclamation," which appeared in the *Srpske novine,* July 14, 1900.

69 *Vl. Al. Ob.*, III, 25–26.

70 *Ibid.*, pp. 36–39.

71 Živanović, IV, 107–14.

72 *Vl. Al. Ob.*, III, 21–23.

73 Živanović, IV, 223–24.

74 *Vl. Al. Ob.*, III, 42–45; Živanović, IV, 226–27.

75 *Vl. Al. Ob.*, III, 46–50.

76 *Večernje novosti,* No. 1, 1905. A fragment from the memoirs of Aleksa Jovanović, head of the "wedding cabinet." See also Živanović, IV, 226.

77 Tasa Milenković, *Kralj Aleksandar i oficirska zavera,* p. 9; *Vl. Al. Ob.*, III, 50–54.

78 Živanović, IV, 229.

79 *Vl. Al. Ob.*, III, 54–55.

80 *Ibid.*, p. 57.

81 *Srpske novine,* August 26, 1900; *Večernje novosti,* No. 1, 1905; *Vl. Al. Ob.*, III, 59; Živanović, IV, 226–27 n.

82 *Srpske novine,* No. 192, August 26, 1900; Živanović, IV, 227; *Vl. Al. Ob.*, III, 61.

83 *Vl. Al. Ob.*, III, 62–63.

84 *Ibid.*, p. 64.

85 *Vl. Al. Ob.*, III, 69–71; Živanović, IV, 231.

[86] *N.S.*, 1903–1904, pp. 135 ff., for details and figures of Serbia's loans; *Vl. Al. Ob.*, III, 88–89.

[87] Milorad Nedeljković, *Istorija srpskih državnih dugova* (Beograd, 1909), pp. 252–53; *Vl. Al. Ob.*, III, 189–90.

[88] Vladan Djordjević, *Kraj jedne dinastije*, Parts 25–26, pp. 676 ff.; Živanovic, IV, 229; *Vl. Al. Ob.*, III, 33.

[89] Mijatovich, pp. 117–19.

[90] *Vl. Al. Ob.*, III, 33, 93.

[91] Mijatovich, pp. 117–19.

[92] *Vl. Al. Ob.*, III, 91–92.

[93] *Vl. Al. Ob.*, III, 93–94, cites Maršićanin, I, 124; Djordjević, III, Ch. 39; Živanovic, IV, 231–32.

[94] Živanović, IV, 232–33.

[95] *Vl. Al. Ob.*, III, 94; Živanović, IV, 232.

[96] Živanović, IV, 233, description of the funeral; *Vl. Al. Ob.*, III, 94.

[97] *Vl. Al. Ob.*, III, 94; Novaković, pp. 213–14.

[98] Jelenić, p. 216.

[99] For a detailed and authoritative discussion of the April Constitution, see Jaša M. Prodanović, *Ustavni razvitak i ustavne borbe u Srbiji*, pp. 375–413; see also *Vl. Al. Ob.*, III, 98–144; Živanović, IV, 235–45; Novaković, pp. 215–20; and Jelenić, pp. 215–17.

[100] Živanović, IV, 246–47; Jelenić, p. 216.

[101] Prodanović, pp. 375–76.

[102] Živanović, IV, 244–45; Novaković, pp. 220–21.

[103] Prodanović, p. 377; Novaković, pp. 224–37, Alexander's letter to Stojan Novaković, in which he gives his reasons for granting the constitution.

[104] *Vl. Al. Ob.*, III, 120–23.

[105] *Srpske novine*, August 26, 1900; Živanović, IV, 227–28.

[106] *Vl. Al. Ob.*, III, 60, quotes Aleksa Jovanović, prime minister of the "wedding cabinet," who published a number of articles on Alexander's marriage in the *Večernje novosti,* 1903–6.

[107] *Vl. Al. Ob.*, III, 123–24; Živanović, IV, 247–49.

[108] *Vl. Al. Ob.*, III, 124–25.

[109] *Dnevnik*, May 5, 1901; Živanović, IV, 248.

[110] *Vl. Al. Ob.*, III, 126; Jelenić, p. 217.

[111] *Vl. Al. Ob.*, III, 127.

[112] Dr. Caulet published his diagnosis in August and the protocols signed by Snegirev, Gubarov, and himself in April and May, 1901. See "La fausse grossesse de la reine de Serbie," *Semaine médicale*, No. 22, 1901.

[113] *Vl. Al. Ob.*, III, 130–31; Živanović, IV, 250–51; see also the article on the occasion of the first anniversary of the marriage in the *Dnevnik*, No. 82, July 23, 1901.

[114] *Vl. Al. Ob.*, III, 142–80, in which the author analyzes each of the laws passed; Živanović, IV, 253–59.

[115] *Vl. Al. Ob.*, III, 213 ff.

[116] *Ibid.*, pp. 222–23.

[117] *Ibid.*, pp. 228–30.

[118] Živanović, IV, 251–52; *Vl. Al. Ob.*, III, 133–36.

[119] *Vl. Al. Ob.*, III, 231–32.

[120] *Vl. Al. Ob.*, III, 235–36; Živanović, IV, 262–64; Triša Kaclerović, *Martovske demonstracije i majski prevrat 1903,* pp. 30–31. The author gives details of the part played by the student socialists.

[121] *Vl. Al. Ob.*, III, 242–45.

[122] *Ibid.*, pp. 251–53; Živanović, IV, 279–80.

[123] Nationalversammlung, Germany, 1919–20. "Untersuchungausschuss über die Weltkriegsverantwortlichkeit" (I). Vol. X: Unterausschuss. *Die Vorgeschichte des Weltkrieges,* 67. Hereafter cited as *Die Vorgeschichte des Weltkrieges.*

[124] *Die Vorgeschichte des Weltkrieges*, pp. 62–63; *Vl. Al. Ob.*, III, 236–37.

[125] *Vl. Al. Ob.*, III, 238; Živanović, IV, 261.

¹²⁶ *Vl. Al. Ob.,* III, 240–42.

¹²⁷ *Ibid.,* p. 242.

¹²⁸ Živanović, IV, 281–84; *Vl. Al. Ob.,* III, 272; Jelenić, p. 217; *Dnevnik,* November 1, 1902. Alexander's disappointment in the "fusion" government was explicit in several of his speeches in September of 1902, published by the *Srpske novine,* September 4, 5, 6, 1902.

¹²⁹ B. Maršićanin, II, 126–28, quoted in *Vl. Al. Ob.,* III, 280–94; Živanović, IV, 297–300. For different views on responsibility for the demonstration see *Srpske novine,* April 2, 1903, and July 10, 1903; *Trgovinski glasnik,* April 1903; *Odjek,* June 17, 1903. One of the principal student leaders in the demonstration was Dimitrije Tucović, a leader of the Serbian Social Democratic party. See Kaclerović, pp. 33–34, 44–46, in which the author discusses the part played by the Socialists in organizing and leading the March Demonstration, and its significance; Moša Pijade, *O Dimitriju Tucoviću;* Dimitrije Tucović, *Izabrani spisi.* On the description of the demonstration, the casualties and losses, and the subsequent official reprisals, see *Sloga,* March 24 and April 3, 1903; and *Srpske novine,* March 30, 1903.

¹³⁰ Živanović, IV, 300–301.

¹³¹ *Vl. Al. Ob.,* III, 297; Živanović, IV, 301–6; *Srpske novine,* special issue, No. 68, March 25, 1903.

¹³² Živanović, IV, 311–16; *Vl. Al. Ob.,* III, 298–99; *Sloga,* May 30, 1902.

Notes to Part Two

¹ Georgi P. Genov, *Iztochniiāt vŭpros,* p. 508; *Kako je postala Bugarska Egzarhija* (Beograd, 1897) contains a series of documents purporting to show how the exarchate originated (pp. 3–80); Tihomir Djordjević, *Macedonia* (London, 1918), pp. 117–18; D. Mishew, *The Bulgarians in the Past,* pp. 429–39; F. Hýbl, *Dějiny národa bulharského,* I, 41; A. Ishirkov, *La Macédoine et la constitution de l'Exarchat bulgare;* Ivan Ivanić, *Maćedonija i Maćedonci,* p. 608. The latter is a bulky tome on all phases of the Macedonian problem, from a Serbian point of view. The bibliography on the Macedonian Question, albeit mostly of propagandistic nature, is almost inexhaustible.

² T. Djordjević, p. 117.

³ A. F. Pribram, *The Secret Treaties of Austria-Hungary, 1879–1914,* I, 54–55. Article VII was the work of Benjamin von Kállay, minister of finance and one-time Austro-Hungarian agent in Beograd. As the expert on Balkan affairs he held that "Serbia's outlook for the future should not be blocked on all sides." See also Grgur Jakšić, "Istorija Tajne Konvencije," *Arhiv za pravne i društvene nauke,* IX, No. 3, 1924.

⁴ Pribram, pp. 136–37.

⁵ *S.K.G.,* XII, 1068–79; T. Djordjević, p. 139; Jovan M. Jovanović, *Južna Srbija od kraja XVIII veka do oslobodjenja* (Beograd, 1941), pp. 77–78. (Cited hereafter as *Južna Srbija.*)

⁶ *Južna Srbija,* pp. 78–79.

⁷ Édouard Driault, *Histoire diplomatique de la Grèce,* IV (Paris, 1926), 291–92.

⁸ *Južna Srbija,* p. 80.

⁹ *Ibid.,* p. 81.

¹⁰ About educational and propaganda work in general, as well as a list of Serbian publications, see T. Djordjević, p. 140, and *Južna Srbija,* pp. 138–39.

¹¹ Genov, p. 508; Hýbl, pp. 155–56; *S.K.G.,* XVIII, 777–81; Ilija Pržić, *Spoljašna politika Srbije (1804–1914),* pp. 118–19.

¹² This so-called "Turkophile policy" was most pronounced during the ministry of S. Nikolajević (March 21 to May 9, 1894); see *Južna Srbija,* p. 81. On Serbo-Turkish relations during the period, see especially Vladan Djordjević, *Srbija i Turska, 1894–1897,* and *Vl. Al. Ob.,* II, 121–32.

¹³ Pržić, p. 120; Novaković, p. 195; *Vl. Al. Ob.,* II, 168–69.

¹⁴ Pržić, p. 121; Živanović, III, 374–84; *Vl. Al. Ob.,* II, 188–205; Toshev, I, 101–3.

¹⁵ Pržić, p. 121; *Vl. Al. Ob.,* II, 230–34.

[16] *Vl. Al. Ob.*, II, 193–97. The best work on the Serbo-Greek relations during this period is Vladan Djordjević's *Srbija i Grčka, 1891–1893*, especially on the first attempts to reach an understanding between Greece and Serbia for checking Bulgarian propaganda in Old Serbia and Macedonia, and on diplomatic relations, 1891–93.

[17] From the Serbian point of view, the best work on this subject is Vladan Djordjević's *Srbija i Turska*, pp. 246–50. V. Djordjević treats extensively Alexander's visit to the Jildiz, the struggle for the Serbian metropolitanate in Macedonia and the episcopal question, the Cretan problem, and the movement to re-establish the patriarchate of Peć. See also *Vl. Al. Ob.*, II, 190–92.

[18] Pržić, pp. 121–22.

[19] *Južna Srbija*, pp. 82–83; Vladan Djordjević, *Kraj jedne dinastije*, covers the author's role as Serbia's prime minister. See also German edition: V. Georgević, *Das Ende der Obrenovitch: Beiträge zur Geschichte Serbiens, 1897–1900*.

[20] *Vl. Al. Ob.*, II, 355–56.

[21] *S.K.G.*, XII, 1172–80; Hýbl, p. 148; *Južna Srbija*, pp. 115–18; *Vl. Al. Ob.*, II, 376.

[22] Vidoe Smilevski, "Osvrt na razvoj makedonskog nacionalnog pitanja," *Komunist*, No. 1, January 1950, pp. 77–113; Dimitar Mitrev, *Pirinska Makedonija vo borba za nacionalno osloboduvanje*, pp. 63–109.

[23] Smilevski, *op. cit.*

[24] *Ibid.* Somewhat different is the view of the Bulgarian nationalist historians; see, for example, Ivan Ormandzhiev, *Nova i naĭ-nova istoriĭa na Bŭlgarskiĭa narod*, pp. 502–14. On the struggle between the IMRO (Centralists) and Vrkhovists (Supremists) see Christ Anastasoff, *The Tragic Peninsula*, pp. 63–68.

[25] *Južna Srbija*, pp. 193–94.

[26] *Vl. Al. Ob.*, II, 361–64.

[27] For details on Serbo-Bulgarian relations, 1900–1902, see A. Toshev, *Balkanskitie voĭni*, I, 103–26, 436; and *Vl. Al. Ob.*, III, 191 ff.

[28] *Odnosi*, p. 17. The author quotes the circular *in extenso*.

[29] *Krasnyi Arkhiv*, "Dnevnik Kuropotkina," II (1922), 16.

[30] *Vl. Al. Ob.*, III, 190–91, 195–96.

[31] *Odnosi*, pp. 16–17.

[32] *Vl. Al. Ob.*, III, 199.

[33] *Ibid.*, p. 200.

[34] *Ibid.*, pp. 200–201; Novaković, pp. 222–23. The author discusses Konstantinović and other possible pretenders.

[35] *Odnosi*, p. 18.

[36] *Vl. Al. Ob.*, III, 201–3.

[37] *Ibid.*

[38] *Ibid.*, p. 204.

[39] *G.P.*, XVIII: 1, Nr. 5465 (May 17, 1902), 160–62—a detailed report on the question of Firmilijan by the German ambassador in Constantinople to his Foreign Office; Toshev, I, 119–20; *Vl. Al. Ob.*, II, 364–76, and III, 205, on relations with Turkey, 1897–1900, with special reference to the question of Firmilijan, Macedonia, and the Albanian terror.

[40] *G.P.*, XVIII: 1, Nr. 5454 (February 19, 1901), 140.

[41] Ministarstvo Inostranih Dela. *Prepiska o arbanaškim nasiljima u Staroj Srbiji, 1898–1899*, p. 16—official correspondence on the subject of Albanian atrocities; *Odnosi*, pp. 13–14.

[42] *D.D.F.*, 2e série, II (1931), 480; *Odnosi*, p. 15; *Vl. Al. Ob.*, III, 205–6.

[43] *Vl. Al. Ob.*, III, 207–9.

[44] *Odnosi*, pp. 15–16.

[45] Čubrilović and Ćorović, pp. 184–85; *Vl. Al. Ob.*, III, 210; *Odnosi*, pp. 18–19, full text of the Serbian note; see also S. Simić, *Maćedonsko pitanje*, pp. 50–54; and H. Marcuse, *Serbien und die Revolutionsbewegung in Makedonien*, pp. 48–51.

[46] *Srpske novine*, No. 192 (August 26, 1900); Živanović, IV, 227; *Vl. Al. Ob.*, III, 61.

[47] *Vl. Al. Ob.*, III, 62.

[48] *Ibid.*, p. 67; Mijatovich, pp. 173–74.

[49] Mijatovich, pp. 173–74.
[50] *G.P.*, XVIII: 1, Nr. 5435 (May 7, 1900), 99–101; see Constantin Dumba, *Memoirs of a Diplomat*, pp. 91–92; Bernard von Bülow, *Denkwürdigkeiten*, I, 626–27.
[51] *G.P.*, XVIII: 1, Nr. 5443 (January 6, 1901), 115–16.
[52] Mijatovich, pp. 123–24; *Odnosi*, pp. 14–15.
[53] N. V. Tcharykow, *Glimpses of High Politics*, p. 232.
[54] *Ibid.*, pp. 232–33.
[55] *Vl. Al. Ob.*, III, 210–11.
[56] *Ibid.*, p. 212.
[57] A. Witte, *Vospominaniiă*, 3 vols., I, 237–41.
[58] *Vl. Al. Ob.*, III, 261–63.
[59] Tcharykow, p. 233.
[60] *Vl. Al. Ob.*, III, 326; *Odnosi*, p. 27.
[61] *Livres jaunes*, No. 51, 6061 (December 31, 1902); Dumba, *Memoirs*, pp. 99–100.
[62] *Vl. Al. Ob.*, III, 312–14.
[63] *Ibid.*
[64] Tcharykow, p. 239.
[65] *Krasnyi Arkhiv*, II (1922), 16.
[66] *Odnosi*, p. 27.
[67] *B.D.*, V, No. 12 (June 10, 1903), 57–59, 102.
[68] *Ibid.*, text of "Vienna scheme," pp. 51–53; *Livres jaunes*, XLII–XLV, No. 19 (February 25, 1903), 12–15; *G.P.*, XVIII: 1, Nr. 5507 (January 3, 1903) and the Appendix, 226–28; *ibid.*, Nr. 5504 (January 4, 1903), p. 222; *ibid.*, Nr. 5475 (November 9, 1902), pp. 180–81.
[69] *Livres jaunes*, XLII–XLV, No. 18 (February 23, 1903), 12.
[70] *B.D.*, V, 57 n.; *Accounts and Papers*, CX (1904), Nos. 34 and 35 (March 31, 1903), 428.
[71] *Vl. Al. Ob.*, III, 315.
[72] *Livres jaunes*, XLII–XLV, No. 4 (February 8, 1903), 3; also *Accounts and Papers*, CX (1904), No. 23 (March 19, 1903), 18.
[73] Dumba, *Memoirs*, p. 101.
[74] *Ibid.*, pp. 100–101; *Vl. Al. Ob.*, III, 315.
[75] *Vl. Al. Ob.*, III, 316–17.
[76] Čubrilović and Ćorović, pp. 186–87. On the mission of Miloš Petronijević, sent to Vienna for the same purpose in January, 1902, and similar offers, see *Odnosi*, p. 26.
[77] *Vl. Al. Ob.*, III, 315.
[78] *Odnosi*, p. 27; *Vl. Al. Ob.*, III, 318–19.
[79] Dumba, *Memoirs*, pp. 105–6.
[80] Vladimir Ćorović, "Misija Andre Djordjevića u Beču 1903 godine," *S.K.G.*, August 1, 1934; Dumba, p. 101; *Vl. Al. Ob.*, III, 319–20. The author quotes Goluchowski's instructions to Dumba, and reports by the Austrian military attaché in Beograd, dated May 30 and June 2, 1903.
[81] *Odnosi*, p. 28.
[82] Dumba, pp. 89–90.
[83] *Ibid.*, pp. 91–92.
[84] *H.A.O.R.*, June 9, 1903, Session XVII, Abgeordneten Klofač.
[85] *Vl. Al. Ob.*, III, 326; *Odnosi*, p. 17.
[86] Dumba, p. 101.
[87] *G.P.*, XVIII: 1, Nr. 5507 (January 13, 1903), 226–27. See also Anlage, pp. 227–28.
[88] *Odnosi*, pp. 19 ff.
[89] *D.D.F.*, 2e série, II, 672.
[90] *Odnosi*, pp. 20–21; *G.P.*, XVIII: 1, Nr. 5467 (August 13, 1902), 164–65; P.O. (Svetislav Simić), *Stara Srbija i Arbanasi*, p. 74; Lj. Jovanović, *Srpski narod i otomanska ustavnost*, p. 8.
[91] Dumba, p. 102.
[92] *G.P.*, XVIII: 1, Nr. 5521 (April 5, 1903), 249–50; *ibid.*, Nr. 5523 (April 11, 1903), pp. 253–54; *ibid.*, Nr. 5529 (April 16, 1903), pp. 259–60; *Odnosi*, p. 21.

⁹³ *G.P.*, XVIII : 1, Nr. 5539 (April 29, 1903), 271–72; *ibid.*, Nr. 5527 (April 15, 1903), p. 258; *ibid.*, Nr. 5528 (April 15, 1903), p. 258.

⁹⁴ *Neue Freie Presse,* April 2, 10, 1903.

⁹⁵ *Accounts and Papers,* CX (1904), No. 43 (March 31, 1903), 433; Ćubrilović and Ćorović, pp. 182–85; *Vl. Al. Ob.*, III, 321–22.

⁹⁶ *Vl. Al. Ob.*, III, 321–22.

⁹⁷ *Ibid.*, p. 325.

⁹⁸ *Livres jaunes*, XLII–XLV, No. 34 (October 30, 1902), 30–31; *ibid.*, No. 43 (December 3, 1902), pp. 44–45.

⁹⁹ *Vl. Al. Ob.*, III, 322.

¹⁰⁰ *B.D.*, V, 104; *Accounts and Papers*, CX (1904), No. 152 (May 19, 1903), 521.

¹⁰¹ *B.D.*, V, 104; *Accounts and Papers,* CX (1904), No. 193 (June 5, 1903), 555–56.

¹⁰² *Vl. Al. Ob.*, III, 327.

¹⁰³ *Accounts and Papers*, CX (1904), No. 187 (June 2, 1903), 552–53.

¹⁰⁴ *Vl. Al. Ob.*, III, 325.

¹⁰⁵ *Ibid.*

¹⁰⁶ *Borba,* p. 160; *B.D.*, V, No. 11 (April 22, 1903), 57.

¹⁰⁷ *G.P.*, XVIII : 1, Nr. 5511 (February 1, 1903), 233–34; *ibid.*, Nr. 5512 (February 2, 1903), pp. 234–37; *B.D.*, V (February 6, 1905), 78.

¹⁰⁸ *G.P.*, XVIII : 1, Nr. 5522 (April 9, 1903), 251–53.

¹⁰⁹ Momtchilo Nintchitch, *La Crise bosniaque (1900–1908) et les puissances européennes*, I, 99; Pribram, I, 199–201.

¹¹⁰ *Borba*, p. 13.

¹¹¹ *Odnosi*, p. 10, a discussion of the Italo-Austrian rivalry in the Balkans.

¹¹² *Borba*, p. 14. This reasoning is also discussed in more detail by the Rumanian writer Ilie Barbulescu (translated by Svetislav Ilić), *Rumuni prema Srbima i Bugarima s pogledom na pitanje Makedonskih Rumuna.*

¹¹³ Vladimir Ćorović, *Borba za nezavisnost Balkana*, p. 120.

¹¹⁴ *Borba*, p. 14.

¹¹⁵ Vasić, pp. 151 ff.

¹¹⁶ *Vl. Al. Ob.*, III, 328–29.

¹¹⁷ *Ibid.*, pp. 330–35. The subject of the king's divorce is also discussed by Vasić, p. 147, and P. Todorović, "Kraljev brak," *Ogledalo*, No. 67 (1904), p. 857, and "Kraljeva tajna," *ibid.*, No. 87 (1904), p. 1087.

Notes to Part Three

¹ The best accounts of the royal tragedy, based on primary sources and in essential agreement on principal points, are: Dragiša Vasić, *Devesto treća (Majski prevrat), Prilozi za istoriju Srbije od 8 jula 1900 do 17 januara 1907*; Slobodan Jovanović, *Vlada Aleksandra Obrenovića*, III, 339–441; Živan Živanović, *Politička istorija Srbije*, IV (1925); and Chedomille Mijatovich, *A Royal Tragedy*. See also Dušan Semiz, "Majevci," *Nova Evropa*, October 11, 1927, pp. 214–24, and the appended translation of a report by a Russian intelligence agent on the events of May 1903 ("Jedan ruski savremeni dokumenat o 29 Maju"), pp. 225–30, hereafter cited as "Majevci." In preparation of this chapter the author relied for the most part on the above sources. The communist version of the "March Demonstration" and the "May Revolution" is given by Triša Kaclerović in his *Martovske demonstracije i majski prevrat 1903*, p. 84. Kaclerović, an old Socialist, was a contemporary and an eyewitness of the 1903 events. He criticizes Sl. Jovanović, Ž. Živanović, and D. Vasić, on many details.

² *Vl. Al. Ob.*, III, 339–41; Vasić, p. 53; Kaclerović, pp. 68–69, listed what he considered to be nine principal causes of the conspiracy.

³ Jelenić, p. 218, a description of the chaotic state of affairs after March 1903; *Vl. Al. Ob.*, III, 342–43.

⁴ Vasić, pp. 54–55; Živanović, IV, 343; Kaclerović, pp. 64–65, discusses the organization of the conspiracy and its leaders.

[5] *Vl. Al. Ob.*, III, 351–52.
[6] Vasić, p. 55.
[7] *Vl. Al. Ob.*, III, 344–45.
[8] Vasić, p. 55.
[9] *Vl. Al. Ob.*, III, 354–55.
[10] Vasić, pp. 59–60; *Vl. Al. Ob.*, III, 355.
[11] *Vl. Al. Ob.*, III, 356.
[12] *Ibid.*, p. 346.
[13] Vasić, p. 56.
[14] Dumba, *Memoirs*, p. 109.
[15] Vasić, pp. 56–57.
[16] *Ibid.*, pp. 61–63; *Vl. Al. Ob.*, III, 346–47.
[17] Vasić, p. 59.
[18] *Vl. Al. Ob.*, III, 347.
[19] *Ibid.*, pp. 349, 352–54; Vasić, pp. 60–62.
[20] Vasić, pp. 61–62; *Vl. Al. Ob.*, III, 352–53.
[21] Vasić, pp. 62–63.
[22] Živanović, IV, 346.
[23] *Vl. Al. Ob.*, III, 349–52.
[24] *Ibid.*, p. 353.
[25] *Ibid.*, p. 354.
[26] Vasić, pp. 63–64. The author gives the names of the principal Niš conspirators.
[27] *Ibid.*, pp. 64–66.
[28] *Ibid.*, p. 66.
[29] Dumba, p. 109.
[30] *Vl. Al. Ob.*, III, 356–57.
[31] *Ibid.*
[32] *Ibid.*, p. 358.
[33] *Ibid.*, p. 359.
[34] *Ibid.*, p. 360, citing Maršićanin, II, 11. See also "Majevci," p. 225.
[35] *Vl. Al. Ob.*, III, 360.
[36] Mijatovich, p. 160.
[37] Vasić, p. 141 ff.; *Vl. Al. Ob.*, III, 361.
[38] "Majevci," p. 226.
[39] *Ibid.*, p. 228. See also Novaković, *Dvadeset godina ustavne politike u Srbiji*, p. 237; Vasić, pp. 141–47; on the king's marriage and divorce, see P. Todorović, "Kraljev brak," *Ogledalo*, No. 67 (1904), p. 857; and "Kraljeva tajna," *Ogledalo*, No. 87 (1904), p. 1087.
[40] Živanović, IV, 346; *Vl. Al. Ob.*, III, 362; Vasić, p. 70.
[41] Živanović, IV, 347; Vasić, p. 75.
[42] Vasić, pp. 70–73.
[43] *Ibid.*, p. 77.
[44] *Ibid.*, p. 73.
[45] Kaclerović, pp. 67–68.
[46] Živanović, IV, 347. See also the article by D. Vasić in *Književna republika*, September 1924, for a description of the developments on the night of May 28–29, 1903. The article was translated and published by the *Frankfurter Zeitung*, November 1924, and summarized in *The Living Age*, January 3, 1925; Major Pomiankowski, Austrian military attaché, gave his version in the *8-Uhr-Abendblatt* (Berlin), Nos. 46–50 (February 23–28, 1928). See also the report on and description of the murder by a Russian intelligence agent, "Majevci," p. 227.
[47] Vasić, p. 80; *Vl. Al. Ob.*, III, 364; Živanović, IV, 348–49.
[48] *Vl. Al. Ob.*, III, 364–65; Živanović, IV, 349.
[49] *Vl. Al. Ob.*, III, 366. The author gives names of various military units that participated in the attack on the palace and the officers in charge of them.
[50] *Ibid.*, p. 367; Živanović, IV, 350; Vasić, p. 80.
[51] *Vl. Al. Ob.*, III, 368–69, and Živanović, IV, 351.

[52] Živanović, IV, 352–53; *Vl. Al. Ob.*, III, 367–70; Vasić, pp. 88–89; "Majevci," p. 227.
[53] *Ibid.*
[54] Vasić, pp. 93–94; *Vl. Al. Ob.*, III, 371.
[55] Vasić, p. 113.
[56] Živanović, IV, 353 n.

Notes to Part Four

[1] Vasić, p. 113; Živanović, IV, 355; *D.D.F.*, 2e série, III, No. 292 (June 11, 1903), 385; *B.D.*, V, No. 89 (June 11, 1903), 126.
[2] Živanović, IV, 355.
[3] Vasić, p. 113.
[4] *Ibid.*, pp. 115–17; see also description of the burial in "Majevci," pp. 227, 230.
[5] Živanović, IV, 353 n.
[6] Vasić, pp. 113, 115, 122–25, in which the author gives the full text of the proclamation; Živanović, IV, 355.
[7] Vasić, pp. 119–22; Živanović, IV, 360.
[8] *Ibid.*
[9] Živanović, IV, 356–57; Vasić, p. 117.
[10] J. M. Prodanović, *Ustavni razvitak i ustavna borba u Srbiji*, pp. 418–25, texts of the constitutions; also Jelenić, pp. 223–24, text of the Constitution of 1903.
[11] Vasić, p. 118; Milan Zečević, *Kraljevske reči. Zbirka govora Kralja Petra I*, p. 2.
[12] Marco (Božin Simić). "Pripremanje 29 maja 1903," *Nova Evropa*, June 1927, p. 416.
[13] "Majevci," pp. 228–29.
[14] *Ibid.*
[15] Zečević, pp. 5–12.
[16] Alfred Stead, "King Peter I of Serbia," *Review of Reviews*, XXXIV (September 1906), 245–50.
[17] Dragoslav Stranjaković, "Detinjstvo, vaspitanje i školovanje Kralja Petra I u Srbiji do 1858 godine," *Jugoslovenski istoriski časopis*, III: 1–4 (1937), 213–35. This article by a very able historian is an excellent coverage of Peter's youth and education in Serbia. Milenko Vukićević, *Kralj Petar od rodjenja do smrti*, a biography of King Peter, which, though incomplete and superficial, is the only one available.
[18] *Vl. Mil. Ob.*, III, 86–92.
[19] V. Ćorović, *Istorija Jugoslavije*, p. 544.
[20] *Ibid.*; see also discussion of the Serbian ascendancy after 1903, discussed by a Montenegrin writer, Nikola Djonović, *Ustavne i političke borbe u Crnoj Gori od 1905 do 1911.*
[21] Ćorović, *Istorija Jugoslavije*, pp. 545–46.
[22] Zečević, pp. 13–14.
[23] Jelenić, p. 225; Zečević, pp. 13–14, 24.
[24] *N.S.*, I (1903–4), 7 ff.; Zečević, pp. 51–52.
[25] Dumba, p. 131.
[26] *N.S.*, 1903–4, p. 71 ff.; Zečević, pp. 57–58; Dušan Lončarević, *Jugoslaviens Entstehung*, pp. 43–44.
[27] *N.S.*, 1903–4, pp. 101–2.
[28] Stead, pp. 247–48.
[29] *Borba*, p. 157.
[30] Živan Mitrović, *Srpske političke stranke*, p. 114; *Borba*, p. 157.
[31] Milivoje Popović, *Borba za parlamentarni režim u Srbiji*, p. 92. For some inconsequential changes in the program of the Independent Radicals, made on April 2, 1905, see Mitrović, pp. 96–97.
[32] Mitrović, pp. 97–98; Popović, p. 53.
[33] Mitrović, p. 98.

[34] Mitrović, p. 101.

[35] Prodanović, pp. 425–26.

[36] A list of works by Žujović is conveniently accessible in *Savremena škola,* I and II (1950), 59–64.

[37] Slobodan Jovanović, *Svetozar Marković,* and Stevan Masleša, *Svetozar Marković,* are the best monographs on Marković. For a bibliography of his works see *Istoriski glasnik,* I (1949), 123–25.

[38] Josip Broz Tito, *Political Report of the Central Committee of the Communist Party of Yugoslavia,* pp. 4 ff.

[39] *Izabrani Spisi Dimitrije Tucovića.* Only Volume I of the projected collection of Tucović's writings has appeared thus far.

[40] *N.S.,* March 3, 1905, pp. 19, 22–26.

[41] *Ibid.* See also various interpellations by Dragiša Lapčević and Milan Marković regarding the persecution of Social Democrats and workers, *N.S.,* August 5, 1905, pp. 20–21, 131, 137, 139, 141.

[42] Vasić, p. 171.

[43] *Ibid.,* pp. 172–73.

[44] Dumba, pp. 129–30; Vasić, pp. 179–80; A. Todorović, *Život i rad Milana J. Novakovića,* as quoted by Vasić, pp. 173–75.

[45] Marco, "Srpska vojska pre i posle 29 maja 1903," *Nova Evropa,* July 11, 1927, pp. 9–20.

[46] Vasić, pp. 176–77.

[47] *Ibid.,* pp. 177–78.

[48] *Ibid.,* p. 179.

[49] *Ibid.,* p. 181. The author gives the list of officers sentenced and the terms they received.

[50] *Ibid.,* pp. 182–83.

[51] Marco, "Srpska vojska pre i posle 29 maja 1903," p. 16.

[52] *Život i rad M. J. Novakovića,* p. 25, as quoted by Vasić, p. 181.

[53] Marco, "Srpska vojska pre i posle 29 maja 1903," p. 17.

Notes to Part Five

[1] *B.D.,* V, No. 100 (June 18, 1903), 132.

[2] *Ibid.*

[3] *US.D.,* 1903, p. 719.

[4] Dumba, p. 114.

[5] Živanović, p. 352; *Vl. Al. Ob.,* III, 348–49.

[6] Dumba, pp. 115–16.

[7] "Majevci," p. 229.

[8] Henry Wickham Steed, *The Hapsburg Monarchy,* pp. 240–41.

[9] *Ibid.*

[10] *Ibid.,* p. 242.

[11] *B.D.,* V, No. 92 (June 12, 1903), 12; Barbulescu, *Rumuni prema Srbima,* p. 21.

[12] Barbulescu, p. 21.

[13] *D.D.F.,* 2e série, III, No. 294 (June 12, 1903), 387; *B.D.,* V (June 13, 1903), 127.

[14] *Journal des Debates,* June 13, 1903; Ellery C. Stowell, *Intervention in International Law* (Washington, 1921), pp. 140–41.

[15] *Borba,* p. 87.

[16] Stowell, p. 141.

[17] *D.D.F.,* 2e série, III, No. 300 (June 15, 1903), 392–93.

[18] *US.D.,* June 29, 1903, pp. 718–19.

[19] Jelenić, *Nova Srbija i Jugoslavija,* p. 170.

[20] Dumba, pp. 89–90.

[21] *Ibid.,* p. 117.

[22] *Ibid.,* pp. 114–16.

[23] *B.D.*, V, No. 90 (June 12, 1903), 126.
[24] *Ibid.*, No. 106 (June 18, 1903), p. 132.
[25] *D.D.F.*, 2e série, III, No. 295 (June 12, 1903), 388; *ibid.*, No. 299 (June 14, 1903), p. 391; *B.D.*, V, No. 91 (June 12, 1903), 126.
[26] *B.D.*, V, No. 99 (June 17, 1903), 129; *ibid.*, No. 105 (June 18, 1903), p. 132; *D.D.F.*, 2e série, III, No. 306 (June 17, 1903), 401–2.
[27] *B.D.*, V, No. 93 (June 13, 1903), 127; *D.D.F.*, 2e série, III (June 13, 1903), 389–90.
[28] Dumba, p. 123.
[29] *B.D.*, V, No. 95 (June 15, 1903), 128.
[30] *Borba*, pp. 95–96.
[31] *B.D.*, V, No. 100 (June 17, 1903), 130.
[32] *Ibid.*, No. 101 (June 17, 1903), p. 130, also No. 104, Statement in House of Commons, June 17, 1903; *Parl. Deb.*, 4th ser., CXXIII, 1171–72.
[33] *D.D.F.*, 2e série, No. 316 (June 20, 1903), p. 410; *B.D.*, V, No. 107 (June 19, 1903), 133.
[34] *B.D.*, V, No. 100 (June 17, 1903), 130.
[35] *Ibid.*, No. 96 (June 17, 1903), p. 129.
[36] *Ibid.*, No. 102 (June 17, 1903), p. 130.
[37] *Ibid.*, No. 96 (June 15, 1903), p. 128.
[38] *Parl. Deb.*, CXXIV (June 22, 1903), 64–66.
[39] *Ibid.*, CXXIII (June 15, 1903), 946; *B.D.*, V, No. 97 (June 15, 1903), 128–29.
[40] *Parl. Deb.*, CXXIV (June 22, 1903), 64–66.
[41] *D.D.F.*, 2e série, III (June 21, 1903), 412.
[42] *B.D.*, V, No. 108 (June 22, 1903), 134.
[43] *Ibid.*, No. 109 (June 23, 1903), p. 134.
[44] *Ibid.*, No. 106 (June 18, 1903), p. 132.
[45] *Ibid.*, No. 105 (June 18, 1903), p. 132; *D.D.F.*, 2e série, III (July 9, 1903), 442. See also *supra*, p. 63.
[46] *B.D.*, V, No. 99 (June 17, 1903), 129.
[47] *Ibid.*, No. 110 (June 23, 1903), p. 135.
[48] *D.D.F.*, 2e série, III, No. 333 (July 4, 1903), 429; *ibid.*, No. 446 (September 29, 1903), pp. 590–92.
[49] *B.D.*, V, No. 99 (June 17, 1903), 129; *ibid.*, No. 106 (June 18, 1903), p. 133, Peter's telegram and Francis Joseph's reply; *Wiener Abend Post*, June 17, 1903; *D.D.F.*, 2e série, III (June 18, 1903), 408.
[50] *Ibid.*
[51] *B.D.*, V, No. 106 (June 18, 1903), 132.
[52] *Ibid.*, No. 103 (June 17, 1903), p. 131; *Borba*, p. 87.
[53] *Borba*, pp. 95–96.
[54] Dumba, pp. 123–27.
[55] *Ibid.*, pp. 123 ff.
[56] *Ibid.*, pp. 124–27.
[57] *D.D.F.*, 2e série, III, No. 330 (July 2, 1903), 426–27; Dumba, p. 116.
[58] Dumba, pp. 124–27.
[59] *B.D.*, V, No. 110 (June 23, 1903), 134.
[60] *D.D.F.*, 2e série, III, No 322 (June 24, 1903), 414.
[61] Dumba, pp. 124–27.
[62] *D.D.F.*, 2e série, III (June 22, 1903), 413–14.
[63] *Ibid.*, No. 321 (June 23, 1903), p. 414.
[64] *Ibid.* (June 22, 1903), pp. 413–14.
[65] Tscharykow, p. 237; Dumba, pp.. 124–27.
[66] *D.D.F.*, 2e série, III, No. 323 (June 25, 1903), 415.
[67] *Ibid.*, No. 329 (July 2, 1903).
[68] Zečević, p. 32.
[69] Dumba, p. 127.
[70] Živanović, p. 358.
[71] Jelenić, p. 226; Zečević, p. 49.

[72] Dumba, pp. 134–36.

[73] *B.D.*, V, No. 113 (January 13, 1904), 137.

[74] Karlo Sforca, *Nikola Pašić i ujedinjenje Jugoslovena*; *Spomenica Nikole Pašića, 1845–1925*; and *Nova Evropa*, XIII (1926), are best on the political activities of Pašić.

[75] N. Marković, *Dr. Laza Paču.*

[76] On Ljubomir Davidović see *Srpski književni glasnik*, LVI (1939); R. Mitković, "Ljubomir Davidović," *Nova Evropa*, XVI:8 (October 26, 1927), 258–62.

[77] M. Popović, p. 94.

[78] Dumba, pp. 134–36.

[79] *B.D.*, V, No. 112 (October 8, 1903), 136–37.

[80] Dumba, p. 144.

[81] *Ibid.*, p. 145.

[82] *Ibid.*

[83] *Ibid.*, p. 146.

[84] *US.D.*, No. 52 (Serbian series, September 26, 1903), p. 803.

[85] *Ibid.*

[86] Dumba, pp. 146–47.

[87] *Ibid.*, p. 147.

[88] *Ibid.*

[89] *N.S.*, I (November 1, 1904–March 3, 1905), 2–3.

[90] *Ibid.*

[91] *Ibid.*

[92] *Ibid.*, p. 3; Zečević, p. 29.

[93] *Borba*, p. 41.

[94] *N.S.*, I (November 1, 1904–March 3, 1905), 3.

[95] *Ibid.*, pp. 323–41.

[96] Popović, p. 94.

[97] *Ibid.*, Zečević, p. 132.

[98] See Ribarac's interpellation and the debates which ensued in the Skupština. *N.S.*, II (January 22, 1905), 1288 ff.

[99] Popović, p. 96; *Srpske novine*, January 11, 12, 1905. See pp. 189–94.

[100] *N.S.*, II (January 31, 1905), 1288 ff., 1354, and II (February 4, 1905), 1415 ff.

[101] Popović, p. 97.

[102] *N.S.*, II (January 21, 1905), 1288 ff. Text of Pašić's note of resignation.

[103] Popović, p. 97.

[104] *N.S.*, II (January 28, 1905), 1295 ff.

[105] *Ibid.*, I (October 22, 1905), 277–78; M. Popović, pp. 99–100.

[106] M. Popović, p. 100.

[107] *N.S.*, I (October 14, 1905), pp. 151–53; *ibid.* (October 16, 1905), p. 181; M. Popović, p. 101.

[108] Vasić, pp. 199–200. For the declaration of the Populist party see *Srpska zastava*, No. 1 (October 16, 1905).

[109] Vasić, pp. 201–2; *Srpska zastava*, Nos. 17, 18 (January 3, 4, 1905).

[110] Vasić, p. 204.

[111] Dumba, pp. 143–44.

[112] *Borba*, p. 97.

[113] See Ribarac's interpellation, *N.S.*, I (October 10, 1905), 85 ff.; and Žujović's defense of his foreign policy and statement regarding relations with England, *N.S.*, I (October 11, 1905), 94–95; *Borba*, p. 99.

[114] *Ibid*.

[115] Vasić, pp. 206–7.

[116] *Borba*, p. 99.

[117] M. Popović, p. 101.

[118] *Ibid.*

[119] Vasić, pp. 184–86; *N.S.*, I (December 14, 1903), 498 ff.

[120] Vasić, pp. 184–86.

[121] *Ibid.*, p. 187.

122 *Ibid.*, p. 189.
123 *Ibid.*, pp. 190–92.
124 *Ibid.*, p. 193.
125 *Ibid.*, pp. 193–95; names and sentences are given.
126 *Ibid.*, pp. 195–96.
127 Kaclerović, *Martovske demonstracije*, pp. 4, 78 ff.; *Radničke novine*, No. 112 (September 20, 1907).
128 See *Tajna prevratna organizacija; izveštaj sa pretresa u Vojnom sudu za oficire u Solunu po beleškama vodjenim na samom pretresu.* An official version of the trial.
129 Dumba, p. 143.
130 *Ibid.*
131 Marco, "Srpska vojska pre i posle 29 maja 1903," *Nova Evropa*, July 11, 1927, pp. 9–20.
132 Marco, "Preporod srpske vojske i borba za ujedinjenje," *Nova Evropa*, July 26, 1927, pp. 51–67.
133 Marco, "Pripremanje 29 maja 1903," *Nova Evropa*, June 11, 1927, pp. 405–19, quoting Čedo Mijatović, "Moje poznanstvo sa kraljem Petrom," *Dnevnik*, January 27, 1923.
134 *Borba*, pp. 103–4.
135 Živanović, IV, 337–38.
136 Dumba, p. 142.
137 *Ibid.*
138 *D.D.F.*, 2e série, III, No. 446 (September 29, 1903), 590–92.
139 Živanović, IV, 338.
140 *Borba*, pp. 103–4.
141 *Ibid.*
142 Kaclerović, p. 79.
143 *Ibid.*, pp. 80–83.
144 *Ibid.*
145 *B.D.*, V, No. 114 (November 17, 1904), 198.
146 *Ibid.*, No. 115 (November 29, 1905), p. 138.
147 *Ibid.*, No. 122 (May 23, 1906), pp. 143–44.
148 *Ibid.*; *Borba*, p. 98; Živanović, IV, 342.
149 *Parl. Deb.*, 4th ser., CLV (April 11, 1906), 1302; *B.D.*, V, No. 117.
150 *B.D.*, V, No. 116 (March, 1906), 139.
151 *Ibid.*, No. 118 (April 18, 1906), p. 140, Thesiger to Grey.
152 *Ibid.*
153 *Ibid.*, No. 120 (May 9, 1906), p. 141, Thesiger to Grey.
154 *Borba*, p. 101.
155 *B.D.*, V, No. 120 (May 9, 1906), 141, Thesiger to Grey.
156 *Ibid.*, No. 121 (May 10, 1906), p. 141, Grey to Thesiger.
157 *Ibid.*, No. 122 (May 23, 1906), pp. 143–44.
158 *Ibid.*, No. 123 (May 24, 1906), p. 144, Edward VII to Grey; *ibid.*, No. 122 (May 23, 1906), memorandum by Grey to the king.
159 *Ibid.*, No. 124 (May 25, 1906), p. 144; *Borba*, pp. 101–2.
160 For text of resignations and Peter's note of acceptance, see *Parl. Deb.*, CLIX (June 22, 1906), 487–90. Regarding the appointment of Milićević as Serbian minister in London, see *The Times* (London), June 11 and July 10, 1906.
161 *Borba*, p. 102; *B.D.*, V, No. 125 (May 30, 1906), 145.
162 *B.D.*, V, No. 126 (May 31, 1906), 145, Grey to Goschen.
163 *Ibid.*, No. 129 (June 1, 1906), p. 146.
164 *Borba*, p. 102.
165 *Parl. Deb.*, CLIX (June 22, 1906), 487–90.
166 *Ibid.*, p. 493. Compare with Jaša M. Prodanović, "Radikalna Stranka," *Nova Evropa*, XIII (1926), 392.
167 *Parl. Deb.*, CLIX (June 22, 1906), 487–90.
168 *Ibid.*, pp. 490–91.

[169] *Parl. Deb.*, CLIX (June 22, 1906), 491–92.
[170] *Ibid.*, CLXI (July 19, 1906), 392; *ibid.*, CLIX (June 28, 1906), 1133.
[171] *Ibid.*, CLXII (August 2, 1906), 1352.
[172] *B.D.*, V, No. 138 (August 23, 1906), 156–58.
[173] *Ibid.*, p. 148.
[174] Wenzelides Arsen, "Hrvatskosrpska Koalicija," *Nova Evropa*, July 1932, pp. 414–22.
[175] M. Popović, pp. 102–3.
[176] *Ibid.*, p. 103.
[177] Jagoš Jovanović, *Stvaranje crnogorske države i razvoj crnogorske nacionalnosti*, pp. 370–71; Nikola Djonović, *op. cit.*
[178] Jagoš Jovanović, pp. 372–73.
[179] *Odnosi*, pp. 135–38.
[180] Conrad von Hötzendorff, *Aus meiner Dienstzeit, 1906–1918*, I (June 30, 1908), 82–83.
[181] These papers were published by *Narod* (Mostar), May 21 and June 4, 1908 (O.S.). See also *Srbobran*, May 2, 1908 (O.S.).
[182] Conrad von Hötzendorff, *Aus meiner Dienstzeit*, I (December 18, 1907), 530.
[183] For details on Nastić see *Odnosi*, pp. 135–40, and two articles by Montenegrin Prime Minister L. Tomanović, "Kralj Nikola i Austrija," *Nova Evropa*, June 11, 1929, and "Austrija i Crna Gora," *ibid.*, April 26, 1929.
[184] See Part Six.
[185] M. Popović, p. 104.
[186] M. Popović, p. 105; Stojan Protić, *Odlomci iz ustavne i narodne borbe*, I, 50–51.
[187] *Ibid.*
[188] M. Popović, p. 106.
[189] *Ibid.*
[190] *Ibid.*

Notes to Part Six

[1] Č. A. Popović, "Organizacija 'Ujedinjenje ili Smrt' ('Crna Ruka')," *Nova Evropa*, June 11, 1927, pp. 396–405; see also *Odnosi*, pp. 537–97.
[2] *B.D.*, V, 105; *Livres jaunes*, XLIII–XLV, No. 22 (August 22, 1903), 23–25.
[3] Dančo Zografski, *Kruševskata republika*, a communist account.
[4] *Parl. Deb.*, CX, No. 378 (1904), 308–10.
[5] *Accounts and Papers*, CX (1904), No. 332 (August 18, 1903), 680–81.
[6] *Ibid.*
[7] *Ibid.*, No. 349 (August 20, 1903), pp. 695–96.
[8] *Ibid.*, No. 377 (August 30, 1903), p. 308.
[9] *Ibid.*, No. 382 (September 2, 1903), pp. 313–15.
[10] *Livres jaunes*, XLII–XLV, No. 32 (September 29, 1903), 33–34.
[11] Dumba, p. 131.
[12] *Livres jaunes*, XLII–XLV, No. 32 (September 29, 1903), 33–34. For this Serbian grievance see also *Accounts and Papers*, CX (1904), No. 24 (March 24, 1903), 19.
[13] *Accounts and Papers*, CX (1904), No. 46 (September 30, 1903), 49–50.
[14] Zografski, *op. cit.*
[15] On the Macedonian Question and the Ilinden insurrection, as well as *comitadji* (band) warfare, see R. A. Reiss, *The Comitadji Question in Southern Serbia*, pp. 1–5; T. Djordjević, *Makedonija*, p. 126; Christ Anastasoff, *The Tragic Peninsula*; *S. K. G.*, XIII (1904), 612–17; Dime Bojanovski-Dize, "Goce Delčev i negovoto vreme," *Nov den*, No. 5 (1948); Lazar Mojsev, *Bugarska Radnička Partija (Komunista): Makedonsko nacionalno pitanje*, pp. 25–26; H. N. Brailsford, *Macedonia: Its Races and Their Future*; Cleanthes Nicolaides, *La Macédoine*.
[16] Elisabeth Barker, *Macedonia. Its Place in Balkan Power Politics*, pp. 16–17.
[17] J. M. Jovanović, *Južna Srbija*, pp. 148–49.

[18] Toshev, I, p. 43.
[19] *Accounts and Papers*, CX (1904), No. 48 (September 30, 1903), 50–51.
[20] *Ibid.*, No. 102 (October 21, 1903), pp. 95–96.
[21] *Ibid.*
[22] Dumba, p. 94.
[23] *Borba*, p. 25.
[24] *B.D.*, V, 107; *Livres jaunes*, XLII–XLV, No. 40 (October 30, 1903), 38–41.
[25] *Borba*, pp. 16–19.
[26] *Ibid.*, p. 19.
[27] S. Krakov, *Plamen Četništva*, p. 82.
[28] Dumba, p. 129; *Južna Srbija*, p. 149.
[29] *Borba*, p. 26.
[30] *Odnosi*, p. 45.
[31] *Ibid.*, p. 53.
[32] *Borba*, p. 30, explains the preponderant influence of the Austro-Hungarian agent.
[33] *B.D.*, V, No. 20, 65–66.
[34] *Livres jaunes*, XLII–XLV, No. 69 (April 6, 1904), 92; Ćorović, *Borba za nezavisnost Balkana*, pp. 125–26.
[35] *Odnosi*, pp. 33–34.
[36] *Ibid.*, pp. 34–35, 49–50.
[37] *Ibid.*
[38] *Ibid.*, pp. 50–51.
[39] *G.P.*, XXII, Nr. 7417 (March 23, 1904), 127–28; L. V. Povolni, *Le problème macédoine et sa solution*, pp. 43–44.
[40] *Odnosi*, p. 36.
[41] W. Giesl, *Zwei Jahrzehnte im Nahen Orient*, p. 148, and Chapter VI, in which the author-soldier-diplomat discusses the question of Macedonian reform.
[42] Dumba, pp. 129, 169.
[43] *Odnosi*, p.. 37.
[44] *Borba*, p. 34.
[45] *Odnosi*, pp. 34–35.
[46] *Ibid.*, p. 36.
[47] *Ibid.*
[48] *Borba*, p. 34.
[49] Sir George Franckenstein, *Diplomat of Destiny, Austrian Ambassador to the Court of St. James*, p. 65; Slobodan Jovanović, "Nicholas Pašić; After Ten Years," *Slavonic Review*, XV (1936), 376.
[50] *Odnosi*, pp. 44–45. The author cites a score of Serbian consular reports.
[51] Slobodan Jovanović, "Nikola Pašić," *Nova Evropa*, XXIX (December 26, 1936), 381–89.
[52] Slobodan Jovanović, "Nicholas Pašić; After Ten Years," *Slavonic Review*, XV (1936), 376.
[53] *Odnosi*, pp. 38–40.
[54] *Ibid.*
[55] *Odnosi*, p. 39 n.
[56] *Ibid.*, p. 39.
[57] *Ibid.*, pp. 39–40; *S.K.G.*, XVII (1906), 533–35; *Borba*, p. 37.
[58] *Borba*, p. 38. The formula was advanced by Milovan Milovanović, minister to Rome.
[59] *Južna Srbija*, p. 158.
[60] *Ibid.*, pp. 149–50.
[61] *Ibid.*, pp. 155–56.
[62] *Ibid.*, p. 159.
[63] On the *četnik* activity see *Narodna Odbrana*, a patriotic Serbian weekly published during the interwar period. Numerous issues of the journal carry descriptions of individual battles and *četnik* heroes. See article entitled "Četnička Akcija," in the *Narodna Enciklopedija* and also biographical sketches of leading *četnici*; Aleksa Jova-

nović (ed.), *Spomenica dvadeset godišnjice oslobodjenja Južne Srbije, 1912–1917,* especially the chapter entitled "Četnički pokret u Južnoj Srbiji pod Turcima," pp. 271–325. There are, of course, numerous other accounts.

[64] *Južna Srbija,* p. 159.

[65] Grgur Jakšić, "Drugi Srpsko-Bugarski savez," *Politika,* January 6–9, 1930. For an excellent study of various attempts to effect a Balkan federation, see L. S. Stavrianos, *Balkan Federation* (Northampton, Mass., 1944).

[66] Tošev, I, 101 ff.; Živanović, III, 377 ff.; Pržić, pp. 121 ff.; *Južna Srbija,* pp. 82 ff.; *supra,* p. 27.

[67] A. Stojanoff, *Die handelspolitische Situation der Balkanstaaten gegenüber Österreich-Ungarn,* p. 1.

[68] Jakšić, p. 11; M. Dj. Milovanović, *Srbi i Bugari,* pp. 3–43.

[69] *Borba,* p. 43.

[70] *Odnosi,* pp. 53–54.

[71] *Ibid.,* p. 54.

[72] Ćorović, *Borba za nezavisnost Balkana,* pp. 127–28; *Borba,* p. 41; *Pržić,* p. 133.

[73] *S.K.G.,* XVII (1906), 77.

[74] *Odnosi,* pp. 55, 58.

[75] *Borba,* p. 42; Pržić, p. 133.

[76] Toshev, I, 163; *Borba,* p. 55.

[77] *Ibid.*

[78] Toshev, I, 164–65.

[79] *Ibid.,* pp. 165–67.

[80] *Ibid.; Borba,* p. 55.

[81] Ćorović, *Borba za nezavisnost Balkana,* p. 128; *Borba,* p. 41; Pržić, p. 133.

[82] *S.K.G.,* XIV (1905), 457–63; *Južna Srbija,* pp. 141–84.

[83] *Odnosi,* p. 55.

[84] *Ibid.,* pp. 56–57.

[85] *B.D.,* V, "Extract from Annual Report for Bulgaria for the Year 1906," 108; *Livres jaunes,* XLII–XV, No. 70, Annexe I, II (April 18, 1904), 93–95; *D.D.F.,* 2e série, V, No. 6 (April 10, 1904), 6–8; *ibid.,* No. 59 (April 25, 1904), pp. 69–70; Hýbl, pp. 152–53.

[86] Toshev, I, 152. Ćorović doubts the accuracy of this statement.

[87] The Bulgarian text reads March 31, 1904.

[88] The agreement of 1904 consisted of a Treaty of Friendship and a Treaty of Alliance. Complete texts of the two treaties were first published by A. Toshev, former Bulgarian minister to Beograd, I, 152–58. Treaty negotiations, as well as texts of the treaties, were published in Serbian by Vladimir Ćorović in two articles (*Politika,* May 1, 1937; and "Pregovori o balkanskim savezima," *G.N.Č.,* pp. 1–24. E. C. Helmreich in his excellent study, *The Diplomacy of the Balkan Wars, 1912–1913,* gives an analysis and the texts of the treaties, which he obtained from *Berliner Monatshefte* (XV, 1937) and A. Toshev. H. G. Hesapchiev discussed the Serbo-Bulgarian understanding in a series of articles in *Mir* (Nos. 8400–8401, July 2, 1928), under the title, "Istoricheskata istina po bŭlgaro-srŭbskite sŭiŭzni dogovori ot 1904 i 1905 g." The author is indebted to Professor Ćorović for most of the details pertaining to the negotiations.

[89] *G.N.Č.,* pp. 10–12.

[90] *Ibid.,* p. 12.

[91] *Ibid.,* pp. 13–14.

[92] *Ibid.,* pp. 14–15; Helmreich, p. 463.

[93] *G.N.Č.,* p. 16.

[94] *Odnosi,* p. 59.

[95] *B.D.,* No. 26 (February 24, 1904), pp. 69–70.

[96] *Danzers Armee-Zeitung,* No. 44 (October 29, 1903); *ibid.,* No. 49 (December 3, 1903); *ibid.,* No. 51 (December 17, 1903).

[97] *Odnosi,* pp. 38, 41–43.

[98] *Ibid.,* p. 29.

[99] Bernard Bülow, *Denkwürdigkeiten,* I, 626–27.

[100] *Odnosi,* p. 29.

[101] *Ibid.*, pp. 43–44.
[102] *Ibid.*, pp. 47–48.
[103] Bülow, I, 578, 608.
[104] *Odnosi*, pp. 31–32.
[105] *Ibid.*, pp. 44, 48.
[106] Bülow, I, 578, 608.
[107] *Odnosi*, pp. 52–53.
[108] Francesco Tommasini, *L'Italia alla vigilia della guerra*, II, 109.
[109] *G.N.Č.*, p. 17 *Odnosi*, pp. 65–67.
[110] *G.N.Č.*, pp. 17–18; *Odnosi*, p. 57.
[111] Marco, "Nikola Hartvig," *Nova Evropa*, XVII, No. 8 (April 26, 1928), 261–62.
[112] D. Semiz, "Pred zoru velikih dana," *Nova Evropa*, XIX (1920).
[113] Toshev, I, 49–51.
[114] Dumba, p. 137.
[115] *Ibid.*, pp. 140–41.
[116] *Ibid.*, p. 138.
[117] *Ibid.*, pp. 138–39.
[118] For the texts of the treaties in English, see Helmreich, *op. cit.*
[119] Toshev, I, 159.
[120] Dumba, p. 139.
[121] *D.D.F.*, 2e série, No. 137 (May 16, 1904), pp. 156–58.
[122] Tommasini, II, 109.
[123] *Ibid.*, p. 110.
[124] *Ibid.*
[125] *D.D.F.*, 2e série, No. 240 (June 21, 1904), pp. 281–82.
[126] *Ibid.;* Tommasini, II, 110.
[127] *D.D.F.*, 2e série, No. 420 (November 1, 1904), p. 494.
[128] *Borba*, p. 45 ; Toshev, I, 159 ; *Nov Vek,* No. 792 (1904).
[129] Toshev, I, 159–60.
[130] *D.D.F.*, 2e série, No. 420 (November 1, 1904), p. 494.
[131] *Ibid.*
[132] *G.N.Č.*, p. 23.
[133] *Ibid.*
[134] *Odnosi,* p. 60.
[135] *Livres jaunes,* XLII–XLV, No. 85 (September 29, 1904), 110.
[136] *G.N.Č.*, p. 23.
[137] *Ibid.*, pp. 23–24.
[138] *Ibid.*
[139] *Ibid.*
[140] Toshev, I, 160–61 ; *Borba,* p. 45.
[141] Toshev, I, 161.
[142] *Odnosi,* p. 61.
[143] *Ibid.*, pp. 61–62. The author gives extensive evidence.
[144] *Ibid.*, p. 61.
[145] Toshev, I, 161.
[146] *Ibid.*, p. 162. The author relies on H. G. Hesapchiev, "Istoricheskata istina po būlgaro-srūbskite sūrūzni dogovori ot 1904 i 1905 g.," *Mir,* No. 8401 (July 3, 1928).
[147] *Ibid.*
[148] *Helmreich,* p. 7.
[149] *Odnosi,* p. 71.
[150] Toshev, I, 163.
[151] *D.D.F.,* 2e série, VI, No. 50 (January 26, 1905), 65–66.
[152] *G.P.*, XXII, Nr. 362 (October 26, 1904), 195–96.
[153] *Ibid.*; *Odnosi*, pp. 59–60 ; *Borba*, p. 129.
[154] *D.D.F.*, 2e série, VII, No. 256 (July 24, 1905), 295–97 ; *ibid.*, No. 322 (August 9, 1905), pp. 386–88.
[155] *Ibid.*, No. 256 (July 24, 1905), pp. 295–97.

[156] *Livres jaunes,* XLII–XLV (February 1, 1905), 141.
[157] *Odnosi,* p. 81.
[158] *D.D.F.,* 2e série, VII, No. 256 (July 24, 1905), 295–97.
[159] *Livres jaunes,* XLVII–XLV, No. 135 (April 19, 1905), 174.
[160] *S.K.G.,* XVII (1906), 77, 128–39.
[161] *D.D.F.,* 2e série, VII, No. 256 (July 24, 1905), pp. 295–97.
[162] *Ibid.,* V, No. 256 (July 10, 1904), 313–14.
[163] *Odnosi,* pp. 81–83 n.; Albertini, I, 143; Tommasini, II, 112–13.
[164] *Ibid.,* p. 56.
[165] *Borba,* p. 50.
[166] *Ibid.,* p. 51.
[167] *Ibid.,* pp. 51–52.
[168] *Odnosi,* p. 68.
[169] *Borba,* p. 53.
[170] *D.D.F.,* 2e série, VIII, No. 121 (November 10, 1905), 170–73.
[171] *Borba,* p. 54.
[172] *Ibid.,* p. 52.
[173] *D.D.F.,* 2e série, VII, No. 322 (August 9, 1905), 386–88.
[174] *Ibid.*
[175] *Ibid.,* No. 313 (August 6, 1905), pp. 369–72.
[176] *Ibid.,* No. 360 (August 20, 1905), pp. 434–35.
[177] *Odnosi,* p. 126.
[178] *Borba,* p. 63.
[179] *Livres jaunes,* XLII–XLV, No. 168 (November 14, 1905), 207–8; *ibid.,* Annexe I, II, 208–12.
[180] *Odnosi,* pp. 126–27.
[181] *Livres jaunes,* XLII–XLV, No. 171 (November 27, 1905), 215; *ibid.,* No. 174, and Annexe I, II (December 5, 1905), 217–20; *ibid.,* No. 179 (December 23, 1905), p. 228.
[182] *Odnosi,* pp. 67–68.
[183] *Borba,* p. 60.
[184] *Odnosi,* p. 67.
[185] *Ibid.,* p. 132.
[186] *D.D.F.,* 2e série, VIII, No. 204 (December 7, 1905), 272–73.
[187] *Ibid.*
[188] *Borba,* p. 63.
[189] Milosch Boghitschewitsch, *Die auswärtige Politik Serbiens, 1903–1914.* Instructions of the Serbian minister of foreign affairs to the representative in Vienna, I, Nr. 120 (July 5, 1909).
[190] *Ibid.; S.K.G.,* XVIII (1907), 775–78.
[191] *S.K.G.,* "Austro-ruska verbalna nota o članu III mircštegskog programa," XIX (1907), 770–75; *B.D.,* V, No. 169 (October 4, 1907), 215–16; *ibid.,* "Extract from Annual Report for Bulgaria for the Year 1907," p. 111.
[192] *S.K.G.,* XIX (1907), 770–75.
[193] *Ibid.,* p. 772.
[194] *Južna Srbija,* p. 167.
[195] *B.D.,* V, No. 84 (February 15, 1907), 117.
[196] *Ibid.,* p. 118.
[197] Toshev, I, 169.
[198] *Ibid.*
[199] *Ibid.,* p. 170.
[200] *Ibid.*
[201] *B.D.,* V, No. 84 (February 15, 1907), 118.
[202] *Južna Srbija,* p. 168.
[203] *Borba,* pp. 61–62.
[204] *Odnosi,* p. 127. The author gives details.
[205] *Ibid.*
[206] *Ibid.,* p. 128.

[207] *Ibid.*, pp. 128–29.
[208] Toshev, I, 173; Steed, pp. 242–44.
[209] *Južna Srbija,* p. 167.
[210] *Ibid.*
[211] Toshev, I, 175–76.
[212] *Južna Srbija,* p. 173.
[213] *Odnosi,* p. 130.
[214] See Part Eight.
[215] Toshev, I, 176.
[216] *Ibid.*, p. 177.
[217] *Ibid.*, pp. 177–78.
[218] *Ibid.*, p. 178.
[219] *Ibid.*
[220] *Borba,* pp. 66–67; *B.D.*, V, No. 231, "Extract from Annual Report for Turkey for the Year 1908"; *G.P.*, XXV: 2, Nr. 8765 (March 9, 1908), 390; *ibid.*, Nr. 8787 (April 22, 1908), pp. 419–26.
[221] Toshev, I, 179.
[222] *Ibid.*, p. 180.
[223] *Ibid.*
[224] *Ibid.*, p. 181.
[225] *Ibid.*, p. 182.
[226] *Ibid.*, p. 183.
[227] *B.D.*, V, No. 195 (Secret), 237; G. Bazhdaroff, *The Macedonian Question Yesterday and Today,* p. 24.
[228] Toshev, I, 184.
[229] *B.D.*, V, "Extract from Annual Report for Turkey for the Year 1908," 250–54.
[230] Boghitschewitsch, I, Nr. 120 (July 5, 1909). Instructions by the Serbian Ministry of Foreign Affairs.
[231] *B.D.*, V, "Extract from Annual Report for Serbia for the Year 1907," 118.
[232] *Ibid.*, No. 84 (February 17, 1907), p. 117.

Notes to Part Seven

[1] A good study of Serbian economic history is still wanting. An excellent review of the nineteenth-century economic history of Serbia, with particular emphasis on Austro-Serbian relations after the Congress of Berlin, is an article by Dr. Mih. V. Vujić entitled "Najnoviji obrt u trgovinskoj politici," *Glas Srpske Kraljevske Akademije,* Drugi razred, LXVI (1903), 151–93. See also the criticism of Vujić's study by M. Ninčić, in *Delo,* XXVII (1903), 134–41. A valuable essay on Serbian trade before 1903 is Momčilo Ninčić's *Srbija pred trgovinskim ugovorima.* Antiquated but still useful is M. Vujić's *Naša ekonomska politika.* Austro-Serbian relations from the Austrian side have been analyzed by Dr. Karl Grünberg, *Die handelspolitischen Beziehungen Österreich-Ungarns zu den Ländern an der unteren Donau.* A severe criticism of Austro-Hungarian policy relative to Serbia and a demand for Serbian economic emancipation was provided by Božidar Nikašinović, *Srpska izvozna trgovina i Austro-Ugarska Monarhija,* reprinted from *Srpski Pijemont,* p. 60. The opposition to Austro-Hungarian economic policy is also given by M. Dj. Milovanović, "Naši trgovinski ugovori," *Delo* (1895), pp. 182–207. Milovanović was one of the delegates sent to Vienna in August 1892 for the purpose of renewing the Austro-Serbian trade treaty of 1881; consequently he presents an authoritative and detailed study of the new treaty. Milovanović devotes considerable space to the Veterinary Convention. On the developments of Serbian trade see B. Dj. Milošević, *O razvoju naše trgovine—ekonomsko-statistička studija,* reprinted from *Trgovinski glasnik.* A study of the Serbian financial position during this period is best presented by Milorad Nedeljković, *Istorija srpskih državnih dugova.* There are several other works on the subject. See for example Nikola S. Petrović, "Les emprunts et la dette publique du Royaume de Serbie," *La Revue de Science et de Législation Financières,* IV (1906), 65–88.

Another study of Serbian economic policy after the Congress of Berlin is that of Arnold Sachse, "Das Königreich Serbien nach seinen wirtschaftlichen und Produktionsverhältnissen," *Preussische Jahrbücher*, LIV (1884), 116–33, 270–90. Although poorly organized and at times carelessly presented, of considerable value is C. Stoyanovitch, *Economic Problems of Serbia*. Very useful and informative is, of course, the multi-volume work on Milan and Alexander Obrenović by Slobodan Jovanović (*op. cit.*).

[2] Stoyanovitch, p. 33.

[3] Gabriel Effendi Noradoughian, *Recueil d'actes internationaux de l'empire Ottoman*, II, 197–200 : the Hatti Sherif concerning the autonomy of Serbia. See especially articles V–IX, which regulated commercial relations between Serbia and the Ottoman Empire.

[4] Čeněk Štěpánek, "Hospodářský vývoj Srbska," *Obzor Národohospodářský*, XIII (December 1908), 139.

[5] De Testa, *Recueil des Traités de la Porte Ottomane avec les Puissances étrangères*, IX, 277.

[6] M. Vujić, "Najnoviji obrt u trgovinskoj politici," *Glas Srpske Kraljevske Akademije*, LXVI (1903), 177 ; Testa, IX, 277.

[7] Noradoughian, III(1902), 70–79.

[8] *Ibid.*, pp. 193–202.

[9] Testa, VII, 126–30.

[10] *Vl. Mil. Ob.*, II, 210.

[11] *Ibid.*, pp. 211–12.

[12] Jovan Ristić, *Diplomatska istorija Srbije . . . 1875–1878*, I, 159–83.

[13] Hertslet, IV, 2788 ; *British and Foreign State Papers*, LXIX, 612.

[14] *Vl. Mil. Ob.*, II, 213–14.

[15] *Ibid.*, pp. 215–16.

[16] *Ibid.*, p. 227.

[17] *Ibid.*, pp. 255–56.

[18] *Ibid.*, pp. 257–58.

[19] On May 9, 1883, the Railway Convention was signed with Austria-Hungary, Turkey, and Bulgaria. Serbia was obligated to ratify it not later than October 1, 1883. Novaković, *Dvadeset godina ustavne politike u Srbiji, 1883–1903*, p. 19.

[20] *Vl. Mil. Ob.*, II, 261–63.

[21] *Ibid.*, pp. 264–65.

[22] Hertslet, IV, 2787–88.

[23] *Vl. Mil. Ob.*, II, 266–68.

[24] *Ibid.*, pp. 269–70.

[25] *Ibid.*, pp. 271–77.

[26] *Ibid.*, pp. 279–80.

[27] *Ibid.*, pp. 295–99.

[28] *Ibid.*, pp. 322–25.

[29] *Ibid.*, pp. 325–26.

[30] *Ibid.*, p. 327 ; M. Dj. Milovanović, *Naši trgovinski ugovori*, p. 184.

[31] *Vl. Mil. Ob.*, II, 329.

[32] Milovanović, p. 183.

[33] *Ibid.*, p. 186.

[34] *Ibid.*, p. 183.

[35] *Vl. Mil. Ob.*, II, 329–30.

[36] Grgur Jakšić, "Istorija Tajne Konvencije," *Arhiv za pravne i društvene nauke*, IX (1924–25), Nos. 35 *et al.* See also Pribram, *The Secret Treaties*, I, 54–55 ; Vaso Čubrilović and Vladimir Ćorović, *Srbija od 1858 do 1903*, pp. 120–27.

[37] *Vl. Mil. Ob.*, II, 334–35.

[38] Pribram, *The Secret Treaties*, I, 54–55.

[39] *Ibid.*

[40] *Ibid.*, pp. 61–63.

[41] *Ibid.*, pp. 57–61.

[42] Stoyanovitch, pp. 35, 76.

[43] *Ibid.*, p. 20.

44 Milovanović, p. 187.
45 *Vl. Al. Ob.,* I, 364–65.
46 Milovanović, pp. 190–91.
47 *Ibid.*
48 Milovanović, pp. 191–92.
49 *Ibid.,* pp. 201–2 ; *Vl. Al. Ob.,* I, 366.
50 Milovanović, p. 201.
51 *Vl. Al. Ob.,* I, 366–67.
52 Milovanović, pp. 202–3.
53 *Ibid.; Vl. Al. Ob.,* I, 367–68.
54 Milovanović, p. 189 ; *Vl. Al. Ob.,* I, 366.
55 Milovanović, pp. 193–95.
56 R. G. D. Laffan, *The Guardians of the Gate,* pp. 50, 71–72 ; Jelenić, p. 214.
57 Stoyanovitch, pp. 36–37.
58 Božidar Nikašinović, *Srpska izvozna trgovina i Austro-Ugarska Monarhija.*
59 Nikašinović, pp. 22–25.
60 *Ibid.,* p. 27.
61 *Odnosi,* p. 47.
62 *Ibid.,* p. 45 ; Nikašinović, pp. 57–59.
63 *G.P.,* XVIII : 1, Nr. 5495 (December 18, 1902), 211–13 ; *ibid.,* Nr. 5505 (January 6, 1903), pp. 223–24 ; and *Krasnyi Arkhiv,* II (1922), 16.
64 *Ibid.; Odnosi,* p. 46.
65 *N.S.* (1903–4), p. 108.
66 M. Dj. Milovanović, *Srbi i Bugari,* p. 23.
67 Zečević, pp. 75–76.
68 *N.F.P.,* Nr. 13809 (February 5, 1903), p. 10 ; Vujić, "Najnoviji obrt u trgovinskoj politici," p. 193.
69 Zečević, pp. 67, 89 ; for Austrian comments see *N.F.P.,* Nr. 14321 (April 6, 1904), p. 8.
70 *Supra,* pp. 142–43.
71 Sl. Jovanović, "Pašić i Dumba," *Politika,* January 6, 1939 (?), p. 11.
72 *Ibid.*
73 Stoyanovitch, p. 37. See also "Trgovinski ugovori izmedju Srbije i Nemačke," *Delo,* XXXIX (1906), 10–23 ; *ibid.,* XL (1906), 178–92 ; Momčilo Ninčić, "Trgovinski bilans izmedju Srbije i Nemačke," *Arhiv za pravne i društvene nauke,* I (1906), 1–2, 45.
74 *Delo,* XLII (1907), 251.
75 A. Tsankov, *Srŭbsko-Bŭlgarskite tŭrgovsko-politicheski otnosheniiā,* p. 183.
76 *Supra,* p. 149 ; Helmreich, p. 7 ; *Odnosi,* p. 71 ; *S.K.G.,* Nr. 3 (February 1, 1906), p. 226 : "An explanation from Sofia, that the Bulgarian government only wished to have the new agreement ratified before the old Serbian treaty expired on January 1, 1906, did nothing to lighten the consequences of this precipitate action." See also *Delo,* XXXVIII (1906), 236 ff.
77 *S.K.G.,* Nr. 3 (February 1, 1906), pp. 224–26 ; A. Stojanoff, *Die handelspolitische Situation der Balkanstaaten gegenüber Österreich-Ungarn,* pp. 1–6.
78 M. Ninčić, *Delo,* XXXI (1904), 314–40.
79 Th. Schiemann, *Deutschland und die grosse Politik,* 1907, p. 36.
80 *S.K.G.,* Nr. 3 (February 1, 1906), p. 227.
81 *Odnosi,* p. 74.
82 Alfred Stead, "The Serbo-Bulgarian Convention and Its Results," *The Fortnightly Review* (new series), LXXIX (1906), 1538.
83 *Ibid.* There are a number of other studies on Serbo-Bulgarian economic relations : K. D. Spisarevski, *Srŭbsko-Bŭlgarskiiā mitnicheski sŭiūz;* "Srpsko-Bugarski carinski savez i Austro-Ugarska," *Delo,* XXXVIII (1906), 463–66 ; Dr. Mom. A. Ninčić, "Carinski savez Srbije i Bugarske," *Delo,* XXXI (1904), 314–40 ; Kir. G. Popov, "Sravnitelen pregled na vŭnshnata tŭrgoviiā na Rumūniiā, Gŭrtsiiā, Sŭrbiiā i Bŭlgariiā," *Spisanie na bŭlgarskoto ikonomichesko druzhestvo,* IX–X (1902), 588–90 ; G. D. M. Iablanski, "Kakva trebva da bŭde ikonomicheskata politika na Bŭlgariiā ?" *Spisanie na bŭlgar-*

skoto ikonomichesko druzhestvo, IV–V (1901) ; M. G. T. Danailov, "Stopanska solidarnost mezhdu Rumŭniâ i Bŭlgariâ i Balkanskiât mitnicheski sŭûz," *Letopisi,* VI–VII (1902) ; "Bugarska trgovina," *S.K.G.,* XVI (1906), 474–75; Alexander v. Matlekovits, "Die sogennante serbisch-bulgarische Zollunion," *N.F.P.,* Nr. 14859 (January 5, 1905), pp. 1–2; Alexander v. Matlekovits, "Serbiens Lage im Zollkriege mit Österreich-Ungarn," *N.F.P.,* Nr. 14878 (January 24, 1905), p. 12; A. D. Dimianoff, "L'union douanière serbo-bulgare et l'Autriche-Hongrie," *Le Mouvement Économique,* IV, No. 21. On various economic developments in the Balkans, see also the periodical *Le Mouvement Économique* (Bucharest), published from 1904 to 1916 in twenty-three volumes; A. Iaranoff, "L'Au-triche-Hongrie et l'union douanière serbo-bulgare," *Revue Économique Internationale,* August 1910, p. 332; Christo Abadjieff, "Die Handelspolitik Bulgariens," *Staats- und sozialwissenschaftliche Forschungen,* Heft 143 (1910), pp. 1–155; René Gonnard, "La politique douanière des états des Balkans," *Revue Économique Internationale,* III (1912), 37–68; Moritz Ströll, "Die Handelspolitik der Balkanstaaten Rumanien, Serbien und Bulgarien," *Schriften des Vereines für Sozialpolitik,* LI, Bd. 3 (1892) ; Moritz Ströll, "Über südosteuropäische Staats- und Volkswirtschaft," *Schmollers Jahrbuch für Gesetz-gebung, Verwaltung und Volkswirtschaft,* XXV, Heft 3 (1901), 253–79; Joseph Grünzel, *Die Handelsbeziehungen Österreich-Ungarns zu den Balkanstaaten;* Karl Grünberg, *op. cit.;* Nicolaus Xenopol, "Die Staaten der Balkanhalbinsel und das Türkische Reich," *Die Weltwirtschaft,* II (1907), 233–40; S. Schilder, "Bulgarische Zollpolitik," *Das Handelsmuseum,* XXIV, No. 43 (October 28, 1909), 670–72; P. Todoroff, "Unsere Handelsbeziehungen mit den Balkanstaaten," *Demokratische Rundschau,* VII (1909), Heft 7; Dr. M. Nitschin, "Eine Zollunion zwischen Bulgarien und Serbien," *National-wirtschaft* (1906), Hefte 14–20; Dr. A. Stojanoff, *Die handelspolitische Situation der Balkanstaaten gegenüber Österreich-Ungarn.*

[84] *Odnosi,* p. 72.

[85] *Ibid.*

[86] D. A. Goluchowski to von Czikann, January 11, 1906, p. 2.

[87] Lončarević, p. 98.

[88] *Ibid.,* pp. 101–2.

[89] *N.F.P.,* January 5, 1906. See similar threats in *N.F.P.,* January 3, 4, 1906. *Odnosi,* pp. 72–73.

[90] *Trgovinski glasnik,* January 17, 1906, pp. 1–2.

[91] Alexander von Matlekovits, "Der autonome Zolltariff und die Handelsverträge," *N.F.P.,* Nr. 13871 (April 10, 1903), p. 11. He argues that it was foolish of Serbia to pursue an independent policy because she has to sell to Austria-Hungary. He considered the Serbian customs tariff a mistake. See also H. Friedjung, *Das Zeitalter des Impe-rialismus, 1884–1914,* I, 351, II, 190, in which this historian wrote that the Customs Union, had it been permitted to come into force, would have "excluded Austria-Hungary eco-nomically and politically from the Balkans."

[92] *Odnosi,* p. 94.

[93] *Ibid.,* p. 74.

[94] *Ibid.,* p. 77.

[95] *Ibid.,* p. 95.

[96] *D.A.,* Czikann to Goluchowski, January 14, 1906, p. 2, and Goluchowski to Czikann, January 17, 1906, p. 3.

[97] *N.S.,* LXXXII (February 2 [January 20], 1906), session on review of trade rela-tions with Austria-Hungary, by Ljubomir Stojanović. See also Lončarević, pp. 102–3.

[98] *D.A.,* Goluchowski to Czikann, January 11, 1906, pp. 1–2.

[99] *Ibid.,* Czikann to Goluchowski, January 19, 1906, p. 4.

[100] *Ibid.,* January 20, 1906, p. 4; *Odnosi,* p. 75.

[101] *N.F.P.,* January 17, 1905. This semiofficial journal was typical of the press.

[102] *D.A.,* Goluchowski to Czikann, January 21, 1906.

[103] *Ibid.,* Vujić to Goluchowski, January 23, 1906, p. 5.

[104] *Trgovinski glasnik* (January 13, 1906), No. 10, p. 1.

[105] *N.S.,* III (1905–6), 1388, 1407.

[106] Jelenić, p. 230.

[107] Lončarević, p. 110.

[108] *S.K.G.,* XVI (1906), 470–75.

[109] *Odnosi,* p. 77.

[110] *Ibid.,* pp. 76–77.

[111] Tommasini, II, 119–21 ; Albertini, I, 145 ; *Odnosi,* pp. 76–77.

[112] *Ibid.,* p. 78.

[113] *Ibid.,* and *Temps,* January 31, 1906, a statement by Austro-Hungarian Ambassador Count Khevenhüller.

[114] *Odnosi,* p. 79.

[115] *D.A.,* Vujić to Goluchowski, February 14, 1906, p. 6.

[116] *Ibid.,* Goluchowski to Vujić, February 16, 1906; *S.K.G.,* XVI (1906), 470–71. "Both Serbia and Bulgaria possess the right in their treaties with Austria to enter into fiscal union without prejudice to the other nations already having treaty relations with them. In these treaties it is laid down that the advantages arising from the most-favored-nation clause 'are not applicable to conditions imposed on the contracting parties by the clauses of any Customs Union already concluded, or which may be concluded in the future.' In 1892 and 1897, therefore, Austria recognized to Serbia and Bulgaria their right to form Customs Unions. It is true that this clause was inserted because at that time there was a possibility of the German and Austrian Empire forming a Customs Union, but that does not alter the fact that permission was granted. Thus the two Balkan States acted in good faith towards Austria in drawing up their present Convention. They even observed the Veterinary Convention between Austria and Serbia postponing the question of cattle until after the treaties with Austria had been concluded." A. Stead, "The Serbo-Bulgarian Convention and Its Results," *The Fortnightly Review,* LXXIX (1906), 540.

[117] *Odnosi,* p. 79.

[118] *Ibid.,* p. 80.

[119] *D.A.,* Vujić to Goluchowski, February 24, 1906, p. 14.

[120] *Diplomatske prepiske o trgovačkom ugovoru s Austro-Ugarskom od marta 16-og do juna 24-og, 1906,* Vujić to Colonel G. Antonić, No. 1 (March 4, 1906), and Protocol 4 (hereafter cited as *D.P.*). See also review of this source in *S.K.G.,* XVII (1906), 238 ff.

[121] *The Times* (London), March 12, 1906.

[122] *Delo,* XLII (1907), 16.

[123] *Ibid.,* XXXVIII (1906), 547.

[124] Alfred Stead, "The Serbo-Bulgarian Convention and Its Results," *The Fortnightly Review,* LXXIX (1906), 541.

[125] *S.K.G.,* XVII (1906), No. 1, excerpt from the exposé made before the Hungarian Parliament.

[126] *D.P.,* No. 2 (April 5, 1906), p. 7.

[127] *Ibid.,* No. 3, 9 (May 9, 1906), Pašić to Vujić; see also *D.A.,* Goluchowski to Czikann, January 19, 1906, p. 4.

[128] Lončarević, p. 123.

[129] *D.D.F.,* 2ᵉ série, No. 329 (April 20, 1905), Jullian to Berteaux, pp. 393–97.

[130] *Odnosi,* p. 80.

[131] *Ibid.,* p. 82.

[132] *Ibid.,* pp. 83–84.

[133] *Ibid.,* p. 84.

[134] *D.D.F.,* 2ᵉ série, No. 329 (April 20, 1905), pp. 393–97; *N.F.P.,* Nr. 14575 (March 21, 1905), p. 3; *ibid.,* Nr. 14548 (February 22), p. 13.

[135] Lončarević, p. 89; *N.F.P.,* Nr. 14514 (January 19, 1905), p. 11; Pržić, p. 136.

[136] *Odnosi,* p. 84.

[137] *Ibid.,* pp. 84–85.

[138] *Trgovinski glasnik,* XVL (January 1, 1906), 1.

[139] *Odnosi,* p. 85.

[140] *Ibid.*

[141] *Ibid.*

[142] M. Popović, p. 101.

[143] *Odnosi*, p. 86. The author cites appropriate documents from the Serbian Foreign Ministry Archives.

[144] *Ibid.*, p. 158. Ćorović disagrees with the thesis expounded in *Die Vorgeschichte des Weltkrieges*, X, 67, to the effect that the Russians pressured the Independent Radicals into resigning after they decided to order guns from Krupp and Škoda.

[145] *Odnosi*, p. 87.

[146] *Ibid.*, pp. 87–88.

[147] *Ibid.*, pp. 88–89.

[148] *Ibid.*, p. 89.

[149] Pržić, p. 139.

[150] Lončarević, pp. 84–88; *B.D.*, V, Enclosure in No. 142 (December 11, 1906), Whitehead to Grey, 162.

[151] *Odnosi*, pp. 89–90.

[152] *Ibid.*, p. 90.

[153] *Ibid.*

[154] *Ibid.*

[155] *Ibid.*, pp. 90–91.

[156] Constantin Dumba, *Dreibund- und Entente-Politik*, pp. 218–19.

[157] *Odnosi*, pp. 93–94.

[158] *D.P.*, No. 3 (May 9, 1906), Pašić to Vujić, p. 13; *D.A.*, May 22, 1906, Vujić.

[159] *D.P.*, No. 5 (June 20, 1906), Pašić to Czikann, p. 12.

[160] *Ibid.*

[161] *Ibid.*, No. 4 (June 30, 1906), Czikann to Pašić, p. 11.

[162] *N.S.*, 1906, p. 268.

[163] *N.F.P.*, Nr. 15069 (August 3, 1906); *ibid.*, Nr. 15065 (August 1, 1906), pp. 4–5; *ibid.*, Nr. 15066 (August 2, 1906), p. 4.

[164] *Odnosi*, p. 95.

[165] *B.D.*, V, No. 132 (April 23, 1906), 151; Pinon, *L'Europe et l'Empire Ottoman*, p. 412.

[166] *B.D.*, V, No. 132 (April 23, 1906), 151.

[167] *Odnosi*, p. 91.

[168] *Ibid.*, p. 92.

[169] Lončarević, pp. 85–86.

[170] W. S. Davis, *The Roots of the War*, p. 423; see also Pinon, p. 405.

[171] *Supra*, pp. 79–80, 105–12.

[172] *B.D.*, V, No. 135 (July 10, 1906), Buchanan to Grey.

[173] *Ibid.*, No. 136 (July 11, 1906), p. 154, Thesiger to Grey.

[174] O. Hoijer, p. 21.

[175] *Odnosi*, p. 100.

[176] J. M. Baernreither, *Fragmente eines politischen Tagebuches* (Berlin, 1928), p. 74.

[177] *Odnosi*, p. 99.

[178] *Ibid.*, p. 100.

[179] *B.D.*, V, No. 140 (November 14, 1908), Whitehead to Grey, 158; Pinon, p. 424.

[180] *Odnosi*, p. 99 n.

[181] Oscar Jászi, *The Dissolution of the Habsburg Monarchy*, p. 58.

[182] *Ibid.*, pp. 186–87.

[183] G. Gratz and R. Schüller, *The Economic Policy of Austria-Hungary*, p. 12.

[184] O. Jászi, pp. 191–92.

[185] *Ibid.*, p. 199.

[186] *Ibid.*, p. 212.

[187] Drage Geoffrey, *Austria-Hungary*, p. 192.

[188] *Ibid.*, p. 203. See also Matlekovits, "Der autonome Zolltariff und die Handelsverträge," *N.F.P.*, April 4, 1903, p. 12; *ibid.*, April 9, 1903, p. 11; *ibid.*, April 10, 1903, p. 11.

[189] Geoffrey, p. 192.

[190] Gratz and Schüller, p. 12.

[191] *H.A.Ö.R.*, 222, Session XVII (April 28, 1903), 20121.

192 *Ibid.*, p. 20138.
193 *Ibid.*, 328, XVII (May 6, 1905), 29226.
194 *Ibid.*, 329, XVII (May 10, 1905), 29290.
195 *Ibid.*, p. 29294.
196 *Ibid.*, 328, XVII (May 6, 1905), 29234–35.
197 *Ibid.*, 329, XVII (May 1905), 29318–19.
198 *Ibid.*, 385, XVII (February 22, 1906), 34647.
199 *Ibid.* (April 24, 1906), p. 3607.
200 *Ibid.*, 223, XVII (May 1, 1903), 20239.
201 Heinrich Kanner, *Kaiserliche Katastrophen-Politik*, p. 27.
202 Quoted in *Odnosi*, p. 93.
203 Economic relations with Turkey were a subject of heated parliamentary discussions; see *N.S.*, I (1903–4), 103–20.
204 *Odnosi*, p. 93.
205 *Izveštaji o trgovini s hranom u Brajili; Doktor Aberaldo Bokalari o kvalitetu srpskih volova* (Beograd, 1906) ; *Carinski rat izmedju Austro-Ugarske i Rumunije* (Beograd, 1906). In the latter work a comparative study of the Serbo-Austrian and the Austro-Rumanian commercial conflict is given. The author argues that conditions in both instances were much the same and concludes therefore that the results should be the same. *Do ut des* is the only way out, the author states. Božidar Nikašinović, *Srpska izvozna trgovina i Austro-Ugarska Monarhija*, shows the various ways by which Serbia could find new outlets and emancipate herself. *Izveštaji delegata Kraljevske vlade o trgovinskim prilikama za naš budući izvoz u novome pravcu* (Beograd, 1906). This is the commission's report to the government after its study of commercial conditions at Sofia, Varna, Constantinople, Salonika, Alexandria, Cairo, and Athens. "Uloga Egipta u ekonomskoj emancipaciji Srbije," *Politika*, July 9, 1939, p. 22. *N.F.P.*, Nr. 15139 (October 14, 1906), p. 5.
206 *G.B.C.R.*, No. 3962 (1906), by Blakeney.
207 *Trgovinski glasnik*, October 1, 1906.
208 *Ibid.*, October 4, 1906.
209 *Politika*, July 9, 1939, p. 22.
210 *Zbirka trgovinskih ugovora, Ministarstvo Finansija*, pp. 357–407 ; "Trgovinski ugovori izmedju Srbije i Njemačke," *Delo*, XXXIX (1906), 10–23. An extensive study of Serbo-German economic relations was made by Momčilo Ninčić, "Trgovinski bilans izmedju Srbije i Njemačke," *Arhiv za pravne i društvene nauke*, I, Parts 1–2.
211 *Odnosi*, p. 78. On Austro-German economic rivalry in Beograd, see Dumba, *Dreibund*, pp. 213–15.
212 *Odnosi*, p. 23.
213 *N.F.P.*, Nr. 14611 (April 27, 1905), p. 12.
214 *Zbirka trgovinskih ugovora*, pp. 408–9; *British and Foreign State Papers*, CI (1907–8), 491–92.
215 *Peace Hand Books*, IV, Part 2, 108.
216 *British and Foreign State Papers*, CI (1906–7), 924–32.
217 *Ibid.*, C (1906–7), 1126–33.
218 *Ibid.*, CI (1907–8), 591–600.
219 *Ibid.*, C (1906–7), 560–74; the *Times* (London), March 7, 1907.
220 *British and Foreign State Papers*, C (1906–7), 712–18.
221 *Das Staatsarchiv*, LXXVII, Nr. 14023, 84.
222 *N.F.P.*, Nr. 15347 (May 14, 1907), p. 2.
223 *Odnosi*, p. 100.
224 *N.F.P.*, Nr. 15373 (June 10, 1907).
225 *Ibid.* (July 1, 1907), p. 11; *ibid.* (July 2, 1907), p. 14; *ibid.* (September 8, 1907), pp. 4–5; *ibid.* (October 23, 1907), p. 11.
226 *G.B.C.R.*, No. 4373 (1909), by Blakeney.
227 *Delo* (1911), pp. 78–96, reviewing the article by J. M. Baernreither in *Österreichische Rundschau*, XXIX (1911), Hefte 1 and 2 ; Lončarević, pp. 164–82 ; *Regierungsvorlage betreffend den Handelsverträge zwischen Österreich-Ungarn und Serbien, von*

27 Juli 1910, nebst Anlagen Schlussprotokoll (Wien, 1911) ; *G.B.C.R.,* No. 4355 (1908), p. 6, by von Schoeller ; Stoyanovitch, p. 39.

[228] "Spoljašnja trgovina Srbije za 1906 godinu," *Delo,* XLV (1907), 413–27 ; *Statistika spoljašnje trgovine Kraljevine Srbije za 1906 godinu* (Beograd, 1907), p. 417.

[229] K. Stojanović, *Govori i rasprave političko-ekonomske,* II, 132, 154 ; *Odnosi,* p. 171.

[230] *Godišnjak,* XII (1907–8), 509–13.

[231] *G.B.C.R.,* No. 3962 (1906), by Blakeney.

[232] *Godišnjak,* XII (1907–8), 509.

[233] *Trgovinski glasnik* (January 12, 1906), br. 9, p. 1.

[234] *Godišnjak,* XII (1907–8), 509.

[235] *Ibid.,* p. 510.

[236] *Ibid.,* p. 509.

[237] *G.B.C.R.,* No. 4373 (1908), p. 4.

[238] *Ibid.,* by Blakeney, p. 4 ; *ibid.,* No. 3900 (1906), by Paul von Schoeller.

[239] *Ibid.,* No. 4373, p. 11.

[240] *Ibid.,* No. 4355 (1908), p. 5, by von Schoeller.

[241] *Ibid.,* No. 4112 (1908), by Whitehead.

[242] Stoyanovitch, p. 24.

[243] *Ibid.,* pp. 24–25.

[244] *Ibid.,* p. 49.

[245] V. Bajkić, *Seljački kredit,* p. 136.

[246] Stoyanovitch, pp. 24–25.

[247] K. Stojanović, I (1910), 124 ; *ibid.,* II (1911), 50, quoted in *Odnosi,* p. 170.

[248] *B.D.,* V, 160.

[249] Heinrich Kanner, *Kaiserliche Katastrophen-Politik,* p. 27 ; *Revue de Hongrie,* XLVII (1931), 12.

Notes to Part Eight

[1] J. Aulneau, "La querelle des chemins de fer balkaniques," *Revue politique et parlementaire,* LVII (1908), 494–95 ; Pavel Milûkov, *Balkanskii krizis,* p. 10 ; R. Riedl, *Sandschakbahn und Transversallinie,* pp. 6–7.

[2] *Borba,* p. 119 ; Wadham Peacock, *Albania,* p. 232 ; Arthur May, "The Novibazar Railway Project," *The Journal of Modern History,* X :4 (December 1938), 496–99 ; H. Lorin, "Les chemins de fer balkaniques," *Revue des deux mondes,* XXX (1915), 900 ; H. Wendel, *Der Kampf der Südslawen um Freiheit und Einheit,* p. 422 ; *D.D.F.,* 2ᵉ série, I, No. 139. On the Turkish and other railways in the Balkans in the nineteenth century, see Radoslave M. Dimtschoff, *Das Eisenbahnwesen auf der Balkan Halb-Insel.*

[3] *Odnosi,* p. 101.

[4] Ćorović, *Istorija Jugoslavije,* p. 548.

[5] Eduard von Wertheimer, *Graf Julius Andrássy: sein Leben und seine Zeit,* III, 276–77 ; *N.F.P.,* October 8, November 1, 3, 6, 8, 1900 ; C. Loiseau, "Les chemins de fer du Balkan occidental," *Revue de Paris,* VIII (1901), 214. "The Novibazar Railway Project" is an exceptionally fine study by Arthur J. May, in *The Journal of Modern History,* X :4 (December 1938), 496–527.

[6] *Odnosi,* p. 25.

[7] *G.P.,* XVIII :1, Nr. 5495 (December 18, 1902), 211–13.

[8] *Ibid.,* p. 213 n. ; *ibid.,* Nr. 5505 (January 6, 1903), pp. 223–24.

[9] *Spomenica Nikole P. Pašića, 10 decembar 1926–10 decembar 1936,* especially the article by Ranislav M. Avramović, entitled "Nikola Pašić kao tehničar u politici i praksi," pp. 66–70. See also D. Petrowitsch, *Entwicklung und Ausbau des jugoslawischen Eisenbahnnetzes,* p. 29 ; and for the topographical study of the proposed route, Remy, "Sandschakbahn und Donau-Adriabahn, ein Kapitel aus der Vorgeschichte des Weltkrieges," *Archiv für Eisenbahnwesen,* L (1927), 1201–6, 1216–19.

[10] *D.D.F.,* 2ᵉ série, I (March 14, 1901), 139 ; *ibid.* (May 18), p. 238 ; *ibid.* (May 24), p. 247 ; *ibid.* (April 10), p. 182 ; *ibid.* (June 29), p. 307 ; *ibid.* (July 10), p. 322. On the

Franco-Italian rivalry in this connection, see Leopold von Chlumecky, *Österreich-Ungarn und Italien*, pp. 64–65. See also *N.F.P.*, November 9, 1900, January 9, 1901, February 17, 1908.

[11] *Odnosi*, p. 102.

[12] Charykov, p. 320.

[13] On the importance of the Adriatic railway to the trade of Serbia and the benefits that were expected to accrue to Italy, France, and Russia, see Jovan Cvijić, "Der Zugang Serbiens zur Adria," *Petermanns Mitteilungen*, LVIII : 2 (1912), 361 ; T. Tittoni, *Italy's Foreign and Colonial Policy*, p. 100 ; Aulneau, p. 513 ; May, "Trans-Balkan Railway Schemes," *The Journal of Modern History*, XXIV :4 (December 1952), 354.

[14] *Odnosi*, p. 101.

[15] *G.P.*, XVIII :1, 213 n.

[16] *Ö.-U.A.*, 3-aide mémoire for the Russian government, May 1, 1908 ; *N.F.P.*, November 29, 30, 1902, January 1, 2, 11, 1903.

[17] *Ibid.* ; *G.P.*, XVIII :1, 213 n. ; *Ö.-U.A.*, 9-aide mémoire of the Russian Foreign Office, July 2, 1908.

[18] Ferdinand Schmid, *Bosnien und Herzegovina unter der Verwaltung Österreichs-Ungarns*, p. 600.

[19] Baernreither, p. 74 ; the *Times* (London), July 17, 1907.

[20] May, "The Novibazar Railway Project," p. 502.

[21] Goldberg, "Die orientalischen Bahnen und die Sandschakbahn," *Rundschau für Technik und Wirtschaft*, I (1908), 109–13 ; Riedl, pp. 7–10 ; Conrad von Hötzendorff, I, 556.

[22] René Pinon, "La crise balkanique : chemins de fers et réformes," *Revue des deux mondes*, XLV (1908), 143–76 ; *The Times* (London), February 26, 1908 ; Riedl, p. 13 ; Conrad von Hötzendorff, I, 72, 99, 591 ; Bernhard Schwertfeger, *Unveröffentliche Dokumente*, III, 64–66, 69 ; *Contemporary Review*, XCIII (1908), 370 ; May, "The Novibazar Railway Project," p. 503 ; Chlumecky, pp. 64–65 ; Jelenić, p. 235.

[23] *G.P.*, XXV :2, Nr. 8682, Marschall to Bülow, 285.

[24] *B.D.*, V (April 11, 1907), 321 ; Pinon, *L'Europe et l'Empire Ottoman*, p. 283 ; *S.K.G.*, XX (1908), 712–15.

[25] *Odnosi*, p. 102.

[26] *B.D.*, V, No. 221 (January 14, 1907), 322 ; *ibid.*, No. 222, pp. 323–25 ; Miliūkov, p. 10 ; Pinon, p. 285 ; *Borba*, p. 120. See also Riedl ; Balkanikus (Stojan Protić), *Albanski problem i Srbija i Austrija-Ugarska*.

[27] *B.D.*, V, No. 223 (March 4, 1907), 325–26.

[28] *Ibid.*, No. 26 (April 11, 1907), pp. 321–22.

[29] *G.P.*, XXV :2, Nr. 8684 (January 21, 1907), 289.

[30] *Ibid.*, Nr. 8735 (March 4, 1908), p. 349 ; *ibid.*, Nr. 8736 (March 5, 1908), p. 350.

[31] *Ibid.*, Nr. 8685 (January 26, 1907), pp. 289–90.

[32] *Ibid.*, Nr. 8683 (December 18, 1906), pp. 286–89.

[33] *Ibid.*, Nr. 8685 (January 26, 1907), pp. 289–90.

[34] *Ibid.*, Nr. 8686 (February 28, 1907), pp. 290–91 ; *ibid.*, Nr. 8687 (March 15, 1907), pp. 291–93.

[35] *Ibid.*, Nr. 8686 (February 28, 1907), pp. 290–91.

[36] *Ibid.* ; *Odnosi*, p. 108.

[37] *G.P.*, XXV :2, Nr. 8687 (March 15, 1907), 291–93.

[38] *Ibid.*, XXII, Nr. 7373 (May 7, 1907), 55–56.

[39] *Ibid.*, XXV :2, Nr. 8687 (March 15, 1907), 291–93.

[40] *Ibid.*, XXII, Nr. 7385 (December 14, 1907), 83–88.

[41] May, "The Novibazar Railway Project," p. 507 ; Schwertfeger, III, 69.

[42] *G.P.*, XXV : 2, Nr. 8755 (July 6, 1908), 374–75 ; *ibid.*, Nr. 8756 (July 15, 1908), p. 376.

[43] *Ibid.*, Nr. 8690, pp. 295–96 n.

[44] *Ibid.*, Nr. 8760 (August 28, 1908), pp. 381–82 ; *Ö.-U.A.*, p. 36, Aehrenthal to Bülow, August 15, 1908.

[45] Steed, I, 266–67 ; *Fortnightly Review*, XCII (1909), 390–91.

[46] *G.P.*, XXV:2, Nr. 8706 (February 12, 1908), 313–14.   Hence Izvolsky's pretense of surprise was not warranted, see *B.D.*, V (June 1908), 195.

[47] *G.P.*, XXV:2, Nr. 8733 (February 27, 1908), 343–45.

[48] *Ibid.*, Nr. 8708 (February 15, 1908), pp. 316–17.

[49] *Ibid.*, Nr. 8716 (February 20, 1908), pp. 324–25.

[50] *Ibid.*, Nr. 8701 (February 9, 1908), pp. 308–9.

[51] *Ibid.*, Nr. 8688 (December 30, 1907), pp. 293–94.

[52] May, "The Novibazar Railway Project," p. 509.

[53] *G.P.*, XXV:2, Nr. 8688 (December 30, 1907), 293–94; *Odnosi*, p. 108.

[54] *N.F.P.*, January 28, 1908; *B.D.*, V, No. 230 (February 10, 1908), 333; *Delo*, XLVI, 117–24; *S.K.G.*, "Austro-Ugarska i Balkan," XX (1908), 470; *Odnosi*, p. 109.

[55] *N.F.P.*, January 28, 1908, pp. 2–3, 4; *ibid.*, January 31, 1908, p. 15; *ibid.*, March 14, 1908, p. 15. The last two references contain statements by Richard von Riedl, an expert on Balkan economic and railway affairs. See also *G.P.*, XXV:2, Nr. 8691 (January 30, 1908), 297–98; Bernadotte E. Schmitt, *The Annexation of Bosnia, 1908–1909*, pp. 7–15; Momtchilo Nintchitch, *La crise bosniaque (1900–1908)*, pp. 123–41.

[56] *Odnosi*, p. 108.

[57] *B.D.*, V, No. 224 (April 8, 1907), 326–27; *G.P.*, XXV:2, Nr. 8716 (February 20, 1908), 324–25.

[58] *B.D.*, V, No. 232 (February 12, 1908), 334; *Odnosi*, p. 103.

[59] *B.D.*, V, No. 224 (April 8, 1907), 326–27; *ibid.*, No. 220 (January 7, 1907), p. 322. The Serbian railway project interested the German diplomats as early as the autumn of 1906, see *G.P.*, XXV: 2, Nr. 8681 (October 22, 1906), 283; *ibid.*, Nr. 8682 (November 19, 1906), pp. 284–86; *ibid.*, Nr. 8683 (December 18, 1906), pp. 286–89.

[60] *Odnosi*, p. 103.

[61] *Ibid.*, p. 104.

[62] *B.D.*, V, No. 225 (April 22, 1907), 327.

[63] *Ibid.*, No. 233 (February 12, 1908), pp. 335–36.

[64] *Odnosi*, pp. 103–4.

[65] *B.D.*, V, No. 224 (April 8, 1907), 326–27.

[66] *G.P.*, XXV:2, Nr. 8687 (March 15, 1907), 291–93; *B.D.*, V, No. 220 (January 7, 1907), 322.

[67] *Odnosi*, p. 104; *supra*, pp. 156–57.

[68] *Ibid.*, pp. 104–5; *Srpska riječ*, No. 167 (August 1–14, 1907).

[69] *Odnosi*, p. 105.

[70] *Ibid.*, pp. 105–6.

[71] *Ibid.*, p. 104.

[72] *Ibid.*, p. 106.

[73] *B.D.*, V, No. 237 (February 19, 1908), 340.

[74] *Odnosi*, p. 107.

[75] *B.D.*, V, No. 237 (February 19, 1908), 340.

[76] Pinon, p. 274.

[77] *Odnosi*, p. 108.

[78] *Ibid.*, p. 113.

[79] *G.P.*, XXV:2, Nr. 8709 (February 17, 1908), 317–18.

[80] *Ibid.*, XXII, Nr. 7736 (February 12, 1908), 507–8.

[81] Schwertfeger, III, 64.

[82] *G.P.*, XXV:2, Nr. 8691 (January 30, 1908), 297–98. See also Nr. 8695 (February 1, 1908), pp. 299–300.

[83] *Odnosi*, p .110.

[84] *S.K.G.*, XX (1908), 473. On the reaction to Aehrenthal's exposé see *Delo*, XLVI (1908), 117–24.

[85] *S.K.G.*, XX (1908), 473.

[86] *Odnosi*, p. 114.

[87] *Ibid.*, pp. 113–14.

[88] *Ibid.*

[89] *Ibid.*, pp. 114–15.

[90] *Ibid.*, p. 115.

[91] *G.P.*, XXV :2, Nr. 8698 (February 2, 1908), 302–4.

[92] *Ibid.*, Nr. 8705 (February 14, 1908), pp. 312–13.

[93] *Odnosi*, p. 116.

[94] *G.P.*, XXV :2, (May 5, 1908), Tschirschky to F. O., 370–72.

[95] *Ibid.*, Nr. 8699 (February 7, 1908), p. 305. The Russian ambassador in Vienna, Prince Urusov, spoke similarly to Serbian Minister Dj. Simić, on February 23, 1908, *Odnosi*, p. 199.

[96] *B.D.*, V, No. 233 (February 12, 1908), 335–36.

[97] *Ibid.*, No. 227 (February 3, 1908), pp. 328–29.

[98] H. Nicholson, *Die Verschwörung der Diplomaten*, p. 282.

[99] *Odnosi*, p. 111.

[100] *G.P.*, XXV :2 (February 26, 1908), Marschall to Bülow, 340–41.

[101] *Odnosi*, p. 111.

[102] Dragomir Arnautović, *Histoire des chemins de fer yougoslaves, 1825–1937*, pp. 200–201 ; May, "Trans-Balkan Railway Schemes," p. 355.

[103] *G.P.*, XXV :2, Nr. 8726 (February 23, 1908), Monts to Bülow, 335–36.

[104] *Ibid.*, Nr. 8701 (February 9, 1908), Monts to Bülow, pp. 309–10.

[105] *Odnosi*, p. 111 n.

[106] *Ibid.*, p. 112.

[107] Baernreither, *The Fragments of a Political Diary*, p. 38 ; *N.F.P.*, February 14, 1908.

[108] *Odnosi*, pp. 115–16.

[109] *B.D.*, V, No. 238 (February 24, 1908), Grey to Lascelles, 341–44 ; *G.P.*, XXV :2, Nr. 8746 (April 25, 1908), Jenisch to F. O., 365 ; *ibid.*, Nr. 8747 (April 25, 1908), Jenisch to F. O., p. 366.

[110] *Odnosi*, p. 112.

[111] *Ibid.*, p. 117.

[112] *G.P.*, XXV :2, Nr. 8735 (March 4, 1908), 349 ; Jelenić, p. 234.

[113] *B.D.*, V, No. 244 (March 4, 1908), 347. For additional information regarding the Russian attitude toward the Sandjak and Adriatic railways see *Ö.-U.A.*, No. 3 (May 1, 1908), pp. 5–6 ; *ibid.*, No. 9 (July 2, 1908), pp. 9–11 ; *Gosudarstvenaîa duma. Stenograficheskie otcheti*. Session I, Sitting 49, April 4, 1908, Izvolsky's exposé of foreign policy in which he discusses the Macedonian reforms and the Sandjak railway project and admits failure. Pavel Milîukov, the famed historian, likewise spoke, criticizing the official policy.

[114] *B.D.*, V, No. 246 (March 5, 1908), 349. For the Italian policy with regard to the Austrian Uvac-Mitrovica line, the Danube-Adriatic and various other Balkan railway proposals, see discussion in the Italian Lower House, *Atti del Parlamento Italiano Camera dei Deputati*, Sessions 1904–8, Ia della XVII (1908), 20149–83. Of particular interest is Tittoni's speech, pp. 20160–66. See also Tittoni, *Italy's Foreign and Colonial Policy*, pp. 98–99.

[115] *B.D.*, V, No. 247 (March 5, 1908), 349–50.

[116] *Ibid.*, No. 243 (March 3, 1908), p. 346.

[117] *Ibid.*, No. 247 (March 5, 1908), pp. 349–50.

[118] *Odnosi*, p. 117.

[119] *Ibid.*

[120] *B.D.*, V, No. 248 (March 17, 1908), 350 ; *ibid.*, No. 251 (April 16, 1908), p. 352 ; *ibid.*, No. 247 (March 5, 1908), pp. 349–50.

[121] Sir Edward Grey, *Speeches on Foreign Affairs 1904–1914*, p. 84.

[122] *B.D.*, V, No. 248 (March 17, 1908), 350.

[123] *Odnosi*, p. 117.

[124] *Ibid.*, p. 202.

[125] *Ibid.*, p. 119.

[126] *G.P.*, XXV :2, Nr. 8735 (March 4, 1908), Schoen to Marschall, 349.

[127] *Odnosi*, pp. 118–19.

[128] *G.P.*, XXV :2, Nr. 8735 (March 4, 1908), Schoen to Marschall, 349.

[129] *Odnosi*, p. 119.

[130] *Odnosi*, p. 118.
[131] *G.P.*, XXV :2, Nr. 8736 (March 5, 1908), Marschall to F. O., 350.
[132] *Odnosi*, p. 119.
[133] *Ibid.*, pp. 119–20.
[134] *Ibid.*, p. 120.
[135] *Ibid.*, p. 121.
[136] *G.P.*, XXV :2, Nr. 8753 (May 18, 1903), 372–73.
[137] *Odnosi*, p. 122.
[138] *Ibid.*, p. 122 n.
[139] *G.P.*, XXV :2, Nr. 8745 (April 19, 1908), 363; *ibid.*, Nr. 8746 (April 25, 1908), p. 365.
[140] *Odnosi*, p. 123.
[141] *G.P.*, XXV :2, Nr. 8745 (April 19, 1908), 363; *ibid.*, Nr. 8746 (April 25, 1908), p. 365.
[142] *Odnosi*, p. 123.
[143] *Ibid.*, pp. 123–24 n.
[144] *Ibid.*, p. 124 n.
[145] *G.P.*, XXV : 2, Nr. 8750 (May 5, 1908), 370–71.
[146] *Odnosi*, p. 125.
[147] *B.D.*, V, No. 257 (November 27, 1908), 355.
[148] *Ibid.*, No. 259 (June 15, 1909), p. 355.
[149] Giovanni Giolitti, *Memoirs of My Life*, pp. 208–10.
[150] *Odnosi*, p. 125.
[151] *Ö.-U.A.*, I, Nr. 32 (August 9, 1908), 25–34; Friedjung, *Das Zeitalter des Imperialismus*, p. 241; Franckenstein, pp. 82–83; Baernreither, *Fragments of a Political Diary*, p. 44.
[152] *Odnosi*, pp. 325–26.
[153] *Ö.-U.A.*, II, 885–86.
[154] *Odnosi*, pp. 326–27.

Notes to Conclusion

[1] Bajkić, p. 143.
[2] *Ibid.*

Bibliography

There is a lack of documentary material pertaining to Serbian diplomatic history since 1903. The Serbian foreign ministry papers and diplomatic correspondence have not been published, and some materials have been lost in each of the two world wars. The author consequently has been forced to rely for the most part on secondary materials and on foreign diplomatic documents. Of the latter, particularly useful were the British (*British Documents on the Origins of the War, 1898–1914*) and the French (*Documents diplomatiques français, 1871–1914*), which cover Serbian affairs at some length. The German documents (*Die Grosse Politik*) are of considerable value on the Macedonian Question and the subject of Balkan railways. The Austro-Hungarian documents on the period 1903 to 1908 have not been published. The tsarist foreign documents, published by the Soviet government (*Mezhdunarodnye otnosheniiā v epokhu imperializma*) likewise do not cover the period, although the series is valuable as background material on the period immediately preceding 1903. The parliamentary debates of Serbia (*Stenografske beleške o sednicama Narodne Skupštine*) and Austria-Hungary (*Stenographische Protokolle über die Sitzungen des Hauses der Abgeordneten*) are of great value and have been used quite extensively in the preparation of this study.

Both Serbia and Austria-Hungary have published documents on specific questions concerning their mutual relations, as for example the documents dealing with the "Pig War." Official statistical compendia of the two countries, especially Serbia's *Statistički godišnjak*, are also of considerable value in studying the economic and social development of Serbia. Of the large number of newspapers and periodicals examined for this study, the author found most valuable the Serbian official gazette (*Srpske novine*) and the organs of the various political parties. Of the foreign newspapers, many Austro-Hungarian publications are useful, but in the author's opinion the *Neue Freie Presse* (Wien) provides the most extensive coverage of Serbian developments, especially those affecting relations with Austria-Hungary.

Materials concerning Serbian political parties and leading political figures have not been systematically collected and preserved. Only a few speeches, diaries, and memoirs of leading personalities have been published. The organs of the political parties and numerous other journals and periodicals are available, but as is the case with all such materials, they are difficult to use because of the lack of indexes. Many articles and brief notes by informed persons and those who were active during the period from 1903 to 1908 are strewn throughout many journals and periodicals. After 1918, fragmentary materials from diaries and memoirs of the politicians and statesmen have been published in *Politika, Borba, Samouprava, Narodna Odbrana, Srpski književni glasnik, Letopis Matice Srpske*, and others. These publications contain also many brief scholarly studies of specific problems and developments in Serbian prewar history.

Aside from the works of Slobodan Jovanović, Živan Živanović, Dragiša Vasić, and Vladimir Ćorović, of which we have spoken in the Preface, one must mention the brief study of Serbian foreign relations between 1903 and 1908 (*Borba za narodno ujedinjenje*) by Jovan M. Jovanović, former diplomat, which, though it contains many minor errors, is valuable because of the official position in the Serbian diplomatic service which the author held during the period. Of the works in foreign languages, only the study of Dušan Lončarević (*Jugoslaviens Entstehung*) gives any serious attention to the period of 1903–8 in Serbian historical development.

No problem has been as popular with journalists and writers as the perennial Macedonian Question. Hundreds of short studies on the subject have appeared, but unfortunately most of these are of propagandist character and ardently nationalistic in tone. Nothing of consequence has been published on King Peter, and very little indeed on the conspirator regicides and their activities in Serbia after 1903. On the "Pig War," only a few brief studies appeared, and most of these are now antiquated. No study of relations with Bulgaria has appeared for the period. Likewise, except for the work of Ćorović, no study of Serbian relations with Austria-Hungary, Russia, England, and France from 1903 to 1908 is available.

Present-day Yugoslav historians, officially guided by Marxian methodology and philosophy, are showing great interest in the period of our concern. Yet they are concerned primarily with rewriting history to suit the ideological needs of the current regime. Their attention is disproportionately centered on the collection of documentary materials and the interpretation of the dominant trends relevant to the growth of the socialist movement.

The listing of the following materials does not represent by any means the entire literature on the subject; it merely represents a selection of more pertinent materials, those used more extensively in preparation of this study.

PRIMARY SOURCES

Austria-Hungary

Bericht über die Verwaltung von Bosnien und der Herzegovina. Wien, 1906.

Berichte der k. u. k. Österr.-Ung. Konsularämter über das Jahr 1903 bis 1907. Verlag der k. u. k. Österr. Handels Museum. Wien, 1903 *et al.*

Diplomatische Aktenstücke über die Handelsvertragsverhandlungen mit Serbien, 1905–1906. K. u. k. Ministerium des Aussern. Wien, 1906.

Hötzendorff, Conrad von. *Aus meiner Dienstzeit, 1906–1918.* 5 vols. Wien, 1922–25.

K. u. k. Ministerium des Aussern Diplomatische Aktenstücke über die Reformaktion in Mazedonien 1902–1906. Rotbuch. Wien, 1906.

Österreich-Ungarns Aussenpolitik von der bosnischen Krise 1908 bis zum Kriegsausbruch 1914. 9 vols. Wien, 1930.

Pribram, A. F. *The Secret Treaties of Austria-Hungary, 1879–1914.* 2 vols. Translated by A. C. Coolidge. Cambridge, 1920.

Regierungsvorlage, betreffend den Handelsvertrag zwischen Österreich-Ungarn und Serbien, von 27 Juli 1910, nebst Anlagen Schlussprotokoll. Wien, 1911.

Statistik des auswärtigen Handels des Österreich-Ungarn. Wien, 1903 *et al.*
Stenographische Protokolle über die Sitzungen des Hauses der Abgeordneten des Österreichischen Reichsrates. Wien, 1862 *et al.*
Stenographische Protokolle über die Sitzungen Herrenhauses des Reichsrates. Wien, 1862 *et al.*

Bulgaria

Glavna direktsiia na statistikata. *Statisticheski godishnik na Bŭlgarskoto Tsarstvo.* Sofia, 1910 *et al.*
Kesiakov, B. D. *Prinos kŭm diplomaticheskata istoriia na Bŭlgariia, 1878–1925.* 4 vols. Sofia, 1925.

France

Ministère des affaires étrangères. *Documents diplomatiques français (1871–1914).* 2ᵉ série. Paris, 1929 *et al.*
Ministère des affaires étrangères. *Livres jaunes, Affaires de Macédoine, 1902–1907.* Paris, 1907.

Germany

Dugdale, E. T. S. *German Diplomatic Documents, 1871–1914.* Selected and translated. 4 vols. London, 1928.
Lepsius, Johannes, *et al. Die Grosse Politik der Europäischen Kabinette, 1871–1914.* 53 vols. Berlin, 1921–27.
Das Staatsarchiv. Sammlung der offiziellen Aktenstücke zur Aussenpolitik der Gegenwart. 86 vols. Leipzig, 1861–1919. New series since 1928.
"Untersuchungausschuss über die Weltkriegsverantwortlichkeit" (I). Vol. X: "Unterausschuss." *Die Vorgeschichte des Weltkrieges.* Berlin, 1930.

Great Britain

Accounts and Papers, CX (1904), London.
Foreign Office. *British and Foreign State Papers.* London, 1812 *et al.*
Foreign Office. *Diplomatic and Consular Reports.* London, 1886 *et al.*
Gooch, G. P., and H. Temperley. *British Documents on the Origins of the War, 1898–1914.* 11 vols. London, 1926–36.
Hertslet, E. *Map of Europe by Treaty.* 4 vols. London, 1875–91.
Parliament. *The Parliamentary Debates.* 4th ser. London, 1892 *et al.*

Ottoman Empire

Noradoughian, Gabriel Effendi. *Recueil d'actes internationaux de l'Empire Ottoman.* 4 vols. Paris, 1897–1903.
Testa, Ignaz de. *Recueil des traités de la Porte Ottomane avec les puissances étrangères.* 11 vols. Paris, 1864–1911.

Russia

Gosudarstvenaiia duma. *Stenograficheskie otcheti.* Chast II. St. Petersburg, 1908.
Krasnyi Arkhiv. "Dnevnik Kuropotkina," II (1922), 16.
Laloy, Émile. *Les documents secrets des archives du ministère des affaires étrangères de Russie publiés par les Bolcheviks.* Paris, 1920.
Ministerstvo Inostrannykh diel. *Diplomaticheska perepiska. Reforma Makedonii: 1902–1903, 1903–1905.* St. Petersburg, 1906.
Narodni komisariat po inostrannym dielam. *Sbornik sekretnikh dokumentov iz arkhiva bivshago ministerstva inostrannykh diel.* St. Petersburg, 1917–18.

Serbia

Bokhitschewitsch, Milosch. *Die auswärtige Politik Serbiens, 1903–1914.* Berlin, 1928.

Ćorović, Vladimir. *Diplomatske prepiske Kraljevine Srbije.* Vol. I. Beograd, 1933. (Serbian diplomatic and consular correspondence covering the period from January 1, 1902, to June 1, 1903.)

Diplomatske prepiske o trgovačkom ugovoru s Austro-Ugarskom od marta 16-og do juna 24-og, 1906. Beograd, 1906.

Dnevnik Senata. Stenografske beleške 1901–02. Beograd, 1901–2.

Izveštaji delegata Kraljevske vlade o trgovinskim prilikama za naš budući izvoz u novome pravcu. Beograd, 1906.

Izveštaji o trgovini s hranom u Brajili. Beograd, 1906.

Ministarstvo Inostranih Dela. *Prepiska o arbanaškim nasiljima u Staroj Srbiji, 1898–1899.* Beograd, 1899.

Narodna Skupština. Stenografske beleške o sednicama Narodne Skupštine. Beograd, 1902 *et al.*

Srpsko pitanje u Turskoj pred Narodnom Skupštinom. (Sjednica skupštinska od 12 julija 1897 god.) Beograd, 1897.

Statistika spoljašnje trgovine Kraljevine Srbije za 1906 godinu. Beograd, 1907.

Statistički godišnjak Kraljevine Srbije. Beograd, 1900 *et al.*

Stenografske beleške o radu Vanredne Narodne Skupštine za 1903 g. Beograd, 1903.

Tajna prevratna organizacija; izveštaj sa pretresa u Vojnom sudu za oficire u Solunu po beleškama vodjenim na samom pretresu. Solun, Štamparija, "Velika Srbija," 1918.

Zbirka trgovinskih ugovora, Ministarstvo Finansija. Beograd, 1908.

Zečević, Milan L. *Kraljevske reči. Zbirka govora Kralja Petra I.* Beograd, 1924.

Žujović, J. M. "Govor prilikom debate o Adresi, 11 oktobra 1905 g.," *Odjek*, No. 237, 1905.

United States

Papers Relating to the Foreign Relations of the United States. Washington, 1903 *et al.*

SECONDARY SOURCES

Albertini, Luigi. *The Origins of the War of 1914.* London, 1952.

Anastasoff, Christ. *The Tragic Peninsula.* St. Louis, 1938.

Andonović, M. J. *Makedonski su Slaveni Srbi.* Beograd, 1913.

Arnautović, Dragomir. *Histoire des chemins de fer yougoslaves, 1825–1937.* Paris, 1937.

B. M., *Stara Srbija i reforme.* Beograd, 1906.

Baerlein, Henry. *The Birth of Yugoslavia.* London, 1922.

Baernreither, J. M. *Fragmente eines politischen Tagebuches.* Berlin, 1928.

———. *Fragments of a Political Diary*, ed. Joseph Redlich. London, 1930.

Bajkić, V. *Seljački kredit.* Beograd, 1928.

Balkanikus (Stojan Protić). *Albanski problem i Srbija i Austrija-Ugarska.* Beograd, 1913.

Balugdžić, Živojin. *Pašić u Beču u službi otadžbine.* Beograd, 1905.

Barbulescu, Ilie. *Romanii fata de Serbi si Bulgari.* Bucharest, 1904. Translated into Serbian by Svetislav Ilić. Beograd, 1908.

Barker, Elizabeth. *Macedonia. Its Place in Balkan Power Politics.* R.I.A., London, 1950.

Bazhdaroff, G. *The Macedonian Question Yesterday and Today.* Sofia, 1926.
Belić, Vlad. J. *Ratovi Srbije i Crne Gore.* Beograd, 1937.
Brailsford, H. N. *Macedonia: Its Races and Their Future.* London, 1906.
Brandenburg, Erick. *From Bismarck to the World War.* Translated by A. E. Adams. London, 1927.
Bülow, Bernard. *Denkwürdigkeiten.* 4 vols. Berlin, 1930–31.
Burmov, T. *Bŭlgarskata tsŭrkovna raspra.* Sofia, 1902.
Carinski rat izmedju Austro-Ugarske i Rumunije. Beograd, 1906.
Charmatz, R. *Österreichs aussere und innere Politik von 1895 bis 1914.* Leipzig, 1918.
———. *Geschichte der auswärtigen Politik Österreichs.* Berlin, 1914.
Chlumecky, Leopold v. *Österreich-Ungarn und Italien.* 2d ed. Leipzig, 1907.
Ćirić, Mihajlo. *Jedan pogled na naš državni život.* Beograd, 1905.
Ćorović, Vladimir. *Borba za nezavisnost Balkana.* Beograd, 1937.
———. *Istorija Jugoslavije.* Zagreb, 1933.
———. *Odnosi izmedju Srbije i Austro-Ugarske u XX veku.* Beograd, 1936.
Čubrilović, Vasa. *Opšti pogled na novu srpsku istoriju.* Beograd, undated.
Čubrilović, Vasa, and V. Ćorović. *Srbija od 1858 do 1878. Srbija od 1878 do 1903.* Beograd, 1938.
Cvijić, Jovan. *L'annexion de la Bosnie-Herzégovine et la question Serbe.* Paris, 1909.
Danev, S. *Ocherk na diplomaticheskata istoriia na Balkanskite dŭrzhavi.* Sofia, 1922.
Denis, E. *La Grande Serbie.* Paris, 1915.
Derzhavin, N. S. *Bŭlgarsko-srŭbskite vzaimni otnosheniia i Makedonskiia vŭpros.* Sofia, 1915.
Dimtschoff, M. *Das Eisenbahnwesen auf der Balkan Halb-Insel.* Bamberg, 1894.
Djonović, Nikola. *Ustavne i političke borbe u Crnoj Gori od 1905 do 1911.* Beograd, 1938.
Djordjević, Tihomir. *Macedonia.* London, 1918. Also Serbian and French editions.
Djordjević, Vladan. *Arnauti i velike sile.* Beograd, 1913.
———. *Das Ende der Obrenovitch: Beiträge zur Geschichte Serbiens, 1897–1900.* Leipzig, 1905.
———. *Kraj jedne dinastije.* 3 vols. Beograd, 1905–6.
———. *Srbija i Grčka, 1891–1893.* Beograd, 1923.
———. *Srbija i Turska, 1894–1897.* Beograd, 1928.
Djurdjević, Vukadin S. *Odnosi izmedju srpstva i Rusije od 1185 do 1903 godine.* Beograd, 1903.
Doktor Aberaldo Bokalari o kvalitetu srpskih volova. Beograd, 1906.
Drage, Geoffrey. *Austria-Hungary.* London, 1909.
Driault, Édouard. *Histoire diplomatique de la Grèce.* Vol. 4. Paris, 1926.
Dučić, Nićifor. *Raško-prizrenska mitropolija i nacionalno-kulturna misija Kraljevine Srbije u Staroj Srbiji i Maćedoniji.* Beograd, 1896.
Duhem, Jules. *La Question Yougoslave; la Monarchie Danubienne et l'Europe.* Paris, 1918.
Dumba, Constantin. *Dreibund- und Entente-Politik in der Alten und Neuen Welt.* Zürich, 1931.
———. *Memoirs of a Diplomat.* Translated by Ian F. D. Morrow. Boston, 1932.
Fay, S. B. *The Origins of the First World War.* New York, 1931.

Franckenstein, Sir George. *Diplomat of Destiny. Austrian Ambassador to the Court of St. James.* New York, 1940.
Friedjung, H. *Das Zeitalter des Imperialismus 1884–1914.* 3 vols. Berlin, 1919–22.
Genov, Georgi P. *Iztochniat vŭpros.* Sofia, 1926.
Georgević, Vladan. *See* Djordjević, Vladan.
Giesl, W. *Zwei Jahrzehnte im Nahen Orient.* Berlin, 1927.
Giolitti, Giovanni. *Memoirs of My Life.* London, 1923.
Gopčević, Spiridon. *Russland und Serbien von 1804–1915.* München, 1916.
Gratz, G., and R. Schüller. *The Economic Policy of Austria-Hungary.* New Haven, 1928.
Gravier, G. *Le Sanjak de Novi Bazar.* Paris, 1913.
Grey, Sir Edward. *Speeches on Foreign Affairs, 1904–1914.* London, 1931.
Grey, Viscount of Fallodon. *Twenty-Five Years, 1892–1916.* London, 1925.
Grünberg, Karl. *Die handelspolitischen Beziehungen Österreich-Ungarns zu den Ländern an der unteren Donau.* Leipzig, 1902.
Grünzel, Joseph. *Die Handelsbeziehungen Österreich-Ungarns zu den Balkanstaaten.* Wien, 1892.
———. *Handelspolitik und Ausgleich in Österreich-Ungarn.* Wien, 1912.
Haumant, E. *La Formation de la Yugoslavie.* Paris, 1930.
Hauser, H. *Histoire diplomatique de l'Europe (1871–1914).* 2 vols. Paris, 1929.
Helmreich, E. C. *The Diplomacy of the Balkan Wars, 1912–1913.* Cambridge, 1938.
Hiller, Gerhard. *Die Entwicklung des Österr.-Serbischen Gegensatzes 1908 bis 1914.* Halle, 1934.
Hoijer, O. *Le Comte d'Aehrenthal et la politique de la violence.* Paris, 1922.
Horvat, Josip. *Politička povijest Hrvatske, 1918–1929.* Zagreb, 1938.
———. *Stranke kod Hrvata i njihova ideologija.* Beograd, 1939.
Hýbl, F. *Dějiny národa bulharského.* Praha, 1930.
Iaranov, Atanas. *Stopanskata politika na Bŭlgariia.* Sofia, 1934.
Ishirkov, A. *La Macédoine et la constitution de l'Exarchat bulgare.* Lausanne, 1918.
Ivanić, Ivan. *Maćedonija i Maćedonci.* Novi Sad, 1908.
Jakšić, Grgur. *Borba za slobodu Srbije 1788–1816.* Beograd, 1938.
———. *Diplomatska istorija Srbije u XIXom vijeku.* Beograd, 1938.
Jakšić, Grgur, and D. Stranjaković. *Srbija od 1813 do 1858 god.* Beograd, 1938.
Janković, Dragoslav. *O političkim strankama u Srbiji.* Beograd, 1951.
Jászi, Oscar. *The Dissolution of the Habsburg Monarchy.* Chicago, 1929.
Jelačić, Aleksije. *Rusija i Balkan, pregled političkih i kulturnih veza Rusije i balkanskih zemalja od 866 do 1940.* Beograd, 1940.
Jelenić, Djurdje. *Nova Srbija i Jugoslavija.* Beograd, 1923.
Jireček, Jovan. *Projekat željeznice Dunav-Niš-Jadransko More.* Beograd, 1908.
Jovanović, Aleksa. *Iz borbe za obnovu naših škola pod Turcima: Arhimandrit Partenije.* Skoplje, 1939.
———. *Postanak egzarhije i Turska, Rusija i Srbija.* Skoplje, 1936.
——— (ed.). *Spomenica dvadeset godišnjice oslobodjenja Južne Srbije, 1912–1917.* Skoplje, 1937.
Jovanović, Jagoš. *Stvaranje crnogorske države i razvoj crnogorske nacionalnosti.* Cetinje, 1948.
Jovanović, Jovan M. *Borba za narodno ujedinjenje od 1903 do 1908.* Beograd, 1938.

————. *Južna Srbija od kraja XVIII veka do oslobodjenja.* Beograd, 1941.
————. "Novaković u diplomatiji," *Spomenica St. Novakovića (Srpska književna zadruga,* XXIII, 151–219). Beograd, 1921.
Jovanović, Lj. *Srpski narod i otomanska ustavnost.* Beograd, 1908.
Jovanović, Slobodan. *Svetozar Marković.* 2d ed. Beograd, 1920.
————. *Vlada Aleksandra Obrenovića.* 3 vols. Beograd, 1936.
————. *Vlada Milana Obrenovića.* 3 vols. Beograd, 1934.
Kaclerović, Triša. *Martovske demonstracije i majski prevrat 1903.* Beograd, 1950.
————. *Ruska politika i srpska omladina. Povodom putovanja grofa Lamsdorfa.* Beograd, 1903.
Kako je postala Bugarska Egzarhija. Beograd, 1897.
Kanner, Heinrich. *Kaiserliche Katastrophen-Politik.* Wien, 1922.
Karić, V. *Srbija i Balkanski Savez.* Beograd, 1893.
Kerner, R. J. *Yugoslav Movement.* Cambridge, 1918.
Krakov, S. *Plamen Četništva.* Beograd, 1930.
Laffan, R. G. D. *The Guardians of the Gate.* Oxford, 1919.
Larmeroux, Jean. *La politique extérieure de l'Autriche, 1876–1914.* Paris, 1918.
Lang, L. *Hundert Jahre Zollpolitik 1805–1905.* Wien, 1906.
Langer, W. L. *The Diplomacy of Imperialism 1890–1902.* 2 vols. New York, 1935.
————. *European Alliances and Alignments.* New York, 1931.
Lončarević, Dušan. *Jugoslaviens Entstehung.* Zürich, 1929.
Mandl, Leopold. *Die Habsburger und die Serbische Frage.* Wien, 1918.
————. *Österreich-Ungarns und Serbiens.* Wien, 1911.
Marcuse, H. *Serbien und die Revolutionsbewegung in Makedonien.* Berlin, 1908.
Markov, Walter M. *Serbien zwischen Österreich und Russland, 1892–1908.* Stuttgart, 1934.
Marković, J. T., and Svet. Tomić. *O Makedoniji i Makedoncima.* Krf, 1918.
Marković, N. *Dr. Laza Paču.* Beograd, 1923.
Masaryk, T. G. *Der Agramer Hochverratsprozess und die Annexion von Bosnien und der Herzegovina.* Wien, 1910.
Masleša, Stevan. *Svetozar Marković.* Beograd, 1945.
Matlekovits, A. von. *Das Königreich Ungarn volkswirtschaftlich und statistisch dargestellt.* 2 vols. Leipzig, 1900.
————. *Die Zollpolitik der österreichisch-ungarischen Monarchie und des deutschen Reiches seit 1868 und der nächsten Zukunft.* Leipzig, 1881.
Michelis, E. *Die Zolltrennung Österreich-Ungarns in handelspolitischer und volkswirtschaftlicher Beleuchtung.* Wien, 1908.
Mijatovich, Chedomille. *The Memoirs of a Balkan Diplomatist.* London, 1917.
————. *A Royal Tragedy.* New York, 1907.
Milenković, Tasa. *Kralj Aleksandar i oficirska zavera.* Beograd.
Milenković, Vladislav. *Ekonomska istorija Beograda.* Beograd, 1932.
Miliukov, Pavel. *Balkanskii krizis.* St. Petersburg, 1910.
Milošević, B. Dj. *O razvoju naše trgovine—ekonomsko-statistička studija.* Reprinted from *Trgovinski glasnik.* Beograd, 1904.
Milovanović, M. Dj. *Srbi i Bugari.* Reprinted from *Delo.* Beograd, 1898.
Mishew, D. *The Bulgarians in the Past.* Lausanne, 1919.
Mitrev, Dimitar. *Pirinska Makedonija vo borba za nacionalno oslobodiuvanje.* Skopje, 1950.

Mitrović, Živan. *Srpske političke stranke.* Beograd, 1939.

Mojsev, Lazar. *Bugarska Radnička Partija (Komunista): Makedonsko nacionalno pitanje.* Beograd, 1948.

Molden, B. *Alois Graf Aehrenthal.* Stuttgart, 1917.

Murray, Beaven. *Austrian Policy Since 1868.* London, 1914.

Nastić, G. *Finale.* 2d ed. Sarajevo, 1908.

Nedeljković, Milorad. *Istorija srpskih državnih dugova.* Beograd, 1909.

Nešić, Milutin. *Srbi i Bugari.* Novi Sad, 1919.

Nešković, Borivoje. *Istina o solunskom procesu.* Beograd, 1953.

Nicholson, H. *Die Verschwörung der Diplomaten.* Frankfurt, 1931.

Nicolaides, Cleanthes. *La Macédoine.* Berlin, 1899.

Nikašinović, Božidar. *Austro-Ugarska politika na Balkanu i Kraljevina Srbija.* Beograd, 1904.

————. *Bosna i Hercegovina pod upravom Austro-Ugarske monarhije i austrougarska balkanska politika.* Beograd, 1901.

————. I. *Engleska, Srbija i zavereničko pitanje.* II. *Kalajeva Union Banka.* Beograd, 1906.

————. *Srpska izvozna trgovina i Austro-Ugarska Monarhija.* Reprinted from *Srpski Pijemont.* Beograd, 1903.

Ninčić, Momčilo. *Srbija pred trgovinskim ugovorima.* Beograd, 1902. (Same as Momtchilo Nintchitch.)

Nintchitch, Momtchilo. *La crise bosniaque (1900–1908) et les puissances européennes.* Paris, 1937. (Same as Momčilo Ninčić.)

Niška carinarnica pred Narodnom Skupštinom. Niš, 1904.

Novaković, Stojan. *Balkanska pitanja.* Beograd, 1906.

————. *Dvadeset godina ustavne politike u Srbiji, 1883–1903.* Beograd, 1912.

————. *Poslanica našim političkim prijateljima i svakome koje čuti rad.* Beograd, 1905.

Nuri-Hadžić, Osman, V. Skarić, and Nikola Stojanović. *Bosna i Hercegovina pod austriskom upravom. Srpski narod* series, Vol. XV. Beograd, 1938.

Nuri-Hadžić, Osman, V. Skarić, and Vasilj Popović. *Bosna i Hercegovina pod turskom upravom. Srpski narod* series, Vols. XIII–XIV. Beograd, 1938.

O tajnoj konvenciji izmedju Srbije i Austro-Ugarske zaključene 1881 god. Novi Sad, 1902.

Ormandzhiev, Ivan. *Nova i nai-nova istoriia na Bŭlgarskiia narod.* Sofia, 1945.

Pantić, Dušan. *Spoljna i trgovinska politika nezavisne Srbije.* Beograd, 1910.

Paulová, Milada. *Tomáš G. Masaryk a Jihoslované.* Praha, 1938.

Peacock, W. *Albania.* New York, 1914.

Petrowitch, D. *Entwicklung und Ausbau des jugoslawischen Eisenbahnnetzes.* Cologne, 1932.

Picheta, Vladimir. *Serbia.* St. Petersburg, 1917.

Pijade, Moša. *O Dimitriju Tucoviću.* Beograd, 1950.

Pinon, R. *L'Europe et l'Empire Ottoman.* Paris, 1917.

Pomiankowski, J. *Der Zusammenbruch des Ottomanischen Reiches.* Wien, 1928.

Popović, Dimitrije. *Borba za narodno ujedinjenje od 1908 do1914 godine. Srpski narod* series, Vol. VII. Beograd, 1938.

————. *Izvoljski i Erental.* Beograd, 1927.

————. *Nikola Pašić i Rusija.* Reprinted from *G.N.Č.,* No. XLVI. Beograd, 1937.

Popović, Milivoje Ž. *Borba za parlamentarni režim u Srbiji.* Beograd, 1939.

Popović, Vasilj. *Evropa i srpsko pitanje. Srpski narod* series, Vol. XIX. Beograd, 1938.
――――. *Istočno pitanje.* Beograd, 1928.
Povolni, L. V. *Le problème macédoine et sa solution.* Paris, 1903.
Pribram, A. F. *Austrian Foreign Policy 1908–1918.* London, 1923.
Prodanović, Jaša M. *Istorija političkih stranaka i struja.* Beograd, 1947.
――――. *Ustavni razvitak i ustavne borbe u Srbiji.* Beograd, 1938.
Protić, Stojan M. *Odlomci iz ustavne i narodne borbe u Srbiji.* 2 vols. Beograd, 1911-12.
Pržić, Ilija. *Spoljašna politika Srbije (1804–1914).* Beograd, 1939.
Radikali i naša nacionalna politika. Beograd, 1904.
Rathmann, E. *Die Balkanfrage 1904–08 und das Werden der Tripelentente.* Halle, 1932.
Reiss, R. A. *The Comitadji Question in Southern Serbia.* London, 1924.
René, Henri. *Les Questions d'Autriche-Hongrie et la question d'Orient.* Paris, 1903.
Riedl, R. *Sandschakbahn und Transversallinie.* Wien, 1908.
Ristić, Jovan. *Diplomatska istorija Srbije za vreme srpskih ratova za oslobodjenje i nezavisnost 1875–1878.* 2 vols. Beograd, 1896–98.
Scheffler, ――――. *Das bulgarische Exarchat und der mazedonischen Kirchenstreit.* Leipzig, 1909.
Schiemann, Th. *Deutschland und die grosse Politik.* Berlin, 1901–14.
Schmid, Ferdinand. *Bosnien und Herzegovina unter der Verwaltung Österreichs-Ungarns.* Leipzig, 1914.
Schmitt, Bernadotte E. *The Annexation of Bosnia, 1908–1909.* Cambridge, 1937.
Schwertfeger, Bernhard. *Unveröffentliche Dokumente.* 5 vols. Berlin, 1919.
Segre, Roberto. *Vienna e Belgrado.* Milano, 1935.
Der Serbische Handelsvertrag. Ein Sieg der Agrarin, ein Wert zur Aufklärung, von einem aufrichtigen Freunde der österreichischen Landwirtschaft. Wien, 1908.
Seton-Watson, R. W. *The Balkans, Italy and the Adriatic.* London, 1912.
――――. *The Emancipation of South-Eastern Europe.* London, 1912
――――. *German, Slav and Magyar.* London, 1916.
――――. *The Rise of Nationality in the Balkans.* London, 1917.
――――. *The Southern Slav Question.* London, 1911.
Seymour, Charles. *Diplomatic Background of the War, 1870–1914.* New Haven, 1916.
Sforca, Karlo. *Nikola Pašić i ujedinjenje Jugoslavena.* Beograd, 1937.
Sieghart, R. *Zolltrennung und Zolleinheit. Geschichte der österr.-ungarischen Zwischenhandels.* Wien, 1915.
Simeonoff, Iwan. *Die Eisenbahnen und Eisenbahnpolitik in Bulgarien.* Halle, 1909.
Simić, Svetislav. *Maćedonsko pitanje.* Beograd, 1908.
――――. *Stara Srbija i Arbanasi.* (Written under the pseudonym "P. O.") Beograd, 1904.
Simitch, Milan. *La dette publique de la Serbie.* Paris, 1925.
Sosnosky, Theodor. *Die Balkanpolitik Österreich-Ungarns seit 1866.* Berlin, 1914.
Spisarevski, K. D. *Srŭbsko-Bŭlgarskiia mitnicheski sŭiuz.* Sofia, 1906.
Spoljna politika. Spoljna politika Vladanova kabineta. Reprinted from *Odjek.* Beograd, 1898.

Spomenica Nikole P. Pašića, 10 decembar 1926–10 decembar 1936. Beograd, 1937.
Spomenica Nikole Pašića, 1845–1925. Beograd, 1926.
Stanev, N. *Nai-nova istoriia na Bŭlgariia 1878–1918.* Sofia, 1925.
Stanojević, A. *O političkim reformama u Staroj Srbiji i Maćedoniji.* Beograd, 1902.
Stavrianos, L. S. *Balkan Federation.* Northampton, Mass., 1944.
Steed, Henry Wickham. *The Hapsburg Monarchy.* 4th ed. London, 1919.
Stojanoff, A. *Die handelspolitische Situation der Balkanstaaten gegenüber Öster-reich-Ungarn.* Wien, 1914.
Stojanović, K. *Govori i rasprave političko-ekonomske.* Beograd, 1910.
———. *Posle svršenih trgovinskih ugovora.* Beograd, 1908.
Stojanović, Ljubo. *Godišnjak zadužbine Ljube Stojanovića za 1937.* Beograd, 1937.
Stojanović, Nikola. *La Serbie d'hier et de demain.* Paris, 1917.
Stoyanovich, C. *Economic Problems of Serbia.* Paris, 1919. (Same as K. Sto-janović.)
Subotić, V. *Dr. Vladan Djordjević.* Beograd, 1910.
Südland, L. v. *Die Südslawische Frage und der Weltkrieg.* Wien, 1918.
Tcharykow, N. V. *Glimpses of High Politics.* New York, 1931.
Tittoni, Tommaso. *Italy's Foreign and Colonial Policy.* Translated by Baron Bernardo Quaranta di San Severino. London, 1914.
Todorović, M. A. *Carinski rat izmedju Srbije i Austro-Ugarske od 1906 do 1910 god.* Beograd, 1911.
Tomitch, Zoran. *La formation de Yougoslavie.* Paris, 1927.
Tommasini, Francesco. *L'Italia alla vigilia della guerra.* 3 vols. Bologna, 1934–37.
Toshev, A. *Balkanskite voini.* 2 vols. Sofia, 1929–31.
Toshev, Georgi D. *Balkanski mitnicheski sŭiuz.* Plovdiv, 1907.
Trumbić, Ante. *Suton Austro-Ugarske i Riječka rezolucija.* Zagreb, 1936.
Tsankov, A. *Srŭbsko-bŭlgarskite tŭrgovsko-politicheski otnosheniia.* Sofia, 1915.
Tucović, Dimitrije. *Izabrani Spisi Dimitrije Tucovića.* Beograd, 1949.
Vasić, Dragiša. *Devesto treća (Majski prevrat): Prilozi za istoriju Srbije od 8 jula 1900 do 17 januara 1907.* Beograd, 1925.
Villari, Luigi (ed.). *The Balkan Question.* New York, 1905.
Vladisavljević, Milan. *Hrvatska autonomija pod Austro-Ugarskom.* Beograd, 1939.
Vošnjak, Bogumil. *A Dying Empire.* London, 1918.
Vujić, M. *Naša ekonomska politika.* Beograd, 1883.
Vukićević, Milenko. *Kralj Petar od rodjenja do smrti.* Beograd, 1924.
Vuković, Gavro. *Memoari.* Sarajevo, 1925.
Wendel, Hermann. *Die Habsburger und die Südslawische Frage.* Leipzig, 1921.
———. *Der Kampf der Südslawen um Freiheit und Einheit.* Wien, 1925.
Wertheimer, E. v. *Graf Julius Andrássy: sein Leben und seine Zeit.* 3 vols. Stuttgart, 1910, 1913.
Witte, A. *Vospominaniia.* 3 vols. Berlin, 1922–23.
Živanović, Ž. *Jovan Ristić kneževski i kraljevski načelnik i mnogogodišnji minis-tar inostranih dela.* Beograd, 1929.
———. *Politička istorija Srbije u drugoj polovini devetnaestog veka, 1897–1903.* 4 vols. Beograd, 1923–25.
Zografski, Dančo. *Kruševskata republika.* Skopje, 1949.

PERIODICAL AND NEWSPAPER ARTICLES

Abadjieff, Christo. "Die Handelspolitik Bulgariens," *Staats- und sozialwissenschaftliche Forschungen,* Heft 143 (1910), 1–155.
Baernreither, Joseph. "Aehrenthal und Milovanovich," *Deutsche Revue,* XLVII (January 1922), 84–89.
――――. "Unsere Handelsbeziehungen zu Serbien," *Österreichische Rundschau,* XXIX (October–November 1911), 1–16, 105–21.
Balugdžić, Ž. "Kralj Petar i Knez Ferdinand," *S.K.G.,* February 1, 1938, pp. 185–92.
Čas. "Celni válka se Srbskem," January 30, 1906, pp. 1 ff.
Caulet, Dr. "La fausse grossesse de la reine de Serbie," *Semaine médicale,* No. 22 (1901).
Chakalov. "Tūrgovskite dogovori na Bŭlgaria od 1897 g. nasam," *Spisanie na bŭlgarskoto ikonomichesko druzhestvo,* VI : 1 (1902).
Ćorović, V. "Misija Andre Djordjevića u Beču 1903 godine," *S.K.G.,* August 1, 1934.
――――. "Pregovori o balkanskim savezima," *G.N.Č.,* 1938, pp. 1–24.
――――. "Srpsko-bugarski odnosi," *Politika,* May 1–4, 1937.
Danailov, M. G. T. "Stopanska solidarnost mezhdu Rumūniia i Bŭlgariia i balkanskiat mitnicheski sūiuz," *Letopisi,* VI–VII (1902).
Delo. "Carinski spor izmedju Srbije i Austro-Ugarske," XLII (1907), 245–56.
――――. "Politička hronika," XLVI (1907), 117–24.
――――. "Spoljna trgovina Srbije za 1906 godinu," XLV (1907), 413–27.
――――. "Srpsko-Bugarski carinski savez i Austro-Ugarska," XXXVIII (1906).
――――. "Trgovinski ugovori izmedju Srbije i Nemačke," XXXIX (1906), 10–23.
Dillon, E. J. "Serbia and the Rival Dynasties," *Contemporary Review,* July 1903, pp. 131–43.
Dimianoff, A. D. "L'union douanière serbo-bulgare et l'Autriche-Hongrie," *Le Mouvement économique,* IV : 21 (1906).
Geršić, G. "Carinski savez u političkom pogledu," *Delo,* LXVIII (1913).
Gonnard, René. "La politique douanière des états des Balkans," *Revue économique internationale,* III (1912), 37–68.
Gribble, F. "Serbia Irredenta," *Edinburgh Review,* CCXX (July 1914), 41–59.
Grünberg, Karl. "Die Neuregelung unseres handelspolitischen Verhältnisses zu Serbiens," *N.F.P.,* February 7, 1906.
Hartwig, Nicholas. "Serbiens Aussenpolitik vor den Weltkrieg," *Kriegschuldfrage,* VI (August 1928), 745–69.
Helmreich, E. C. "Die Serbisch-Bulgarischen Verträge von 1914," *Berliner Monatshefte,* XI : 2 (July–December 1933), 772–80.
Hesapchiev, H. G. "Istoricheskata istina po bŭlgaro-srŭbskite sūiuzni dogovori ot 1904 i 1905 g.," *Mir,* Nos. 8400, 8401 (July 2–3, 1928).
Iablanski, G. D. M. "Kakva trebva da bŭde ikonomicheskata politika na Bŭlgariia ?" *Spisanie na bŭlgarskoto ikonomichesko druzhestvo,* IV–V (1901).
Iaranoff, A. "L'Autriche-Hongrie et l'union douanière serbo-bulgare," *Revue économique internationale,* August 1910, pp. 332 ff.
――――. "Srŭbskiiat iznos prez Solun," *Spisanie na bŭlgarskoto ikonomichesko druzhestvo,* XIII : 7–8 (1909), 578 ff.
Inostrani (Jovan M. Jovanović). "Austro-Ugarska i Srbija," *S.K.G.,* XVII (1906), 629–31.
――――. "Boris Sarafov," *S.K.G.,* XX (1908), 229–30.

Inostrani (Jovan M. Jovanović). "Carinski savez Srbije s Bugarskom," *S.K.G.*, XVII (1906), 222–28.
——. "Demokrati u Bugarskoj," *S.K.G.*, XX (1908), 870–73.
——. "Kongres maćedonskih revolucionara," *S.K.G.*, XV (1905), 951–56.
——. "Maćedonska revoluciona organizacija," *S.K.G.*, XIII (1904), 612–17.
——. "Maćedonski revolucionari u Bugarskoj," *S.K.G.*, XX (1908), 290–93.
——. "1907 godina," *S.K.G.*, XX (1908), 146–50.
——. "Novi skopaljski mitropolit," *S.K.G.*, XV (1905), 868–72.
——. "Opet Austro-Ugarska i Srbija," *S.K.G.*, XVII (1906), 790–93.
——. "Rascep medju maćedonskim revolucionarima," *S.K.G.*, XIV (1905), 457–63.
——. "Srpsko-Bugarski odnosi," *S.K.G.*, July 16, 1907, pp. 145–48.
——. "Veleško-debarsko mitropolitsko pitanje," *S.K.G.*, XVIII (1907), 777–81.
Ivanovich, M. R. "The Serbian Massacre," *Contemporary Review,* July 1903, pp. 62–78.
Jakšić, Grgur. "Drugi srpsko-bugarski savez," *Politika,* January 6, 7, 8, 9, 1930.
——. "Istorija Tajne Konvencije," *Arhiv za pravne i društvene nauke,* IX (1924–25), No. 35 *et al.*
Janković, V. "O budućem trgovinskom ugovoru sa Austro-Ugarskom," *Delo,* IV (1910), 448 ff.
Jánossy, Dionys. "Der handelspolitische Konflikt zwischen der österreichisch-ungarischen Monarchie und Serbien in den Jahren 1904–1910," *Jahrbuch des Wiener ungarischen historischen Instituts* II (1932), 285–312.
Jovanović, Jovan M. "Dr. Milovan Dj. Milovanović i srpsko-bugarski savez," *Politika,* March 3, 1932, pp. 2–3.
——. "Kralj Nikola i bombaška afera," *Nova Evropa,* II (1921), 27 ff.
——. "Kralj Petar kao čovek i kao vladar," *ibid.,* III (1921), 395 ff.
——. "Kralj Petar I (Beleške i uspomene)," *Bratstvo,* XVII (1921), 176 ff.
——. "Obnova srpske mitropolije u Skoplju (1891–1902)," *Bratstvo,* XXIX (1938), 65 ff.
——. "Srpsko-engleski odnosi," *S.K.G.,* XXXII (1931), 141–45.
——. *See also* Inostrani.
Jovanović, Slobodan. "Jugoslovenska misao u prošlosti i budućnosti," *S.K.G.,* January 1, 1940, pp. 28–38.
——. "Milovan Milovanović," *S.K.G.,* July 1, 1937, pp. 337–48.
——. "Nicholas Pašić: After Ten Years," *Slavonic Review,* XV (1936), 368–76. The article also appeared in Serbian: "Nikola Pašić," *Nova Evropa,* XXIX (December 26, 1936), 381–89.
Liapchev, A. "Kŭm predstoiashtite tŭrgovski dogovori," *Spisanie,* III: 4 (1903), 231–74; *ibid.,* III: 6, 383–401; *ibid.,* III: 7, 479–507.
Loiseau, C. "Les chemins de fer du Balkan occidental," *Revue de Paris,* VIII (1901).
Lorin, H. "Les chemins de fer balkaniques," *Revue des deux mondes,* XXX (1915), 900.
Marco (Božin Simić). "Nikola Hartvig," *Nova Evropa,* XVIII (April 26, 1928).
——. "Preporod srpske vojske i borba za ujedinjenje," *Nova Evropa,* XVI: 2 (July 26, 1927), 51–67.
——. "Pripremanje 29 maja 1903," *Nova Evropa,* XV: 12 (June 11, 1927), 405–19.

——. "Srpska vojska pre i posle 29 maja 1903," *Nova Evropa*, XVI:1 (May 11, 1926).

Masaryk, T. G. "Vnitřní politický stav v Rakousku," *Čas*, 11 června 1908, pp. 1 ff.

Matlekovits, Alexander v. "Der autonome Zolltariff und die Handelsverträge," *N.F.P.*, April 4, 1903, p. 12; April 9, 10, 11.

——. "Serbiens Lage im Zollkriege mit Österreich-Ungarn," *N.F.P.*, January 24, 1905, p. 12.

——. "Die sogennante serbische-bulgarische Zollunion," *N.F.P.*, January 5, 1905, pp. 1–2.

May, Arthur J. "The Novibazar Railway Project," *The Journal of Modern History*, X:4 (December 1938), 496–527.

——. "Trans-Balkan Railway Schemes," *The Journal of Modern History*, XXIV:4 (December 1952), 352–67.

Mijatović, Č. "Moje poznanstvo sa kraljem Petrom," *Dnevnik*, January 27, 1923.

Milovanović, M. Dj. "Naši trgovinski ugovori," *Delo* (1895), pp. 182–207.

Mitković, R. "Ljubomir Davidović," *Nova Evropa*, XVI:8 (October 26, 1927), 258–62.

Neue Freie Presse. "Die Bestimmungen der serbisch-bulgarischen Zollunion," January 5, 1906, p. 11.

Ninčić, M. A. "Carinski savez Srbije i Bugarske," *Delo*, XXXI (1904), 314–40.

——. "Trgovinski bilans izmedju Srbije i Njemačke," *Arhiv za pravne i društvene nauke*, I (1906), Nos. 1–2.

Nitschin, M. "Eine Zollunion zwischen Bulgarien und Serbien," *Nationalwirtschaft*, Hefte 14–20, 1906.

Nova Evropa. "Jedan ruski savremeni dokumenat o 29 maju," October 11, 1947, pp. 235–39.

P. O. "Pogled na naš prosvetno-politički rad u St. Srbiji i Makedoniji," *S.K.G.*, XII (1904), 1068–79.

Pašić, Nikola. A series of articles on Pašić in honor of his eightieth birthday. *Nova Evropa*, XIII (1926).

Petrovitch, N. S. "Les emprunts et la dette publique du royaume de Serbie," *La revue de science et de législation financières*, IV (1906), 65–88.

Pinon, René. "Le conflit austro-serbe," *Revue des deux mondes*, XXXVII (February 1907), 638–68.

——. "La crise balkanique: chemins de fers et réformes," *Revue des deux mondes*, XLV (1908).

Politika. "Uloga Egipta u ekonomskoj emancipaciji Srbije," July 9, 1939, p. 22.

Popov, K. G. "Sravnitelen pregled na vŭnshnata tŭrgoviia na Rumŭniia, Gŭrtsiia, Sŭrbiia i Bŭlgariia," *Spisanie na bŭlgarskoto ikonomichesko druzhestvo*, IX–X (1902), 568–90.

——. "Vŭnshnata tŭrgoviia na Bŭlgariia prez 1902 g.," *ibid.*, III:1 (1903), 48–60.

Popović, Č. A. "Organizacija 'Ujedinjenje ili Smrt' ('Crna ruka')," *Nova Evropa*, XV:12 (June 11, 1927), 396–405.

——. "Rad organizacija 'Ujedinjenje ili smrt,'" *Nova Evropa*, XVI:5 (September 11, 1927), 139–52.

Popović, Dimitrije. "Milovan Milovanović i Aneksija," *S.K.G.*, April 1, 1938, pp. 493–510.

Prodanović, Jaša M. "Radikalna stranka," *Nova Evropa*, XIII (1926).

Protić, S. "The Secret Treaty Between Serbia and Austria-Hungary," *Fortnightly Review*, XCI (May 1909), 838–49.

Randi, Oscar. "Nicola P. Pašić," *L'Europe Orientale*, VII (1927), 1–41, 155–82, 231–55.

Remy, ———. "Sandschakbahn und Donau-Adriabahn, ein Kapitel aus der Vorgeschichte des Weltkrieges," *Archiv für Eisenbahnwesen*, L (1927).

Riedl, Richard v. "Sandschak- und Transversallinie," *N.F.P.*, March 14, 1908, p. 15.

———. "Der zweite Schienenweg nach Salonichi," *N.F.P.*, January 31, 1908, p. 15.

Sachse, Arnold. "Das Königreich Serbien nach seinen wirtschaftlichen und Produktionsverhältnissen," *Preussische Jahrbücher*, LIV (1884), 116–33, 270–90.

Sasse, Heinz. "Nikola Pašić," *Berliner Monatshefte*, XIV (January 1936), 23–42.

Savić, M. "Opća carinska tarifa od 1904 godine, njena primjena i njen uticaj na proizvodnju," *Delo*, LXIX (1913), 285–91.

Schilder, S. "Bulgarische Zollpolitik," *Das Handelsmuseum*, XXIV: 43 (October 28, 1909), 670–72.

Schultz, Maurice. "La politique économique d'Aehrenthhal envers la Serbie," *Revue d'histoire de la guerre mondiale*, XIII (1935), 325–47, XIV (1936), 23–42.

Semiz, Dušan. "Majevci," *Nova Evropa*, October 11, 1927, pp. 214–24.

———. "Pred zoru velikih dana," *Nova Evropa*, XIX (1929).

Seton-Watson, R. W. "Les relations diplomatiques austro-serbes," *Le Monde slave*, III (1926), 273–88.

Simić, Božin. "Nikola Hartvig," *Politika*, November 12, 1939, p. 6.

Smilevski, Vidoe. "Osvrt na razvoj makedonskog nacionalnog pitanja," *Komunist*, I (January 1950).

Snowden, A. L. "Present and Future of Serbia," *Independent*, June 1903, pp. 1487–96.

Spalajković, Miroslav. "O aneksiji Bosne i Hercegovine sa diplomatskog gledišta," *Politika*, January 7, 1938.

Srpski književni glasnik. "Austro-ruska verbalna nota o članu III mircštegskog programa," XIX (1907), 770–75.

———. "Austro-Ugarska i Balkan," XX (1908).

———. "Bugarska i srpska trgovina," XVII (1906), 463–66.

———. "Bugarska trgovina," XVI (1906), 474–75.

———. "Naš medjunarodni položaj," XVI (1906), 447–52; *ibid.*, XVII (1906), 606–19, 928–40.

———. "Put Kneza Nikole u Rusiju," XX (1908), 712–15.

———. "Srpska Plava Knjiga," XVII (1906), 238 ff.

———. "Srpsko-austriski odnosi," XVII (1906), 146–50.

———. "Srpsko-bugarski odnosi," XVIII (1907), 775–78.

———. "Trgovinski ugovor s Austro-Ugarskom," XVI (1906), 470–74.

———. "Živio Jugoslovenski Kralj," XII (1904), 309 ff.

Stanojević Lazar. "Jedna nedovoljno poznata strana naše novije istorije," *Letopis Matice Srpske*, May–June 1935.

Stanojević, St. "Borba Srba za srpsko-hrvatsko ujedinjenje," *Narodna Odbrana*, July 26, 1930, pp. 468–69.

Stead, Alfred. "King Peter I of Serbia," *Review of Reviews*, September 1906, pp. 245–50.

——. "The Serbo-Bulgarian Convention and Its Results," *The Fortnightly Review*, LXXIX (new series, 1906), 537–45.

——. "The Situation in the Near East," *The Fortnightly Review*, LXXXVII (1907), 695–707.

Štěpánek, Čeněk. "Hospodářský vývoj Srbska," *Obzor Národohospodářský*, XIII (1908).

Stojadinović, M. "Budućnost austro-srpskih trgovinskih odnosa," *Delo*, LXVII (1913), 125–29.

Stranjaković, D. "Arbanija i Srbija u XIX veku," *S.K.G.*, December 16, 1937, pp. 11 ff.

——. "Detinjstvo, vaspitanje i školovanje Kralja Petra I u Srbiji do 1858 godine," *Jugoslovenski istoriski časopis*, III: 1–4 (1937), 213–35.

Ströll, Moritz. "Die Handelspolitik der Balkanstaaten Rumanien, Serbien und Bulgarien," *Schriften des Vereins für Sozialpolitik*, LI (1892), No. 3.

——. "Über südosteuropäische Staats- und Volkswirtschaft," *Schmollers Jahrbuch für Gesetzgebung, Verwaltung und Volkswirtschaft*, XXV: 3 (1901), 253–79.

Tartaglia, Oskar. "Dragutin Dimitrijević 'Apis,' " *Nova Evropa*, XVI: 2 (July 26, 1927), 67–74.

Todoroff, P. "Unsere Handelsbeziehungen mit den Balkanstaaten," *Demokratische Rundschau*, VII (1909), Heft 7.

Todorović, M. "Dejstva carinskog rata izmedju Srbije i Austro-Ugarske (1906–1910) s pogledom na našu spoljašnu trgovinu," *Delo*, LIX (1911), 208 ff., 396 ff.

Todorović, P. "Kraljev brak," *Ogledalo*, No. 67 (1904), pp. 857 ff. See also continuation in Nos. 58–70 (1904).

——. "Kraljeva tajna," *Ogledalo*, No. 87 (1904), pp. 1087 ff.

Trifunović, Miša. "Nikola Pašić," *S.K.G.*, XX (new series, February 1, 1927), 197–206.

V. M. "Istorija srpsko-bugarskog zbližavanja od osamdesetih godina XIX veka do ostvarenja Balkanskog saveza u 1912 godini," *Narodna Odbrana*, February 2, 1930, pp. 77–78, and in several subsequent issues.

V. V. "Balkanskata federatsiia kato ideal na srūbsko-būlgarskata mladezh," *Spisanie na Būlgarskoto Ikonomichesko Druzhestvo*, III: 2 (1904), 101–13.

——. "Poseshtenieto na srūbskiia kral i srūbsko-būlgarskoto sblizhenie," *Spisanie na būlgarskoto ikonomichesko druzhestvo*, III: 2 (1904), 654–62.

Vujić, M. "Najnoviji obrt u trgovinskoj politici," *Glas Srpske Kraljevske Akademije*, Drugi razred, LXVI (1903).

Xenopol, Nicolaus, "Die Staaten der Balkanhalbinsel und das Türkische Reich," *Die Weltwirtschaft*, II: 3 (1907), 233–40.

Index

Abadjieff, Christo, 260

Abdul Hamid, 24, 25, 26, 30, 32, 33, 42, 43, 66, 154, 157, 158, 160, 161, 162, 163, 215, 216, 218–19, 220, 227, 228

Adrianople, 28, 43, 122, 136, 143 ff.; reform program, 153–54; Treaty of, 1; vilayet of, 43, 136, 154

Adriatic railway. *See* Danube-Adriatic railway

Adriatic Sea, 210, 211, 213, 214

Aegean Sea, 177, 212, 216, 219

Aehrenthal, Alois Lexa, Count von, 82, 265, 266; Balkan railways, 213; Bosna-Adriatic railway, 221, 226; Danube-Adriatic railway, 214, 226; exposé, 215, 216, 220, 224; Italy policy, 223, 227; Montenegro policy, 219, 220; Ottoman Empire policy, 216; railway policy, 227; reforms in Macedonia, 220; Russia policy, 215, 222; Sandjak railway, 119, 160, 163, 198, 215; Serbia policy, 157–58, 203, 204, 224

Afera lista "Za Otadžbinu" i moja, 101

Alavantić affair, 22

Alavantić, Rade, 22

Albania: attacks on Serbs, 27, 30, 32–34, 41, 42, 89, 129, 150, 154, 158, 161, 230, 233, 234, 243; Balkan wars, 105; bands, 42; Danube-Adriatic railway, 213; delimitation, 144; disturbance, 139, 142, 160, 230; independence, 138, 152, 230; Montenegrin railways, 219; nationalism, 32, 128, 129; Ottoman railways, 213; policy of, 128, 153; relations with Austria-Hungary, 33, 41, 122, 129, 138, 152, 154, 212; relations with Italy, 89, 151, 152

Albanian League, 129

Albanians: Catholic, 33, 41, 76, 153; mixed districts, 128, 130

Albertini, Luigi, 185, 255, 261

Aleksić, Andjelko, 132

Alexander (Karadjordjecić), King of Serbia, 1

Alexander I (Karadjordjević), King of Yugoslavia, 64, 105 ff.

Alexander (Obrenović), King of Serbia, 8, 47, 239; April Constitution, 16–17, 20, 23, 38; army, 10–11, 37, 50, 195; autopsy and burial, 44, 59, 60–61; conspiracy against, 14, 22, 50–51, 53–55, 73, 101, 103, 232; Djordjević (Vladan), 5, 8, 12, 14; March Demonstration, 52; marriage, 2, 4–8, 9, 10, 35, 108; Milan Obrenović, 1, 5, 8, 10, 13–16, 31, 35; murder, 58, 58 n., 63, 70, 78, 80, 84, 239; opposition, 232; Peter Karadjordjević, 102; press, 15; radicals, 12, 18, 232; rule, 8–9, 12–14, 16, 19, 21, 23, 38, 48, 231; Skupština, 8–9, 14, 20; succession question, 1, 17, 20, 21; tours Serbia, 19. *See also* Mašin, Draga
—foreign relations: Austria-Hungary, 16, 32, 34, 35, 38–39, 40, 44, 63, 65; Bulgaria, 27, 34, 42; England, 44; Germany, 35; Greece, 1, 5; Italy, 96; Macedonia, 122; Montenegro, 1, 5, 27, 77; Ottoman Empire, 43, 243; Rumania, 38, 44, 77; Russia, 6, 11, 34–36, 38, 44, 55, 63, 76

Alexandria, 202

Anastasoff, Christ, 243, 252

andarte, 163

Andonović, 12

Andrássy, Count Julius, 165, 166, 167, 169

Andrejević, Milan, 85 n.

Andrijevica, 213

Anglo-Serbian Syndicate, 214

Annexation crisis. *See* Bosna-Hercegovina

Antić, Antonije, 47–49, 51, 240

Antivari (Bar), 210, 213, 214

Antivari-Scutari railway, 217, 219

Antivari-Virpazar railway, 223

Antonić, G., 261

Antonić, Vasilije, 98

Arandjelović, Radomir, 47 n.

Arhiv za pravne i društvene nauke, 259, 263

Arnautovic, Dragomir, 267

Aroumanians. *See* Kutsovlachs

Arzano, 214

Asaf Pasha, 33

Asia Minor, 207

Atanacković, Jovan, 8, 9, 47, 51, 60 n., 71, 73, 84, 97, 107–8, 109

Athens, 216

Aulneau, J., 264, 265

Ausgleich, 199

Austria-Hungary, foreign affairs:
—Albania, 33, 41, 129, 139, 154, 212, 230
—Balkans, 37, 40–41, 44, 96, 113, 130, 138–